HOMOSEXUALITY

**Lesbians and Gay Men
in Society, History and Literature**

HOMOSEXUALITY

Lesbians and Gay Men
in Society, History and Literature

General Editor
JONATHAN KATZ

Editorial Board
Louis Crompton
Barbara Gittings
Dolores Noll
James Steakley

Research Associate
J. Michael Siegelaub

See last pages of this volume
for a complete list of titles

HERE

LIES

THE

HEART

Mercedes de Acosta

ARNO PRESS

A NEW YORK TIMES COMPANY

New York — 1975

Editorial Supervision: LESLIE PARR

———◆———

Reprint Edition 1975 by Arno Press Inc.

Copyright © 1960 by Mercedes de Acosta
Reprinted by permission of
  William Morrow & Company, Inc.

Reprinted from a copy in
  The New York Public Library

HOMOSEXUALITY: Lesbians and Gay Men in
Society, History and Literature
ISBN for complete set: 0-405-07348-8
See last pages of this volume for titles.

Manufactured in the United States of America

———◆———

Library of Congress Cataloging in Publication Data

Acosta, Mercedes de.
    Here lies the heart.

    (Homosexuality)
    Autobiographical.
    Reprint of the ed. published by Reynal, New York.
    1. Acosta, Mercedes de--Biography. I. Title.
II. Series.
[PS3501.C7Z52 1975]   818'.5'209 [B]   75-13709
ISBN 0-405-07360-7

Here Lies the Heart

HERE

LIES

THE

HEART

Mercedes de Acosta

REYNAL & COMPANY

NEW YORK

When I was young, the Spanish painter, Ignacio Zuloaga said to me, "All great people function with the heart." He placed his hand over my physical heart and continued, "Here lies the heart. Always remember to think with it, to feel with it, and above all, to judge with it."

Many years later when I was in India in 1938, the great Sage, Ramana Maharshi, placed his hand on my right breast and said, "Here lies the Heart—the Dynamic, Spiritual Heart. Learn to find The Self in it."

The Enlightened One raised the artist's counsel to a higher level. Both, at just the right moment, showed me The Way.

One

I was conceived in France and born in New York. If it is true, as it is maintained in India, that the place of one's conception has a marked influence on the subconscious, this, then, may be the reason why I have been drawn back time and again to France as though I had some affinity with that country.

I am by blood a pure Spaniard, my mother and father both having been Castilians as far back ancestrally as they could trace.

I was brought up mostly in America and France, but I have lived in many other countries and I am at home in many of them, and, I might add, equally lonely in all of them. I am, however, always grateful that I am a Spaniard in spite of the fact that, to my way of thinking, it is a handicap to possess a Spanish character. It imposes upon the consciousness a far too tragic sense of life.

Pure Spaniards are totally apart from other races and very little understood, and to have this heritage and at the same time to have been born in the United States is in itself a cause for psychological contradictions and "complexes." The Spaniard, as a rule, is not adaptable. My mother and father, both transplanted from Spain to America, communicated to my brothers and sisters, and to me, a consciousness of a sort of "homelessness"—that is, of not actually belonging to America. But having acquired a modern way of life there, we could not feel when we returned to Spain that we belonged to that country either.

1

It is strange how far apart the brain and the heart can be. In my case, I believe that my mentality is truly international but somehow, try as I may to change them, my impulses and my heart too often remain Spanish.

I was the eighth child in my family of three boys and five girls—we were Joaquin Ignacio, Rita Lina Hernandez de Alba, Ricardo Miguel, Aida Marta, Maria Cécelia, Enriqué José, Angéla Aloysius, (who has always been called "Baba"), and myself. Perhaps as the last child of so large a family, I suffered from the "material having run out," as I expressed it. This theory I advanced at an early age as the reason for my spiritual and physical suffering.

The first thing I really remember was when I was six months old. A bear looked down at me as I lay in my pram in a place called Quoque, Long Island, where my parents had rented a cottage for the summer. In my childhood, it was not unusual to see men strolling the American countryside with trained bears. It was only a little unusual that he peered into my pram—not only peered but put his face close to mine to get a good sniff of me. I was not frightened. I am told that I tried to put my arms around his neck. I can distinctly recall the delight I felt in touching him, and the despair I sank into when the keeper pulled him away.

When I was about four, Maggie, my nanny, took me every morning to nine-o'clock Mass at Saint Patrick's Cathedral. At this time there was a Catholic orphan asylum opposite the Cathedral on Fifty-first Street. The children and some of the nuns of the asylum also came to the Mass. They occupied the pews on the left side of the main aisle. For some reason of her own Maggie always made straight for the first unoccupied pew directly back of the children and, pushing me into it, knelt down, so that it seemed to any observer that we were part of the orphanage.

While Maggie followed the Mass, engrossed in her prayers, I usually entertained myself by standing up to look over the people in the pews behind. One gentleman in particular received my special attention. I always stuck out my tongue at him. The gentleman happened to be Augustin Daly, who owned the famous Daly Theatre on Broadway and was considered the foremost theatrical producer of his time.

After some weeks of flirting and making faces at each other, Mr. Daly went to the Mother Superior of the orphanage and inquired if he could adopt me. From his description of me the Mother Superior was not unnaturally mystified as to which child of the orphanage it could be, so one day during Mass he brought her to the Cathedral and pointed me out to her.

"This child does not belong to the orphanage. I know her mother very well," the Mother Superior said. Mr. Daly was disappointed but, being a man who always got what he wanted, he persisted.

"Maybe it could be arranged to let me adopt her anyway," said he. "I have my heart set on bringing her up. I feel there is a great mutual sympathy between us. I am willing to make any financial arrangement with the mother that will enable me to adopt her. I am quite in love with her."

Mr. Daly had been quite used to bargaining with actresses, actors and authors, and had found that if he offered enough money, usually they could finally be coaxed to sign contracts. He was quite confident that a mother could be persuaded to give up her child by the same means.

My mother had been one of the first pew owners in Saint Patrick's. She was a friend of the archbishop and a close friend of Father Lavalle who later became Monsignor. She knew all the priests of the Cathedral as well as she knew all the nuns in the orphanage, then attached to it.

Mother Ada Martha had a sense of humor. She decided to play a joke on my mother and at the same time, no doubt, teach Mr. Daly the lesson that there are some things in life not to be bought with money. She told Mr. Daly that she would arrange a meeting for him with my mother on condition that he would plead his own case. With his usual confidence he agreed. She then invited my mother to have tea with her to meet "a charming gentleman who wished to ask her a favor."

My mother, in spite of her years in America, remained somehow unmistakably foreign, aristocratic, and very unusual looking. She spoke English abominably, with the worst kind of Spanish accent. Mr. Daly had not imagined facing a woman like this. When, after presenting him, Mother Ada Martha left the room, Mr. Daly, no doubt for the first time in his life, found it difficult to talk money.

"Madame, I would like to offer you a contract on your own terms for the legal adoption of your little daughter," was perhaps what he said.

My mother, thinking that Mr. Daly was out of his mind or, more likely, that she had misunderstood him, called for Mother Ada Martha to come back into the room and explain what this peculiar gentleman was saying. In simple English Mother Ada Martha, her tongue in her cheek, repeated Mr. Daly's offer. The reaction of my mother may easily be imagined.

But Mr. Daly was a fine-looking man. When he found that for once money couldn't get him what he wanted, he tried charm. This procured him a small compromise. My mother, touched at his seeming love for me, and perhaps also flattered, made a curious agreement with him. She said that during the winter months he could come every Sunday at two o'clock to fetch me, and that I could spend the afternoon with him.

Considering that my mother knew very little about theatrical people and nothing at all about Mr. Daly, I can only say that her consent to this agreement speaks well for Mr. Daly and for the confidence she had in Mother Ada Martha, who no doubt assured her that Mr. and Mrs. Daly were devout Catholics and reputable people.

The famous actress Ada Rehan was at this time under contract to Augustin Daly and was his leading lady. It was also well known that she was his mistress—of which fact, no doubt, Mother Ada Martha was not aware. Certainly my mother did not even faintly suspect it.

For some months after my mother's meeting with Mr. Daly all went well. He called for me promptly every Sunday and brought me home promptly at six. Instead, however, of taking me to his own house, we went to Ada Rehan's.

I cannot say that I remember Ada Rehan very clearly. I have only a vague recollection of her but I do vividly recall sitting on the floor of her living room with Mr. Daly and watching him make little theatrical maquettes according to stories which he encouraged me to tell him. Together we would paint the scenery and backdrops, and cut out in paper the personages who fitted into my plots. Then we would perform the play, he bringing the characters onto the stage by manipulating them with strings, like marionettes. I would recount the plot and improvise the dialogue as we went along. I returned home every Sunday afternoon proudly carrying my "little theatres," as I called them, and all the following week my mind would be teeming with new plots with which to surprise Mr. Daly.

Then the blow fell. My mother thought it high time that she should call on Mrs. Daly to thank her for her precious care of her darling child during all those Sunday afternoons!

Mrs. Daly was a large, fat, good-natured and red-haired Irishwoman. When my mother called on her, she admitted she had never heard of the Sunday afternoons. Weeping, she told my horror-stricken mother that Mr. Daly always spent his Sunday afternoons with his mistress. He had, however, spoken of some child, a little girl that he seemed to love and wish were his. Any mention of a child, Mrs. Daly confided to my mother, always caused trouble between her and her husband as they had been unable to have one of their own.

As a result of this meeting Mrs. Daly and my mother became friends, but Mr. Daly was no longer allowed to call for me on Sunday afternoons. In the end, however, his pleadings won him another concession. I was finally allowed to go with him backstage to matinees at Daly's Theatre. Sometimes on a morning when he had a rehearsal he would pass by our house and beg my mother to let me go with him. Occasionally she consented and I would sit on his lap out front and watch the rehearsal. Sometimes he would carry me about on his shoulder and show me off, calling me his "own little baby" and telling everyone that some day I was going to be a great actress or dramatist. I was, of course, dreadfully spoiled by all the company, including the stagehands, and I learned to know and love the people of the theatre and to feel at home with them.

Unfortunately Daly died while I was still a child. He left me the gold pen with which he had signed all his contracts, but as things of the theatre held no interest for my mother she never gave it to me, and when I was old enough to ask for it, it had disappeared. When we moved, my "Little theatres" disappeared too, alas.

Most powerful of all my infant memories was the vision of my sister Rita, who was about to be married to William Earl Dodge Stokes, descending the stairway in our house wearing a white lace veil and dressed in a white wedding gown with a fantastically long train which I —darting out from the sidelines and rushing after her—promptly sat down upon. Needless to say I was snatched up and carried away kicking violently.

Rita was my first conscious glimpse of beauty and all through my life she symbolized beauty to me. I must speak of her here at once because on looking back on my life, I can truly say that I have known a number of extraordinary and beautiful women the world over, but Rita, considered objectively and without any prejudice in her favor, seemed to me more striking, more unfailing in perfect grace and beauty than any other woman. And with these physical characteristics she combined a remarkably magnetic personality.

She also had a quality—a curious one which I have never found in anyone else—of radiating artistic creativeness. Not only did she herself radiate it, but she had the ability to inspire art in anyone susceptible to it. Perhaps this was the principal reason for her great influence upon me.

Mrs. Jack Gardner, of the famous Gardner Collection in Boston, once remarked to the famous painter John Singer Sargent that it was amazing that Rita, whom she considered so creative, had never expressed herself in some form of art. He answered: "Why should she? She herself is art."

Two

 When I was a child my mother often used to tell me about her childhood. She would tell me of her lonely life in a big house in Madrid where she seldom was allowed to play or amuse herself. There were good reasons for this. In later years I questioned her about her life in detail. Gradually she told it all.

On both the maternal and paternal side she was descended from ancient and noble Castilian families from the Dukes of Alba. Her full name was Micaela Hernandez de Alba y de Alba.

It is customary in Spain for children to be christened with the names of saints, thereby securing, so the Church claims, the protection of the particular saints whose name the child bears. My mother had a number of saints' names given her in baptism and her first one, Micaela, placed her under the special care of the Archangel Michael. She always had a very special devotion to the archangels.

Her mother, Rita Hernandez y de Alba, after whom my sister Rita was named, had been famed in Madrid for her beauty and even more for her daring and revolutionary way of life. Women in Spain at that time, particularly the aristocrats, led almost entirely secluded lives. In most cases they were married off at an early age to a man chosen by their parents. But "Rita la Linda," as my grandmother was popularly known, had her own ideas and held to them. She did not marry until what was then considered the late age of twenty-four—and my grandfather was the man of her choice.

When her mother and father died, leaving her an heiress, she at once spent a good part of her inheritance in building and maintaining in Madrid a free public clinic. Such a thing was unheard of in Spain at this time. There were a few badly run state hospitals where the poor died off like sick flies without adequate medical care or hygiene. Private hospitals were only for the extreme upper classes and nobility. A free clinic, where it was possible for the poor to receive medical care and medicines without having to pay even a peseta, was indeed extraordinary.

But "la Linda" dared even more than this—she walked alone in the streets of Madrid. Most gentlewomen walked rarely and then only when strictly guarded by a duenna, a parent, or a nun. These guardians took great care to see that their charges did not so much as raise an eyebrow if a gentleman were bold enough to look at them. My grandmother looked people in the eye and spoke to them if she had any reason to.

Such a violation of custom caused a furious scandal in the circle in which she moved. Like my sisters and brothers, in the twentieth century, she was ahead of convention. Some years ago when I was in Spain I met an extremely old lady—she was past ninety—who told me that in her girlhood she had often seen "Rita la Linda" walking unescorted in the streets, distributing gold coins to the beggars and cripples who crowded around her. She told me how often she had heard of my grandmother's generosity and prodigious extravagance. Unfortunately, this wealth eventually brought disaster and death to herself and her husband.

When she married her handsome husband, Rafael, who was then twenty-six, Rita knew she was risking the loss of her entire inheritance, for if she proved childless, it was to revert to an uncle—a sinister character who literally played the role of archvillain in the drama of her young life.

By the light of modern psychology this uncle was undoubtedly a pathological case. He was wealthy in his own right and had no reason to covet his niece's money, but he was well known for his avarice and for his intensely jealous nature. Rita realized that she had a great enemy in him, but there was little she could do to defend herself against him because, being a Spanish woman, she had no rights by law.

Through the servants the uncle succeeded in poisoning Rita's husband shortly after their marriage. The poison not only produced impotency but also attacked the brain cells, causing a mental breakdown. The uncle then had him committed to a private institution for the insane, and even succeeded in making it impossible for my grandmother to visit her own husband. But a part of these plans proved futile: Rita was already pregnant.

Hearing that Rita had borne a child, the uncle escaped with most of her inheritance to Paris. She was advised to follow him, as his signature was necessary to release her husband from the ghastly place where he was confined. She embarked at Cadiz with my mother (then only three months old), a maid and a wet nurse, on a ship bound for Le Havre. The boat was about to sail when a messenger came on board with a letter. Rita was already in bed in her cabin, exhausted by the emotional and physical strain of the journey from Madrid. This was the final blow. The letter said that Rafael had died of a heart attack.

My grandmother was unable to disembark and the ship sailed with her. She died a few days before it reached port. The frightful rolling of the ship in the Bay of Biscay had made her violently seasick, and she burst a blood vessel. It was a poignant finish to the life of a noble woman who had not yet reached her twenty-sixth year.

As my mother was now an orphan, the law required a guardian to bring her up. An old and intimate friend of the family—Don Delgado—accepted the responsibility and left for Le Havre where the two broken-hearted servants and the infant were waiting for him in a hotel. My mother returned with her guardian to Madrid wearing a long white dress with a black crepe sash around her waist and two large black bows hanging from her shoulders.

Don Delgado was handsome, kind, and distinguished, but unimaginative. Undoubtedly he became fond of his ward in his limited way, and did what he thought best to protect her. He had a constant fear that the uncle who had ruined Rita's life might attempt to kidnap or poison her child and he saw to it that my mother associated only with a few trusted servants and teachers. Her food was examined and tasted by Don Delgado before she was allowed to touch it and the windows were barred even more thoroughly than usual in Spanish houses.

Luckily, my mother's great-uncle died when she was fourteen. It was then discovered that most of the wealth he had stolen from her had been invested in America. A year later Don Delgado took her to New York to appeal to the Supreme Court for the return of her fortune, all of which the insane old man had registered under his own name.

The inheritance of gold may diminish in its passage from generation to generation but I have seen the spiritual inheritance from my grandmother, Rita de Alba, repeat itself undiminished in the lives of my brothers and sisters. And again like my grandmother, they have not been afraid of life or death—or, at the expense of breaking conventions, to walk alone.

Three

Although my father had little influence over me, we had much in common intellectually. He had a great thirst for knowledge which, from my earliest years, I shared. He was an untiring reader. When I was not yet old enough to read myself, he read me Shakespeare, Cervantes, and Goethe.

My father seemed to me a source toward which I could turn for knowledge and stimulation; but due, perhaps, to my mother's influence, he did not interest me as a person, nor did I feel sorry for him though I have many times since. He was miscast in life. He was not a businessman, but he had to try to become one in order to bring up a family of eight children. He had an excellent, scholarly brain, but he was, comparatively speaking, a weak man unable to assert his own tastes as against my mother's.

As a young man my paternal grandfather had gone from Spain to Cuba, where he settled down, became a planter in a place near Matanzas called La Jagua—married and raised a family of four sons and two daughters. Some years later his wife died and he married again, this time a Spanish girl not much older than a child. He himself was forty.

My father was the child of this second marriage. He was born in Cuba, but while he was still an infant his parents returned home.

As a child in Madrid he often heard his father telling nostalgically fascinating tales of Cuban life, tales of the life of a planter working in a tropical land under glowing hot sun, of ravishing foliage and strange birds of rare color—and these inflamed his romantic young mind. There were stories, too, of the oppression of the Cuban people and the cruelties they suffered under the reign of terror of the Spanish.

No doubt all of these varying pictures of Cuban life dramatically portrayed by his father stamped on my father's susceptible mind a sympathetic impression of this small West Indian island where he had been born, and made him want to defend its downtrodden cause. He made up his mind before he was eight years old that he would fight for the liberation of Cuba as soon as he was old enough.

When his parents decided to return to Cuba, before leaving Madrid he hatched a plan with eighteen of his fellow students to follow him with the idea of creating a revolt.

On arriving, the family went to their plantation at La Jagua and the following two years, my father often declared, were the only truly happy years of his life. Of this he wrote in his diary:

"Our coffee plantation, 'Dolores,' at La Jagua, was a little paradise. Friends and guests whom my father had previously known came from Havana and other places to spend the holidays. They came to enjoy the characteristic hospitality for which our house was reputed. I now remember like a dream the many gatherings of happy people during those few short years before tragedy descended on my family and myself. . . . The plantation was one of the most beautiful in Cuba, embellished with all kinds of tropical fruit trees and flowers. The avenue leading to the main entrance on the highway was half a mile long, and superb. On this avenue my father would tie vines on the trees and throw them across from tree to tree, hanging upon them all kinds of fruit and flowers to be gathered by the guests on their holiday visits. The whole plantation was encircled by a charming hedge of lemon trees evenly trimmed at the top and sides. My father used to ride around this hedge early every morning. Sometimes I would accompany him, riding along beside him on my beautiful black horse. I would feel like a king."

Shortly after arriving in La Jagua, my father went to Havana to see his Spanish fellow students who had followed him as planned. His parents never dreamed what lay behind these visits.

The young revolutionaries organized clandestine meetings as well as printing pamphlets and distributing them among the students in the various colleges. Gradually their plans matured. They hoped to instigate a revolt of all Cuban students, to overpower the Spanish garrison stationed in Morro Castle, and to gain control of the entire city.

Then one evening the first bolt of tragedy flashed across the sky at La Jagua.

My grandfather had returned home one evening from Matanzas where he had drawn a large sum of money to pay the workers on the plantation. He was eating his usual late supper with his wife seated opposite him when through the open doors he saw a figure approaching the house. Casually he remarked that it was probably some runaway Negro, perhaps from one of the adjoining plantations, coming to implore his aid, as they often did.

The stranger approached steadily, but on entering the house, he suddenly drew a pistol out of his cloak and fired at my grandfather. An accomplice appeared, and as my grandmother tried to defend her husband she was knocked down and kicked out of the way. The attackers seized my grandfather when he tried to rise, and dragging him to the veranda, tied him to one of the columns that supported the porch. After pounding him with a club they took the money from his pockets.

Some workmen heard the shot and rushed toward the house as the robbers fled. They were pursued and apprehended and they turned out to be a trusted foreman and his son. A few days later, my grandfather died.

The day after the funeral my father was summoned back to Havana. The hour of the student uprising had been set. Heartbroken though he was, there was no choice.

Although every detail seemed to be in order, the revolt did not mature. A Cuban student betrayed the plot to the Spaniards and the original revolutionaries, including my father, were arrested and imprisoned. Incriminating papers and pamphlets were found on each of them and there seemed every chance that they would be shot.

Meanwhile my grandmother had been forced to move to Havana because my grandfather had died without leaving a will. She tried to be brave when she came to visit her son in prison, but he told me that instead of the gay young woman of a few weeks ago, she was broken and matured. Calmly she told my father that she had made a vow to "La Señora de la Merced" that if by some miracle his life was spared, she would cut off the beautiful hair of which she was so proud and donate it to the Virgin. She would live for the rest of her life with a shaven head.

In due course the nineteen students were condemned to be shot on the battlements of Morro Castle overlooking the sea. My grandmother did not wait for the miracle. Cutting off her hair, she sent it to the priest in charge of the church in Matanzas, to be used for the statue of the Virgin.

The Spanish captain who was detailed to command the execution was a very ardent Catholic. When he saw my grandmother in her son's cell with her shaven head and heard about her vow, he was deeply touched. He secretly told my father that he had thought of a plan that might save him. His plan was to place my father at the end of the line of condemned men. When he was about to give the command "Fire!" my father was to leap into the sea. There was a chance in a million that he might escape—there are rocks beneath the battlements of Morro Castle.

The day of the execution arrived. The nineteen were led onto the battlement. As the captain gave the command "Fire!" my father jumped over the wall, narrowly missed the rocks, swam for a long time, and was picked up by an American schooner bound for Boston.

The miracle had come to pass.

When the schooner reached Boston, my father, who could speak only a little English he had learned at school in Madrid, made his way into the city. It was winter and snow covered the ground. Without much difficulty he got a job clearing the streets.

Being rather delicate and poetic-looking, and also very thinly dressed, he drew the attention of a passer-by. This gentleman stopped and spoke to him, and discovering that he was a Spaniard, gave him his card and requested him to call on him if he needed help.

My father went through many vicissitudes during his first months in the United States. He lived sparingly and, with the small savings he earned snow-shoveling, bought a ticket to New York. Knowing no one and having only fifteen cents in his pockets, he spent his first night in the city dozing on a bench in the station.

He had written to his mother after his arrival in Boston to assure her that he was well and safe, and to advise her—very grandly indeed—that she should "keep up her heart" because shortly he would have enough money to bring her to America. He did not mention that his only manner of making money at this time was shoveling snow.

Of his first day in the city he wrote:

A stranger in New York—my first day with but fifteen cents in my pocket . . . I passed a horrible night. I remained sleepless thinking what to do the next morning. When the cold dim rays of the sun crept through the window, I arose, looked outside and exclaimed out loud in despair, "My God, is this the same glorious sun I left behind me in Cuba!"

He had the wit that morning to go to a newsstand and buy a Spanish newspaper with his last nickel. Asking his way in very poor English, he walked to the address where the newspaper was printed and asked for a job, saying he was a writer and that he also wrote poetry. He was asked his name but, afraid that it might be connected with the attempted revolt in Cuba, he answered "Odracir," which is Ricardo spelled backwards. After that he always signed himself *Odracir.*

He was employed at a dollar a day to write editorials and poems, but still afraid that his identity would be discovered, he soon left the newspaper and took a job with a business house. It was while working there that he received a letter informing him that his mother had developed tuberculosis. Not long after came a second letter announcing her death.

I have now no reason to make money, he wrote in despair.

But he did make money. It happened by chance that he met again the man who had given him his card in Boston. This man was the owner of a steamship line which ran between New York and the West Indies. He was glad to employ my father, who was soon promoted to an important position in the company. By the time he met my mother some years later he was fairly well off. He had also learned to speak perfect English and had become an American citizen.

His meeting with my mother came about when a friend of his, an American lawyer, asked him as a great favor to act as interpreter for "a rich and beautiful Spanish girl of noble birth," whom he was representing in a lawsuit to help her regain her fortune. My father was presented to the young woman and her guardian at the St. Nicholas Hotel.

"She was not yet sixteen," my father told me in later years, "and she was remarkably beautiful." Needless to say, he had fallen instantly in love.

My mother's appeal was successful. The court ruled that the investments her great-uncle Rodriguez had made in his own name in America were rightfully hers. She came into about four million dollars, at that time a fairly large fortune.

The case was closed and my mother was about to return to Spain, but my father pleaded with her to stay in America and marry him. Don Delgado was extremely generous in not insisting that my mother, still a minor, should return to Spain with him. He had come to consider her as his own daughter and to be separated from her must have involved a great sacrifice on his part. My mother on her side was very attached to Don Delgado and it could not have been easy for her to see him return to Spain alone.

Nevertheless she accepted my father. Her guardian graciously gave them his blessing and, shortly after their marriage, returned to Spain. This union in America of a de Alba and a de Acosta was to be the bridge between the Old World and The New over which their children were to cross back and forth in ceaseless search of a home.

Four

We lived in a house on Forty-seventh Street between Fifth Avenue and Sixth. This area of the West Side from Forty-second Street to Fifty-ninth Street was, at that time, restricted to private houses and was fashionable.

Next door to us was the house of Joseph Choate, who made such a brilliant ambassador to Great Britain. On. the other side and farther down the street Theodore Roosevelt had a house. He had lived in this house when my older brothers and sisters were growing up, and after he was President he sometimes came back to it. When I was a young child, Rita took me along with her several times when she went to see "Teddy" in Oyster Bay. He laughed a great deal and, as everyone knows, showed his teeth prominently. I once asked Rita, before him, in quite a loud voice, if his teeth were false. This childhood remark did not prevent his flashing the famous smile at me many times in years to come.

About this time Maude Adams created the role of Peter Pan and lived for a short time on our street. Every child was hysterical about her as the little boy who never grew up and I was no exception. To me she *was* Peter Pan and when I saw her in the part I was thrown into a state of ecstasy. On one occasion I managed to slip away from home to stand with a group of children outside the stage door at a matinee, waiting for her to come out. She always gave away little silver thimbles to the waiting children which, in the manner of Peter Pan, represented a kiss. I was determined to have one. Unfortunately it was a freezing day and the ground was covered with ice. My feet have always been very sensitive to cold. The result was that while I did see Miss Adams and got a much coveted silver thimble, I also got chilblains.

I became friends with Miss Adams in later years and she gave me her volume of *Kim* which Kipling had marked for her with marginal notes.

On Fifth Avenue at the north corner of the street the August Belmonts had their house, a great and gloomy brownstone. According to the term used at that period a house of this type was called a "mansion." Since those days the whole character of New York has shifted and changed as anyone—even a person much younger than I—can testify.

It seems now almost unreal to think of being pushed in my carriage by my nurse, and later, when I could walk, running beside or ahead of her over a bridge across Park Avenue at Forty-seventh Street where the trains ran underneath, in the open, up and down the Avenue. I can even now conjure up in my memory the picture of gleaming icicles as they hung from the iron railings of the bridge. I can see them glistening in the sunlight and hear the crackling of the hard snow beneath my feet. It was an unending joy to stand on this bridge and listen to the nostalgic whistles of the trains and hear the metallic clanking of their bells, and at the same time to be enveloped and hidden by the great puffs of white steam and black smoke that poured out of the engine as it sped beneath. Considering the amount of soot and smoke I must have swallowed on this bridge, I later wondered why Maggie referred to those walks as "inhaling good fresh air!"

I remember driving in a cart pulled by a Shetland pony on the estate of Mr. and Mrs. George Mathews where my mother often took me to play with their children. This estate was on the East River between Seventy-fourth and Seventy-fifth Streets, extending west to York Avenue. The property ran down to the river where the ships cut through the water, causing gentle waves to break on a little beach directly in front of the house.

I looked upon these exciting visits as trips to the country, for indeed this place was the country, with its poplar and oak trees, its winding dirt road and smell of the earth. Actually it was not much more than a mile and a half from our house on Forty-seventh Street. The city took this property away from the Mathews by right of eminent domain and a powerhouse was built there. Today the East River Drive runs through it and thousands of cars rush over it every hour.

I first remember going to Beekman Place about 1911. Rita had bought a house there on the corner of Fiftieth Street which she gave as a home for delinquent girls. Beekman Place was then a small village with green trees flowering on the rim of the sidewalks and cobblestone streets. No tall apartments cast their shadows over it, hemming and enclosing it as they do now.

Actors and actresses later "discovered" this part of town. Margalo Gilmore's mother and father and Katharine Cornell and Guthrie McClintic were among the pioneers. Later Laurette Taylor and Greta Kemble Cooper joined them. During the first World War, I went to see Jack Barrymore there in a house which my husband and I were to buy in 1929. Jack used to refer to Beekman Place at this time as "my slums."

Until the end of the early twenties, Italian organ grinders roamed the streets of New York, holding on chains sad-eyed and flea-infested monkeys dressed in red velvet jackets. In the most touching manner they used to stretch out their cold clammy little hands to grab at fingers and lift their caps when anyone gave them a penny. Italians also sold gay-colored paper pinwheels on Fifth Avenue and held, on bamboo sticks, brightly painted balloons that waved and bobbed in the breeze—symbols, perhaps, of the last touch of fantasy in a city doomed to commercialism.

And of course there was the old Battery Park. Who of my generation has not sat in this park and watched the waves splashing up, wetting the feet of the city.

I am certainly not unique in my memories of New York. Anyone who lived there from 1900 until late into the twenties can remember the same things I can. But it seems a shame that the young now know it merely as a great commercial city—infinitely impersonal. It is not surprising that they are unable to visualize it as intimate and informal, with, for example, Alfred Vanderbilt driving a four-in-hand up Fifth Avenue, his coach brightly painted and two small footmen standing at the back dressed in gay green livery, wearing high silk hats and blowing lovely notes on long, golden horns. I suppose this sounds like a fairy tale to them.

Recently I went to the Frick Museum with Cecil Beaton. We were amused at the many things there in the way of furnishings that we had known in our childhood in our own homes. The brocade silk on the walls with the fleur-de-lys pattern was the identical brocade I remember in pink hanging in the living room of our house on Forty-seventh Street. On the mantel stood the classic gilded clock, elaborate in design, with cupids sitting on it. On either side of it stood twin vases which matched the clock. In the corner cabinets we saw again the little figurines and bits of jade, gold snuffboxes and various objects in crystal and amethyst we had seen all too many times before in the houses of our youth. And there were also the tiny Chinese figures exquisitely carved in ivory.

As we stood before the clock Cecil remarked, "No wonder we of our generation are neurotic. To have passed so quickly from the gentle ticking of this clock to jet planes, atomic bombs—it has all been too rapid. The transitions of our age have been too violent and too great."

Rita by Ignacio Zuloaga: *"There was no one like Rita. No woman of her distinction, style or wit. But, more outstanding then these, was her great heart and generous nature. She was a true Spaniard in the finest sense of our race."*

My father when he first came to this country

My sister Aida

My brother Enriqué José

Katie, Mercedes, Baba and Maggie in Houlgate, France

My brother Ricardo Miguel

My sister Baba

My mother when I was born

My sister Rita
from a photograph by Baron de Meyer

My sister Maria
from a drawing by John Singer Sargent

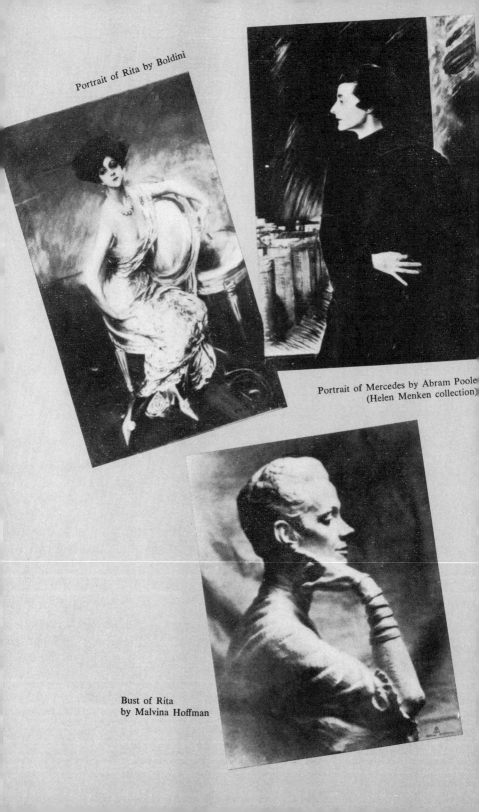

Portrait of Rita by Boldini

Portrait of Mercedes by Abram Poole
(Helen Menken collection)

Bust of Rita
by Malvina Hoffman

Snapshot by Cecil Beaton

Portrait by Abram Poole

Snapshot by Marlene Dietrich

MERCEDES

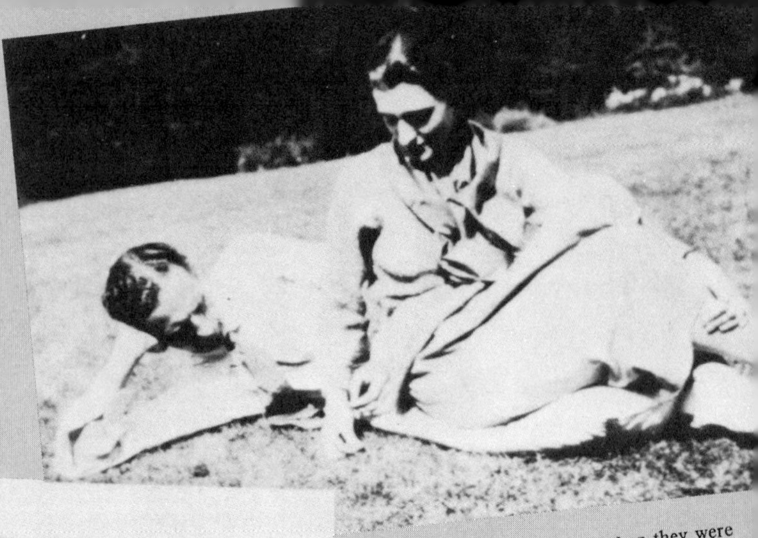

Alfred Stieglitz,
Georgia O'Keefe
and Mercedes
in New York
*(Photographed by
Cecil Beaton)*

Abram Poole and Mercedes when they were
first married

Ethel
Barrymore

Michael Strange

To Mercedes —
with love from
Ethel Barrymore 1909

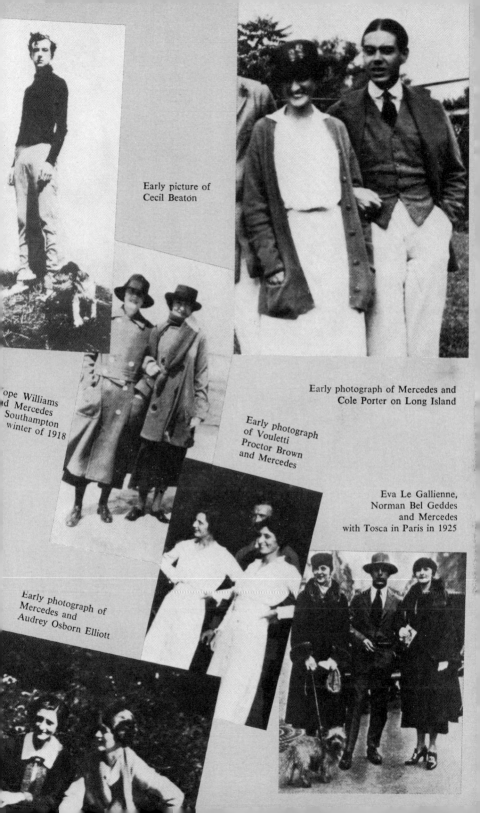

Early picture of
Cecil Beaton

Early photograph of Mercedes and
Cole Porter on Long Island

ope Williams
d Mercedes
Southampton
winter of 1918

Early photograph
of Vouletti
Proctor Brown
and Mercedes

Eva Le Gallienne,
Norman Bel Geddes
and Mercedes
with Tosca in Paris in 1925

Early photograph of
Mercedes and
Audrey Osborn Elliott

Greta Garbo at Silver Lake

Greta at
my house in
Santa Monica

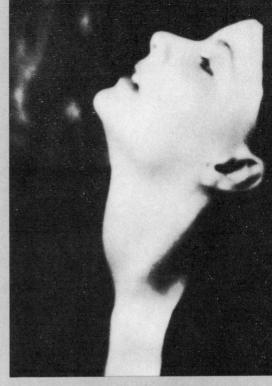

My favorite portrait of Greta by Arnold Genthe
which he gave me in 1925

Greta with Bambina

Garbo in pants! Mercedes
de Acosta and Greta Garbo
striding swiftly along Hollywood
Boulevard.

Greta and Chotzie
taken by Mercedes

Mercedes and Chotzie taken
by Greta

Snapshots of Marlene Dietrich in her beach
house in Santa Monica

Anna with our brood

Adrian

Marion Stevenson

Isadora Duncan overlooking Paris from her house in Belview

"Mercedes, Lead me with your little strong
hands and I will follow you—
To the top of a Mountain
To the end of the world
Wherever you wish—
Isadora, June 28, 1926"

Eugene Berman, Igor Stravinsky,
Vera Stravinsky and Baron de Meyer on
the Stravinsky's lawn in Hollywood

Igor Stravinsky and Mercedes
with Adolf Bolm in the background—Hollywood

Snapshot of Jeanne Eagles
and Tony Bushell taken a
few days before her death
at her country home
in Ossining

Mercedes with Marie Laurencin
at her studio in Paris

Aldous Huxley in Hollywood

Dr. Daisetz T. Suzuki and Mihoko Okamura by Barbara Morgan

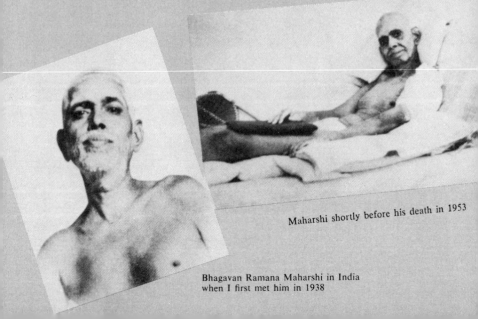

Maharshi shortly before his death in 1953

Bhagavan Ramana Maharshi in India
when I first met him in 1938

Maria Annunziata (Poppy) Kirk

Claire, the Marquise de Forbin

Alice B. Toklas in Paris

Tamara Karsavina in London

Eleonora Duse—from a
snapshot taken on the
balcony of her house
in Asolo, Italy just
before her tour
in America on which
she died.
She is gazing over her
beloved mountains
at a spot where she
is now buried.

Five

My mother's first child, christened Joaquin, was only a legend to me as he died at fifteen, before my birth. His death was caused by a blow accidentally dealt him while playing baseball with a friend. It always seemed to me an ironic act of fate that the child of two people so fundamentally un-American should be killed playing so essentially American a game. Neither my mother or my father ever really recovered from Joaquin's death.

My sister Rita was their second child and, after Joaquin died, my mother's favorite child. This was natural as she was part of my mother's youth and all through her life remained extremely Spanish. She always spoke Spanish to my mother, whereas we other children often spoke to her in English. I do not remember ever hearing Rita at any time address one word of English to my mother. My other brothers and sisters became more Americanized, with the exception of Baba, who became British by her second marriage.

My mother had counted on Rita's marrying a Roman Catholic as a true Spaniard should most certainly have done. That she married a Protestant was a great shock and a deep sorrow to my mother. Because she married a non-Catholic, the marriage itself had to take place in our own home, although Archbishop Corrigan, from St. Patrick's Cathedral, officiated.

While the rest of us called Rita's husband "Will," my mother never

21

accorded him that familiarity. He was just "Stokes" to her, and that is what she called him.

There were other reasons why she objected to this marriage. Will was nearly twenty years older than Rita. He was a man of the world and before his marriage had had many experiences with women. He owned a racing stable in Kentucky, where he also had a house and a big stud farm. He belonged, in my mother's opinion, to a "fast" racing set. But her strongest reason against Rita's marriage, apart from his being a Protestant, was the fact that "Stokes" was a multi-millionaire. My mother felt that such vast wealth could never bring Rita happiness. It did not.

Stokes came from a good American family. He had two very distinguished and proper older sisters and a charming uncle, Anson Phelps Stokes, all of whom considered him the black sheep. Contrary to my mother's feeling about the marriage, the Stokes family welcomed it and were pleased that "Wild Will," as they called him, was finally settling down with such a delightful girl.

Oddly enough, during the many intimate conversations between us I never asked Rita if she was in love with Will Stokes. I do not think she ever was. She was perhaps fascinated by the glamour of his worldly experience, and by the wild charm which he indisputably possessed.

Rita's nature was dual-sided. One side loved power and worldly position, while the other side despised and rejected them. She was ceaselessly torn between the two, and was rarely at peace. I think she was only at peace in the presence of beauty. Then and then only her dual nature ceased to battle.

When she finally decided to marry Will Stokes it was, I believe, because she felt his wealth could open doors to certain ambitions she undoubtedly possessed, but she paid a high price for any material gain she obtained from him and it was not long before she became tragically disillusioned in her marriage. When she gave birth to her son, named after his father but called by her and my family "Weddie," she could not dissociate him from the dislike she felt for his father and never felt in any way maternal toward him.

When she came to New York after Weddie's birth, she made every effort to conceal the fact that she was unhappy with Will. For a time she may have succeeded in deceiving everyone but my mother, who not only knew the truth at once, but had probably known it before Rita was aware of it herself. My mother was far too intuitive about any of her children's suffering not to have been aware when one of us was unhappy.

Rita had always had an admiration for Russia and anything Russian. At this time, finding things going hopelessly astray between herself and Will, she decided a trip there might help to bring them together.

She returned from the trip full of enthusiasms. She had been presented at court and had met the Czar and Czarina. She brought back some lovely presents, among them a complete cossack costume for me. I all but slept in it.

When Rita returned from Russia it became apparent to everyone that she was unhappy with Will. Nevertheless they frequently came to dinner.

This was a great joy to me. I could count on one or both of them stealing upstairs to see me in bed after dinner. Usually they smuggled up a plate of ice cream. I welcomed these visits because on these nights I would not be left alone in the dark.

During this time Rita's situation was one more thing to make me feel uneasy and nervous; I also felt a disharmony between my mother and father. It is, of course, only fair to say that they had been married many years before I was born and at this time I was hardly old enough consciously to understand their attitude toward each other. In fact it is only now, by piecing together certain facts and evaluating feelings and intuitions of my childhood, that I am able to weigh and partially determine their relationship.

From early childhood I can remember sensing that my parents were unlike the parents of the American children I knew. They seemed to me superior. This evaluation was not egotistical on my part nor did I arrive at it simply because they were *my* parents. Quite objectively I was conscious that they belonged to a different world from the American one in which we lived. To begin with, they were both pronounced Latin types and could not possibly have been less American-looking.

My mother had remarkable hair—blue-black and thick. Her skin was alabaster-white and transparent. Her brown eyes, under an exquisite brow, were wide apart and soft. She had a finely chiseled, sensitive nose. Her face was delicate and her small head was well placed on an exceptionally lovely neck and shoulders. Her arms and hands were unusually graceful. Slender, and of medium height, she added to her beauty a most original personality.

My father, in contrast to my mother, had the golden hair and gray eyes that are quite often found in the very northern Spaniard. In his youth he was slender and extremely poetic-looking. As I remember him he was, of course, already an old man. His hair was white and he had grown heavy, but he was still very handsome.

The feeling that my parents were unique and apart from other people made me regard myself as different too, as though it were only right that I be alienated from the common herd.

My mother possessed, even more strongly than my father, that Spanish characteristic of inadaptability. Living in America had undoubtedly made her life more difficult. She could never forget that she was a Spaniard. Nor did she wish to be anything else. She was strong enough to resist the American influence and hold to her own Spanish habits and mannerisms until the moment of her death. I rarely saw her without a fan in her hand. Day and night, winter and summer, she fanned herself, completely unaware that to do so was considered unusual by Americans. I can still hear the click of her fan as she suddenly and quickly closed it when she wanted to emphasize a point in talking.

I unquestionably had a mother complex—a complex often found in boys but less common in girls. It was curious that I had this extravagant feeling for my mother, because intellectually we had little in common. From my youngest years I hungered for knowledge. As I grew older and learned to read I devoured books, and I have always been passionately interested in arts and sciences—particularly art. Except for music, my mother regarded most art as "trash," a word she picked up in English and constantly used even when speaking Spanish.

My mother's interest lay in her children and her religion. Nevertheless, so strong is the tie of the heart that in spite of our intellectual differences she had an exceptionally strong influence on me.

My father, though he sought every avenue of knowledge and was absorbed in learning, had no influence on me, as I have said. He was able to stimulate my intellect, but to my mother I gave a passionately emotional side of my nature, the side that always won in any battle against my brain.

Six

To give a picture of the household of my childhood I must sketch brief portraits of the numerous people who—in one capacity or another—lived with us or constantly came to our house.

To begin with, there were what I would like to term "the servers," who were as much a part of our family as the family itself. I cannot apply such a word as "servants" to any of these wonderful women who brought me up and who played a major part in my childhood.

I could not apply it in particular to three such blessed women as Catherine Coffey, who was like a second mother and guardian angel rolled into one, or Annie Cahill—or to Maggie Kelly, who watched over me, not as nurse alone, but as a kind of heartfelt barricade against any ill that might befall me.

Catherine Coffey, who was the same age as my mother, went to live with her as a sort of jack-of-all-trades and companion when they were both sixteen years old—just after my mother's marriage, in fact. Katie, as we called her (often we called her Cat), forced my mother to try to speak English, helped her dress, went about with her and was, in a manner of speaking, a playmate for her, as they were both at this time very immature for their years.

Katie also accompanied my mother to Mass. Needless to say, she was a devout and pious Catholic. She lived every second of her life fully aware of the Divine Presence. She existed only for God and for any help she could give His creatures. Every morning at six o'clock she rose and went to Mass to receive Holy Communion and in the evenings she went to Vespers or Benediction.

But it was not her churchgoing habits which made one conscious of her goodness and saintliness. It was her pure character, her self-efface-ment and patience, which made one aware that she had chosen the path of anonymity walked only by the rare ones who are conscious at all times of eternal values as opposed to temporal ones. I cannot recall a single time when Katie ever showed the slightest impatience or lost her self-control, which she might so understandingly have done considering the many annoyances our quick Spanish tempers must have caused her.

It was Katie who took care of me when I was ill and sat up all night long with me if I needed her, as she had done for all my brothers and sisters before me. It was Katie, too, who acted as a kind of middleman between me and God because, when she prayed for me or for anything I wanted, I always felt quite sure that God was going to listen to her and do whatever she asked Him to. Whenever I had a problem, it comforted me to know that Katie was in church praying for me. I knew that in some magical way she would arrange with God to solve it.

Annie Cahill was more worldly-wise although also devout in her Catholicism. She had, however, a philosophy of her own which gave her a different understanding of life far beyond Katie's—and even beyond my mother's—comprehension. She had run away from Ireland when she was a child and come to New York, where she worked in a number of places before she came to my mother, about four years after Katie.

Annie was uneducated, but she had a deep natural intelligence and remarkable intuition. I would say that she was an inspirational person, relying always on inspiration or intuition to guide her. Had she been edu-cated, I think she would have had a brilliant career as a psychologist. Long before Coué, she expounded the theory he taught. When I was a child she used to tell me to repeat to myself over and over again, just before falling asleep, whatever I wanted to bring about, and at the same time to visualize it.

Annie had the gift of healing hands. When I was ill she used to lay her hands on me, closing her eyes and visualizing me as well. At the same time, she would repeat the words "You are well—you are well" over and over again.

All my life I have had migraine headaches. In my childhood and youth they seemed to me a sort of curse. I never went on a trip or did any-thing exciting without coming down with one of them. The slightest emotional disturbance would bring one on. Annie understood this and she wisely tried through this method of her own—the importance of which she herself was only partly aware—to make me control my emotions.

Annie believed that since we were put here in this world by the will of God, we should partake of the gifts and pleasures of it. She encouraged me in anything I wanted to do no matter how wild it might seem to the commonplace mind. When my mother refused to let me go to certain parties, Annie schemed to help me get to them. I was not allowed to go or come home from any party alone, and it was Annie who took me to them and sat in the servants' quarters of many private houses or in the dressing rooms of Sherry's, Delmonico's and all the other ballrooms until the small hours of the morning. Around three o'clock I used to go out to the dressing room to see how she was. I would find her half asleep, nodding on a chair and when—rather guiltily but with the selfishness of youth—I asked her if she wanted me to come home, she would say, "Certainly not, my darling, not if you're enjoying yourself. You are only young once, so stay as long as you like." Back to the ballroom I would go, to stay at least two hours longer. Many times Annie took me home at dawn and helped me steal to bed so my mother wouldn't know the hour we had come in.

Annie believed in romance and she understood all my problems of the heart. She would discuss them with me and weigh them from every angle, always advising me wisely, but at the same time with daring. She would say, "Be as wise as a serpent and as gentle as a dove."

Maggie Kelly was not only my nanny; she was also our laundress, as people in those days never dreamed of sending laundry out. Maggie was gentle and completely selfless. Like Katie, she went to Mass every morning, and when we went into the park she used to sit on the bench and say her rosary while I played. My sister Maria was her favorite child and for her she had a pathetic kind of servitude and devotion. There was something touching about her. She seemed to have no defenses and one felt that any storm in life could blow her away and find her mutely unresisting. She was too gentle, but she was also highly emotional and on many occasions lost her head. I always had a desire to defend her and I always did when my mother found fault with her.

Like Katie and Annie, Maggie had been with my mother from the earliest days of her marriage. But unlike Katie and Annie, she never voiced an opinion on any subject. One felt, nevertheless, a curious strength in her silence and an unbreakable loyalty to my mother and everyone in my family. She would have died for any of us.

Bridget Sweeney, our fat and good-natured Irish cook, had learned to cook at a Spanish school of cooking and could make certain Spanish dishes like a chef. Her rice was a marvel and, in the tradition of Spain, it was served in our house at every meal.

Then there was José Arias, a young Spaniard my father had brought from Cuba. He was our butler—or rather, that was what he was supposed to be. He also polished our shoes, mended anything in the house that needed mending, pressed my father's clothes, fed our fox terrier Pinta and took her out for a walk in the early morning, ran to and from the post office more often than the postman himself, and went to school at night to study English.

Besides this collection of faithful servers, an old lady by the name of Miss Adelaide Barling lived with us. She was British to the core and, long before I opened half an eye to peep at the world, she was already past her seventieth year and concealed, beneath a wig of gray curls, a bald head which I was always trying to catch a glimpse of. From the first week of my mother's arrival in New York Miss Barling had been her duenna. She had nobly tried to teach my mother English and a reverence for Queen Victoria. She had lamentably failed in both.

"Barley," as my mother called her, had a fixation about Queen Victoria. She resembled the old queen, and the question could be disputed whether the fixation had caused her to resemble Victoria or whether the resemblance had caused the fixation. She had a mania for royalty in general and she knew the name, date of birth, and intimate life of every crowned head in Europe. She referred to them as her close friends and spoke of them by their first names. All through the years she had a room in our house, and having lived so long with my mother, she seemed a part of the family, in spite of the fact that she claimed she could never understand Spaniards. "They are so different from us British," she used to say, and by her tone of voice there was no doubt as to which was superior.

Another character who figured in the drama of our house was Ezequiel Rojas, the former President of Venezuela. He was my godfather and during my childhood was ambassador in Washington. On the slightest excuse he would come to New York and spend all his time in our house. He had met and fallen in love with my mother when she was a young woman. She was the love of his life and, because of her, he never married or even looked at another woman. His loyalty and devotion to my mother belonged to a past romantic age, or perhaps it belongs to every age but is merely rare to encounter.

He was everything a great gentleman should be, the very essence of the term *un grand seigneur.* In his novel *White Mice,* Richard Harding Davis modeled his hero on him.

Mr. Rojas had had a very eventful and colorful life. He had been involved in a number of revolutions in Venezuela and at one time was thrown into a prison under the sea and kept in complete darkness and near starvation for several years. When he was rescued as the result of another revolution, he had almost lost his sight and his voice in the darkness and dampness.

He was a charming, interesting man, very small, with the most delicate hands and feet. His hair was silky white and he had a small pointed white beard. Because of his imprisonment, he could never speak above a whisper and sometimes, if the weather was bad, he lost his voice completely. He was always exquisitely dressed and took great pride in his clothes and shoes, which were all made in London. He was a strange contradiction for a man who had lived such a rough and dangerous life. I never knew anyone more considerate of the feelings of others, more distinguished and possessed of better manners.

During all my young years and until his death, my father had a Spanish assistant in his office by the name of Pancho. Pancho must have had a last name, but in the many years he came to our house no one except my father ever knew it or was interested enough to ask. My father said that in his office Pancho was a genius, but this must have been the kindness of my father's heart boosting his feeble ego. Pancho may have been a genius in the office but in our house he seemed closer to an idiot. He had a doglike devotion to my mother, but in her presence he was so intensely shy that he rarely ever spoke, and when he did he stammered.

My mother and father's warm Spanish hospitality was inexhaustible and many people—their friends as well as those of my brothers', sisters', and my own—kept a human stream of all ages and occupations flowing through the house.

Aida—who had already made her debut and was considered a great beauty—had many admirers who, it seemed to me, were always coming and going, bearing flowers and presents and colliding with each other.

My brother Dick, who was at Harvard, used to come down over the weekends, arriving for dinner with half a dozen friends in his wake. I remember his bringing the Waterbury brothers who played brilliantly for America on the International Polo Team. I also recall a rather slender and delicate young man named Franklin Delano Roosevelt.

My sister Maria often brought a friend of hers to our house called

Dorothy Taylor, who married Graham White and, after divorcing him, became Countess Frasso. Maria and Dorothy were considered "wild" because in Newport and Southampton—after swimming—they used to dry their hair by driving in an open car as fast as a car would then go. Maria had thick long beautiful hair that flowed back from her head as she and Dorothy raced over the roads. This harmless pastime caused quite a scandal among the stuffy society women.

Hennie, as we called my brother Enriqué, and Baba had their friends too, and I had some of my own.

Although my mother might have been regarded as a conventional Spaniard, actually she was anything but conventional. Except in matters of religion, I would say that we were brought up not only in a most unconventional manner, but also in a most undisciplined one. As a child I never recall any definitely set hour for my bedtime. As for meals, whenever I hear of servants complaining of work today I wonder what they would have done if they had been our Bridget, who rarely cooked a meal in our house for less than ten or fifteen people and never had the slightest idea of what hour my mother or any of us was going to sit down to table. It was no uncommon thing for us to have dinner as late as ten o'clock at night and still be sitting at the table after midnight. My father liked to sit and talk while drinking innumerable cups of coffee long after the meal was finished. Then, too, no guest ever came to our house at any hour of the day or night without being served some form of food or drink, and this necessitated a constant vigil in the kitchen by one or several servants and the coal stove always burning. Bridget used to say good-naturedly that if the fire in the stove ever went out it could only mean that she was dead.

Seven

I never owned or played with a doll. The toy I remember cherishing most was a large white rocking horse Rita gave me which I christened White Hawk and loved for its fiery red nostrils, flowing mane, and tail made of real black horsehair. I used to stand in the stirrups and lasso everything in the room.

I also played at being a newsboy, undoubtedly a painful experience to the members of our household while this obsession possessed me, as I would pass from the basement to the top floor and back again with newspapers under my arm and one of my brother's caps pulled over my eyes shouting:

"EXTRA! EXTRA! A GREAT DEFEAT
THE SINKING OF THE BRITISH FLEET
AND AN M.P. SENT TO JAIL!"

I never varied my news and I must have been a great bore.

In my childhood, Houlgate in Normandy, where my mother and father took our family every summer, was a small place. The casino was then intimate and informal. At night, music was played in the ballroom, while on Sunday afternoons in the same room the Bal d'Enfants took place. Children, willingly and unwillingly, were dragged there by their mothers and nannies and made to dance with each other.

I suffered at these parties not only from shyness but from being dressed up in a stiff, starched frock with the usual sash in pink or blue round my tiny waist, and uncomfortable leather pumps cramming together my toes and feet which had become used to being bare on the beach all day. I detested being mauled and pulled about by some dreadful little boy who in most cases could not lead me as well as I could have led him.

How wonderful it was to sometimes break away and dance lightly by myself round and round the ballroom floor to the strains of "The Blue Danube," free and released until a grownup rushed out to give me a good shaking and push me into the arms of some little boy as shy as myself. According to the grownups the children were brought there to have a good time. It was the grownups, however, who saw to it that they didn't.

These children's balls were like a scene from Noel Coward's *This Year of Grace* when Beatrice Lillie played a mother with her child on the beach at Brighton. When the child did not do exactly what she wished him to do she gave him a good whack on his head, exclaiming, "I brought you here to have a good time and a good time you'll have!"

It was in Houlgate that I first met Audrey Osborn, who is now Mrs. John Elliott. She had come to Houlgate with her devoted nurse Mary, just after the death of her mother who had been the first society woman in New York to go into business. She started and successfully ran a *maison de couture.*

We first noticed Audrey wandering around on the beach or in the casino with Mary, charming looking, sad-eyed and lonely. We were all interested in her and felt sorry for her. Katie, who had seen Mary at Mass, spoke to her and from their acquaintance we met Audrey. My mother and all of us took her at once very much into our hearts, and from then on we have always considered her as a member of our family.

Audrey was my first friend. I was very proud of this friendship and I can remember there in Houlgate when we first met saying to myself, "Now I have a friend." I was proud, too, of showing her off, especially as in appearance we were a great contrast. Audrey is extremely blond with golden hair and blue eyes whereas I have very black hair and dark eyes. When we were older it was said on several occasions that we were so inseparable in order to offset one another when we went to parties.

In character and taste we are also very unlike, although in some mysterious way we understand each other, and I believe we would never fail one another in a crisis. To hear us argue, anyone who does not know us would think we were never going to speak again and no doubt be surprised, when the storm is over, to see us thick as thieves and as though we had never been anything else.

We enjoy the wonderful luxury—which is rare between friends—of being able to speak our minds to each other in no uncertain terms without offending. When we were young, we argued about nearly everything. (I'm afraid that sometimes we still do.) Once Audrey corrected me for using the word "yip" and promptly I denied having used it. Thereupon she shouted, "Yap you said yip!" After this, Audrey's chaperone, Miss McLean, who overheard the argument, used to call us "Yip" and "Yap."

Eight

As soon as I could read and write I read every book I could possibly lay my hands on no matter how much over my head the contents seemed to be. It would be more truthful to say I devoured them, so ferocious was my longing for knowledge. Wallowing in the poets, I too began to write poetry. No subject daunted me, and in the most peculiar spelling I poured out in verse my deepest emotions on any event or aspect of life.

At this period it would seem that I did not have enough to occupy my mind, so I began to teach myself to read everything backwards. I read books, newspapers, advertisements and signs in reverse. As soon as I heard a name pronounced or read it in print I mentally spelled it backwards. I signed my own name "Sedecrem." My mother then decided it was high time I went to school and I was sent to a day convent in New York run by the order of the Sisters of Charity. Here I made my first confession and received my First Communion, and here many other events took place that remain vividly in my memory, though my connection with the school was brief.

And it was here that I met Alice de Zaldo—a great friend for many years. On her mother's side she descends from Dutch people, but her father was Spanish, and happily, Alice looks very Spanish. She has raven black hair and remarkably white skin, and the slender and fragile hands which I have always associated with her. Alice was deeply devoted to me and I had the same devotion for her and often fought her battles in one way or another, sometimes to the point of fist fights, as she was very delicate and would have been pushed about by the other children had it not been for my protection.

It was while I was studying at this convent that Rita divorced Stokes. Much was written in the newspapers about the divorce, especially in the society columns. Some of the children in school were told about it by their parents and they tried to make me feel that a black disgrace had fallen upon me. Of course from their limited and bigoted Catholic point of view it had. I found it impossible to accept this point of view and became rambunctiously furious if anyone said a word against Rita.

One child in the convent, a daughter of James Butler whose grocery store has since developed into a chain of stores, sang an insulting song to me about my divorced sister. I retaliated by answering, "I would rather have a sister who has a divorce than a father who has a grocery store." How cruel children can be!

Soon after this incident I was forced by the nuns to go to a party at James Butler's house. Having had these unpleasant words with his daughter, I did not want to go. Maggie, who was to take me, for some reason did not want to either and tried to influence my mother not to send me. But the nuns won and we both had to go. On the way home I asked Maggie why she had not wanted to take me to the Butlers' house. Her answer was that at one time when she had been a young girl in Ireland she had been engaged to marry James Butler. She had not wanted to go to the party for fear that "Jimmy" would discover her sitting downstairs in the role of a nursemaid.

Aida was not married yet and my great joy at this time was to hang about her room in the evening and help her dress for what was then generally spoken of as a "Ball." I can remember her on many of these occasions, dressed in a lovely decolleté dress of the period—usually white satin with a train sweeping after it—her black hair worn high as women wore it in the early part of the century, brushed up in back and a "pompadour" in front, a coiffure made famous by Charles Dana Gibson in America and by Helleu in France.

Aida was the first woman to make a solo flight in a dirigible. She made this flight over Paris in Santos Dumont's dirigible. I used to love to have her tell me how she felt in the air and I asked her about this flight over and over again.

It was Sister Isabel who brought about my sudden exit from the school of the Sisters of Charity. She was the instructress of my grade, and she had a great attachment for another nun called Sister Clara. For some reason she found me sympathetic and singled me out from all the other children in the class to be her innocent accomplice in this attachment by carrying notes to Sister Clara. I used the utmost caution and discretion in this errand for fear of meeting the Sister Superior, who constantly roamed the corridors to "keep an eye" as she expressed it "on everything going on." I used to go first to the washroom on the pretext of washing my hands and to make sure the coast was clear. Then I would go into Sister Clara's room pretending I wanted to borrow a book, or that I had to look up a word in her large dictionary, or that I wanted to use her special pencil-sharpener.

I was very fond of Sister Isabel. She was a very gentle young nun, and since these letters seemed to mean so much to her and she loved Sister Clara so much, as she often told me, I saw no reason why I shouldn't help her. Sometimes I even stayed in after class to "keep an eye" on the corridors while Sister Clara stole in to have a few private words with her. I did not then fully realize that nuns are not supposed to have private lives or personal attachments. I was only unconsciously aware of the human element in the whole matter, and I felt the craving in Sister Isabel to give human love and have it returned.

When these letter carryings and secret meetings had been going on for some time, a sad thing happened. Sister Clara received a notice that she was to be transferred to China at once. The notice said that the transfer would be for life. Apparently the Mother Superior had been aware of what was going on and had been instrumental in the transfer. Sister Clara had to leave the following day. She was allowed five minutes at the eleven-o'clock recess to say good-by to Sister Isabel in her room. Confiding all this to me, Sister Isabel asked me to remain in the room —perhaps because she was afraid she might throw herself out of the window when Sister Clara was gone.

Sister Clara came in rapidly and for a second they stood mutely before each other. Then suddenly Sister Clara folded Sister Isabel in her arms and they clung to each other. Not a word was exchanged between them and then Sister Clara pulled herself violently away and rushed from the room. A cry like the cry of death came from Isabel and she crumpled and fell to the floor. I rushed to her. The Mother Superior and two other nuns came in, and I was taken away weeping hysterically myself. I remember sobbing wildly in the Mother Superior's office, and beating my head against the wall while two nuns tried to calm me and make me drink a cup of tea.

Later on I went back to class and when I saw another sister presiding and calmly sitting in Sister Isabel's place, I ran out of the room and pulled the fire-alarm bell. We had fire drill every week so all the children knew what to do. They filed into the corridors and had begun descending the stairs in formation when it was discovered that it had been a false alarm.

I have no recollection of what happened then but evidently my mother thought it best to take me out of this school. Events followed fast after this.

For one thing, Rita married the handsome Philip Lydig. She was married in Grace Church—a Protestant church—in a princess gown of heavy cream lace with one of the exceptionally high collars she had begun to wear, and long sleeves. The dress was molded to her beautiful figure, reached to the ground and had a short train. Wrapped around her was a sable boa, and her hat was a huge flat black one characteristic of the period. I went to the wedding in a carriage with Maria, Hennie and Baba, who wept all the way to the church because Rita was going to be married in a Protestant service. What suffering this wedding must have caused my mother. Luckily I don't remember that. Memory plays strange tricks, because while I remember Rita's first wedding when I was still practically an infant, this one I hardly remember at all. It is probable that I only remember her dress so clearly because Helleu made a drawing of her in it, and Boldini painted the life-size portrait of her in a similar costume—walking with Philip Lydig in the Bois—that now hangs in the Louvre.

Nine

During these years I began from time to time to be afflicted with a malady which, has stayed with me all through my life, until recently and caused me untold agony. In my childhood days I invented a name for it. I called it my "moaning sickness."

In those days little was known about child psychology and absolutely nothing was known about it in my home. My mother and Katie attributed every one of my childish pains to indigestion or a cold in my stomach or to just plain cantankerous behavior. My mother never heard of such a word as the psyche in English, and even if she had heard of it in Spanish she would have fought to the last ditch the idea that any one of her children could be troubled by such an absurd and illusory thing.

Thus when at an early age I had violent attacks of psychological suffering and, going into a corner of the room, put my face to the wall and moaned, not much importance was attached to it. It may be that my mother and Katie thought it wiser to ignore the whole matter. Perhaps they thought I would outgrow "this foolishness." It was not, unfortunately, as simple as that.

Considering how I used to moan in these attacks, it is extraordinary that something was not done to help me. But it was not until years later, when I had long ceased to moan and merely suffered in a kind of hopeless silence, that Rita took me to two psychiatrists who did not help me at all.

Later on, these attacks usually started about five o'clock in the morning when I would wake up with a sense of painful bewilderment and sometimes with a sense of acute fear, and feeling as though I had returned from a long and fatiguing journey. I would want to fall back into sleep and a state of forgetfulness, but an active part of me—a sense of preservation—struggled to rouse me and keep me from falling into unconsciousness. This conflict added to my suffering. I would be unable to move and for hours I would lie listless. It was only gradually as the morning wore on that I was able to pull myself together. As a result, through most of my adult years I have kept very late hours and many nights skipped sleep altogether in the hope of avoiding an attack.

Through the years I evolved a technique which in many instances helped me. I discovered that whenever I discussed mystical or spiritual subjects with someone who understood them, for some days and even weeks afterwards these attacks failed to appear. Driving fast in a car, traveling in trains or planes, being in the sunlight, running on the beach, and especially swimming in the sea also helped me.

I write of this very personal suffering in such detail as it was the cause of many things I did in my life, and of an almost suicidal obsession I had for years. How much there is still to be discovered about the spirit!

Fortunately, Eastern teachers have gone into many studies of the spirit and take their findings quite naturally. For example, the art of astral traveling, where the spirit or ego leaves the body while one sleeps and yet remains connected to the life force, is accepted as natural. People in the West are inclined to scoff at these things, but this is only because of their ignorance on the subject. Nearly everyone does at some time travel astrally while asleep. In the West it happens involuntarily and often causes psychic disturbances when the person wakes up. In the East this traveling is done fully consciously. And when an adept or advanced person wakens after having gone out on the astral plane, he has a complete memory of his experiences. He knows these experiences were *not* a dream, whereas the ignorant person thinks he has been dreaming.

Everyone has fallen asleep and awakened with a jerk. Eastern teaching tells us that this indicates a too sudden parting of the astral from the physical body. In my own experience, I believe I have gone out so far on the astral plane that it has been hard for me to find my way back, so that when I woke up I was dazed and felt lost. I believe this is an explanation of much of my moaning sickness and morning depressions, which in turn have caused my migraine headaches.

When I left the convent of the Sisters of Charity I was sent to another, a boarding school outside of Morristown, New Jersey, where Baba had been living for a year. When I arrived at this convent I immediately had one of my most melancholy attacks. Whether it was brought on by the sight of the nuns, who reminded me of the unhappy episode of Sister Isabel, or because it was the first time I had ever been separated from my mother, I don't know, but so violent was my suffering that I went on a hunger strike and also a strike of complete silence. Not having any idea what to do in such a case, the nuns simply left me alone, parking me out, so to speak, on the steps of the convent garden.

It was autumn and Indian summer, and the warmth of the sun somewhat eased my anguish; but the fox hunt going on in the vast park of the Twombly estate across the way, the howling of the dogs, and the thought of the wretched fox trying to escape with his life from these assassins did not help my state of mind.

Baba was sent for by the nuns to try to reason with me.

"Please come and eat your lunch. The nuns are kind people and want you to eat. You will grow weak and ill. All the pupils know how badly you are behaving, and you are upsetting the whole school. Please come and eat," she pleaded.

Poor Baba! Through no fault of my own I have always been a trial to her. She was always worried because I did not eat enough, or because I did not sleep enough, or because I had strange friends. Hatched in the same nest, Baba and I are as unlike as though we had been born on different planets. We have always worried about each other, although we both see life quite differently.

There on the convent steps she failed to move me because, as at many other times in our lives, I knew she was looking at my problems through her own eyes and not through mine. Neither did she have the remotest idea what I was suffering. Reason was not what I wanted. Three days went by without eating or speaking and only very fitful sleep; three times three long twenty-four hours, nine of which each day I spent alone on the steps. Then they sent for my mother, and when she arrived told her in no uncertain language what they thought of me. My mother came out on the steps intending to be angry with me, but when she saw my pinched white face she turned on the Sister Superior and was angry with her instead. She told the nuns what she thought of *them* for allowing me to sit for three days on stone steps in the cold. The unfortunate sisters probably understood very little of what she said in her excitement because of her strong accent, but I am quite sure they heaved a sigh of relief when she departed *with* me.

I well remember leaving the convent with her and walking down the road through masses of red and yellow leaves. As we walked out of the huge iron gate she took my hand and instantly the attack lifted. The blood began to circulate through my body and I experienced a sense of relief as though fresh clear air had been let into my heart.

I can at this moment close my eyes and relive vividly the ride back in the train. I can feel the sensation of leaning against my mother on the coach seat. Her physical presence calmed my overexcited nerves. She put her arms around me and I fell asleep, but not deeply. I was troubled because I felt it was unfair that we had left Baba in the convent. I fretted about it and begged her to take Baba away too. Surprisingly enough, my mother agreed at once and, as if to seal her promise, she bought me a box of "Velvets." These were candies made of molasses which came in bright yellow boxes with red monkeys scampering all over the covers. I coveted the red monkeys almost as much as the candies, but I was only allowed to have the candies on very special occasions. My mother evidently regarded this as one of them.

In spite of all this, my mother did not despair of further convent life for me. I was sent to the nuns of the Order of the Sacred Heart instead of the Sisters of Charity. This day school was in New York in a house on the northeast corner of Fifty-fourth Street and Madison Avenue, which later became the Monte Carlo night club.

For some unexplainable reason the atmosphere of convent life did not agree with me and I was not happy in this convent either. Also, Rita had put the idea into my head that whereas European convents provided good education and friendships for a future life, convents in America did neither. As I had a passion for knowledge, the fact that I was not getting the best education disturbed me. To make up for any deficiency, I sat up all night long reading books far beyond my age. I became absorbed in philosophy and I read Kant, Spinoza, Goethe, Schopenhauer—and William James, whose *Varieties of Religious Experience* had a great influence on my future thinking.

I do not remember receiving anything in this convent except a thorough knowledge of the Catholic Church. Perhaps because of an historic interest in the Church, or because of a profound interest I was later to develop in all religions, I took a course in its history. It was naturally taught from the Catholic point of view, but it did give me a basic understanding of its dogmas.

During this time Alice de Zaldo and I kept up our friendship. Much to my envy, Alice had been sent to a "proper school." Her family had in the meantime moved to a house in our block. We met every day after school and we used to walk from Forty-seventh Street to Washington Square and back. Everyone at this time walked on Fifth Avenue, which was then almost entirely an avenue of private houses. But Alice and I walked like hunters out for game—we hunted our favorite actors and actresses.

Alice very nearly swooned if she saw John Barrymore and I felt the same about Ethel. Alice and I had great arguments about the Barrymores. She maintained that Jack was the most handsome person in the world. I did not go so far as this about Ethel, but I maintained that she was more beautiful than Jack.

Rita was then living in a house which Stanford White had designed for her on Fifty-second Street between Park and Madison Avenues. It was a uniquely beautiful house, Italian in style, and she filled it with priceless Italian art and furnished it with unerring taste. Here in this house she received all the great singers and musicians of the day— Caruso, Scotti, Geraldine Farrar, Sembrich, Emma Eames, Mary Garden, Lina Cavalieri, Toscanini, Paderewski and many others. Meeting these artists so often, I began to regard them as everyday people in my life.

I especially remember Caruso—gay, sometimes comic, always reacting with heart to people and events. Scotti was distinguished, rapierlike; Sembrich very much the prima donna; Geraldine Farrar, charming, sensuous, feline; Mary Garden was highly intelligent, magnetic, almost puritanical—entirely the reverse of her reputation as she was reported to be a dangerous *femme fatale*. Cavalieri was fantastically beautiful, calculating but remarkably stupid. Emma Eames was reserved, charming, well-bred; Toscanini flirtatious, alive, keenly aware of women; Paderewski idealistic, fragile, with a remarkably handsome head.

I went to the opera often with my mother or with Rita, and sometimes we went backstage during the entr'acte. When we went to Caruso's dressing room he used to draw caricatures for me. I took them for granted too, and didn't have the good sense to keep them.

Ethel Barrymore, who was a friend of Rita's, came sometimes to our house. Rita had most likely told her of my admiration, and noticing me staring at her breathless and awed, she invited me to lunch. She came to fetch me in an electric hansom cab and took me, all of atremble, to Sherry's. I sat before her at the table, too shy and excited to be anything but stupid, and praying all the while that I wouldn't suddenly turn peagreen and be overcome with a migraine headache.

Shortly after this, John Barrymore married Phil Lydig's first cousin, Catherine Harris. Alice de Zaldo was dismayed by this—she liked to dream about Jack single—but I was delighted because now I could feel, if only through my brother-in-law, that I was related to Ethel and Jack.

Besides getting a liberal education in opera, Alice and I had a mania for going to the theatre. On the sly we went to matinees when our families thought we were out exercising in the air. My mother and Katie disapproved of the theatre and there certainly were many plays I would never have seen had they had anything to say about it. My mother said that the theatre filled my head with "trash." Katie remarked from time to time that my interest in it would lead me to a bad end. I couldn't see why, if I was allowed to go to the opera, I couldn't go to the theatre, but my mother's answer to this was that the opera was music, the theatre was just plain *trash*—which was not entirely complimentary to the opera either!

There were other difficulties for me pertaining to the trash and these were financial. Although Alice and I sat in the first balcony and sometimes the second, we never could scrape up enough money between us to see every play. I decided to be businesslike and make some. I had seen an advertisement in the newspapers to the effect that for ten dollars you could have a certain number of china plates with decalcomanias delivered to you. The idea was to put the decalcomanias on the plates, in other words perform the labor, and the firm was then supposed to buy them back at twice the price you paid for them. I was delighted with this idea, but I didn't have ten dollars. However, I hit on an idea to get it. Knowing that my father had a great many books he hardly ever read, there seemed no reason why I shouldn't do a little business with them. I put a collection of them in a suitcase and as they were too heavy to carry, I took a cab and drove down to a secondhand bookshop on Fourteenth Street, confident that they would bring me a lot of money. To my dismay, after fingering the books and making hideous faces, the man offered me three dollars. I was too embarrassed to refuse or bargain with him, so I took the money and left the books. When I went outside to pay the cab, the fare was three dollars.

I walked home, crushed but not defeated. I was still determined to make—if not a great one—at least a small fortune in plates. When I got home I showed Maria the advertisement in the newspaper. Maria is very artistic. She should have been an actress and according to that great authority, the Moscow Art Theatre actress, Maria Ouspenskaya, she could have been a great one. But instead of pursuing a career on the stage, she married. We have always been sympathetic and like the same things. I made her feel on this occasion that this was an artistic adventure as well as a commercial one. I had a few dollars myself, she advanced me the rest, and I answered the advertisement. She promised that I could open shop in her room which was on the top floor of the house.

I waited anxiously for the plates to arrive, oozing an air of mystery as though I knew where the crown jewels were hidden. Unfortunately the plates arrived while I was at school. The expressage was collect and José had to pay it. My mother arrived home to find a great case in the hall. The bird was out of the cage, so I mildly told her (trying to keep my head and say the right thing) only about the plates and that I had gone into business. My mother was exasperated and told José to open the box. There, inside, were dozens of the most ordinary plates and packages of dreadful decalcomanias that would obviously come off when they were washed. My mother told José to give the plates to the ashman.

It was not long before the absence of the books was discovered and I had to tell the whole truth about them, as well as about the money José had paid and all my doings. My mother was angry, but my father only shook his head and said, "One can see that she is never going to be a businesswoman."

Ten

Woven into these years were continual trips to Europe. Along with our annual visits to Paris and Houlgate in the summer we often included excursions to other countries.

I never will forget the curious and overwhelming excitement I experienced the first time I saw the great Dutch paintings in the museums of Amsterdam. Once before, when I walked through the Prado in Madrid for the first time, I actually wept, so poignant and intense were my feelings on being surrounded by the incomparable art of Velasquez, Greco and Goya. This time a passing monk kindly stopped and asked me why I was weeping. I replied that I was weeping mostly because I was so overcome by the impact of such beauty and genius, "But," I added, "if I must tell the strict truth, I am really weeping because I did not paint these paintings myself." Such egocentricity must have shocked the little monk. I only hope it prompted him to pray that I might attain a more detached and impersonal point of view.

I saw my first bullfight in Spain at about this time and I was horrified. No amount of explaining to me about tradition, pageantry, no exalting of the footwork and technique of the matador, or praise of his bravery could reconcile me to the sport. Spanish friends made fun of me and said I was not a true Spaniard.

"If killing pathetic horses and bulls is being a Spaniard," I said, "then I renounce forever being one."

The thought of killing animals or even the smallest insect has always been painful to me, and I have never enjoyed eating meat. Even when I was a child having early supper by myself, I used to throw my meat behind the sideboard as soon as Maggie left the dining room.

In France people often breed rabbits and after making pets of them, eat them. As a child this always seemed to me the lowest form of treachery. In Houlgate we had friends who bred rabbits and gave them pet names like Mimi and Fifi. I once was at lunch with these friends when they served rabbit and bluntly inquired if we were eating Mimi and Fifi. My hostess looked guilty and embarrassed while my mother gave me a silencing look, but I refused to accept quietly what I then considered murder. Jumping up from the table, I rushed out to the rabbit shed. Of course there was not a sign of Mimi or Fifi. I stood there paralyzed with horror and visualized these pets whom I had played with a few days before mashed up and disintegrating inside the people who were devouring them. Luckily my mother did not eat rabbit, but I refused to forgive my hostess for her part in the affair and could never be induced to return to that house again.

During these years Rita lived a great deal in Europe and spent several months of the year in Paris. She had become an outstanding figure, not only in the social world and because she was a patroness of art and artists, but really because of her remarkable personality and style. I don't think the word *glamour* was used then as it is now, but if it had been, Rita would have been considered glamorous in its fullest and richest sense. In any case, her presence raised the vibration of the most commonplace event. For this reason she had a sort of magnetic appeal for all kinds of people. Without the advance publicity of a movie star, without the recognition which comes from films and photographs, she attracted people whenever she appeared in public. She rarely went into stores and never into a department store because crowds followed and surrounded her.

At this time the great *couture* houses were Worth, Paquin, Callot Soeurs, Vionet, and Poiret. Rita designed most of her own clothes and they were made for her by Callot Soeurs. Whatever style she created or wore was copied by the fashion world, and spies were sent out by the different houses to discover her new creations. She once said to me, "I should play a joke on these foolish sheep women by wearing some monstrous costume. They would all rush to copy it and then imagine they looked well in it!"

Rita had an exceptionally beautiful back. It was she who invented the décolleté evening gown cut down to the waistline at the back with only two narrow straps over the shoulder to hold it up. She wore this gown for the first time in her box in the Diamond Horseshoe of the Metropolitan Opera House. As the lights went on after the first act Rita was sitting with her back half turned to the audience. Frank Crowninshield, who was in the box with her, said there was a gasp from the audience and then there was a flutter as binoculars and lorgnettes were lifted to a thousand pairs of eyes. It was a sensation. Newspapers came out the next day calling it and Rita "scandalous" and "indecent." But it was not long before this type of evening dress was copied by fashionable women all over the world.

When I was only ten, Rita took me to see many great artists in Paris. She treated me like a grownup and used to introduce me then as her "canary." Later on she always referred to herself and me as "The Sisters Karamazov." I met Rodin, Bourdelle, Henri Bergson, Brieux, Anatole France, Boldini, Yvette Guilbert, D'Annunzio, Edith Wharton, Helleu, Sarah Bernhardt, Jacques Copeau and many others—some with less celebrated names but burning, nevertheless, the *feu sacré* within their hearts as brightly as the more famous ones who had, in the worldly sense, succeeded. We went often to Zuloaga's studio in Montmartre, where he mixed gypsies and bullfighters with intellectuals such as Benevente, Ortega y Gasset and Unamuno.

With Rita I met many celebrities other than artists—King Alfonso, Queen Marie of Roumania, Count Boni de Castellane, Princess Hohenlohe, and not the least, Yantorny—who was a remarkable bootmaker. He was the shoe curator of the Cluny Museum in Paris and there was nothing he didn't know about shoes of every period. By birth he was an East Indian but he lived most of his life in France, following his own way of life, which was very ascetic. He was a vegetarian and seldom ate more than one meal a day. He went into designing and making shoes because he had a passion for them. He had his own ideas about making them, and he didn't make them for everyone. If Yantorny decided to make you a pair he would make a cast of your feet in plaster, at the same time measuring every inch of both feet. He would observe them walking barefoot to ascertain just where the weight was placed, and he would feel them, holding and balancing them in his hands. He would ask you to contract them and make them limp and then put you through a series of toe-spreadings. If he finally decided to make you your shoes, you could count on the first pair being delivered in about two years. If he liked you very much, as he did Rita, you might hope to get them in a year, or, if a miracle occurred, in six months.

The most beautiful things about all the shoes he made for Rita were the trees. He wanted to fashion them out of the lightest wood possible, so he made them out of violins. Rita bought old violins and he transformed them into shoetrees so exquisite that they are works of art in themselves. Stark Young asked if he might have a pair of the trees to put on a table in his living room. He said he considered them equal to any work of art.

Yantorny told me that he loved making shoes for Rita because, he said, "She walks perfectly and is the only person I know who, as she walks, places her feet absolutely correctly on the ground."

I always loved going to Rodin's studio with Rita. I know that modern sculptors consider his art uninteresting. It is uninteresting to them in the same way that realistic painting is uninteresting today to the abstract painter. Nevertheless, to have seen Rodin at work in his studio, to have felt the dynamic power of his personality and seen him wrestling with stone—transforming it from its material aspect into a work of art—makes me feel an appreciation of his genius that the self-termed "modernist" probably cannot share.

Except for certain pieces of Greek and Eastern sculpture I am, as a rule, not aesthetically moved by it, and yet I do not know any other art which makes one so aware of a superpower in man. This working with stone, transposing its material quality to a higher octave, conquering the gigantic physical difficulties involved in carving great blocks of stone—all this creates in me a certain sense of awe for this art if not actually an artistic pleasure. Certainly the sculpture in the caves of Ajanta and Ellora in India awed me more than any other great works of art in the world.

Awe was my reaction to Rodin—awe for the man for his superhuman work.

Boldini painted a number of portraits of Rita and I went with her occasionally to his studio when she was posing for him. When he painted he sometimes wore a bowler hat. He was a highly nervous, energetic and astute little man with a flair for style and chic that no other portrait painter in this century ever surpassed.

As I was impassioned by the theatre I suppose it is only natural that I remember Sarah Bernhardt more vividly than any person I met in those early days in Paris. I made many visits to her house with Rita. In spite of my attraction to the theatre and theatre people I was, nevertheless, not much drawn toward Bernhardt. I could not help admiring her amazing technique, her breath control in long speeches, her astounding production of sound and words (I have heard her at a moment's notice recite long pages from *Phèdre, L'Aiglon,* or some one of her other great roles), and her fantastic vitality. But to me she was like a person who had swallowed ten lions, and they were all raging within her. I watched her—listening at the same time to that curious voice and that amazing language and avalanche of words—but my emotions remained unmoved.

One day she was expecting an official to come and present her with a decoration, and there was a great stir in the household. The servants rushed around in wild excitement while Bernhardt gave crisp orders in a loud voice. The presentation was supposed to have been a surprise, but of course the Divine One had been tipped off about it. She called a dress rehearsal and took her place in the living room before the mantel so that her reflection could be seen in the mirror. She rehearsed a scene of surprise for us and improvised a wonderful and warm speech thanking an imaginary person for the decoration. All of us in the room—Rita, the servants, her doctor and myself—were supposed to enter into the spirit of the scene. Then the doorbell rang. Bernhardt sprang into position as if she were behind a rising curtain on the stage. But it was merely a poor little man with an ordinary package. Bernhardt's servant, unfortunately for him, had made a mistake. When she saw the little man with the package she shouted a volley of abuse at the servant and he was hustled out. When the real bearer of the decoration arrived, no one in the world could have put on a better act of complete surprise than Bernhardt. I didn't understand actresses then. I lacked the humor to appreciate the scene, and I remember feeling ashamed for her—at what seemed to me hypocrisy.

Bernhardt greatly admired Rita's carriage and manner of walking. She used to ask Rita to give her lessons in walking. Rita, only too happy to do a bit of acting herself, would walk up and down the room saying, "One's weight must never be placed on the heels. One's heels must only lightly touch the ground to insure the balance. It is on the balls of the feet that the weight of the body must rest and even there not too heavily. One must feel a spring in the foot and be conscious of this spring as one lightly touches the ground with each step, feeling the sense of it in one's entire spine. Head held high, breathe deeply and spring!"

These lessons were very funny and usually ended with all three of us rocking with laughter.

Eleonora Duse was quite a different woman and artist. I will never forget the mystic magic with which Duse's art touched me and the white-flame quality I felt in contact with her personality.

It is strange how destiny weaves a circle in one's life. In my own life, when people have meant much to me they have appeared in it and disappeared out of it in the same way—arriving at the last point exactly as at the starting point. For instance, when I saw Isadora Duncan for the first time in my life she waved a scarf at me, and the last time I saw her she waved a scarf at me. And it was a scarf that killed her!

It was so too with Eleonora Duse. I was a child in Venice the first time I saw her, gliding past me in a black gondola. The last time I had contact with her mortal body was when she was carried off dead in a black ship to Italy, and I watched that dark ship glide out from the pier and steam down the river.

My first sight of her is as clear in my mind as spring water. I was alone in a gondola, and it was the hour in the day when Venice is more magical than any other place in the world. It was not yet exactly evening but rather late afternoon just after the sun had gone down—an hour when one is most aware of shadows and the presence of the past. As we were turning into one of the narrow canals I leaned a little to one side of the gondola, placing my hand along the outside. As we turned we collided with a gondola coming the other way. Startled, I quickly drew in my hand and the two gondoliers hurled the usual insults at each other. The other gondola was suddenly beside ours. It was painted completely black and in it sat a woman dressed in black. I looked up at a strikingly tragic face. For a second I was almost close enough to touch her. Then, as our eyes met, she smiled and made a quick gesture with her hand toward my hand and shook her head, indicating that I should keep my hand away from the side of the gondola. Then her gondola turned the corner of the house and glided down the canal. It was only a brief flash but I can still see her face today in my mind's eye as I saw it that moment. A tortured but inspired face that stirred and awakened in me, even as a child, a profound emotion.

"La Duse! *La grande attrice* Eleonora Duse!" my gondolier exclaimed.

That evening, and all that night whenever I woke up, I thought of her. I felt as one might feel who had suddenly received Grace—as though a change had taken place inside of me. I had the sensation that a well of feeling had been struck in my heart, a well that was to grow deeper with the years. That chance meeting started a quest in my life—I dreamed from then on only of knowing her.

In spite of the obsession I developed for Duse I did not actually meet her for many years—not until she came to the United States only a few months before her death in 1924. The reason for this was that, until she went to London in 1923, she lived in Asolo in complete seclusion over a period of about fourteen years. During this time she saw no one and the world heard nothing about her. Strangely enough, however, when Isadora Duncan's children were killed she generously wired Isadora to come to her in Asolo, knowing that she was beside herself with grief. Isadora often spoke to me about this visit which unfortunately ended disastrously.

Isadora said that while staying with Duse she walked alone up into the hills and lay down in the grass under a tree. Thinking of her children as she stretched out on the ground with her face buried in the grass, she began to sob. Suddenly she felt a hand placed gently on her shoulder. She looked up and, as she expressed it to me, "beheld a Greek god." In reality he was a young Italian painter who lived in a little house nearby and was going naked for a plunge in a mountainstream. He asked Isadora why she was crying and took her in his arms to console her. She told him about the loss of her children. He said, "Let me give you another one." With no further words Isadora gave herself to him. (She actually had a child by him which was born dead the day war was declared in 1914.) She told me that she returned to Duse's house beside herself with joy. She said, "I floated back to Eleonora on wings, because I knew God would surely not be so unkind as not to give me another child." She burst into Duse's room and recounted her meeting with the Greek god. Duse, far from entering into the spirit of this adventure, was scandalized. Her disgust and disappointment in Isadora were so profound that there was nothing further for Isadora to do but leave her house. Duse never forgave this act of what she considered promiscuity, nor could she forgive the fact that while Isadora was grieving for her children she could, at the same time, have a sexual adventure. Isadora claimed it was not a "sexual adventure" but only a means toward an end in having another child.

Isadora and Duse met years later but they were never again real friends. Isadora spoke to me many times about this incident and, although it had occurred many years in the past, it seemed to be often in her mind. I realized how much she had suffered in losing Duse's friendship. Being such a complex person, she was rather puritanical at heart despite her outward behavior, and regardless of what she said about Duse, I believe she felt a deep guilt about the whole matter. She said,

"I never could have imagined that such a supreme artist as Duse could be so narrow-minded."

These two great women so alike in so much, as they both uniquely expressed their art in vast dimensions, were actually as far apart in their concept of life as the North Pole is from the South. Duse could never comprehend Isadora's often humorous and sometimes pagan approach to life; and Ísadora could never remotely understand Duse, whose Catholic background gave her a sense of sin and an emphasis on death rather than life. Isadora loved and embraced life—Duse more often turned from it.

Eleven

   The news of our father's death came to Hennie, Baba and me while we were in Houlgate in Katie's care. My mother, Dick, Aida and Maria had gone back to America with him when he complained of not feeling well. He was the first person close to me with whom I associated death. I had read about it in books and wept over Shelley and Keats, and had even written poems to death myself—but this was different. Now it became visualized in a familiar face and body that I had loved and touched. Fortunately we were not then told how he had died.

   For some years he had been melancholy. He often mentioned owing a debt to the comrades of his youth who had been shot in Cuba. It seemed to prey on his mind that his life had been spared while theirs had not. He spoke of having lived his life on a false basis. He said that he had only borrowed it and that sooner or later he would be called upon to return it and pay off his debt. He said these things whenever he drank too much red wine, which he sometimes did when he was over-tired. Incidentally, I never saw him drink anything else—only red wine, which he always drank at dinner.

   This habit of my father's of talking about his life debt was not taken very seriously by any of us. That particular summer he had gone up to the Adirondack Mountains with the intention, so he said, of resting. Instead, he jumped from a high cliff onto a plateau of rocks below. He was killed instantly. Evidently to his way of thinking this was some sort of expiation for the years he had lived beyond the lives of his comrades. In a way it was a repetition of the leap he had made into the sea so many years before, which had been a leap to life.

After his death there was not enough money to warrant the manner in which we were living. True to his Spanish character, he had given a great deal away which my mother never attempted to recover. My mother and father always believed in giving money whenever they could, but they did not believe in lending it.

To reduce expenses, my mother decided to put the house on the market, and it was not long before it was sold. When many years later I saw *The Cherry Orchard,* it was very real to me. One by one every piece of furniture was taken away—the packing cases, boxes, and trunks as they were carried out seemed like a long procession of coffins. On the last day I went upstairs for a look at each room. My mother was waiting for me as I came down the stairs. This for her was a parting from all the ties of her youth, her married life and the associations with all our childhoods. My oldest brother had died in this house and many of us children had been born there. She held her head high and taking my hand she led me through the front door and closed it behind us forever. As we drove away she made no comment and she did not look back.

With the selling of the house many other changes took place. Our old cook Bridget had just recently died, and so had our fox terrier Pinta. As the apartment we were moving into was much smaller, Maggie decided to go and live with her sister and take in washing. So out of the original number of old servers only Katie and Annie moved with us to the new place at Sixty-sixth Street and Madison Avenue. Rita, in the meantime, had sold her house on Fifty-second Street and moved to a Georgian house on the corner of Washington Square. My brother Dick had recently married Alice de Zaldo's oldest sister. Then quite suddenly my mother decided to send Baba and me to a boarding school in France.

"This time your school will not be a convent," she said.

The school to which Baba and I were sent was called the Château de Dieudonne. It was near Beauvais on the Oise. The Château itself, which had been built during the reign of Louis XIV, was small, but back of it was a large forest—at least it seemed large to me then. This forest played an important part in my life at the school.

It was here, while still buttoned up in winter clothes and wearing woolen gloves, that I became aware of the first signs of spring and knew that the bitterness of winter was gone. It was as though some inner voice were chanting: "Death has passed." I would stand and listen to the melting ice dripping down the sides of the dark trees and then I would kneel and smell the earth, and somehow the odor would magically be changed from what it had been only the day before. Now there was a new message in the earth—a message which vitalized me and made me sharp and alert.

Often at night when everyone in the school was sleeping I stole out into the forest and, as though plunging into some fantastic land, held my breath in terror as the black trees creaked and groaned in the wind and cast their great shadows over my head. I would go forth into the darkness tortured by the fear it held for me and in some curious way enjoying this fear as a poignant ecstasy, even though it struck into my heart a sense of doom, the same sense of doom I have experienced in later years when I have dreamed of that forest—because this dream has invariably brought some kind of disaster into my life.

It was into this forest that I escaped when I was overwhelmed by a kind of cosmic despair—a feeling as if the weight of life was too much to bear. I would throw myself down on the ground and weep from the intense pain in my heart, and slipping into a state of semiconsciousness, fall asleep on a soil seemingly softened and fertilized by my own tears.

The school was run by an old Spanish lady, the Marquesa de San Carlos de Pedroso. She ran the school because she had lost her money, and she used to say that she "took in pupils" and was always annoyed if anyone said she "ran a school." Perhaps she was right as, according to my memory of the Marquesa's management, there was not much "running" nor was there much "school," either, about the whole thing. All of us pupils were supposed to converse in French with one another, but as we were a mixture of nationalities—French, German, Irish, Scotch, with English in the majority—our French was most peculiar, many of the accents sounding more like Chinese. Many of the English girls translated literally from English into French. When it came to a phrase like "by the way, I forgot to tell you," they would translate "by the way" as *"par le chemin."* Unfortunately, no one ever corrected this nonsense. Some of the pupils studied the piano, others painted, and we all read the French classics; but generally speaking, I do not believe any one pupil learned much of anything, although ancient professors from Paris tottered in and out of the Château on odd Wednesdays or Fridays, supposedly to teach us history, mathematics, or some special science.

Baba and I were the only Spanish children in the school and this, no doubt, brought us closer to the Marquesa and her daughters than the other pupils. We were also Roman Catholics and that was another reason for the Marquesa's sympathy toward us. We assisted at Mass in her private chapel and I was allowed to take care of the altar.

The Marquesa was an extraordinary old lady with a face more like a man's than a woman's. She wore a mantilla over her white hair and dressed in black—"Traditional to Spanish women," she said. We pupils were fed and nourished by her daughters on the idea of how charming and unselfish she was. Looking back on those days now I realize she indeed was charming when she wished to be, but certainly never unselfish. She ruled with a strong will, a biting tongue, and Machiavellian methods.

I remember her once saying to me in Spanish while smiling charmingly at some of the English girls: "Look how clumsy they are and how badly they hold themselves. Spanish children would never move their bodies in such an ugly way or have such big feet." She said all this in such honeyed tones that the poor English girls, not understanding a word of Spanish, thought she was praising them and looked extremely pleased.

The Marquesa not only allowed me to take care of the altar in the chapel but I was also allowed to dust, renew the candles, polish the candlesticks and sanctuary lamp, arrange the flowers and take care of the incense. The village priest permitted me to ring the bell on Sundays when he said the Mass. My happiest moments were spent in the chapel. This was my realm where no one interfered, and where I felt that no one but God had an eye on me. I did so much polishing and cleaning it was a miracle I didn't wear everything out. The little gold bell I rang at the Mass shone so brilliantly that when I raised it up to ring it I could see my face fantastically elongated and peering from its sparkling surface. I loved this bell. It was always a thrilling moment waiting to ring it. I would watch the priest as he genuflected and then just a second before he picked up the chalice and turned to elevate the Host, my heart would begin to thump. This was the moment to ring—not a second too soon—not a second too late! I peered out of the corner of my eye at the people kneeling in the chapel: the Marquesa, her daughters, Baba, Erika and Lily Hohenlohe (the only other children who were also Catholics), Alfonso, the servants, and generally some peasants. At the sound of my bell they all bowed their heads in reverence. Once, twice, three times my bell tinkled out while a profound silence seemed to embrace the entire chapel. With the last faint tinkle, as the echo of its sound died away, came the general stirring, coughing and relaxing of all the kneeling people.

One day when my dusting mania in the chapel was in full swing, I saw a speck of dirt on the face of the statue of the Madonna. I stood on tiptoe and tried to brush it away with a cloth, but I lost my balance and before I could prevent it fell forward, knocking the Virgin to the floor. I heard the crash and closed my eyes. A terrible roaring sound like the sea rushing through a giant shell flooded through my ears. Then I heard a quick and what seemed to me an amazingly loud hammering. I was sitting on the floor from weakness and giving my undivided attention to what was causing this knocking. Suddenly I was aware that it was coming from my own heart. At my feet lay the statue of the Madonna. She was stretched out on her back, her calm eyes undisturbed and gazing up at the ceiling. In her arms she still held the little child whose delicately painted eyes also gently and wisely gazed up at the ceiling, as if they were remotely unconscious that for nearly two thousand years He had stirred the world to sacrifices, to bloody wars and massacres, to love, strife, hate, inspiration and peace.

At a little distance from the statue of the Madonna and her child lay a tiny plaster hand. I viewed it with dismay and saw that it had broken off from the left arm of the Virgin. There it lay pathetically with the palm turned upward. I picked it up and gently tried to fit it onto the wrist. It was such a clean break that I was able to fit it perfectly into place. But of course it wouldn't stay there. I cast about for some substance that would hold it, and saw a lighted candle—a tiny wax candle burning on the altar with a shimmering small flame. It seemed fit to once more unite this virginal hand to its wrist. I sighed with relief. But as I placed the Madonna and her Child back where they had originally been I realized that across her wrist there was a crack that not even a dim light could conceal. I thought of all the remarks the Marquesa would make when she discovered my clumsiness. "Flowers!" cried out my brain. "Flowers tucked in the arms of the Virgin will surely hide the crack!" I ran outdoors, but instead of flowers I picked laurel leaves. This I felt was wiser. Laurel leaves lasted while flowers withered quickly, and the incessant changing of flowers would undoubtedly draw attention to the very spot I wished to conceal. I slipped the laurel leaves into the Madonna's arms where they spilled over and hid the broken hand. I felt safe.

A few days later while all the pupils were assembled at the usual fortnightly conferences I heard from out of a state of daydreaming the Marquesa's voice. She was saying, "Quite recently I have noticed a lovely spray of laurel leaves in the arms of the Madonna in our chapel. I wish all you Protestant children would learn a lesson from the great devotion Mercedes gives to the Mother of God. This touching tribute is an example."

I felt the blood drain away from my heart and for a fleeting second I was tempted to sink low in my chair and remain very quiet. But the deep inner Me (something profoundly deeper than either heart or brain) lifted my body to my feet. I remember then shouting in a loud clear voice (and I have always been grateful to "Me" that I didn't evade this test): "You are mistaken, madame—I placed the laurel leaves in the arms of the Madonna not as a tribute, but as a deception in order to hide her hand which broke off when I knocked the statue over. I stuck the wrist on again with candle wax."

As my voice trailed away there was a profound silence, broken only by the sound of the Protestant pupils drawing in their breaths in agitation. They did not know about the Madonna, but in my voice they sensed a tremendous declaration—for all they knew, a declaration that might carry me away from the school and cause me to be cast into a dungeon in the Vatican.

"Come here," the Marquesa commanded.

I moved forward, my knees shaking as I stood before her.

"Kneel," she said.

I knelt as if I were about to be beheaded. Then, instead of the falling ax, I felt the hand of the Marquesa very tenderly laid on my head.

"You have proved yourself worthy of being a Spaniard. No matter what your motive, you nevertheless paid a tribute to the Madonna by placing laurel leaves in her arms. For is not laurel the symbol of victory?"

I rose to my feet to protest and explain my true intentions, but my words were drowned by a sudden outburst of applause from the Protestant pupils. They sensed a dramatic climax and they felt the need of a physical gesture to express it. I was still not permitted to explain that I had not picked laurel leaves for victory but merely because I thought they would last longer.

Twelve

When I returned from school in France my sister Aida introduced me to Mrs. William Ross Proctor's daughter Vouletti, and we formed a close friendship which has lasted to this day.

Mr. and Mrs. Proctor originally came from Pittsburgh. Mrs. Proctor before her marriage was a Miss Singer and her father was Andrew Carnegie's partner and, like him, an outstanding figure in the steel world. (Curiously enough, Vouletti's own father's family, the Proctors, had made their money in the Singer Sewing Machine Company, but there was no connection between the two families.) In spite of their wealth the Proctors lived with simplicity and the utmost good taste. On his estate at Shohola Mr. Proctor had built an Elizabethan house overlooking a large lake. The estate covered thousands of acres and included a large farm with many barns where he raised cows. He modeled his way of living after the English gentleman-farmers, but he fraternized with his tenants and the little country people as only an American could. Vouletti and her brother were brought up unaware of their wealth and never even remotely made anyone conscious of it. Vouletti, like her mother, has always managed to help people without any show and without appearing to be helping.

I spent the happiest days of my youth in the Proctors' two houses, one on Thirty-ninth Street in the then-fashionable Murray Hill district in New York and the other in Shohola. There in this wooded Pennsylvania land, broken only by the lovely streams rushing down from its mountains and hills, we often came upon wild deer, beaver, raccoons, bears and snakes. Whatever my worries were or my adolescent yearnings, there, removed from the city's touch, I often forgot them or was at least able to arrive at a correct evaluation of them.

During the winter months the lake in Shohola often froze completely over with black ice. It was so smooth that an iceboat could travel on it at a terrific speed. I remember iceboating there, the only time I have ever done so in my life. We used to skate, too—sometimes all day—and when evening fell we'd go home to a great roaring fire.

It is often the case that rich people, no matter how talented they are, are unable to discover or use their talents. If Vouletti had not had wealth I am convinced that she could have been a great ballet dancer. She had a passionate love of dancing—a pathetic love, since she had no way of professionally expressing it.

At the time when I first met Vouletti many changes were taking place in my home life. My three sisters married, one by one, which left only Enriqué and me at home with our mother. Aida married Oren Root, the nephew of Elihu Root who had been Secretary of State under Mc-Kinley and Roosevelt. Maria married Andrew Robeson Sargent from Boston. He was the nephew of the painter John Singer Sargent, and his father, Professor Sargent, was a distinguished botanist. Bo was an enormous man, six feet seven inches tall. His heart was equally big and he was a generous and lovable character. Baba also married a Boston man—William Sewall. He was much older than Baba and had lived for some years in Kenya where he had a large ranch. My mother was unhappy because she felt that Billy was too old for Baba and she hated to have her live so far away, but Baba was determined to go to Africa and there was nothing to be done about it.

As she and I had always been much together, her marriage made a change in my life. It brought my brother Enriqué, or Hennie as we called him, closer, since we were the last ones left at home. There was a difference of about eight years in our ages, but we discovered at this time that there were many similarities in our characters and reactions to various things, and a curious affinity in our manner of thinking. We found, for example, that when we were reading a copy of the same book at the same moment we often marked exactly the same lines. We both discovered and bought a copy of a book called *The Gadfly,* written by E. L. Voynich and published many years earlier, in 1897, by Henry Holt and Company. This book had a terrific effect and influence on both of us, but it was only some time later that we realized this and then found out that we had each bought and read the book during the same week. So powerful was the impression made on me by this book that, though I considered it a strong factor in the death of my brother Enriqué, I have never since been able to reread it. I still have my copy of it and several times in later years I have tried to look through its pages to see what could have been in it that influenced us so morbidly. But some force within or without myself—I do not know which—has prevented me from doing it. The contents of the book perhaps holds something which subconsciously I do not want to face, so that each time I have tried to reread it my emotion has been too great and I have been forced to put it away again. The curious part is, that nowadays I only vaguely remember the characters in it and not at all its actual story.

I find it difficult at this present writing to conjure up a picture of Hennie in my mind, and believe now that I never really knew him, and no doubt he did not know me. We were both desperately unhappy and unadjusted people, centered in our own despair and unable to help one another. We were like deaf mutes making frenzied signs, but using different symbols and scarcely knowing that we did not really understand each other. If I had known then as much as I do now about life in general and psychology in particular, the whole tragedy for Hennie and myself might never have happened. But I was ignorant in those days— blindly ignorant on many levels. I was wandering then, it now seems to me, through a forest of darkness, wandering and stumbling and benumbed by pain. Unquestionably Hennie was in the same state, so how could we possibly have helped each other, much less have been aware of the sharp blades we held, each to the other's throat?

Hennie was always delicate. From his childhood he was supposed to have had a "floating kidney." When I heard my mother discussing this ailment it was never very clear in my mind exactly what it was. I imagined Hennie's kidney floating inside him, tossed from one side of his body to the other like a small ship in a storm. As I remember him before his death, he was over six feet tall, slender and sensitive-looking. He had beautiful and poetic hands with long, tapering fingers. I realize now that they were hands that were incapable of handling life. Hennie, like myself, wanted to be a poet. We regarded all other people who were not poets as inferior human beings. He was very antisocial and liked few people. When he went to school he detested every minute of it. He used to say, "The average school is only for idiots and is designed to increase the student's imbecility." At home he never ceased studying and reading. It seemed to me that he was brilliantly informed on all subjects. He left Harvard at the end of his freshman year and refused to go back, saying that it could easily produce brokers, lawyers and bankers, but not men of true culture or thought. After this it was hard to know what to do with him. To me it was quite obvious that his career should have been writing. At least he could have gone into a publishing firm or worked on a newspaper. But our brother-in-law Phil Lydig, who represented everything Hennie disliked in life, brought pressure to bear so that he had to take a job in a bank—a job for which he was about as well fitted as a nightingale in a five-and-ten-cent store.

At this time my mother, Katie, Annie, Hennie and myself moved from the apartment on Sixty-sixth Street to a private house on Madison Avenue and Seventy-ninth Street. The house was a small one. I had a room at the back of the third floor, while Hennie slept on the top floor at the front. He used to come into my room at night and we often talked until dawn. He told me that he did not like to touch or even see money at the bank. He said he hated life. I agreed with him about this, because I hated it too. He said many times that life was just a trap and that he saw no reason to go on with it. He felt strongly that children owed their parents absolutely nothing, but that parents owed children everything for having brought them into the world. He said it was criminal to have children, and when I sometimes asked him what would happen to the world if people did not have children he replied, "Humanity would be finished, and a damn good thing."

I should say that both Hennie and I lived in an inner state of melancholia. Outwardly I carried on my life in spite of this bleakness and desolation of heart and put on a front of being interested in things. A good front it must have been too, because no one seemed to be aware of my intense suffering, nor were they aware of Hennie's either.

I do not recall this whole period in detail—I remember it only as a sort of process of agony. What caused this agony, what it was that created this intense suffering I do not know to this day, although I have questioned psychologists who have been as incapable of explaining it as I myself.

In September, Hennie took a holiday. He, mother and I went down to Hot Springs, Virginia. Here, I think, our mutual depression reached its peak. I remember sitting one beautiful and sunny afternoon on a hill in the long grass with Hennie. We looked over the valley below and talked of death, God, and immortality. We talked at great length about suicide.

Hennie said that God could not be against suicide, and that He would know when one had been tried enough, and would permit the use of free will to further escape the trap. He said, "For those who want to stay on here only to take more suffering, grow old and finally die, why, let them. This is their choice. I won't be one of this mass production— of this bleating herd." Then he added: "You surely don't want to go on only to be expected to marry and have children."

"Good God, no," I said. "I hope I will never be guilty of bringing another soul into the world to suffer as I have. At least I know better than that."

Two weeks later we returned to New York with Mother. It was the beginning of October and a very warm Indian summer. This particular night after dinner my mother went right upstairs to bed. Hennie and I sat before the piano in the living room. We again talked of suicide while I aimlessly played a tune, striking the notes with one finger. Then I showed Hennie some samples in color of material that Rita had sent me to choose from for an evening dress.

Abruptly he said, "You won't need any of them. If you do, the color should be black."

We got up and went slowly upstairs. Often I try to piece together what I thought of during that long voyage up the stairs, but I have no real recollection of what went through my mind. I only had the sensation of sleepwalking. When we reached my room, Hennie came a little way across the threshold and quite suddenly took me in his arms and held me tightly; then, just as suddenly, he broke away from me and ran rapidly up the stairs. I heard him go into his room and close the door. I heard him turn the key in the lock. Ever since then all through my life, the sound of a door being closed and a lock being turned is like a dagger plunged into my heart.

I do not know how I undressed. I remember closing the windows and the door and, after putting out the light, I turned on the gas logs in the fireplace and got into bed. I must have fallen into a semi-doze when clearly I saw my mother's face. Tears were pouring down it. I jumped up and was wide awake. I leapt to the fireplace and turned off the gas, then I opened the windows and leaned far out for air. I felt sick and lay down on the bed again and fell asleep.

When I woke up it was just dawn. Outside an early Madison Avenue streetcar was passing slowly. Gradually I became conscious of a strong smell of gas. I jumped up. Hadn't I turned off the gas? I knew I had and I rushed out into the hallway. The smell was overpowering. I followed it quickly up the stairs, where it grew stronger. I knew only too well what it was. I banged on Hennie's door. I shouted at him. When there was no answer I ran into a tool room in the hall and seized a hammer. I broke in a panel of the door, and putting my hand inside I turned the key. The room was dark, the curtains were drawn, and at first it was difficult to see anything. I rushed and drew back the curtains and opened wide the windows. Besides the bed a dark figure was kneeling. It was Hennie in a dark blue suit in which he had carefully dressed. I took him in my arms and his already rigid body grasping a crucifix in his hand fell back against me. I shouted for my poor mother, then frantically I rushed downstairs and to the house next door, where I knew a doctor was living. When finally he came, after what seemed to my mother and me like an eternity of waiting, he said that Hennie had been dead for three hours.

Whatever actual part I shared in this tragedy, whatever even partial burden of responsibility for it rested on my shoulders, I paid for a thousandfold through my mother's agony. Her suffering was appalling. It was all the more heartbreaking to see because of the heroic way in which she bore it. It was she who did all the terrible but necessary last things for Hennie. She and I together closed his coffin, but it was she who comforted me at this moment and all through the bleak months that followed.

I did not know then as I do now that there is no excuse for suicide. Unfortunately, it took me years to learn this. We may invent many reasons for excusing suicide. None of them is valid. It is an act that can never be purely personal or isolated from our fellow men. The cause of every suicide is essentially and solely ignorance, no matter what the motive appears to be. No one with spiritual knowledge could commit such an act no matter what suffering or stress he was under.

Spiritual knowledge is an awareness of the two great truths taught by all great religions and great teachers down through the ages—Karma (cause and effect of every act and thought) and Reincarnation (a wheel of rebirths put in motion by previous actions in past lives). All of the great Eastern religions have always taught and still teach Karma and Reincarnation. The early Christian fathers taught the same truths.

So in the light of these truths suicide is no solution to anyone's problems, because whatever difficulty or suffering one is trying to escape, these same difficulties or sufferings will reappear again, I believe, in another life. If people fully realized this, no matter what pressure they were under they would cherish the short span of life given them and would face their problems rather than try to escape them, and so these very problems would in some way be solved.

After Hennie's death I sank into deeper melancholy. I could not bear to be alone, I could not bear the nights because I could not sleep, and the sight of a coat thrown across the side of a bed cause me untold anguish. Rita decided that mother and I should move from this ill-fated house. She took a small duplex apartment at 830 Park Avenue and completely furnished it anew for us so that we would have no association with anything from the house. Then she suggested that mother and I take a trip to Cuba to try to sell some property my father had left her which she had never done anything about.

My mother, unfortunately, had about as much business sense as a sparrow. She sold several valuable sugar plantations in the interior of Cuba and a seventy-foot house on the Malecon for fourteen thousand dollars, and the lawyer cheated her out of six thousand of it. A few years later this house was resold for a million dollars and the plantations for fabulous sums.

While we were in Cuba I took a trip to Matanzas, and there in the Cathedral, on the main altar, I saw my grandmother's hair on the statue of La Señora de la Merced!

After this, my mother and I went to France until the summer of 1914 when we went to Southampton and lived at the Meadow Club. Vouletti Proctor and her mother were also staying there at this time. Southampton was very fashionable then and restricted to what socially—or let us say snobbishly—were called the best families. On a smaller scale it was becoming a rival of Newport, the cradle of the "Four Hundred," where Rita had a house and I often visited her. She went there every summer for several weeks before returning to Europe where she usually went to Carlsbad or Marienbad in Austria for a "cure." This was the era of the "cure" when royalty, the top society of all countries, snobs, hypochondriacs and gamblers flocked to watering places and contrary to their usual habits rose at six in the morning to go to a spa, where they drank evil-smelling and foul-tasting waters and afterwards sat for hours in baths of mud.

This summer of 1914 when Vouletti and I sat so quietly on the dunes at Flying Point where the beach, like a white thread tapers off and melts into the blue sea, the shadow of war was already insinuating itself over Europe. We had heard with mild interest about an archduke being assassinated. Then one day—August the fourth—I ran downstairs to buy the morning paper. As I picked it up I read across the front page in large letters: WAR! GERMANY INVADES BELGIUM.

My reaction was purely selfish. I said to myself, "It may prevent me from returning to France." But it couldn't be for long, I reflected. "France can beat any country singlehanded," I remarked to the club steward. I was sure of this. That day many so-called businessmen said, "This will be a war of only a few weeks—possibly only a few days." People discussed it as if it were a remote happening on another planet. No one seemed worried.

Thirteen

When I delve now back in memory through the years from 1914 to 1929, it seems to me as though I am searching for lost relics on another planet.

These were the years guided by the spirit of the New. They were a time of rebellion against the mediocre, the prudish, the unworthy. We could not tolerate what we tolerate now—mass production and herd followers. This was a time of search, of expectancy, of faith and of promise. We were on fire with fire, with burning ideas, with a passion to create and a daring to achieve.

These years have been called "The Jazz Years," "The Wild Twenties," "The *Enfant Terrible* Years," but they were greatly more than these glib titles label them. It seems to me that they had a substance and a character that life does not have today.

There were new movements everywhere. The little theatre movement in New York, as well as in London, Paris, and other European cities, cropped up in every back yard. In America and in England the fight for the rights of women gave impetus to a heated argument in any one hundred per cent male gathering. In New York the battle waged for birth control gave women like Margaret Sanger a glorious torch to carry—and they carried it valiantly, even into prison. After the war, people all over the United States defied the government behind locked doors in "speak-easies" and drank what and how they liked, not always just because they wanted to. Mixed up with all the fun and excitement of speak-easies was a tacit agreement on the part of both owners and consumers to resist a law against personal liberty and freedom of choice. Sordid as it often was, the resistance to prohibition was a great movement of individuals to protect the individual, and a manifestation that in a democratic world it is possible for the individual to defy the government. It was in its way a strange battle cry of freedom.

Then, too, during these years the young—especially in England—kicked over the last vestiges of Victorian influence which had circumscribed and inhibited their lives. They escaped from the influence of that old lady who had made hypocrites of more than a generation. Now at last impulses concealed or suppressed were allowed to assert themselves, and young people of both sexes, thrilled with their new personal freedom, bounded out into the open. Who can blame them if they sometimes bounded a little too high and sometimes fell a little too low?

Freud and Jung began to be read and comprehended. They appeared holding high a light of hope for the maladjusted and misunderstood and showed, not only to the medical profession but also to the clergy and the layman, that the psyche—although often a dark forest—is not necessarily a criminal one.

Art of all kinds was breaking away from tradition and creating new forms. Painting, sculpture, architecture, literature, music—all struck out onto new trails or sounded new notes. Progressive education cropped up everywhere; new forms of dance and new magazines appeared: in New York the *New Republic, The Nation, Vanity Fair,* and later the *New Yorker.* In Chicago the *Little Review* and *Poetry* launched unknown writers and poets. New names were suddenly heard of in America and in Europe: James Joyce, Proust, D. H. Lawrence, Frost, Pound, Fitzgerald, Stevens, Virginia Woolf, Hemingway, Elinor Wylie, Katherine Mansfield, Gertrude Stein and many more. In the New York theatre there were the moving performances of Alla Nazimova in *War Brides,* Eva Le Gallienne in *Liliom,* Glen Hunter in *Young Woodley* and Jeanne Eagels in *Rain;* and, of course, the unforgettable memory of Eleonora Duse when she returned to the stage in London in the summer of 1923 after an absence of fifteen years, and later came to America to appear and die.

And during this period there were the unsurpassed performances of Diaghilev's ballet in Paris, London and New York. Pavlova, like a winged white bird, enraptured audiences round the world. Karsavina, supreme as ever in the dance, nevertheless, divided herself between it and the diplomatic life of her husband.

In New York in the twenties Stanislavsky appeared with his Moscow Art Theatre—a theatre which revolutionized acting on the English and American stage. Also in the twenties Max Reinhardt produced *The Miracle* with Lady Diana Manners alternating with Princess Norina Matchabelli in the role of the Madonna, while Rosamond Pinchot played superbly the role of the Nun. Remarkably gifted stage designers experimented in their art—among them Gordon Craig in London, Robert Edmond Jones and Norman Bel-Geddes in New York. In America new forms of architecture felt their way to the sky. In the cinema, history-making names—Valentino, Chaplin, Garbo—skyrocketed into prominence as the medium itself advanced from silence into sound.

In the midst of all these events my own small personal life moved along. My fear that I would not be returning to Europe for a long time proved well founded. The war that was expected to be over in a few weeks lasted five years. Strangely enough, I believe that if many people told the truth they would say that they were inspired and stimulating ones. Everyone believed then that they were doing "their bit" for a Cause and saving the world for Democracy. The issues were quite clear. The Yanks and Tommies were right and the Jerries were wrong. It was as simple as that.

During the four years of that war I spent practically all my time trying to get myself overseas in some capacity. New York was full of women in beautiful uniforms on their way to France and I saw no reason why I shouldn't be among them. I pictured myself in the trenches doing heroic deeds. I decided to bide my time and get there somehow.

Life in New York under this atmosphere went on at a great pace. Certain events in the theatre which took place at this time stand out in my memory over many others—and that is saying much, because the theatre during these war years and the twenties teemed with new talent and new plays—and I have always been theatre conscious. There has never been such an inspired period before and there has never been one since. 1914 to 1929 was a Golden Age in America, a kind of renaissance.

There was the opening of the Washington Square Players, a little theatre movement that was exciting and characteristic of the times, and the shadow casting itself on the wall of the Theatre Guild which was to follow. They opened their season at the Band Box, a little *avant-garde* theatre on East 57th Street. In the cast was a new and promising actress by the name of Katharine Cornell. Something in the personality of this actress and the quality of her performance made the audience aware of a smoldering flame, and even then that voice was arresting, curiously beautiful and disturbing.

In the repertory of this group was a one-act play about New York called *The Magical City,* a first play by a new playwright, Zoë Akins. In it an enchanting actress, Margaret Mower, gave a very beautiful performance.

Every little theatre movement at this time was an adventure and brought new vision to actors and writers, but the Washington Square players brought a vitality to the theatre that was immediately felt, perhaps because of the outstanding personalities of its founders: Theresa Helburn, Philip Moeller, Lawrence Langner, Maurice Wertheim, Helen Westley and a number of others, some of whom became my friends. Helen was a wonderful, eccentric character and a fine actress.

During this winter Maude Adams was reviving *Peter Pan,* and with it blossomed again the enthusiasm I had felt for her as a child when I went to receive a thimble at her stage door. Elizabeth Marbury—"Bessie" the agent—whom I had met previously with Rita, by this time was fed up with my ravings and relayed them to Miss Adams. To my surprise and joy she received me in her dressing room and kept me waiting until her other visitors had gone. I was alone in the room when she came forward to greet me. At this moment I thought I would actually die from shyness and I almost turned and ran, but the door was shut behind me and I stood rooted to the spot. I was so absurdly and tragically intense that it's a small wonder I didn't blow up the whole dressing room. Years later Miss Adams confessed to me that she had cast an eye at the closed door, too I have no recollection of what was said. I only remember that she finally did rush to the door and call out to someone in that curiously touching voice of hers, which always had a catch in it. She called in her Wendy, a tiny young actress named Ruth Gordon. With her entrance into the room Miss Adams and I relaxed. I because I didn't have to make conversation alone and she, no doubt, in gratitude that she had not been burned up by my intensity.

I believe—and I can only say this from my own experience—that Maude Adams and Eleonora Duse were both genuinely humble, a rare thing for an actress. They were two women who were in the theatre but not of the theatre. They had both been in the theatre all their lives and yet the theatre had not remotely touched them. I did not meet Duse until later when she was old, but I am confident that she always walked through her stage career with downcast eyes—as though she had never been aware of anything except her own inner pain. In the case of Miss Adams there was a self-effacement rare in anyone but a saint. They later both chose anonymity.

Besides Miss Adams I met many celebrated people through Elizabeth Marbury for Bessie was untiringly interested in anyone of talent and was responsible for a number of successful careers. She had been the literary agent in the United States of several important English writers, among them H. G. Wells, Hugh Walpole and Somerset Maugham. She was Oscar Wilde's friend and agent when he first visited New York in 1882 and afterwards when he toured the country. She brought him to life for me with the fascinating incidents and personal details she told me about him, such as the manner in which he used his hands, and how he rose slowly when he got up from a chair as though he were conscious of his weight.

She was old enough to have met George Eliot and she described this meeting which had occurred when she was a child and which I felt she did not too well remember, as a number of times she changed the color of George Eliot's dress in telling me the story.

Bessie was extremely kind to me all through our friendship. Her interest never failed in anything I did or in any personal problems I brought to her, and in spite of the difference in our ages we were close friends till the day of her death. She was an extraordinary mixture of worldliness and childishness; of shrewdness and Victorian innocence. She was a Roman Catholic, a natural Jesuit, and in New York where she held court she was thoroughly enmeshed with the powers of the Church from the Cardinal down. She was a sly and astute politician and, in the days when I knew her, she had a considerable influence in all the intrigues of Tammany Hall. She had the brain of a man, well balanced and keen, lodged in a massive, masculine-shaped head. Her eyes were small, bright and humorous, and she loved a joke—especially if it was what she termed "spicy." Unfortunately, she was enormously fat—so fat that her feet, which were abnormally small, could not carry her weight. She was forced not only to wear steel braces on her legs to support her heaviness, but when she walked she used two canes. She was a short woman but when she was seated, as she generally was, she gave the impression of being tall because of the heavy formation of her head and the bulkiness of her shoulders. Her hands, like her feet, were absurdly small —small and chubby.

Bessie used to refer to herself as my grandmother, but at quite an early age I made her laugh by saying she seemed such a man to me that I felt she was more like my grandfather. She was so delighted with this that afterwards she often signed her letters to me "Granny Pa."

Many people thought her ruthless. I never found her so. In fact it often seemed to me that in her personal relationships the contrary was the case—other people were often ruthless to her. When Elsie de Wolfe lived with Bessie, it was always Elsie who relentlessly got her way. It was Bessie who did all the giving in spite of the fact that she had more ability in her smallest and chubbiest finger than Elsie ever had all her life long. I remember Bessie telling me that when she and Elsie first met, Elsie was an unsuccessful actress. "Elsie," said Bessie, "was an exceptionally untalented actress. As soon as I met her, both for her own sake and the sake of the suffering audiences, I took her off the stage and started her on a career of interior decorating." Luckily for Elsie, she came into this field when it was practically virgin ground and although she made a name for herself through the years, I never felt she did anything really creative or original. Her chief claim to distinction is having introduced French period furniture into the homes of New York society people who until then had enjoyed a conglomeration of ugly heirlooms, mostly Victorian, or more often just a general salad of bad taste without the consistency of any period. Before Elsie took a hand in things, French furniture in New York and throughout the whole United States was considered frivolous, and even a little immoral. Probably in the opinion of the general public it smacked of sophisticated ladies stretched enticingly on a chaise longue and up to no good. There was also a suspicion that the French commode was just a little nasty. After all, the place for such an unmentionable thing as the pot was under the bed.

So we can all be grateful for Elsie! Not so much for having stood on her head in the later part of her life (which actually brought her more fame than decorating), but because she did import French furniture into this country and saw to it that the so-called Four Hundred bought it.

Shortly after my meeting with Miss Adams, Bessie gave me a ticket for a matinée performance of Alla Nazimova in *War Brides* at the Princess Theatre in which she had an interest. I had seen photographs of Nazimova in her Ibsen roles and in *Bella Donna* and I thought she was beautiful and exotic-looking. Bessie, who knew her well, told me how she had arrived from Russia with an actor by the name of Orleneff, and how in 1905 they had made their first appearance in the Bowery playing Ibsen in Russian. It was the first time Ibsen had ever been played in New York in any language and the extraordinary personality of Nazimova, aided by her remarkable acting, had immediately caused a sensation. The following season Margaret Anglin and Henry Miller brought her up to the Princess to do Ibsen in English, although at the time she didn't know a word of it. Bessie told me how she learned three roles in nineteen days in English—Hedda Gabler, Hilda in *The Master Builder,* and Nora in *The Doll's House.* Playing in English she made even more of a sensation than she had in Russian, and New York went wild about her, at the same time discovering Ibsen.

Having heard all this about Nazimova, I built her up to a pitch in my imagination and after her truly great performance in *War Brides,* which went far beyond anyone's expectations, I could dream of nothing but meeting her and was convinced she was a great soul as well as a great artist.

In those days I had very little judgment of the true character of those I met. I was carried away by personality, by beauty, by art. It never occurred to me that a great artist could have anything less than a great soul. I have since had many disillusions in this respect. I have known many great artists but I have rarely found in them the blending of great art and great spiritual development. The answer to this problem may be that artists—artists of all mediums—are generally always self-centered and egocentric. Their approach to themselves is often too personal. They do not realize that any spiritually developed person must strive to lose the ego and become detached.

After seeing Nazimova in *War Brides* I rushed back to Bessie's house and announced what she, and everyone else, already knew—that Nazimova was a great actress. Then I told Bessie that I must meet her. But I did not have to wait for Bessie to introduce us. Fate brought Alla Nazimova into my life in a different way.

A friend of mine named Jane Wallach asked me to help her with a large benefit to be given in Madison Square Garden. Nazimova was going to be in it.

My excitement was such that of the entire performance, which was an elaborate and lengthy one, I remember not a single thing or person except Nazimova. Representing Russia (which was then still Imperial Russia), she made a sudden entrance through the door of the vast arena, then at Twenty-seventh Street, dressed as a cossack and resembling the photographs we had all seen of the Czarevitch. As the band struck up the Imperial Anthem she waved the Russian flag as a great spotlight played over her. Then the music changed to a wild cossack strain and, still carrying the flag high, she ran the entire distance around the arena, leaping into the air every few steps. To run and leap around this enormous arena with such grace was a feat few dancers, or athletes, could have accomplished. She brought the house down.

Jane had asked me to take care of Nazimova when she left the arena and I went back to her dressing room in a trance. She herself opened the door. She had taken off her fur hat but was still in costume. She had thick black hair which stood out from her head and her eyes were the only truly purple-colored eyes I have ever seen. Her lashes were black and thick, providing a setting for the intense purple they surrounded. I was always fascinated and conscious of Nazimova's eyes, and at this first meeting they made a great impression on me. She held out both her hands to me and said she had heard about me from Bessie and Jane. She was unlike anything I had expected. In the photographs of *Hedda Gabler* and *Bella Donna* she had worn a long train and I had imagined her as tall. In these roles, too, she had seemed exotic, a *femme fatale*. Here before me in flat Russian boots she seemed tiny and more like a naughty little boy. We took to each other instantly. I felt completely at ease and as if we had always known each other.

I was then in what I called my Russian period. For several years I had been devouring Russian literature. For months I had lived in the world of Dostoevsky, Tolstoy, Gogol, Pushkin, Turgenev, Chekhov, Gorky, and all the other Russian authors I could lay my hands on. I felt closer to *The Brothers Karamazov* and *The Idiot* than to the people I met in my everyday life. When I met Nazimova she linked all this up in my imagination. Not many people had read the Russians at this time and there had been few to share my enthusiasm. When I talked to her of Pushkin and Chekhov and the others, she was surprised and pleased and said she had met no one in America who was familiar with them. I told her that I felt a great kinship between Russian and Spanish music and between Russian and Spanish mysticism.

"You know, all this is very strange," she said, "because I am originally Spanish. My family were Spanish Jews who immigrated to Russia. My actual name is Lavendera, but when I began to study for the theatre with Nemirovich Danchenko I took the name of Nazimova from the Russian word Zima—meaning winter."

I think we each felt as if we had found a long-lost relative. She asked me to walk home with her.

"Aren't you tired after running and leaping around all Madison Square Garden?" I asked.

"Heavens, no," she answered. "I'm as strong as a lion and I need as much exercise as a tiger."

Which was true, I found in the years to come. So we walked home together feeling the sympathy between us of old friends, but with that underlying excitement of having found a new one.

Fourteen

Although at this time the United States had not yet come into the war, these were abnormal years in New York. All the young men I knew were off in training camps, and most of the young women were doing volunteer work. I too was trying to do my "bit." I was taking a course at the Presbyterian Hospital and, although nursing the wounded would have been a difficult job for me as I cannot bear to see anyone suffer, I managed to struggle through it and get a diploma which made me a qualified Nurse's Aide.

I remember feeling a certain shame while I was taking the Nurse's Aide course because I did it quite unwillingly and hated it. I was really only interested in writing, which I did at night—often starting at midnight and ending in the early hours of the morning. My mother sometimes saw my light and was angry with me for staying up so late. She made it difficult for me to write by continually telling me that my writing was all a lot of nonsense, and undermining my belief in myself. Like most mothers then she thought a woman's career was in the home and marriage—a view I did not share. I believed, without a shred of humor, in every form of independence for women and I was already an enrolled worker for Women's Suffrage. I had also written several poems which had been accepted and published in various magazines, and I had begun to work on a novel. It was somehow rather sad that I felt I had to keep the publication of the poems a dead secret. I didn't even show them to

Bessie Marbury or Rita. I believed I would be laughed at for writing poetry or for attempting to write at all. How I wish now that I had had someone to encourage me then and give me some good, thoughtful criticism.

In the midst of these various activities I was always brought back to the consciousness of war and would have given anything to go overseas, to be in the thick of any sort of battle. I envied my sister Baba who was working in a hospital in France. I envied anyone who was sent to Europe, no matter in what humble or drab job. Now I realize that in many ways I was fortunate to have stayed in America, because this was a period in which I met a number of people who remained my friends and through the years immeasurably enriched my life.

One of these—Ivor Novello—I met in 1916 in the ballroom of the Ritz. He was in uniform and had just arrived from England to raise money for a war drive. A uniquely handsome man, his sensitive face had perfectly balanced features, the dark eyes beautifully cut into it and set off by black and shining hair. He wore his uniform with style and dash and altogether looked enchanting. Everyone was immediately charmed by him. He sat down at the piano that afternoon and played "Keep the Home Fires Burning," the stirring song that had made him famous overnight when it was first played in London. As he played and sang everyone in the ballroom joined in the chorus and cheered wildly. I went with him from the Ritz to Bessie's. In the street, in order to reach the cab, we had to force our way through a throng of people who were waiting for him, and he sang his song as we drove away.

He was gay and elated. He hadn't expected such a warm reception in New York. During all the years I knew him after this first meeting he never failed to have enthusiasm and childlike excitement for any project and for any appreciation given him. It was this enthusiasm which was basically, I believe, the secret of his charm.

At Bessie's that afternoon I met Constance Collier and Clifton Webb for the first time. Constance was already well known in London, not only because of her acting but also because of her great beauty. I was charmed by her and felt something kind and warm radiating from her. Clifton was a special pet of Bessie's and was then acting in a play she had helped produce. These were his dancing days when he danced with the agility and grace of a young sprite. He was slender and willowy and had a flair for wearing clothes, on and off the stage. Clifton has always had great style—and a turned-up impish nose.

That summer my mother and I spent several weeks at the Meadow

Club in Southampton. While we were there Irene and Vernon Castle came for a few days to exhibit their dogs in the Meadow Club Show. Although the word *Americana* is perhaps not usually applied to people, I think it should be to the Castles. To me they and their story were Americana. They stood out during this particular era in clear relief as typically American, in spite of the fact that Vernon Castle was born in Britain. When they danced a tango the very tango itself became the Castles and this combination—tango and Castles—created a dance which was transformed into something profoundly American. They could not have flowered at this time in any other country although they started a vogue for ballroom dancing which was taken up all over the world.

Down through the ages the custom for women of letting their hair grow long had always been considered by men as a source of sexual excitement and a symbol of woman's enslavement. Even the Catholic Church in the early centuries thought about woman's hair in terms of sex and made rules to protect the chastity of any angels who might accidentally become entangled with it. Few Catholic women know it now, but it was to save any stray male angels who might be flying around them from temptation that they were originally forced to cover their heads in church!

That Irene Castle cut off her hair at this time was not accidental. I believe she was used by whatever Forces control such things as a symbol of this particular time. Perhaps she was even aware of this—I don't know—but within a short time of her first public appearance with short hair thousands of women in America and then in Europe had jubilantly sheared off their crowning glory. This was the grand gesture of liberation! And certainly the wearing of short hair has had a psychological effect on women, making them feel freer and younger and look younger too.

This was a memorable summer for me because it brought that self-termed "Priestess of the Dance"—Isadora Duncan—into my life. To me, she seemed more than the reincarnation of a Greek priestess. I looked upon her then as a great genius. Today, after the experience of nearly a lifetime, I would hesitate to use such a word. Isadora was not a genius but she *had* genius—moments of illumination—the stuff of which genius is made. All true artists, like all true mystics (who are, in a sense, artists transformed to a higher level), have illumination in a lesser or a greater degree.

The meeting with Isadora came about through Simone Puget, an attractive young Frenchwoman whose husband, a poet, had just been killed in the war. She had come to America with the intention of reading his poems in order to raise money for the French war cause.

Simone was a great help to me. She read some of my poems and eventually helped me to get them published. Just before she left Southampton for New York she said to me, "You know, you don't belong in a place like this. You belong with artists."

"Possibly. I don't really know where I belong. Artists should be universal. They should belong anywhere," I answered.

"Well, Southampton is not anywhere. In my opinion it is *nowhere*. I still think you don't belong to it." Then she added, "I need 'air,' and so do you. Let's go and see Isadora. I have just discovered she is living near here in a place called Amagansett."

It was a marvelously sunny day, one of those autumnal days with a cool snap in the air so characteristic of this season in the East of the United States. Isadora's house was on the sea. White sand dunes unrolled in front of it with pale green reeds rising from them, swaying and shimmering in the sunlight like quicksilver.

All this made a vivid impression on my mind because when we drove up the drive in front of the house I caught my first sight of Isadora standing in the sun, and at once I felt that the dunes, the reeds, the beach, the sea—all of these—in some strange way mingled with her and she was part of them. In one mysterious flash, like the second-quick opening and shutting of the lens in a camera, my inner eye saw her as all of these— as the very elements—as Nature itself. This experience made such a deep and abiding impression on me that it influenced my whole relationship with Isadora all through the many years of our long friendship. Because of this split second in time I approached Isadora altogether differently from any other person in my life. I not only approached her differently but I also evaluated her differently and, in a manner of speaking, I *saw* her differently. I am quite sure of this. And it was because of this experience that in after years when many people were critical of her, I was always tolerant—tolerant of her violence, her recklessness, of all her wild and uncontrolled love affairs. I understood all these passions in her as I could say I understand thunder, or a hurricane, or, in the case of her love affairs, as I understood a great cosmic maternal urge. Isadora was always the great mother in all her expressions of love—she could never truly be a mistress or a wife. She wanted ceaselessly to give of herself to all her loves as a mother gives to her child. And she gave herself indiscriminately because mothers, of which she was the supreme one, do not discriminate among their children.

When I stopped the car Isadora moved toward us. She was dressed in her customary Greek costume and was barefoot. A scarf (which became a symbol to me of her and which, in the end, caused her death) was streaming in the wind behind her. We jumped from the car and before Simone had time to present me, Isadora stretched her arms wide with a quick, spontaneous gesture as if we had known each other all our lives. Probably Simone had told her something about me on the telephone, and she wanted to make me feel at home. She took me by the hand and led me into the house.

In the room we entered, several men and women were gathered in front of the fireplace, some of them stretched comfortably on the floor. In the confusion and excitement of that day I only remember one face among them—Mary Desti. Mary was a close friend of Isadora's and worshiped her to such an extent that in a curious way she had taken on some essence of Isadora, although there was certainly no physical resemblance between these two women and they were totally different in character. Mary had dark hair and rather large features. Isadora had auburn hair and small features. Often Mary seemed to run things while Isadora behaved like a soft, purring kitten. But things were just the contrary. Isadora completely dominated Mary and, although it was true that she purred, it was the purring of a spoiled child—the egotist who had learned the trick of breaking wills with just this purring and softness. Isadora always got her way. She could make anyone who opposed her wish seem like an absolute brute.

I liked Mary, and we became friends. At this first meeting she spoke to me about her son, Preston Sturges. She was worried about his career. A few years after this he became well known as the writer of that most successful play, *Strictly Dishonorable,* and later on in Hollywood, he was equally successful in films.

During this conversation with Mary I noticed that Isadora was restless. She asked me to go down to the beach with her. When I followed her onto the sand she told me to take off my shoes. Barefooted, we walked to the edge of the water on the hard sand. Then she turned to me and gave me what I afterwards called "my first lesson." She said: "Always go barefooted whenever you can. With your feet free your whole body assumes a natural grace. Contacting the earth barefooted revitalizes brain and body. It is a wonderful health cure." Then she said, "Let me see how you move your body. Come, let's run."

We ran up the beach. When we stopped for breath, she said, "Not bad—not bad. I wish I could have trained you when you were four years old. I could have made a dancer of you."

We sat down on the sand, and suddenly Isadora began telling me about her dead children. Sitting there with the sea at our feet, she described them. She told me how they had looked, how they had danced—what they used to say. She said, "There is fallacy in the saying that time heals any grief. I do not believe this. I think in time we learn to hide grief so as not to become tiresome and boring to others. When my children were killed, I died too. At first I talked constantly about them because they were never out of my mind, but people said, 'Oh Isadora, you must try now to forget your children,' so I simply ceased to speak about them, or to mention the fact that I, too, am dead."

Tears poured down her face, and mine, too. She apologized for making me sad.

"I never talk like this. I don't know what made me open my heart to you. What can I do now to make up for your tears?"

I reflected a moment and then something compelled me to ask her to dance for me. Without a word she led me across the sand, back through a cornfield and into an empty old barn. It was quite dark inside and rather dirty. Along the walls, boxes and barrels were piled high. Isadora closed the door and we stood in semidarkness. She indicated an upturned box for me to sit on, and moved slowly to the center of the floor. She stood a second in silence, then she asked: "What shall I dance for you? It is difficult without music."

An inspiration came to me. I answered, "Dance the resurrection of your children."

She gave a startled look and a curiously tragic expression swept across her face. Then she dropped down to her knees and hung her head, her face almost touching the ground. She began to hum—that curious humming I was to hear so many times in after years. Gradually she rose to a kneeling position, then to a standing one. Then she began to dance. Watching her, I forgot time and place. I don't know how long she danced, but she ended with a great sweeping gesture of resurrection her arms extended high and her head thrown back. She seemed possessed by the dance and entirely carried out of herself. When she finished, she dropped her arms to her sides and stood motionless. I lowered my eyes. In that pause I think we both lived many lives. Then she returned, as from a far land. She became conscious of me. I moved toward her, and it seemed as if I walked on a beam of light.

Years after this Isadora told me that she felt she had danced more perfectly that day than she had danced at any other time in her life.

Fifteen

In the autumn of 1916 Rita arranged a large exhibition of Ignacio Zuloaga's paintings. Some of them were already in the United States, and these Rita borrowed from private or museum collections, but many Ignacio brought himself from Europe.

The exhibition opened in Boston, went to the Brooklyn Museum and then to the Duveen Galleries on Fifth Avenue in New York. After closing there it toured the whole United States. It was a very important one-man show and caused a great stir, especially as it took place during the war when the canvases from Europe might have been torpedoed and sunk. Ignacio himself was very frightened crossing the ocean and was greatly relieved when he found himself safe in Rita's house on Washington Square, where he stayed during his visit.

He was close to my family and we were all very excited to have him in New York. Rita had an interesting catalogue printed with reproductions, a Foreword by John Singer Sargent and an Introduction by Christian Brinton, but when the exhibition came to the Duveen Galleries in New York she did not think the color of the walls in the gallery in good taste. She felt that they detracted from the paintings and she asked Duveen to repaint them. He agreed that they were not the right color, but he said that no one but a perfectionist like Rita would notice it and he did not want to spend the money to change them. She said, "You admit the walls are the wrong color so even if it's only a cat who notices them, how can you let them remain? You notice them and I notice them. They are in bad taste. Isn't that enough?" It was not enough for Duveen. So, of course, Rita had them repainted at her own expense, which was what the wily dealer had been waiting for all along.

I went with Rita and Ignacio to the opening in Boston, where John Sargent and Mrs. Jack Gardner joined us. Mrs. Gardner was by then an old lady and had been famous for many years, not only for her art collection but for her personal eccentricities. John Sargent was related to my sister Maria by marriage and had made some interesting drawings of her. He was fond of her and of Rita and so was charming to me. In the catalogue of this exhibition he wrote a glowing appreciation of Zuloaga and his art. It seems strange now to reread his words and to think that Zuloaga was considered "advanced" at this time. I remember reading a review which that painter and mystic, Roerich, wrote about him when the exhibition opened in New York in which he even referred to Zuloaga as the *"avant-garde."* It would seem that nothing marks the passage of time more clearly than the changing expressions of art. What today is considered advanced, tomorrow is considered old-fashioned. Then slowly the circle repeats itself with a slightly new face. And so it goes with "nothing new under the sun."

During this period many amateur performances of one kind or another were given for war charities. I was a junior member of a committee called the Lafayette Fund, organized to raise money for France. We held a series of supper-dances in the ballroom of the then fashionable Vanderbilt Hotel. We young women were supposed to do most of the work and provide the guest artist for the weekly dance.

I remember well the artists I personally invited to perform. Ruth Draper was one of them and she was kind enough to do some of her wonderful monologues. But I achieved the memorable feat of getting Anna Pavlova to dance on one very special evening when the Imperial Russian Ambassador came with all his Embassy staff.

I had met Pavlova at a party given by Malvina Hoffman in her studio on East Thirty-fifth Street. When it occurred to me to ask her to be a guest artist on one particular evening of the Lafayette Fund, Malvina encouraged me—probably she spoke to Pavlova for me. Pavlova accepted! The ballroom was festive with all the Allied flags flying. Halfway toward the end of supper the room was thrown into darkness and suddenly a spotlight played on the dance floor. Pavlova, in a Russian costume with a magnificent headdress, appeared in its circle. Everyone applauded wildly and only stopped when the orchestra began a spirited

Russian folk dance and she began to move. The evening was a wild success.

At about two o'clock in the morning I was very tired. I managed to leave my partner during an intermission in the general dancing and go up the stairs to one of the boxes above the ballroom. Sitting there unobserved in semidarkness I could look down at the confusion of people on the floor below. It was a relief to watch the crowd and not be of it and to hear the rhythm of the jazzes and tangos only faintly at a distance. Dancing around the room in uniform were officers of many different countries. I wondered how many of them would get through the war alive. Suddenly I had a feeling that someone had slipped noiselessly into the box and was sitting behind me. I turned around, and there sat Pavlova in almost total darkness.

"I hope I am not intruding. I happened to see you come up to this box, and I thought what a good idea it is to get away a little from all those people," she said.

Of course I told her I was delighted she had come.

"Of what were you thinking, if I may ask, sitting up here all by yourself?" She asked the question shyly and as though I could refuse to answer it if I wished to.

"I was thinking of death. Looking down on the dancing crowd I was thinking that no one could say with any certainty how many of these people would be dead within a year."

Pavlova was thoughtful.

"So you, too, think of death," she said.

"Very often—especially in crowds," I replied.

"This is strange, because I do too."

"It must be the Spanish and Russian in us. I'm afraid both our races are rather melancholy," I said.

There in that box, with people laughing and dancing below us, we talked of death, of immortality, and of God. We talked so deeply and so earnestly that I no longer even heard the strains of the music. I was aware only of Pavlova's voice, her words, her eyes.

Then she jumped to her feet, exclaiming, "Heavens! I was to have gone home early. My friends will be frantic looking for me."

I walked out into the dark corridor with her. Then, before I could stop myself, I said, "Anna Pavlova, don't go back to the dance floor tonight. Death is surely there among all those people and I would not want him to touch you."

Without answering she bent forward and, barely touching my cheek, gently brushed it with her lips. Then she turned and I heard her light quick steps descending the stairs. The incident was over within a fleeting second, but as I stood there alone in the darkness I had the sensation that a white moth had brushed my cheek—not the lips of a living woman.

During the last of these war years and until women actually achieved the vote I worked for Women's Suffrage as if it were the only thing that mattered in my life. I was made Captain of my district. Dauntlessly I canvassed every house and verbally armed with every reason why women should have the vote, rang each doorbell. Sometimes I converted a frightened housemaid. Sometimes I argued with an amused male or roundly lectured an angry one. Sometimes I relaxed when I found a sympathetic household—and sometimes I just plain retreated. But always, and under every situation, I left a shower of leaflets and pamphlets strewn behind me. Hounds would not have been necessary to trace me by my scent in those days. Anyone could have found me by following up the stream of literature on Women's Rights I left in my wake. This canvassing of unknown houses and people was agonizing as I was exceptionally shy, but a strong force drove me on and stirred me into action "for all the downtrodden women who have no rights." That was my story and I stuck to it!

After my first meeting with Isadora in Amagansett she and Mary Desti came to see me in Southampton on their way to New York, but I never saw Isadora in any intimate way in New York. I only saw her dance at the Century Theatre and I read in the newspapers about her being arrested for taking her eight adopted children—all of them were dancers and danced with her—out walking on Fifth Avenue in bare legs and sandals. She used to take them out dressed in Greek costumes with bright-colored wool capes. This was the beginning of women wearing sandals and going without stockings, but it was anathema to the idiotic authorities, and Isadora was accused not only of cruelty to the young but of immorally influencing her children. She was completely bewildered by these accusations. She told me about it some years later and she was still bitter about it. She said, "Walt Whitman saw America dancing. He must surely have seen her dancing with bare legs and bare feet. How then could anyone have wanted to put my dancing children's legs into stockings and imprison their beautiful feet in hideous, torturing modern shoes?"

During these various war and Rights for Women activities I managed to finish a novel which was finally published in 1919. I was writing a lot of poetry, too. When I got a rejection slip I was in the depths of despair for days until one was accepted, when I would be in a state of elation until the next rejection slip appeared. Certainly in those days I knew nothing of Buddha's Middle Path.

Luckily for me Harriet Monroe, who edited *Poetry,* was very kind. She published the poems of practically every good living poet while she was the editor of this magazine in Chicago. Many of them she discovered. *Poetry* was known all over the world and it was the ambition of most poets to be published in it. Harriet Monroe was a remarkable woman. If she bothered herself with every young and aspiring poet as much as she did with me, she was more than remarkable—she was nothing less than a miracle.

She accepted the first poem I sent her—not only accepted it but wrote me a letter praising the poem and telling me the date she intended to publish it in the magazine. She asked me to send her another, but that one she rejected. With the rejection, however, came another letter telling me what she considered wrong with it. Up until 1931, when *Poetry* published the last poem I submitted, I sent poems to Harriet Monroe, many of which she published, but never once did I get an acceptance or a refusal that was not accompanied by a few lines. No coldly printed rejection slip ever came from her. No wonder young poets flowered under her gentle watering, and no wonder that the mature and great ones flooded her magazine with their work—poets such as Yeats, Synge, T. S. Eliot, and Robinson Jeffers.

Sixteen

The year 1917, the same year the United States entered the war, Sarah Bernhardt came to the New York theatre in a one-act play in which she played a French soldier who had lost a leg in battle. She was dressed in the uniform of a French *poilu* and held a battered and torn flag in her hand while standing unsupported on one leg. But for once in her life she wasn't really acting. She had, because of an infection, had one leg amputated. She had been in a French hospital for months but had insisted on coming to the United States to act in this play, the proceeds of which she gave to the wounded French soldiers. Theatrically, and I think also from the standpoint of human interest, it was an event.

The first few weeks in New York, Bernhardt, her doctor, and maid stayed with Rita. One evening before the play had opened Rita gave a small reception for her—or rather, what had started as a small reception in the end became a large and very interesting one. All the artists in New York began to ask for invitations and Rita didn't have the heart to refuse them.

She wanted the "Divine One" to receive the guests sitting down. This she refused to do. Instead she supported herself on her one leg by holding onto the back of a chair. Making light of this leg, she said, "Like many others of my countrymen I, too, am a wounded soldier of France."

Rita asked me to keep an eye on Sarah during the evening in case she might want something, but I never got near her after she sat down in a large armchair. People pressed around her from all angles, hanging over the back of her chair and kneeling before her. I caught a glimpse of the great diseuse, Yvette Guilbert among them; she was leaning over to kiss Sarah's hand.

Late at night when all the guests had left, Sarah was still wide awake and wanted to discuss the evening, to ask questions about some of the artists she didn't know. Rita hinted that it was very late and suggested that I stay there for the night. That suited Sarah. "We young people," she said, indicating me and herself, "don't want to go to bed. We still have a lot to talk about." Rita laughed and said that she was going upstairs immediately and I could tell her everything we discussed in the morning. She kissed Sarah and me and left.

Alone with an audience consisting of but one young person, the Divine One was undaunted. I thought she looked desperately weary in spite of her inexhaustible vitality. In her too-red wig and layers of make-up, she suddenly seemed to me like a clock wound up to run a thousand years and just now beginning to show faint signs of running down, and because of this, ticking even louder and faster on its last stretch. I felt terribly sorry for her. I knew her doctor had managed to keep her alive with morphia for several years now. In fact he was dozing in a chair in the dining room, waiting patiently for her to go to bed. I ventured to persuade her to let me rouse him so that he could help her up to bed, but she was so offended I had to back down hastily and change the subject. Whereupon—like turning the handle of a magic spout—she began to recite for me.

She recited long verses from *Phèdre* and almost the entire trial scene from Schiller's *Jehanne d'Arc*. She recited lines from Verlaine and several other poets. She poured out, rather than recited, the whole Wagram scene from *L'Aiglon,* ending finally with Hamlet's soliloquy.

That Bernhardt, at this advanced age, could remember all these roles, and at a moment's notice recite every line without one mistake, was not only a tribute to her memory and artistry, but also to her training. Of course, she and all the leading actresses and actors of her period abroad were trained at an early age in the classics. They seemed to become part of them and could turn on any scene from any great role they had played as easily as an ordinary person could say his name.

After this, Sarah actually seemed revived! When I summoned her maid and woke up the doctor, she said she still did not feel at all like going to bed. I drew the curtains, and before the doctor and the maid helped her upstairs she insisted on looking out the window. It was dawn in Washington Square. Then as she pathetically began to climb the stairs she turned and called out to me, "Head high, breathe deeply, and —spring!"

This was the last time I saw Sarah alone. After she returned to France I never saw her again. She died in 1923.

Two other visiting artists came to New York around this time, two frightened little Spaniards—Enriqué Granados and Miguel Llobet. The Metropolitan was about to produce the opera *Goyescas,* which Granados had composed, and they had invited him to its world première. Granados, terrified of the sea, had persuaded Llobet to make the trip with him, but it was like the blind leading the halt as they were equally afraid of the sea and of leaving Spain and of everything outside of it.

Many people in Spain considered Llobet the greatest guitarist who has ever played that instrument. Besides this, he was also considered a sort of saint. To understand what he was like, one would perhaps have to know the Spanish temperament and especially the temperament of his particular type. Since he rarely traveled, he was very little known outside of Spain. Physically he was small and thin. His face, with its dark and tragic eyes, looked like an El Greco portrait. He was gentle, timid, completely unworldly, unassuming and modest. He believed that everything good—soil, wine, music, flamencos, beauty and even God—could be found only in Spain. There was no need to look for anything outside Spain, and if one did, no good could come of it. His was a completely insular point of view, but you could no more have changed it than you could have moved the rock of Gibraltar.

Unannounced, without telephoning beforehand, the two men appeared one day to see my mother and me just after their arrival in New York. Ignacio Zuloaga had told them to come and see us. When my mother and I received them they looked like frightened mice, but when we began to speak Spanish they became almost hysterical with joy. From this second and until they left New York—poor Granados to meet his death and Llobet to return to Spain—I had them under my wing.

They were living in a cheap little hotel on the West Side, and after they had managed to learn how to talk on the telephone they used to call me at all hours of the day and night to tell me they were going to be blown up. This was because of the noise the radiator made. They were frightened of turning it on or off and Llobet actually cried one day while telling me, by telephone, that the radiator had hissed at him. He was convinced it was inhabited by some kind of devil. They hated

New York and could not find their way around. They could not drink American coffee or eat American food. They were cold, homesick and miserable. Their only joy was to come to see my mother and me and sit before our wood-burning fire while drinking dozens of cups of Spanish coffee and eating Spanish rice. Some evenings after dinner Llobet would play the guitar and Granados would accompany him on the piano. These were wonderful evenings and I think their happiest in New York.

Rita wanted to put them up at a good hotel, but they viewed this offer with suspicion and refused it. In their opinion a woman who paid a man's hotel bill was up to no good. I tried to explain that Rita often helped artists financially with no thought of any return because of her great appreciation of them, but they had different ideas on the subject. They were always cold and often when they left our apartment my mother and I would bundle them up in all our sweaters, scarves, tablecloths, bedspreads and anything else we could find. Sometimes we sent them home looking so odd it's a wonder they were not arrested.

Fortunately for him, Llobet returned to Spain before Granados, who wanted to be present at two or three more performances of his opera. When it was time for Granados to sail I and several of his friends begged him to let us cable home the small amount of money he had earned in America. He wouldn't hear of it. He couldn't comprehend how money could be cabled. He said he had worked hard to make this money for his family and that he would simply put it safely inside his coat pocket, which was wiser than to risk losing it on any such modern device as a cable. I went down to see him off but was only able to say good-by to him on the pier, since in wartime no one was allowed to board the ship. As I walked from the pier I had a strong premonition of doom. Some days later we heard that the ship had been torpedoed off England and beached. Many people were saved, but as Granados could not swim, he was drowned.

Not long after this a benefit performance was given at the Metropolitan to raise money for Granados' family. He had often said that he only came to America to try to make a little money for them. I remember Casals playing and Andrés de Segurola singing. At the end, with the house in darkness, a spotlight was thrown on Paderewski as he played Chopin's Funeral March. Eleven thousand dollars was raised at this benefit—far more than poor Granados had pinned in his pocket when the ship went down with him.

Besides such sad events of the war I had my own personal worries, and try as I might, I could not help feeling spiritually lost, as though I were traveling a dark road. Curiously enough, light was shed on my road from a most unexpected source.

Jack Barrymore and I were friends. Through the years in which I knew him and until he died, our friendship was of such a character that, in the ordinary sense, it might have been termed unrealistic. With the exception of Michael Strange, Kahlil Gibran, and Ned Sheldon, I never saw Jack wih other people. I never went to a play or a party with him and I never went anywhere with him in public. Yet I think I can say that on a certain level—in fact on a number of levels—I knew him intimately. Often over the years, whenever he was unhappy or in trouble, he used to call me on the telephone, generally late at night, and talk about his personal problems for hours. It was a one-sided friendship because Jack, being a supreme egotist, hardly ever asked me anything about myself. I didn't resent it. From the beginning it seemed quite natural that it was he who turned to me for advice and comfort. I hardly remember ever calling him or making any effort to see him. Sometimes there were long stretches—even years—when I didn't hear from him at all, but I always knew that sooner or later he would turn up again in my life.

At this particular time he called me one night very late. He said he had been asked by a publisher to pose for a black and white drawing to be done by an artist called Kahlil Gibran. Jack said, "The fellow is Persian or Syrian—some such country—and he wants to include me in a book of drawings. I have to pose tomorrow morning and I wish you would come with me. I'm frightened out of my wits to go alone." So he called for me the next morning and together we went down to Kahlil Gibran's studio on West Tenth Street. I am ashamed to say that at this time I was as ignorant about Gibran as Jack was, which is enough to have crossed us both off as a pair of idiots.

Kahlil Gibran received Jack and me quietly and graciously in his studio. I apologized for having come uninvited, but he put me at ease at once and made me feel it was the most natural thing in the world that I should be there. To prove this he expressed a wish to do a drawing of me, too. I was deeply impressed by his looks and by his personality.

In stature he was a small man, but as his head was massive and remarkably shaped, he looked taller than he actually was. I never saw a nobler brow than his. The most impressive thing about him was his eyes. He seemed to look at you with a gaze that came from some deeper region than the physical. When later I came to understand certain things better I felt that—like Buddha—he must have had a third eye. He was a poet, artist, musician, philosopher, mystic, and beyond all these—a great spiritual teacher. He was an initiate who came at a certain moment to bring a spiritual message to the Western world, as the thousands of pilgrims who yearly visit his grave in the Monastery of Mar Sarkis in Bsherri demonstrate. Anyone who wishes to know him can read his numerous books, among them *The Madman, The Forerunner,* and *The Prophet.*

This particular morning, when he began to work, he had not drawn ten lines before Jack and I knew he was a master artist. Jack himself could draw well and was a gifted artist. I saw him relax as Gibran continued the portrait, and at the end, after several hours, a strong and fine head of Jack was on the paper. During these hours Gibran had only spoken once or twice, yet his silence seemed light and not at all awkward. Jack said afterwards, "Actors could learn the force of silence from this man."

As we left the studio, almost as though it was an afterthought, Kahlil Gibran handed me a book. He said, "Read this . . . and when you have finished it call me and tell me what you think of it."

That night in bed I opened the book. On the title page I read *The Bhagavad Gita.* I had only vaguely heard of it—an admission that I am now ashamed to make. That same night I started to read it, and when I had finished the last page full daylight was streaming into my room. I do not pretend that I fully understood all that I read, but I drank in the words somewhat like a parched camel who suddenly comes upon a spring at which he can quench his thirst. When I closed the book, instead of feeling exhausted after so many hours reading I felt revitalized and exalted. I knew that this book contained knowledge that could sustain me all my life.

As soon as I felt I could call Kahlil Gibran without waking him up, I rang his number. It was he who answered and heard the excitement in my voice, although I tried to sound calm. I asked him if I could come at once to see him. When he said I could, I rushed from the house barely dressed and without breakfast. As he opened the door and I burst into his studio I said, "Why has no one ever told me about this book before? It has already revolutionized my life!"

Quietly and gently he sat me down. He said that he had hoped I would have just this reaction. He added that had I not reacted favorably, he would not have seen me again. We sat together for several hours while he explained passages from the Gita and answered my questions. These hours seemed timeless. He also told me about the great Hindu epic poem "The Mahabharata," a kind of moral encyclopedic teaching in accordance with the Vedas. I remember he told me that Christianity—as taught by the churches—would have to be restated. He said that Christianity, in the accepted sense, had failed—but that Christ had not, and never would.

When I left his studio that day he gave me another appointment and promised me further instruction. He gave me the Upanishads to take home with me and laughingly said, "If you devour this book the way you did the Gita, you will surely have spiritual indigestion."

When I reached home, for the first time in my life I had a sense of inner peace, a thing I had never achieved in a church. My feelings since my early life have altered very much on this subject and on the subject of creeds in general. I am, however, in many ways grateful that the formation of my life was laid within the embrace of the Catholic Church. On the other hand, I attribute much of the mental and psychological suffering that I have experienced in my life to the Spanish-Catholic influence of my childhood.

I do not mean anything derogatory in general toward the Catholic Church when I say that it would perhaps have been better for me had I not had this dark Catholic influence in my youth. By nature I was too sensitive, impressionable and melancholy to have been raised with a religious belief that so emphasizes the agony of suffering and punishment. I needed a joyful approach to God and not one that stressed my own morbidity. As I started life physically fragile and nervously highstrung, it is a question whether my health was toughened or weakened by being dragged out of bed on icy cold mornings to attend Mass on an empty stomach in order to receive Holy Communion, and also to spend a great deal of time on my knees in dark and gloomy churches instead of running and playing in the air and sunlight.

In any case there is no doubt that in my childhood and adolescent years I took to this austere religious life as a duck takes to water. I can well remember making the Stations of the Cross many times from my own choice, praying, and moving on my knees on the cold stone of the church from one Station to the other.

At seventeen I suddenly became suspicious of the Roman Catholic Church, and of all churches for that matter, and then I became suspicious, too, of myself and of my blind belief in all that I had been taught religiously. I realized I had not thought for myself. I then underwent a sort of "clearing out," which got me rid of a vast amount of rubbish in my own mind about myself and prompted me to give quite a "dusting off" to the Catholic Church, too.

I had always blindly believed in the infallible truth of the Church, and of course I believed, too, that truth was a noble virtue. Now, for the first time in my life regarding such matters, I looked about and observed. I began to realize that the Catholic Church and all other churches as well did not always tell the truth in the strictest sense, but managed many times through superstition and fear to build around entirely false thinking a sort of glorified righteousness, investing it as truth. This made me sharply aware of the falseness and shallowness of so-called creeds. I then understood the profound difference between the word *religion* in its purest sense and the word *creed* and that one bore no relation to the other. I knew then that noble people can only live their lives in two ways—either religiously or poetically—and both these ways, in a measure, are the same, or at least pursue the same path.

Then I came to realize that distortions of the truth are a vital possession not only to the Catholic Church and Christianity in general, but also to national governments, politicians, society at large, and to the average person; and that most so-called morals which society upholds are based on false thinking. And it seemed then that all the ground which had seemed secure to me—especially that territory which the Catholic Church had stood for in my life—was swept away from beneath my feet.

When I was at length able to gather up my wounded self and consider the matter, I saw the Catholic Church was not altogether wrong in its approach to the ignorant masses, and that intelligent lies are many times nearer the truth than half-truths. I understood that Eternal and Divine Truth is comprehended only by the few, and to the ordinary human being truth is relative and fluctuating.

From this moment it became clear to me that I must identify myself with great saints and mystics of every religion, but never again with any creed. I knew then as I know now that in seeking mystical truth I must look for it, ultimately, only within myself. I know that mystical truth has the same accuracy as arithmetical or geometrical truth and does not vary according to the concept of diverse creeds.

At this time I asked myself, am I willing to devote my life to finding and living the deepest Spiritual Truth? Am I striving for the Truth because of a deep desire for it? Or am I hiding behind lies because I am too cowardly to seek the Truth? Am I trying to be so-called truthful because I have not the courage to lie?

Seventeen

The United States was in the war and we entered into a new phase. Most of the young men among my friends and throughout the nation who had been in training camps disappeared one by one into the darkness of the night to board ships painted gray and black which sailed secretly, surrounded by convoys, from unnamed ports.

At this time I was transferred from my department in the Red Cross to another one under Malvina Hoffman. To this office came wounded and blinded men from all the Allied Nations. These men had, of course, already been dismissed from the hospitals. They were sent out to face life and, ironically enough, pronounced "cured."

Despite the war sadness of 1917 and 1918, parties were still given in New York. It was said by those who gave them that these festivities helped to sustain morale. One in particular that I went to stands out clearly because it was then that I met Hope Williams. It was a meeting which resulted in a friendship which has grown and ripened throughout the years.

This party was given by Mrs. John Jacob Astor at her house on Fifth Avenue. I was talking to her son Vincent's cousin, Thornton Wilson, and Ethel Harriman when I glimpsed Hope and asked who she was. She had a charmingly shaped head and I was amused by her delicate and slightly turned-up nose. She was lovely-looking and even at that early age she was a strong personality. We were introduced and "clicked" at once.

It did not take me long to discover that Hope had a passion for the theatre. Here we met on mutual ground, the only difference being that she longed to act. She told me she sometimes acted with an amateur organization called The Comedy Club. I went to see her perform and in less than five minutes of watching her act a bit part I was convinced that she had great talent—especially for comedy. I told her she was wasting her time in amateur performances and advised her to go on the professional stage. She said this was out of the question; her mother would never hear of it.

When I told Bessie about Hope, she cited Dorothy Bigelow, who had recently made a success in Cole Porter's first Broadway show, *See America First,* as an example of one society girl the critics had respected. She said, "If your friend Hope has all you think she has, I'm sure that, like Dorothy, the critics will acclaim her."

"I believe that real talent will always break down every prejudice," I said.

"How right you are," Bessie answered. "Why don't you yourself write a play for Hope? I will help you produce it." Then she said, with a sly twinkle in her eyes, "Of course, you will have to raise the money. Don't expect me to put a penny in it. But you can go into my Princess Theatre on very special terms if it happens to be dark when you're ready to begin rehearsing."

From this conversation one thing led to another in a chain of events which enabled me to gather together—somewhat like a cake—all the ingredients necessary to produce a musical comedy with Hope in the leading role.

Fortunately I had been working in the Red Cross with Mrs. Frank Frueauff, the former Antoinette Perry who will always be remembered as the beautiful ingenue in "The Music Master" with David Warfield. During one of our conversations, I found that she secretly longed to become a producer. Having been told that her husband was rich, I suggested that she ask him to back this ambition. "What is the use of having a rich husband if you don't persuade him to indulge your ambition?" I asked her. Her answer to this was that her husband would give her all the money she wanted for charity, or an amateur theatrical production, but he would never give her a penny for a professional one. I groaned. Did one now have to contend with amateur-point-of-view husbands as well as mothers?

When Bessie remarked that I should write the play myself and raise the money to produce it, I thought of Antoinette Frueauff. I trotted off to see her. Again she said that her husband would never finance a professional production—but I took her to Bessie's house and introduced them.

Granny Pa had a solution—she always did. She said that since Hope's mother wouldn't let her appear in a professional production and Antoinette's husband wouldn't finance one, we should give the proceeds to charity and sprinkle the chorus with society girls. "Use as many professionals as possible. Have professionals write the music and direct the dances. Produce the whole thing as professionally as possible but claim that, being wartime, there's a shortage of professionals and use some amateurs. That way you may please everyone—the professionals, the critics, and those tiresome mothers and husbands."

As both Bessie and I were very fond of Cole Porter, he was our choice for the music. But either he was in the army then or writing another play. He was unavailable but helpfully suggested Deems Taylor for the music, Charles Shaw for the lyrics and Gaillard Thomas to work on the book with me. After they had all accepted we started working like beavers.

Antoinette was responsive and alive to suggestions and a hard worker, which she proved later when she went into producing with Brock Pemberton under her maiden name, Antoinette Perry.

Hope occasionally dropped into the Frueauff apartment when Deems had finished a special number he wanted her to hear. Feeling that she was a born comedienne, I suggested writing a part for her of a Swedish servant girl to whom we gave the name of Brunehilde. It was somewhat of a slapstick part, but it also had subtlety and required finesse to portray. It was a role that Beatrice Lillie might easily have played. Hope and Beatrice Lillie were much alike, as everyone later knew.

When it came to deciding on a professional dancer for the leading dance role, I thought of Bessie McCoy. To a young person that name probably means nothing. For me it conjures up a picture of a woman dressed in a Pierrot costume, sitting astride a half-moon, whom I thought wonderful beyond words when I was young, and still do. She created the song "The Yama Yama Man," and was the first person to dance on the stage in large white gloves. Her voice was the original woman's "husky" voice, which huskiness was later emphasized by Jeanne Eagels as Sadie Thompson in *Rain* and again practiced and consciously developed by Tallulah Bankhead, but which actually came so much into vogue in 1929 when Garbo's voice—so rich, so moving and naturally low—stirred the public in her first talking film, *Anna Christie*.

Bessie McCoy was already retired from the stage. I expressed my hopes of bringing her back to it in a letter and received a most amusing reply written on a large piece of brown wrapping paper. She said that she no longer wanted to dance, but that she would willingly do the choreography for the dances and direct them. She suggested a dancer by the name of Bunny Glass for the lead in the dancing numbers. Strangely enough, Bunny Glass's husband was Ben Ali Haggin, who had just agreed to do the stage sets and design the costumes.

About a year before the production of *What Next?* I met Alfredo Sides, who from this early period of my life until his death in 1952 was to weave in and out of it in one circumstance or another. Whatever were Alfredo's merits or faults, he was original in both. I have never known any man remotely like him. During all the years I knew him I was never able to discover his origin. He was a French subject and had a French passport. When I first met him in New York I was told that he was a Turkish Jew. When we became friends he denied both of these, but on several different occasions he told me conflicting stories about his background. At one time he said he was Spanish, but a few years later he told me he was Italian. This left me baffled as he spoke them both, and also French, like a native. There is no doubt that his looks, his attitude of mind, and his approach to life were all oriental. But it didn't matter what he was, aside from unsatisfied curiosity, because his outlook on life was so broad, so original and refreshing, and he himself so much of a personality and at the same time such a warm friend, that such minor things as birthplace, race, or nationality were of no importance.

Alfredo had a fanatic prejudice in favor of women and all through his life he remained consistent in this. I never saw him weaken or make a compromise or concession toward any man. In Paris, to his renowned flat in rue Gît le Coeur overlooking the Seine with a view of Notre Dame, he never invited a man—if he could possibly help it. Sometimes he was obliged to invite a husband with a wife. If this "misfortune" befell him, and that was the word he used for it, he would just as likely as not make faces at the unwelcome man behind his back. In New York, where he was often invited to dinner parties given by society women, he would refuse to stay in the dining room to have coffee with the men. He would follow the women into the other room, generally remarking at the same time: "What a blessing it is to be rid of those terrible males and their black cigars." He hated anyone smoking and never smoked himself. With the exception of wine, he didn't drink either. Once before a suffrage parade he wrote into headquarters suggesting that he be allowed to carry a banner with an inscription on it reading: *I am for killing all men and letting women run the world.*

Needless to say, the average male did not like Alfredo, although some of them were amused by him. He never minded if a man disliked him. He took it as a compliment. He said, "Men have so little intuition, they are always sure to like or dislike the wrong people."

If men disliked him, he had enough women friends in his life to make up for their absence. He was always surrounded by women, listening to their problems, advising, consoling, encouraging, adoring and flattering them.

As was to be expected, Alfredo assisted daily at all the rehearsals of *What Next?* surrounded by women in the wings, or sitting with one in the darkness of the theatre out front. As this was before Equity we were able to carry out Bessie Marbury's suggestion and we "sprinkled" the chorus with as many beautiful society girls as possible. They were so inspired by Bessie McCoy's training that they danced like professionals. The critics were completely baffled at the opening night of the play and almost persuaded themselves that the chorus was made up not of society girls but real chorus girls trying to put something over on them.

What Next? served several good purposes. It led Hope onto the professional stage. Eight years later Arthur Hopkins, remembering *What Next?* thought of her for the role in *Paris Bound*. That in the meantime she lost so many years which could have been fruitful to her career can only be blamed on the ignorance of this era, which was just emerging from Victorianism—that period in history when parents by directing and ordering the lives of their children always "meant well," and usually succeeded in ruining them. For Deems Taylor *What Next?* probably served no purpose at all except, perhaps, to afford him a little fun. I hope so. His various talents would have come through and been recognized anyway, regardless of his efforts in this play.

It was around this time that Rita with Otto Kahn, who helped finance the project, brought over Jacques Copeau and his company of the Théâtre du Vieux Colombier from Paris. She entirely remodeled the Garrick Theatre for these plays. Among others in the company was the famous actor Louis Jouvet and the talented actress Valentine Tessier —both of whom appeared on the American stage for the first time.

But that summer of 1918 Rita was ill. Since she could not go to Europe for a change as the doctors advised, she took a house in Santa Barbara, California. It was the beginning for her of a long series of illnesses and operations resulting from an accident she had been in many years before while driving in a Hempstead cart in Westbury, Long Island, with Aida. The horse Rita was driving ran away and fell against an embankment, at the same time kicking the dashboard to pieces so that they both plunged out of the cart and landed on the ground beneath his feet.

Aida nearly died as a result of this accident. She had to have several major operations and this was the cause many years later of the glaucoma which lost her the total sight of one eye and the partial sight of the other. Paradoxically enough, had she not lost her own sight she would never have become interested in the blind and been instrumental in organizing the Eye Bank, as later she did.

At the time of the accident Rita appeared to be only slightly injured, but it was just this injury that created internal complications which years later, in 1929, caused her death.

While Rita was in California my mother constantly worried about her and she finally decided to take Katie, Alice de Zaldo, Fai Yen (her Pekingese), and me out to the Coast to see her. We suffered desperately from the heat as, of course, the trains were not then air-conditioned, and during most of the trip the temperature was over 112 degrees. I spent most of my time holding a piece of ice on Fai Yen's head. Otherwise my mother's little dog might have died.

Apart from the heat of the trip, I chiefly remember a visit to Hollywood, where I was taken by a Santa Barbara society woman, Mrs. Graham, and her very beautiful daughter, Geraldine. We went to see Douglas Fairbanks, who took us all around their studio. My knowledge of motion pictures in those days was extremely sketchy as my heart was only in the theatre. With the exception of seeing Nazimova and some foreign films, I rarely went to the movies in New York, and never to the Hollywood ones until the appearance of Garbo. That first tour of Hollywood left me quite indifferent and I wouldn't have believed then had someone predicted that in the early thirties I would be out there working.

Eighteen

This winter of 1918-1919 was a memorable one for me. Howard Cook, the young, progressive, and enthusiastic editor of a small publishing house, Moffat and Yard, was well regarded in the literary world, especially during the twenties. So I gathered up my courage one day and, with two manuscripts under my arm (*Wind Chaff*, a first novel and *Moods*, a book of prose poems), went down to call on him. I consulted no one. In fact, no one knew I had written them. I had spent sleepless nights imagining an interview with a very aged editor (under the impression that all editors must be old) in which I tried to convince him that I was a budding genius.

The young woman in the outer entrance room eyed my manuscripts suspiciously and asked me what she could do for me. I said I wished to see the editor. Through a half-open door leading into an inner room I heard a man's voice say, "Here I am. Come in." The woman gestured and with shaking knees I moved forward. A very attractive young man rose to his feet to greet me. In a stammering voice I repeated that I wished to see the editor.

"He stands before you in the person of Howard Willard Cook." Howard Cook then made a low bow to me and said, "Let me relieve you of your package, which I'm sure is a manuscript." He pulled out a chair for me and sat down in his own. He tried to put me at my ease. He certainly succeeded. Under the spell of his charm and warmth, and probably also out of nervous reaction, I told him my life story—such as it was. When the moment came to discuss my manuscripts, he took them from me with interest and promised to read them as soon as possible. He gave me a slender volume of Sara Teasdale's poems, which he had edited and published, remarking as he did so that he considered her, Edna St. Vincent Millay and Elinor Wylie the three best modern American poets. "In this choice I should probably include Amy Lowell. She is more of a scholar than any of these three. At the same time, she has none of their lightness." Then he charmingly added, "Perhaps after I read your poems, they will also be included in my choice."

"Oh, I will never be anything but a minor poet," said I.

"Great poets are the rarest thing in the world. Minor poets can, nevertheless, give much in their own way. Go on working, regardless of what you think of your work. Don't worry about your poetic rank—great, minor, or zero. Just let your verses flow without feeling self-conscious about them."

With this good advice, I left his office. Out on the street, walking on my toes from sheer excitement, I wondered why the whole editorial profession wasn't decorated and even knighted. One week later I had a letter from him saying he would publish both my books and that he was listing them for autumn publication.

Every once in a while at this time Jack Barrymore took me to see his great friend Ned Sheldon, the playwright.

Ned was already an invalid when I first saw him. His illness began with partial paralysis which gradually overtook his whole body so that he was completely incapable of moving any part of it. As the years passed he became totally blind. He could speak and hear and his mind was as clear as a bell, but he lay motionless on his bed, his hands and face giving the impression that they were carved in ivory. His was an extraordinary case which doctors could neither diagnose nor cure. So Ned lay for years stretched out on his bed with only his brilliant mind active. People from all corners of the world came to see him and bring him their problems. He worked on plays with other dramatists. He wrote *Lulu Belle* with Charlie McArthur, Helen Hayes' husband. Long before he died he had become a legend. Some people thought of him as a saint and approached him as such. Not many years ago, with his body practically petrified and still totally blind, he died.

Ned adored Jack and spoiled him dreadfully. He regarded him as the center of his universe and made him feel he could do no wrong. I always remember him lying motionless on his bed, waiting for Jack to come and see him. There was something infinitely heartbreaking in the patience of his waiting. I believe Jack was the love of his life and the suffering and emotional frustration he went through on account of it caused his illness.

It was at Ned's that I first met Michael Strange, who had come to Ned's that afternoon with Jack for the purpose of meeting me. Jack was in love with her and had talked a lot about her and wanted us to be friends. I thought her beguiling, full of humor, and rather like a healthy young Arab boy, as I told her. Her hair was brown, her eyes dark, and her skin deep olive and clear. I was impressed then and afterwards by her radiant vitality and health. There was vitality and health in all her movements and in her outlook on life. One had the impression that she was in the ring cracking the whip. She cracked it for Jack and he certainly jumped. Jack in some ways was inwardly feminine and had a great sensitivity. He had a need to be dominated but at the same time he revolted—in a love-hate pattern—against any woman who did dominate him, even when he had chosen to fall in love for just this very reason. I believe this inner conflict and ceaseless warring between the masculine and feminine elements of his nature were the cause of his drinking.

He despised himself for it, but it was utterly beyond his power to control his relationship with Michael Strange. He could only have dominated a weak woman and such a woman he would not have respected or loved. Michael and he should have complemented each other, but they both were so intensely egotistical that neither ever gave the other a chance to do so.

When Michael came and told me she was going to marry Jack, I said, "When you do, I wonder who'll kill the other first."

"What do you mean by that?" she asked.

"You are both such egomaniacs that you will some day start a fight to the finish, and one of you will do the other in," I answered. "I'm not sure which one."

"I can tell you that right now. It will *not* be me," Michael laughed.

In a way she was right. It was she who did do Jack in, yet she did herself in at the same time. I never knew two people who loved each other more and hated each other so much. I never knew two people more incapable of living together who could not live apart. I am convinced neither one ever loved anyone else and that, spiritually speaking, neither one survived their divorce.

To me Michael Strange was always stimulating. She had humor about herself as well as other things, which made it possible to laugh with her while laughing at her. I remember a story she told on herself about her manner of dressing. At this particular time she used to wear velvet jackets which she had made in the style of Alfred de Musset. With these jackets she wore a shirt with a wide-open collar. This was a Walt Whitman shirt, she said. She would then wear or carry heavy leather riding gloves with wide cuffs. "Gauntlets," I called them, but she referred to them as "the type of glove George Sand wore." Then on top of her head she would balance a man's soft hat, generally one of Jack's, and carry a walking stick with a heavy knob— "The kind carried by an old gentleman on the way to his club," I used to add. Women had not yet taken to slacks, otherwise Michael would surely have worn them. She had to complete her outfit modestly with a tight tweed skirt and low-heeled walking shoes.

At this time her younger son Robin began to refer to himself continually as a girl. He used to make up stories which he would relate to Michael and me. In most of his stories he imagined a princess who, he said, was himself. He was about five years old then and one day Michael announced that she was going to take him to a psychologist. Grasping Robin by the hand, she marched off to see the doctor in the costume described above.

I waited in the house. They returned much sooner than I expected, and Michael reported her very brief interview.

"I asked the doctor if he could tell me what, for the love of heaven, makes Robin believe he is a girl and always speak of himself as one. He fixed a cold eye on me and what do you suppose he said?" She laughed and imitated the doctor's voice. "He said, 'Madame, evidently you have never looked at yourself in the mirror. Had you done so you could, no doubt, answer this question for yourself without wasting my time and your money.' "

During the winter of 1919 Baba returned to New York. She had not been back to America since her marriage, and until the war had been living in Kenya with her husband, Billy Sewall. During the war she volunteered her services in a hospital in France and did a magnificent job there. But in postwar New York, she found it difficult.

These were confusing days for people all over the world. They had dreamed in the thick of war that with victory it was all going to be "so different." Now they stood with victory and perceived the old patterns, like sinister ghosts, reappearing. They stood on a crust of the "new," but underneath, an old era was still stirring in its crumbling. Here in America we frequented dark basements behind locked doors—where, literally, soft voices spoke "easy." They offered a kind of solace in alcohol, forbidden and either bad or good (it did not much matter which), they offered a solace and a kind of revived excitement—a war hangover excitement and, in its extremes, oblivion from it all. But prosperity was in our midst. Prosperity on roller skates—skating toward 1929!

Baba found it difficult to breathe in New York. Like every other building, she said my mother's small apartment was overheated. She opened the windows and hung far out for air. She was also unhappy as she had come to New York mainly to break the news to my mother that she wanted a divorce from Billy. This would alienate her from the Church and inflict great suffering on my mother as well as herself, for she was a devout Catholic. Nevertheless she said to me, "I am young. I want to remarry. Above all, I want children." Knowing how maternal she had always been with me, I understood how much she needed them and could only hope she would, some day, have them.

I was unhappy myself, for more complex reasons. They had to do with the Church and the effect my new feelings about it would have on my mother. I had talked with Kahlil Gibran many times since our first meeting. I had bought and absorbed countless books on Eastern religions and philosophy. I had read the life of the great nineteenth-century Hindu saint Ramakrishna, and I had begun reading all the writings of his disciple, Vivekananda. I had been studying the teachings of Buddha, and I was deeply impressed by his Eight-Fold Path. And like so many beginners who are seeking truth, I read Blavatsky's *Secret Doctrine* and began delving into Theosophy. Although I had wandered from the Church, I had not forsaken its mystics. I continued reading John of the Cross and Teresa of Avila. These I mixed in with Lao Tzu, the Suffi classics, Meister Eckhart, the Tibetan Book of the Dead and quantities of other spiritual books.

If my reading was a veritable salad derived from all the great religious teachings it was, nevertheless, an enlightened one, opening my eyes to that fact Ramakrishna so perfectly expressed: "Truth is one. Men call it by different names."

But by this small spiritual growth I was placed in a great dilemma. My mother had already had so much sorrow in her life, and for her there was only one Church and one religion. How could I tell her that I no longer wished to belong to that Church, nor to any organized church, and that I wished to find God in my own way? She would feel me eternally lost. Nevertheless I felt cowardly and a hypocrite if I didn't follow and live my own idea of truth as I saw it, right or wrong.

In addition to this I had other problems. During my ardent work for the cause of suffrage many people, including women, had made fun of me. I had stood up against this derision and all the nonsense it entailed such as "a woman's place is in the home" and various other threadbare clichés. But I had always, since my first reasoning years, held a strong belief that a married woman should keep her own name, which would be the name of the mother since I also believed a child should carry the mother's name. Having had no way in which to express this belief or make it workable, it was with great joy that at this time I met Ruth Hale and her husband, Heywood Broun. Ruth, like myself, believed in women always retaining their own names and she was president of the Lucy Stone League, an organization for the rights of women to uphold this practice. Ruth, Heywood and I became strong friends and, backed by Ruth, I began to express my opinions, thereby meeting another avalanche of resistance and ridicule from people who pronounced her theories just plain insane.

Added to the things I had to battle against was my feeling about marriage. Everyone seemed to think I should marry but to me the marriage ceremony seemed archaic and uncivilized. I argued that if two people loved one another it would be sufficient to promise each other whatever they wished to promise without calling in the law, the clergy, and the whole world to witness it. I felt that in the matter of children they belong more to the mother, since it is she who carries them and suffers the physical agony of birth. This should automatically give her priority over them, and since they would have her name the whole matter was simple. So simple, indeed, that it was beyond me why people were forever getting married just to have to spend time and money to get divorced and begin the round all over again.

All these matters now, from a distance of years, seem small, but at the time they were large, perplexing, and tragic. I looked at them with that great fault of intense youth—lack of humor, which was my real tragedy but of course I couldn't see it then.

In the midst of these problems, most of them caused by my own absurd nature, I found solace in a peculiar friend. This was a small Colt revolver I had inveigled out of Jimmy Fargo, who was in love with me. I found comfort in this little weapon. I toyed with the idea that if things got too bad, I could point it at the roof of my mouth and pop myself off this baffling planet.

One day when Baba was staying with us I came home extremely depressed. For comfort I went to have a look at my revolver. It wasn't there. I was stunned; then I completely lost my head. I began shouting, "Who has stolen my revolver!" Baba came into the room and stood petrified with fear. Suddenly I knew she had taken it and moved menacingly toward her. "You took it!" I said, and leaped at her. The weight of my body knocked her over backwards and we fell down. I grabbed her throat and banged her head over and over again on the floor. "Give it back to me!" I yelled. She managed to push me off and struggle to her feet. "I did it for your good. Can't you understand that? You should not have a revolver," she cried. We faced each other, white and shaking. Then I repeated very slowly, as if, upon each word, hung life and death: "Where have you hidden it?"

"I threw it in the East River," poor Baba sobbingly answered.

I crumpled up agonizingly on the floor. Baba knelt beside me, begging me to forgive her. Hearing our wild voices, Katie came into the room. Overhearing Baba's words, and taking in the general scene, she decided that prayer was needed. Dropping to her knees beside us and placing her hands in the attitude of prayer, she began to recite the Litany to the Virgin Mary.

Katie's soft voice, and the repetition of those beautiful words— "Mother of Jesus, have mercy on us"—calmed me down.

In the meantime Annie had come into the room. Seeing this gathering praying and weeping she, with her practical mind, resorted to practical means. She got a cold wet cloth in the bathroom and placed it on my forehead. With Katie's soft voice still reciting the Litany, Baba explained the situation to Annie. But what they could not understand was that possessing the revolver—knowing it was there, loaded, in my drawer— gave me balance. And this was a balance I could not find otherwise.

Not long after this Baba sailed back to France. I immediately began angling for another revolver. I could not buy one without a license, which I had no chance of getting. My only hope was Jimmy Fargo again. I told Clara, his beautiful sister, that I had mislaid a revolver Jimmy had given me and couldn't find it anywhere. I said I wanted him to give me another but thought he would think it strange that I had lost it and even sinister that I wanted it replaced. "You can never tell when a woman might need a gun," said she complacently, and she spoke to Jimmy and evidently handled it so well that he was prepared for my request. He gave me his own army Colt with a full box of cartridges, and my lost balance was restored.

Early in the spring I went with Jimmy Fargo to a party given by his sister, Clara and her husband, Joe Thomas, at their charming house in

East Nineteenth Street. Most of the men were still in uniform. During the evening Clara presented me to an American captain who, she said, had just returned from France and had expressed a desire to meet me. "This is Abram Poole, firstly an artist, and secondly a captain," she said. "You should be flattered, because out of all my guests he was only anxious to meet you." I looked the captain over. He seemed to me more like an eighteenth-century gentleman than a modern warrior. He was of medium height and slender, with features that were sensitive and well drawn. Without any effort he wore his uniform with dash and chic. I thought him very handsome. He was older than any of the young men I knew and I was at once attracted to him. The orchestra started playing a popular tune, "My Baby's Arms." Abram and I started dancing. All through the evening, and until dawn, he cut in on every man who danced with me.

Early the following morning he telephoned to ask me to lunch with him and then during lunch he asked me to have dinner with him. I was amused at this but I accepted. It was a relief to me that he was an artist. I was tired of aspiring young businessmen. When he came to call for me that evening I introduced him to my mother. Later when I came home she remarked that she had liked him. This was a most unusual statement for her. Never before had she said that she liked any of my young men. I thought that probably she had liked him because he was older than any of the others, but this was not the case. She said, "I like him—that's all." This simple remark made a great impression on me and did more to influence me in Abram's favor than anything else could have done.

Oddly enough, Abram had used almost the exact same words in referring to my mother. "Your mother is wonderful, and so amazingly Spanish. I would love to paint her. I have seldom been so attracted to anyone. I just like her—that's all." He couldn't know how much he was endearing himself to me by saying these things about my mother.

My mother at this time often said she had a strong feeling that she wouldn't live much longer. She used to say, "I would die in peace if I knew you were happily married." This would plunge me into the deepest imaginable depression. I would wake up in the middle of the night convinced that she was dead; I would tiptoe into her room and bend over her to make sure she was breathing. I ended by sleeping in her room to make sure she was all right. If she went out and came home ten minutes late, I would be leaning out the window. Once when she was an hour late I had called the police and was about to ring every hospital in town when she finally appeared.

She worried at this time about money. As I have already said, she knew nothing about money, but she used to tell me that if she died she would leave me very little. She would say, "Where has it gone? We used to have plenty. Oh, where has it all gone?" I would try to comfort her by saying, "After all, you have brought up eight children. This costs quite a lot." She would not be comforted and would say, "I should have managed it better."

It would have been wiser to have discussed finances with a squirrel in those days than with me. I thought then that banks were a form of club to which one belonged and from which one could draw whatever sums of money one wanted to be refunded later when and if convenient.

The fact was that somehow or other my mother's fortune had disappeared. Perhaps it was badly invested—I do not know. At this time whenever my mother was in money difficulties, Rita helped her. To me money was some kind of strange rather dirty paper with which I could coax out of someone the things I wanted. I had a firm belief that all economy was wrong. I used to ask, "Why not exchange goods, brains, or the work of one's hands instead of dirty paper? There is enough wheat, enough fruit, there is enough soil to grow vegetables for the whole world. Why not divide all this? Why must we have to deal in money?" No one gave me the answer. I saw, nevertheless, that this horrible thing called money tortured my mother. "Dinero! Dinero!" I used to shout to her from my bed in the middle of the night. "It is the curse of this world!"

When spring came, my mother and I went down to the Irving House in Southampton for a few weeks. Abram went with us. By this time he and my mother were thick as thieves. He had asked me to marry him but I had said I couldn't make up my mind so quickly. As a matter of fact I was in a strange turmoil about world affairs, my own writing, suffrage, sex, and my inner spiritual development. Marriage at the moment seemed irrelevant in comparison to these. I was in a vague mood and treated Abram accordingly.

Several times he packed his suitcases and decided to leave, vowing he would never see me again. But always, just as he was making for a taxi with his suitcases in hand, I would appear and say, "Where on earth are you going with those suitcases? Come back and unpack them." Which he always did. He said I had some kind of psychic power or clairvoyance by which I could tell he was leaving, and that in some mysterious way I always turned up just in time to prevent it. Curiously enough I think this was true. All through our life together I could tell what he was planning at any specific time, and often I would find myself advising him on subjects which he had not consulted me about, but which he would then admit were much on his mind.

Nineteen

I went that summer for a short visit to Spain to stay with Zuloaga at his home in Zumaya, a small fishing town some miles from San Sebastian where Ignacio met me. He greeted me with his usual great warmth, and before taking me home to Zumaya, we went to see friends of his—*Gitanes*—who were living up in the mountains. He had parked his car near the beach and we walked to it along the water front. I had always considered San Sebastian rather an ugly city by daylight, but a curious transformation seemed to take place there at night. The jagged mountains loomed up in the distance against the dark sky and the bright, glaringly yellow lights of the water front made the women's dresses and the soldiers' uniforms appear gaudily gay, while, in contrast, the crouching figures of beggars and cripples seemed terribly sinister. Out in the harbor, through a warm heavy haze, dark ships floated, giving an impression of great birds resting on the water. It was all very dramatic to me.

Because I was Ignacio's friend the gypsies welcomed me—something they would not otherwise have done as the gypsies do not welcome strangers. At first they were shy with me, but later when they began to dance to the accompaniment of flamenco music they lost this shyness. Their grace of movement and aristocratic bearing were impressive. All of them, men and women, young and old, and even the ugly ones (or ones who might be termed ugly in the conventional sense) had a vibrant and colorful beauty.

Unfortunately, we had just missed a wedding which would have been a unique experience for an outsider to witness. The Gitanes considered Ignacio as one of them. He had known three generations of this particular family. He had painted Gitanes and Gitanas all over Spain. He had fought for certain land privileges for them. He often said to me, "You know, I am really a gypsy. Actually I am only happy when I am with them."

Gypsy women are always chaste. There is no prostitution among them. A woman before her marriage is unquestionably a virgin. Her virginity is not allowed to be profaned—even by her husband. To symbolize this, the marriage ceremony begins the night before the actual marriage, or before the final vows are taken. Thirteen young women are chosen to enact the religious ceremony of the symbolic taking of her virginity. Twelve dance around the bed in which the bride is lying, dressed in a specific symbolic costume. They dance a ritual dance, throwing almonds on the bride. The thirteenth girl moves close to the bed and making certain symbolic gestures, breaks the bride's maidenhead with her right hand. When this is done, the groom is brought in. He places offerings and presents at the feet of his bride. Then he, too, dances a ritualistic dance, finally dancing himself out of the presence of his bride, whom he does not see again until the final marriage ceremony the following night.

We arrived in the mountains just after this final ceremony, witnessed the wedding dances, and were given special food eaten only on such occasions.

It was daybreak when Ignacio and I descended the mountain and followed the coast to Zumaya. Before entering the house he took me into a small stone chapel which he had built near it. Hanging in this chapel were his thirteen famous El Grecos. One of them, "Sacred and Profane Love," is a remarkable painting and was little known until he sent his El Grecos to London during the Spanish Civil War. (It is now in the Metropolitan Museum and for some unexplainable reason it is called "The Vision of St. John.") Over the main altar a large crucifix was hanging. Ignacio had made the cross from the wood of a tree he himself had cut down. He had also sculptured the Crucified Christ hanging from it.

That evening, seeing peasants running toward the beach, we followed them. There, on the sand, a ship painted entirely black had beached. There was no one on board and there was no name on the bow or the stern. With their innate sense of superstition the peasants and fishermen saw an evil omen in the landing of this ship. In 1936 during the Spanish civil war I remembered it and felt that it had most certainly been a symbol of impending disaster—a disaster which was already casting its shadow on the white sands of this coast.

The King invited Ignacio and me to a bullfight in San Sebastian. Alfonso was reigning at this time, unaware that his days on the throne were running out. I did not wish to accept this invitation, but Ignacio said that a refusal to sit in the royal box would make it very awkward for him.

Looking at the King that day, I intuitively felt he would surely lose his throne. He was too steeped in the tradition of his realm and the Church to read the writing across the sky of Spain. Writers, poets and thinkers such as Miguel Unamuno, José Ortega y Gasset, Pió Baroja, and many younger men had been exiled because of their free writings against the Church when, in reality, they were doing a service to their country. It was the old story of ignorance. History repeats itself and so do kings—they do not learn their lesson either.

That autumn both my books were published. My novel was, on the whole, treated rather kindly by the critics, who spoke of it as a first novel, which seemed to mean that its shortcomings could be excused. Rereading it last year, I am amazed that the reviewers didn't throw it out of the window.

Moods, my book of prose poems, was published at the same time. Charles Hanson Towne, a writer, editor, critic and poet, wrote the Preface for this volume. It was reviewed with glowing praise.

That winter Katie died very suddenly of pneumonia, almost before my mother or I realized how ill she was. It was a terrific shock to my mother. She neither wept nor broke down, but she was inconsolable and her quiet silences made me feel that this sorrow was too heavy to carry even the weight of tears or words. I had a strong presentiment that she would not long survive Katie.

That same winter I decided to marry Abram and it was agreed that we would live in New York. It went without saying that my mother would live with us. His family home was in Chicago, but already three of his sisters and his brother Ernest were living in New York. Ernest was a novelist and had at this time just published a very successful novel, *The Harbor.* Before the war Abram had lived a number of years in Paris, where he studied painting with Julian. He had also studied in Germany and was extremely talented, especially as a decorative painter. But he hadn't, so far, worked very hard. His family was rich and well known, he possessed talent as well as good looks, and naturally had been,rather spoiled—especially by women. His four sisters adored him and the society women in Chicago considered him a catch. He accepted all this attention rather casually, but this indifference did not hold him down to work and, not needing money, he painted only when he felt like it. It was a shock to him when I told him I considered him a dilettante and that when he married me he would have to work seriously. I said I expected him to become a great painter.

Although Abram was an artist, he was very conventional. Actually he was a strange mixture, for secretly, I believe, he admired unconventional people—he would not have fallen in love with me had this not been so. But the training of his early American background in a city like Chicago, and the inheritance of his blood—half English and half Dutch— surely tended to inhibit the chance he might have had for a broader point of view. He always worried a great deal about what people thought. All during our years together I was forever hearing his fears as to what THEY would think. But whenever I asked him who THEY were he would just wave his hand in the air. Evidently in his mind THEY was some vague outside authority to whom he had to give a proper accounting of his actions.

All this was a pity as far as our relationship was concerned as I never cared a fig what anyone thought. As long as I feel "right" within myself, so called "society's" opinion never influences me for a second. Even in my youngest days I already knew how easily this opinion could be swung and altered—just as easily as one could change the opinion of any mob.

When I broke the news to him that I intended to keep my own name after we were married, he was very upset. What would THEY say? And his family would be shocked. I said I was not marrying his family. We came to a deadlock and I hit on a plan which I considered fair, although a compromise for me. I said we should toss a coin. If he won I would have to take his name. If he lost he would have to take mine. The prospect of taking mine so frightened him that he agreed at once to my keeping mine. He promised on his sacred word of honor that he would never call me any other name but my own or be a party to anyone else calling me any name but my own. I said that I would marry him the eleventh of May.

Three days before my own wedding my friend Audrey Osborn was married to John Elliott, a most attractive man and a friend of mine. (Later Abram and I bought a house on East Forty-seventh Street and

Audrey and Jack bought one next door.) Another friend of mine, Betty Pierson, was married to Schuyler Parsons on the same day as Audrey and Jack, and a few days before her wedding Betty rang me on the telephone and asked me to lunch with her at the Ritz. She said she had a friend—an actress—who wanted very much to meet me. I did not inquire the name of this friend, but I accepted the invitation.

On arriving at the Ritz she presented me to a very charming-looking and seemingly shy young woman named Eva Le Gallienne. When we were seated at a table, Eva said that she had wanted to meet me because Betty had told her how I felt about Eleonora Duse. During lunch Betty got no chance to open her mouth as Eva and I feverishly compared notes on everything we knew or had ever heard about Duse. By the time lunch was over we had worked ourselves into such a pitch of excitement that Betty left us, and we stayed on until we had to leave the table, still discussing Duse.

I was married very quietly in my mother's apartment with only a few friends attending. I did not want a large wedding, and in any case, since Abram was a Protestant and I was married by a Roman Catholic priest, it could not have taken place in a Catholic Church. I did not want to wear a white wedding dress, or a veil. I wore a gray chiffon dress. I did not want music either but Rita, afraid the wedding might seem dreary without it, concealed a small orchestra in the dining room.

While I was dressing, Alfredo Sides put his head in the door and said, laughing, "You and I are two people who never should be married. You have about ten minutes to change your mind." This did not help my emotions but I was surprised out of them when a few minutes later I heard music. It was Rita's orchestra beginning the Wedding March.

As I descended the stairs and moved toward the priest, Mrs. Otto Kahn stepped forward and placed a small box in my hand. It was a curious thing to do just then. Taking my place beside Abram, I handed him the box. He looked puzzled and handed it to his brother Ernest, his best man. Ernest looked bewildered and, having no idea what to do with it, placed it on the floor, unfortunately where I could see it. I was conscious of it all during the ceremony. After the wedding I opened the box and found that it contained a charming, small lapis lazuli and sapphire clock from Cartier's. Some years later, for a few seconds, it played quite a part in my life. In the fifteen years of our marriage it was the only object I ever hurled at Abram.

The day after our wedding Abram and I planned to leave for Chicago to spend two weeks in his house before returning to New York on our way to Europe. We were to spend the night before at the Hotel Vanderbilt, then very new and smart. But my mother looked so forlorn when I kissed her good-by after the reception that that evening after dinner in our rooms I couldn't forget her unhappy face. I spoke of it to Abram, secretly wishing I could go back and see her. He must have read my mind, because he instantly suggested that I go home and spend the night with her. He said, "Tonight is probably the loneliest one for her. If you go home tonight, the others will be easier for her to face without you." I felt then, as I have felt since, that this was one of the most touchingly generous gestures a man could make. He took me home in a taxi and left me downstairs in our apartment. I went up in the lift with the puzzled face of the attendant plainly showing that he was saying to himself: "A quarrel so soon!"

I very quietly unlocked the front door of our flat, and tiptoed inside. It was in darkness except for the glow of a dying fire in the living room. My mother, with her hand over her eyes, was seated before it. I hesitated for a second, afraid of frightening her, then I moved very quietly toward her and enveloped her in my arms. This was an unforgettable moment in my life. A rare psychic moment because my mother and I, during this brief but long, timeless time, which was in reality outside of time, changed identities. I became her mother and she, my child. In some unexplainable way she slipped onto my knees, and holding her as a mother would a child, I rocked her gently in my arms. Neither of us spoke. To this day I do not remember any words passing between us. I only know that I took my mother to bed, and all night long, as though she were still my child, I held her in my arms. A strange wedding night— indeed.

The next day we took the train to Chicago and went to Abram's house on Lake Shore Drive. It was as charming a house as I had expected it to be. Abram has most distinguished taste. He had put it up for sale and asked me to choose anything out of it that I wanted. During the first few days I was busy meeting his family and friends. Next to David Adler, his closest friend was George Porter. I understood George better than Abram did, and he confided in me right up until his death, when he tragically shot himself. I also met David Adler's wife, Catherine. She was beautiful, blond and slender. I can't remember having as much fun with anyone in my life as I did with Catherine. For some reason she drew a comic side out of me.

Of course, one of the first people I went to see in Chicago was Harriet Monroe. We spent hours together discussing poets and poetry. I showed her a collection of new poems I had written which Moffat and Yard had accepted for publication the following autumn in a volume entitled *Archways of Life.* Harriet Monroe was my happiest and most vivid experience during these weeks in Chicago.

There was naturally a good deal of entertaining done for me, and one formal dinner had its amusing aspects. This was a dinner given by John Carpenter, the composer, and his wife, Rue. I was seated to the right of General Leonard Wood, who was expected to run for the Presidency the following year. Almost at once he picked up my card and said, "I thought you were Mrs. Abram Poole." Whereupon I (probably foolishly) launched into a discourse about keeping my own name. He responded with a glum silence as I should have expected. I turned to the gentleman on my other side and, after a brief conversation, thought I would try my luck with General Wood again. I turned around to him and he said, "And now that you are keeping your own name, what do you intend to do with it?"

Since the Russian Revolution I had been following all the events in Russia closely and I was passionately interested in them. So I thought it would be fun to answer the acid question as lightly as I could, and said, "Just as you hope to become the President of the United States I, too, hope to become a president—of Russia."

General Wood, perhaps because he thought I was out of my mind, repeated this conversation with the result that the newspapers the next day came out with *Mercedes de Acosta, recent bride of Abram Poole, expects to be the first president of Russia.*

This was only the beginning of Abram's tribulations with me in Chicago. A few days later his oldest brother Ralph and his wife were giving a dinner for us. The morning of the dinner two friends of mine came to see me. One of them was that talented actress Estelle Winwood, and the other was Lorna Linsley, an old friend. They remarked that they had been invited to the dinner to meet Abram and me. Estelle pulled the invitation out of her bag. Not having received one myself, I looked at it. After the customary formal wording it ended *To meet Mr. and Mrs. Abram Poole.* I tried to conceal my anger from Estelle and Lorna. But when they had left I packed my bags and ordered a ticket on the Twentieth Century to New York. As Abram was out I left a letter for him with the butler: *You have broken your word to me. I will not be at the dinner tonight and I hope you will tell your brother why. I am returning to New York and leaving you.*

Abram caught the next train to New York. When I refused to see him, he went to the St. Regis and bombarded me with letters and tele-grams. For Abram to telegraph required nothing less than life or death. When he first met me and found that I sometimes sent telegrams as long as letters, often quoting poems in them, he was amazed. I found it equally amazing that he could not take a telegram somewhat naturally and not always expect it to carry words of gloom. Besides his astonish-ing telegrams and letters he also begged Rita and my mother to inter-cede for him. Finally Vouletti persuaded me to see him, taking advantage of my soft heart by saying he looked ill. As soon as I saw him, of course I forgave him. He promised again to respect my right to keep my name, which from that day he did.

My behavior at this time may seem fantastic and lacking in humor, and looking at it from today's point of view it certainly was. But it must not be forgotten that this was a very different period for women. We had to battle every inch of the way for rights which are now taken for granted. Young women who vote today can never imagine the frustra-tion and indignity of being considered inferior to men and not allowed to go to the polls. And today, when women can fill any job, it is impossi-ble to realize what it meant to be completely dependent financially on a husband or family simply because jobs were closed to them because of their sex. Birth control, which some governments forcibly advocate nowadays, was in my time taboo. Another unmentionable subject was venereal disease. Even Ibsen's *Ghosts* was discussed only in lowered tones. My youth—the tail end of Victorianism—was still the Dark Ages!

Soon after this my mother, Abram and I sailed for Europe. Baba was in Paris where my mother intended to join her, going later for some weeks to Houlgate while Abram and I traveled. In Paris Abram and I had a small suite on the top floor of the Crillon overlooking one of the most beautiful views in the world—the Place de la Concorde.

During these weeks in Paris I made three lasting friends, Jean Coc-teau, Yvonne George, and Prince Agoutinsky.

Yvonne George is probably little known among Americans although she came to New York twice. Both times that she appeared on the stage here she was under contract to Lee Shubert. During both these engage-ments she was already desperately ill and unable to sing at a number of performances. This failure to appear, sometimes at the last moment, gave her a bad name. With the exception of a handful of people, she was not appreciated here. France, an older and wiser country, knew her worth and in spite of her tragic weakness (she took drugs) people crowded to see her and hear her sing. If she did not appear one night, they just came back again the next one, hoping for better luck.

Anyone who has heard her sing "Pars" (as I did for the first time that spring and many times after) would understand why her great talent was immediately recognized in Paris. She was taken up at once by the intellectual group. Cocteau cast her in the role of the nurse in his production of *Romeo and Juliet*. But somehow Yvonne was marked for tragedy. I felt this immediately on meeting her as I did shortly afterwards when I met Jeanne Eagels.

During the twenties in Paris and until his death during the war, Prince Agoutinsky was one of my closest and warmest friends. This wonderful man, during the time of the late Czar, had been fabulously rich in Russia and was known as a great patron of art. He was a connoisseur of paintings and owned a famous collection of old Russian china which he presented to the Hermitage Museum before his escape from Russia after the Revolution. He arrived in Paris without a cent, but somehow he managed to settle down in a small flat in the rue François Prémier, and before long he became a sort of "little father" to all the other Russian refugees.

His flat was an extraordinary place. Any Russian who had something to sell brought it to him. The place was crowded with icons, amazing paintings, both good and bad, old books, furniture, silver and gold tea sets, gold plates, rugs, and every object imaginable. Sometimes when I arrived at his flat I would find him sitting in the midst of these objects looking rather like a Buddha. He was silent and wise, like a Buddha. His eyes would twinkle and he would say, "Would you like to see something beautiful?" Diving under the bed or into an overcrowded cupboard, he would bring forth a drawing by Leonardo or Rembrandt, or some priceless object which had belonged to a czar.

"If we could only find a rich American to buy this," he would say. "I would like to help my friend who needs money."

It was Agoutinsky who introduced me to Alexandre Benois, (who had been his lifelong friend) Diaghilev, Bakst, Nijinsky, and Stravinsky —in fact, the entire Russian Ballet group, all of whom were his intimate friends.

I met Stravinsky for the first time that summer and I did not at first like him as much as I did many years later, when he came out to Hollywood, and I grew to love him. At this first meeting I thought him conceited and ungracious. Diaghilev seemed just the contrary. He had beautiful manners and was exceedingly gracious. In his great enthusiasm he was like an overgrown child and one could easily understand his being able to direct all this genius as a great conductor leads a great orchestra, bringing it out at moments in full volume, modifying it— coaxing it lightly—sometimes drawing sadness from it but always making out of it one superbly inspired piece of complete unison and harmony. Diaghilev knew how to play on his human instruments as well as he knew how to direct them.

Among all the artists inspired by Diaghilev, the one I came to know best and the one I loved, was Tamara Karsavina.

Looking back over my life I am curious just why so many dancers have been my friends. I believe I am attracted to them by some peculiar thing they emanate—a shadow of some wingéd essence which clings to their spirit—a spark of untiring energy which like the rustle of a con- tinuous wind manifests itself from their souls to their physical entity. Great dancers who express art through their bodies—at the moment of giving themselves to the dance—already soar away and beyond the body into that mysterious realm of rhythm through the gateway of motion. To dance is a gesture of the body by which the spirit reaches out for cosmic strength. It is the flinging of one's secret love into the arena of life. A spending of one's power that by the very law of action and reaction must revert itself twofold back to the spender. Dancing is music of the body. Great dancing is an inspired orchestra of the soul in full play.

Tamara Karsavina was to me, at this time, a revelation of harmony between the spirit and body. I saw her dance for the first time in Paris in "L'Oiseau de Feu" and I was haunted by her beauty and supreme artistry. Later I saw her in "Le Spectre de la Rose" and "Petrouchka." In these two ballets I was deeply moved by a curious, touching quality which she projected when she danced. When later I came to know her well I could see that this quality was part of her—the very fabric of her deeply mystic and Russian soul. Since leaving Russia her home has been in London, and England is a country she loves. Nevertheless, she is essentially Russian and in spite of her attempts to adapt to English ways, she has never been anything else. I have seen her, over the years, unconsciously betray a profound nostalgia for the soil of her own country. She once wrote: *I have never lost the attachment to the country of my birth, though I realize I would now feel a stranger in it.*

Rita was in Paris for a few weeks that summer. While she was there, Ignacio gave several Spanish parties for us. Miguel Unamuno was stay- ing with him then and I met him for the first time. I also met José

Ortega y Gasset, Pió Baroja and the dramatist Benavente. There were always innumerable Spaniards coming and going at Ignacio's studio.

I met José Maria Sert and Misia Sert during these weeks, and started a friendship with Misia which lasted until her death. Polish Misia, emotional and warm, was beloved by artists and had been at the center of French painting for half a century. A great friend of Diaghilev's she was always caught up in the Russian Ballet's gossip and problems.

Abram and I went to see Picasso and Matisse that summer. It was interesting to encounter two such great painters so little known at this time but who seemed to me to symbolize their period. I recall being struck by the power I felt in the works of both these men. The cubist period of Picasso was laughed at. (So were Gertrude Stein and James Joyce at this time.) These artists were the center of endless discussions and arguments and my enthusiasm for them and insistence that they both had genius was not well received by most people.

Visiting the houses where Picasso and Matisse lived led me to an observation which I have verified through the years. I have noticed that creative people very often do not have what is commonly known as "taste" in their manner of living. I noticed then that neither Picasso nor Matisse had a need for beauty in their surroundings. With the exception of their own paintings they had nothing in their houses which in any way lifted the spirit by form, color, or design. Their rooms were not stark but they were ugly. I have many times noticed how various artists—painters, writers, musicians, and so forth—can live in ugly surroundings and remain untouched by them. The paradox is that these same artists can themselves create beauty within their own art. Perhaps they are so greatly absorbed in their art that they have no need to look outside of it. On the other hand, I have observed that there are people who are not remotely creative and yet are extremely artistic. These people have irreproachable taste and are only happy when surrounded by beauty. They can decorate a house beautifully, arrange flowers charmingly, design exquisite clothes, and blend colors faultlessly. It would seem that creativeness in the artist is something quite different from the mere production of beauty.

That summer I caught a fleeting glimpse of Isadora at a party given by the Princess Violette Murat. Isadora was there, walking about with Nijinsky and holding him by the hand. The orchestra played "The Blue Danube." They rose to dance. Isadora clasped her hands behind her head, forcing Nijinsky to lead her by placing his hands around her waist. She became oblivious, lost in the beat of the waltz. With her eyes closed she allowed Nijinsky to guide her in and out among the other waltzing couples. Gradually everyone else stopped dancing to watch. It was an unforgettable sight to see these two geniuses of the dance—each representing his art from opposite poles—waltzing madly around and, at that, waltzing rather badly. Nijinsky found it difficult to lead Isadora as she made no effort to follow him and seemed to be off in a world of her own. When the music stopped we all applauded, and they waltzed again. This time Nijinsky showed fatigue and could hardly keep up with his partner. As the last note of the music ended, Isadora flung herself onto a sofa, dragging him with her. Everyone laughed and applauded again and they scrambled to their feet. Holding her hand out to Nijinsky in a gesture of affection, she said, "What a shame he wasn't my pupil when he was two. Then I could have taught him to dance!"

Later on Abram and I went to Spain. He had never been there, and I knew what excitement lay before him in the Prado in Madrid. He developed a passion for Spanish painting, especially Goya and El Greco. In Toledo he started to paint. I posed for him and he feverishly painted two portraits of me.

After Spain, we went to Italy—to Venice, where we had arranged to rent a charming flat on the Grand Canal, just opposite D'Annunzio's house. I tried to find out where Duse was hiding and learned that she was in her own house in Asolo, that she never went out or was seen by anyone. She had been in total retirement for over ten years.

Abram and I went to see the Marchesa Casati. I wanted to meet her because I had heard so much about her eccentricities. She received us in her garden, dressed in white with black strips of court plaster around and outlining her eyes. As she advanced to meet us she carried a lily in one hand, with the other she led by a chain a small lioness cub. I thought she was "bad theatre," although her performance then was not as "ham" as it would be now. These were different times, and people allowed themselves flights of imagination by dressing up as something they secretly wished to be. I myself had often dressed as a Cossack or a Hussar, and I once went so far as to affect a Franciscan tunic—rope sandals and all—so perhaps I should not criticize the Casati, who evidently thought of herself as a virgin carrying a symbolic lily.

That summer Hope Williams had come to Europe alone, so she joined Abram and me in Venice. Abram was very fond of her. That following winter she married Bartow Read.

Abram had another favorite, a friend of mine by the name of Billie McKeever. Billie's family was well known in New York and by the standards of such families she was supposed to make her debut into society and do all the conventional things expected of a well-brought-up young lady. Billie had other ideas. She was like quicksilver. She slipped out of her family's hands and out of all the social engagements they made for her. She would come to our house and hide in Abram's studio and beg us not to give her away or tell anyone where she was. She was wild, untamed, and had a delicious fey quality. She could completely twist Abram round her little finger, and we called her our "Gypsy child." Some years later, while I was out in Hollywood, she died suddenly. Her death was a great loss to me.

Twenty

In the meantime Baba had decided to remarry. She had met a wonderful man, Frederick Shaw, the son of Sir Robert Shaw and a cousin of George Bernard Shaw's. Frederick's family came from Tere-nure, just outside of Dublin. Baba and Freddie intended to return to Africa, where they had first met and where they both wanted to live.

Before returning to New York, Abram and I went to London to buy some English furniture for our house. While there we met the painter Augustus John, and spent several afternoons with him in his studio. I saw Ivor Novello again, and met his close friend Bobbie Andrews. Cecile Sartoris had given me a letter of introduction to Gabrielle Enthoven saying that Gabrielle knew Duse very well. This, of course, was enough to make me rush to see her at the earliest moment. She became one of my closest friends in London.

Gabrielle was a woman of rare culture, of heart, and remarkable intelligence. A woman, too, of great humor. There were few like her.

Apart from our mutual admiration for Duse, of whom we talked for hours at our first meeting, I found that, like myself, Gabrielle had a passion for the theatre. When I met her, she was going every day to the Victoria and Albert Museum where she was compiling a collection of London playbills to form complete sequences for every London theatre, with examples from the earliest centuries—especially the eighteenth. She had collected and compiled over 80,000 of them, in addition to thousands of engravings and photographs of actors and actresses, scenes from plays, interiors and exteriors of theatres, and a great many printed texts including 150 prompt copies of eighteenth-century plays used by the Theatre Royal, Drury Lane. Gabrielle needed money and she was offered 30,000 pounds by Harvard University for this collection. She preferred, however, to donate it to the Victoria and Albert Museum, which she did in 1924—a gift to the nation.

Before I left London, Gabrielle and I discussed a plan by which she thought she could entice Duse back to the stage. She carried out this plan, and in 1923 it was she who was instrumental in bringing Duse to London and arranging with Charles Cochran to finance and produce her farewell engagement there.

Back in New York we moved into our house, which had a good-sized studio where Abram could paint. On the fourth floor I had a study and on this floor there was also my mother's room and bath. I had planned it this way so that she could come into my study whenever she wished. I knew that Mother had another great worry. At this time Rita was constantly seeing Dr. Percy Stickney Grant, the Rector of the Church of the Ascension at Fifth Avenue and Tenth Street. She did not conceal from us that she was deeply interested in him and was even considering marrying him. After two failures in marriage and two divorces, my mother naturally felt uneasy about it. The possibility of a marriage with a Protestant clergyman was in her opinion the last straw.

I could understand Rita's attraction to Dr. Grant. They had many intellectual sympathies. She was widely read in philosophy and her opinions inclined toward socialism. Every Sunday evening Dr. Grant conducted a forum in his parish house where social and political problems were freely discussed. Rita loved just such discussions. In fact it was generally believed that she wrote most of the papers that Dr. Grant read at these meetings. She could phrase anything in scholarly language and she also had courage and humor. Rita believed that practically any situation in life could be altered for the better by humor.

That autumn my second volume of poems—*Archways of Life*—was published and a third edition of *Moods*. The new book was also well received.

Eva Le Gallienne had opened during the summer in *Liliom* with great success. When I returned from Europe she had already been playing for some weeks, but I had not had time to get in touch with her or see the play. One day Betty Parsons called. She said Eva was so overtired that the doctor had ordered her out of the theatre for a few days. "Why don't you call her?" she said. "I know it would cheer her up." I did, and when Eva said she would be back playing again the following Monday I promised to go and see her that night. I had never seen her act and was not prepared for such a remarkably fine performance. The entire play touched me profoundly. When all the visitors had gone and she had taken off her make-up, I went home with her to her flat and we talked long into the morning about our hopes in the theatre and again at length, about Duse.

I went down to the Village a great deal that year. Cecile Sartoris and Gabrielle Enthoven had come over to New York and were sharing a flat on Washington Square South. Teddy Gerrard, the English musical comedy actress, lived there too, in another flat. I never knew anything about her background. Teddy was just Teddy. Everyone loved her. She moved like a panther. She was gay, wild, beautiful, generous, full of fun, and a trifle mad.

She had staying with her at this time Napier Alington—Lord Alington. "Naps" had come to America at the invitation of old Mrs. Cornelius Vanderbilt, but his visit did not last long at the Vanderbilt "Mansion." He had not bargained on formal dinner parties every night, or on escorting Mrs. Vanderbilt ("All dressed up and looking like a peppermint candystick," he used to say) to the opera. One night both he and the second butler failed to appear at a large and formal dinner. Naps' place at the table, on Mrs. Vanderbilt's right, was empty, the pantry was in a flurry over the missing butler, and it was not difficult for Mrs. Vanderbilt to conclude that wherever these two missing young men were, they were together. The following day they were both dismissed. Naps thought it a great joke and told everyone how he and the butler "got the sack together." Teddy took him in and he stayed with her. In a curious way he was very much like her—full of charm, gaiety, and madness.

In rather a childish, wild way, we had a lot of fun in Teddy's flat that winter—Cecile, Gabrielle, Naps, Mary Rumsey (Averill Harriman's sister), Muriel Draper, Jo Davidson, Sinclair Lewis, and Poldowski, who (in nonprofessional life), was Lady Irene Dean-Paul and a close friend of Naps.

There was snow on the ground on Christmas Eve and we each took a lighted candle and walked around Washington Square singing, in bare feet. Naps loved not wearing shoes and persuaded us that it was healthy to go barefoot in snow. The rest of us nearly cried, our feet were so cold.

At a party in Greenwich Village I was placed at the dinner table next to Sinclair Lewis, whom I had never seen before, nor had I read his much-discussed *Main Street*. Someone introduced us and as I was about to sit down, Red Lewis pulled the chair away. I not only fell flat on my back on the floor, but I also hit my head a dreadful crack against the table. For a minute I saw stars and there was a sudden dead silence in the room. Somehow, although it was quite a shock, I had enough sense not to lose my temper. Scrambling to my feet as though nothing had happened, I said casually, "It's so nice to have a little acrobatic exercise before dinner." The tension was eased, and everyone laughed. It seemed that Red was known for pranks like this. The rest of the evening he couldn't have been nicer and we became friends.

Some years later I was in London when he married Dorothy Thompson. The night before the wedding at three o'clock in the morning, he called me on the telephone. He said he felt like talking to me. "You know," he said, "I have never forgotten how graciously you behaved that evening when I was so beastly. Your humor, and the fact that you didn't get angry, endeared you to me instantly. In fact it's probably why I'm calling you now." I went to his wedding the next day.

This winter I began going to Bob Chanler's on East Nineteenth Street. He was part of the social, artistic and Bohemian fabric of New York in the twenties and his parties became legendary. Bob was one of four brothers, each distinguished in his own line. He was a painter and a fine one. He loved painting exotic animals. His "Giraffes" used to hang in the Luxembourg in Paris. Some years later my sister Maria married Bob's nephew, the composer Theodore Chanler.

Bob was gargantuan. Everything about him—hands, feet, shoulders, head—all were enormous. And his hair, thick and tightly curled, stood out about five inches from his head, making him seem that much taller and his head that much bigger. His voice bellowed out like the roaring of ten bulls and it could be heard a block away. He was a curious mixture of sophistication, worldliness, childlike trust, simplicity, roughness and gentleness.

Bob was very proud of his family. He said, "There are two species of the human race—one is people, the other is Chanlers." He had them all at his parties. Hating to be alone for one second, he held open house several evenings a week. He mixed intellectuals, artists, races, colors, titles, society people, theatrical people, circus people, vagabonds, alcoholics, homosexuals, rich and poor—in a word, humanity. As long as they behaved themselves he didn't care who they were.

He himself sat, dressed in a Russian blouse and wearing bedroom slippers, in a huge chair placed against the wall. Always on the floor beside him stood a large bell with a handle and not far away were several Negro servants. If anyone got what Bob called "out of order," he would seize the bell and ring it wildly. When the servants appeared Bob would point to the offender, who was pounced upon, rushed downstairs and out of the house before he could open his mouth. This happened quite often at first, but Bob was always right in his judgment, and when it got around that he would not tolerate any rowdiness in his house it was remarkable how well this mixed group of people behaved.

Bob had a passion for the names of the states of America. He used to say that such names as Ohio, Alabama, Oklahoma, Wyoming and so forth, were beautiful words. Often while sitting in his huge chair, or even at the dining room table, his great voice would suddenly bellow out over the noisy conversation. "O-HI-O, O-HI-O," he would shout over and over again, or "U-TAH, U-TAH." We were all used to him and no one paid the slightest attention. Sometimes he shouted for fifteen minutes, varying the states. If he was in his big chair in the living room, he rang his bell at the same time.

Bob insisted that winter on painting my portrait. I posed full-length in a black topcoat, fitted at the waist and with a circular skirt, which Poiret had designed for me in Paris. Incidentally, since Poiret made this coat for me I have never worn any other model but have it copied repeatedly in different colors and materials. It has come into vogue and gone out of vogue, but at this time it was considered extremely eccentric as the waistline for women in the early twenties was almost at the knee. In 1931 in Hollywood, Greta Garbo asked me to let her copy the coat. She wore it on her return to Sweden and was, unwillingly, photographed in it by the press. As soon as the photograph appeared, padded shoulders and circular skirts came full swing into vogue. Last year I was *démodée* in it, but soon, no doubt, I will be in fashion again.

When Bob finished my portrait he called it "The Retreat from Moscow." Not exactly a title for America today! He painted several other portraits of me. I was indifferent about them, but I enjoyed posing for him because when we were alone he was at his best. He was amazingly gentle. He talked incessantly about his ex-wife, Lina Cavalieri, often called the most beautiful woman in the world. She had married him some years before, but after persuading him, immediately after the marriage, to sign a paper giving her everything he possessed including his money, she left him—that same night—and never lived with him.

It was then that his brother, Lewis, temporarily confined to a sanatorium, sent him the cablegram which has become a byword: *Who's loony now?* Cavalieri died as she lived. During the last war she was killed by a bomb in Florence when she ran back to save her jewels. (The priest who found her body in the debris of her house was stunned by her beauty.)

These were the days when the speak-easies were in full bloom. Harlem, too, had already come into its own. Everyone rushed up to Harlem at night to sit around places thick with smoke and the smell of bad gin, where Negroes danced about with each other until the small hours of the morning. What we all saw in it is difficult to understand now. I suppose outwitting the government and getting the better of the police lent a zest to our lives.

The Green Hat, a novel by Michael Arlen which was afterwards dramatized and played in New York by Katharine Cornell, completely symbolized the spirit of this time. A spirit which went overboard in bravado, sentimentality and taste. It was a play in which the heroine was utterly reckless but always gallant. *Gallant* and *dangerous* were in a sense the passwords of the twenties. One could do anything then, as long as one lived gallantly and dangerously. At the end of *The Green Hat* Iris March gallantly drove her Hispano Suiza off a mountaintop. Practically everyone of my generation was influenced by this story. Michael Arlen was supposed to have taken the idea of Iris from the character of Nancy Cunard, whom I greatly admired.

This period seemed to produce people with an inner violence and an overcharged excess of emotion that marked them for a tragic end. One night Jeanne Eagels and Sonny Whitney came into a speak-easy where I was sitting with John Colton. The minute I saw her I said to John, "She will end tragically." When she played with great talent the role of Sadie Thompson in *Rain*—which he had dramatized for her—she was only playing herself. There was an affinity between her and Sadie Thompson. This, too, was a violent, reckless and daredevil character— one that gallantly said: "I'm sorry for the whole goddamned world."

I went to a ball that winter at the Hotel Astor given for the benefit of the Actors' Equity and saw an astonishingly beautiful performance by Natacha Rambova and Rudolph Valentino, in Spanish costumes, dancing a tango and a Spanish folk dance. I had seen Valentino in the cinema, but I had never before seen him or Natacha Rambova in person. Except for the Castles, they were the most striking dance couple I have ever seen. Just by accident (which I use only as a figure of speech, because I believe there is no such thing as accident) I was standing near the exit when they finished their number and paused by it while the audience applauded for an encore. It was certainly not the moment to introduce them to anyone, but Charlie Towne, who was Master of Ceremonies and was standing next to me, in his usual kindly and well-meaning way seized Rambova's hand, swung her around and said, "Natacha, this is Mercedes." Rambova smiled as Valentino dragged her back into the ballroom for the encore. I did not know then that a very great influence would come into my life from this seemingly chance meeting.

After Christmas Rita announced her engagement to Dr. Grant. It precipitated a storm of publicity as Dr. Grant had already been in conflict with the Episcopalian Bishop Manning over the radicalism of his forum. He was known to hold liberal views on divorce, while the Bishop held quite the opposite. At this time both Will Stokes and Phil Lydig were alive, and Rita had divorced Phil on grounds considered ecclesiastically trifling—incompatibility. Rita's case brought up the point whether an Episcopalian clergyman could marry a divorced woman. Bishop Manning held fast that this the Church could not permit. The matter came to a deadlock.

Shortly after this an exhibition took place at the National Arts Club. One of the paintings in this exhibition was entitled "Lady Vibrating to Jack-in-the-Pulpit." It was clearly a caricature of Rita and Dr. Grant. Rita's wit and humor were equal to the occasion. She had been tipped off about it and she bought it before the exhibition opened. When it did open, the painting bore the label *Bought by Rita Lydig.* One paper said, "One would have to get up pretty early in the morning to outwit Rita Lydig or to match her rare humor."

This battle between Bishop Manning and Dr. Grant and the publicity it aroused caused Rita untold nervous strain. It was said that she had caused Dr. Grant to revolutionize and make over his church. This was based on the fact that she had given Dr. Grant a sixteenth-century piece of Flemish lace for the altar. She had also supplied him with leather-bound hymnbooks and had paid the salary of a first-rate organist. To give these things to Dr. Grant for his church seemed perfectly natural to her because the church was what he most cared about. She made no secret about giving them. She gave things to the man she loved, whether they were for a church or not. Of course the press took it all up and the facts were distorted in the usual way. As a matter of fact, the congregation was very grateful to her for improving the church and especially for contributing such a fine organist.

Toward spring, Eva and Clare Eames acted together for two matinée performances in Maeterlinck's *Aglavaine and Selysette*. Eva played Selysette and she asked me to design a costume for her. This was a happy request for me, as it brought into my life a friend who was destined to be very close to me until her death in 1952. I needed someone to make the costume I had designed. Eva's great friend Mary Benson said she knew just the right person—Marion Stevenson—who it appeared was a marvel at cutting and sewing. Marion came to see me. She was small, dressed entirely in Victorian clothes, and her long, thick hair was braided and wound around her head. She was like someone from another era, except in her way of thinking. In every thought Marion was in advance of her time. She was related to Robert Louis Stevenson on her father's side of the family. Her father had been a sea captain and every time he sailed to China he brought her beautiful Chinese things. Marion loved everything Chinese. In fact she loved everything oriental, which made a bond between us. She seemed to me like an inspired little mouse with a bomb inside—for indeed, Marion could blow up when she wanted to. She had more force of character in her small person than anyone I have ever met. She was unmarried and living alone and so she immediately adopted me as her child. From that day until her death she thoroughly spoiled me.

During all these months Abram was doing fine work. He had had an order from Mrs. Crane, who had a large and beautiful house in Ipswich, Massachusetts, to do a painting for the ceiling of her living room, and to paint four large panels for her entrance hall. He painted several portraits that winter and a full-length one of me. He also painted Adele Astaire, who was a great source of fun. She is a lover of gingerbread and I always had my cook make some for her which she devoured in great quantities. We only found out later that she was forbidden sweets of any kind, in order to keep her weight down as she was dancing with Fred in a sensational success, *Lady Be Good*.

Often Eva and I went to 35 Broad Street where Stark Young and Bill Bowman lived. I always loved these visits. Stark was one of the editors of *The New Republic*. He was also at this time a most outstanding and brilliant theatrical critic and he was writing for *The New York Times*. There are few people with as distinguished a mind as his. To talk with him on any subject is as stimulating as a breath of mountain air. Besides hundreds of critical articles on the theatre, art or artists, he has written many well-known books, plays, and adaptations of plays, and he has had great success as a sensitive painter. As a human being he is more than all these talents put together—a man of spirit and of heart; and Bill, too. He is an architect, a man of flawless taste and full of fun. When he was young he resembled the then Prince of Wales, so his friends called him "Wales." Even today he still looks like the Duke of Windsor.

All that winter I had been seeing Cecile and Gabrielle. We had had many parties in their studio, at which Cecile often recited my poems while Irene Poldowski played the piano accompaniment she had set them to. These were happy evenings. In June they invited me down to meet a young English playwright. They told me the young man had no money and they were going to take him under their wing. Teddy and Naps also knew him and were invited to the dinner that night. Cecile's flat was simple, with whitewashed walls. She loved flowers and candlelight. That evening all the candles were lit to welcome this guest and before he came Cecile and Gabrielle assured each other that they were going to insist that he lodge with them. "Why should Noel spend money which he hasn't got on a hotel when he can stay with us?" Cecile asked Teddy. Who was Noel? When he walked in, Cecile presented him to me and said, "Darling, this is Noel Coward."

It was indeed Noel Coward, touchingly poor, charmingly unsure of himself, refreshingly unknown and beguilingly insecure, with a bundle of manuscripts under his arm, shyly looking over his shoulder toward Broadway. But he had to be patient and wait, or be impatient and wait. Wait until 1925, when Broadway looked over its shoulder at him.

That summer Rita took a house in Bedford Hills. She took it so that Dr. Grant could visit her there, and she asked my mother to spend the summer with her so that no one could say she and Dr. Grant were living there alone. I wanted to go to Europe. Abram had too much work to do. Eva had gone on the road in *Liliom* but she wrote me that she was getting so tired that she was going to ask the Shuberts to let her have a short holiday in July. We hoped that she could arrange this and that she would join me in Paris.

I went first to London. If in June there is sunshine in London, I do not know any more beautiful place to be. This was a June with sunshine. My talented and beautiful friend Marie Doro was there, having just finished a picture in Italy.

During the early years of my friendship with Marie Doro, she had a way of weaving in and out of my life. When she reappeared it was always as though she had never been away, and when she disappeared once more I accepted it as one might accept the vanishing of a comet which we have been assured will surely return within our lifetime. Some people remember Marie as one of Charles Frohman's stars, (along with Ethel Barrymore and Maude Adams). But acting was the very least of the talents she possessed. Originally she had wanted to be a concert pianist and, before going on the stage, had studied for it, but Charles Frohman saw her and, struck by her beauty, altered the course of her life by insisting that she become one of his stars. If you never knew Marie intimately—and this was almost a lifework—you could never have known all her tricks for hiding her beauty. I was immediately aware of her, even when she dressed herself up like a pixie to conceal it!

At this time I met Cecil Beaton. He was extremely slender and willowy. It was the vogue then for young men of artistic pursuits to appear to be falling apart. And this resemblance to a swaying reed or willow tree gave an impression of fragility, although actually many of them proved unusually durable.

It is rare, as I look back on life, to find many people who, consistently year after year, have developed—in their talents, in their point of view, in their capacity for friendship, in their comprehension of spiritual values, in their looks and in their very character. All these Cecil has done. Little by little he has expressed a diversity of talents unique in one person. He possesses that rare combination of creativeness and artistic sense which also includes the daily living of his life. In physical appearance he has become more distinguished and handsome and in time I believe his books, paintings, and photography will be considered as some of the most sensitive expressions of our age.

Iris Tree, a poet, actress, a fascinating personality and one of the three daughters of Sir Beerbohm Tree, called when I was in London this time and asked me to go to some galleries with her. When I arrived at her flat she was in a dressing gown, and said, "Do you mind waiting while I make myself a new dress? I long for a new dress!" I undoubtedly looked a little startled, but "Don't look so glum," she said, "it will only take a minute." She was right. She spread a double piece of red flannel on the floor, and with an enormous pair of scissors, cut out—as though she were cutting out a large paper doll—a dress. In any case she called it a dress. With large safetypins she pinned the seams along the sides together, and when she had done this she simply slipped it over her head. Out of a drawer she pulled a large red leather belt, and fastening it tightly around her waist, said, "You see?" and we sauntered out to Piccadilly.

I became friends at this time with Osbert Sitwell, who has since become Sir Osbert Sitwell. John Becket was in London then too. He was a close friend of Osbert's and the three of us went often to the Eiffel Tower—then a sort of Bohemian restaurant in Soho where artists met at night for dinner or after the theatre. I also met at this time Madge Garland, who is now Lady Ashton. She was working at *Vogue,* looking very blond and pretty. Madge is very feminine. In those early days one did not suspect a dynamic drive hidden under all those blue bows and ruffles. But as the years progressed and she superbly executed one difficult job after another we realized she was not the kitten we at first thought she was.

This was the period of "bottle parties." Parties were given and everyone was expected to bring a bottle of gin, Scotch, rye, brandy or wine. Syrie Maugham—Somerset Maugham's wife—had a charming house in Chelsea. She used to give lovely parties and it was then that she started what I call "The White Period." Syrie was an interior decorator and she began to decorate everything in white—white flowers, white rugs, white walls and pickled furniture. Syrie pickled every piece of furniture she could lay her hands on. I remember at one of her parties she and Cecil Beaton were huddled in a corner engrossed in a deep conversation. A man asked, "I wonder what they can so seriously be talking about?" The answer was easy. They were discussing white paint!

Not long after this I received a cable from Eva saying she was arriving the following week. With literally a bundle thrown over each of our backs (containing a pair of pajamas, a change of underclothes and a toothbrush) we started off on a walking trip in Brittany looking like a pair of gypsies. We took a train to Paimpol and then walked along the countryside, until we came to a place on the coast called L'Arquest. There we saw a little fisherman's house which took our fancy, and we timidly knocked at the door. A woman with a strong and beautiful face, dressed in the black Breton costume and wearing the traditional white cap, opened it to us, and we asked if she would consider taking us in as boarders. Mère Cardin could not have been kinder. She installed us in a loft at the top of the house and got out her linen wedding sheets which had been packed away in an old chest for twenty-five years.

She had lost her husband and her two sons at sea. One by one they had gone out with the fishing fleet, and one by one they had not returned. Mère Cardin said, with that strange resignation to disaster and tragedy which simple people who deal with the sea often have, "The sea feeds us fishermen's wives, and then devours our men in payment."

Here, walking by the sea and bathing in it, living in this little house, eating the good fresh fish which Mère Cardin cooked, Eva and I became revitalized.

Twenty-One

On my return from Europe, Abram and I went to the Cranes' house in Ipswich, Massachusetts, where Abram had to finish the ceiling in the living room. On this ceiling, within a classical treatment, he had painted the entire Crane family. He had, unfortunately, forgotten a very important member of it—a Siamese cat. This was an omission which very much upset Mrs. Crane, and our trip was made for the purpose of correcting it. A place had to be found for the cat without disturbing the composition. David Adler, the architect, and his wife Catherine came up with us. We had great fun making suggestions and when Abram finally finished the ceiling the cat occupied his place indeed. As he looked serenely down on us, he seemed to dominate the scene. From my point of view this was just as it should be, and fortunately Mrs. Crane thought so too.

I was anxious to return to New York as I wanted my mother to come home from Bedford Hills. She always loved being with Rita but she was glad to be home again with Abram and me. She did not look well. Dr. Lambert came to see her, and said she had high blood pressure and should stay quietly in bed. This my mother would not do. Except for childbirth she had never gone to bed for any illness in her life. She always got up at seven in the morning, and winter or summer nothing kept her in bed five minutes beyond this hour. She agreed, however, not to go up and down stairs and to have her meals in my study. These few

134

months before her death she was constantly there and we talked on many subjects.

It had been difficult for her to live in the same house with a Protestant clergyman for such a long time, but Rita regarded Dr. Grant as the man she loved and intended to marry, and expected my mother to treat him as one of the family.

My mother asked my opinion on the whole problem. I told her what I regretfully believed—that Dr. Grant would never have the courage to marry Rita. I was convinced that Bishop Manning would never sanction their marriage, and that if Dr. Grant really intended to marry he would have to give up his position in the church. Rita believed that he would have the courage to do this and hoped to see him at the head of a great liberal religious movement. She had even discussed it with me, saying, "The moment has arrived when someone should rise and truthfully give out the teachings of Jesus without the yoke of a church around his neck." I agreed with what she said, but unfortunately I did not believe, as she did, that Dr. Grant was the man to do it.

This autumn Moffat and Yard brought out another volume of my poems, *Streets and Shadows*. Until 1931 poems of mine were published in *Poetry* magazine and several of them were read over the radio, but after these I never submitted another. I felt that there were already enough minor poets in the world. After that I decided to write poems for myself but never again for publication.

Of all things in life, I would like to have been a great poet or a great saint. But there is no "becoming" either of these. For each of these states one must be born "in perfection." They are not unsimilar, because both poet and saint are unable to see the world as it is (if anyone can truly say what it is, or what it is not). To both, nothing is final, there is always that mysterious "going on"—that seeking of wings to soar, each in his own way, to the infinite.

Toward the end of November my mother suddenly said she would like to go out to the country to be with Rita again. Dr. Grant was not to be there, and possibly she thought she would have an opportunity to persuade her not to marry him. Or perhaps she felt that she might die before Christmas and did not want to sadden our house by dying in it. She was unselfish enough to have thought of this. In any case, she went out to the country with Rita, "just for a few weeks," she said. She never returned.

A few days after this she showed a distinct physical decline. Annie and I went out to be with her and Rita. Abram came out every few days. Toward the end my mother spoke only Spanish. It was as though she had never heard English. She went suddenly into a coma.

About three o'clock, early on the morning of December 21st, Annie and I were in her room. Rita had gone to bed for a few hours' rest. Annie was dozing in a chair. I went to the window and looked out. Feathery flakes of snow were gently falling, and seeming to rest lightly as they touched the ground. I turned from the window and bent over my mother's face. As I did so a tiny tear trickled down one cheek. I listened for her breath and knew that she had stopped breathing.

If my heart did not also stop beating at this same second, I think I might say that my soul did. For a brief second—within time, or for an eternity—outside of time, my soul seemed to wander to some land where there was neither pain nor joy. Perhaps a land where it could just quietly rest at the feet of God.

I remembered nothing after this for some days. I was told that when my brother Dick attempted to touch my mother, while her body was still lying on her bed, I seized a fruit knife and tried to stab him. Fortunately, Annie caught my wrist in time. I was also told that I attended my mother's funeral, and that a High Requiem Mass was celebrated on the main altar of St. Patrick's Cathedral, the Bishop and our old family friend, Monseigneur Lavelle, officiating. My mother had been one of the first pew holders in the Cathedral and the Bishop insisted that her funeral should be accorded the highest rites.

Returning home on Christmas Eve, after my mother was buried, I locked myself in my room and refused to come out of it or answer anyone who knocked or called. Abram tried to persuade me, and Rita pleaded with me only to answer. Vouletti, Audrey, and Hope, each in turn, begged me to open the door and let them bring me some food. I evidently did not hear them. Finally, just before New Year, that inspired pianist George Copeland appeared and asked Abram to let him go up to our living room. He knew the piano there which my mother had given me when I was married.

He sat down and began to play Granados, de Falla, and fifteenth- and sixteenth-century Spanish church compositions. In my room I heard the music—Spanish music on my mother's piano. I opened the door and crept downstairs. George took no notice of me. I curled up on the sofa and he played, without stopping, far into the night. His music was healing, and before he stopped playing I seemed to hear it in my mother's voice saying, "All is well."

I began to work on a play, *Jehanne d'Arc*. Jehanne was a character Eva longed to portray and I longed to dramatize, in spite of all the other plays which had already been written about her. She seemed to me an inexhaustible subject.

But my writing was temporarily interrupted by Tamara Karsavina, who appeared in New York from Paris with a letter of introduction to me from my good friend Agoutinsky. She was on her way to Chicago with her partner, Peter Vladimirov, as they were engaged to dance there in Adolf Bolm's Company. She told me on the telephone that she was only stopping over one day in New York so I, of course, invited her to come and see me at once. Meeting her was a great event in my life and one I had long looked forward to. Fortunately, Eva was there already in my house as I knew she too wanted to meet Karsavina.

When Tamara rang the bell I went down to open the door myself. I was struck by her dark beauty which, seeing it directly before me, seemed even more poignant than it did on the stage. She put out a warm hand of greeting. We had heard so much about each other from our mutual friend Agoutinsky that we did not feel strangers. We even embraced. Then a funny thing happened. Bob Chanler, who had been seeing Abram in his studio, suddenly appeared at the top of the stairway. To Karsavina, who had never before seen him and did not have the remotest idea who he was, he must have seemed like a giant looming up out of nowhere. Looking up at him, he looked even more grotesquely big than he actually was. He peered down at us and was in one of his shouting moods. Before I could introduce him to Tamara or even explain who he was he descended upon us, bellowing forth the names of some of his favorite states. "O-hi-o, U-tah, A-ri-zo-na," he shouted. Tamara looked frightened but I began to laugh and she then quickly saw the absurdity of the situation and laughed too. When I finally silenced Bob and told him who Tamara was, he gazed searchingly in her face shouting again "O-hi-o" and rushed out the door. I led Tamara up to my study where Eva was waiting and where Abram soon joined us.

I felt this was an occasion for champagne so I rang for the maid to bring up a bottle and some glasses. When she appeared with the champagne glasses they suddenly looked too small for such an overwhelming event. Rushing down to the pantry I reappeared with some beautiful large glass finger bowls—so large that we rarely used them. I poured out the champagne in these. Holding up a bowl to Tamara I said, "Even these are not big enough to drink your health in." But after several rounds of champagne we decided they *were* indeed big enough.

On Fifty-seventh Street between Madison and Park, a Russian general had opened a restaurant called the Russian Eagle where all the waiters, waitresses, cooks, doormen and musicians were refugees. This restaurant had much charm and was greatly frequented by artists. When Stanislavsky brought his Russian Moscow Art Theatre to New York, the members of his company had supper there frequently. One did not have to dress, and the atmosphere was warm and intimate. It was like dropping into a club where one knew everybody.

When Karsavina returned from her Chicago engagement to New York she danced at the Manhattan Opera House. On the opening night I stood in the wings and watched her and Vladimirov dance. It was exciting to watch them at such close range and to peer out and see the faces of the audience obscure and shadowlike in the darkness of the house. I had never seen Vladimirov dance but Karsavina afterwards told me that she considered him the most virile dancer of his generation. She said he was a "strong partner," and that she felt "confidence in his secure support."

The audience was wildly enthusiastic and well they might have been because it was rare indeed to see a dancer with all the qualities that Karsavina combined. Great facial beauty, extreme grace, perfect technique and supreme artistry were just a few of them. No ballet dancer today can remotely approach her mastery of body control, her arm movements, her elevations and the spiritual as well as physical beauty she projected across the footlights.

After the performance I took Karsavina to the Russian Eagle for supper. It was a memorable evening. Stanislavsky was there at a table with all his company. At another table Max Reinhardt, Diana Cooper and Rudolf Kommer were sitting. When we came in, the General gave us the table I had reserved in a corner and Stanislavsky immediately rose and quickly came over to Karsavina. Greeting us both he then spoke to Tamara in Russian. I understood he was asking us to join his table but Karsavina said she was too tired and preferred to remain at a small table.

This was the period of prohibition but with a few secret signs to the General he brought us a little decanter of seeming water, but which

Tamara was amused to discover was actually vodka. After we tossed down a few glasses that wonderful actress, Maria Ouspenskaya, came over to our table with a pitcher which proved to contain Scotch. She insisted we drink a toast with her, and then insisted we drink another. On top of the vodka these glasses of Scotch soon began to make me see strange lights. I looked at Tamara. She said, "Don't look at me. I'm tipsy. I must have something at once to eat." The waiter brought us some soup. Then Reinhardt came over and sat with us. I don't think either of us made much sense in talking to him. Soon after, we rose to go home. Neither Karsavina or I could walk straight. I was very embarrassed and hoped no one noticed us. Outside we had difficulty going down the stairs. I said, "This is really awful. We never should have had all those drinks on empty stomachs." I took Tamara to the Plaza Hotel where she was staying and managed to get myself home. When I was in bed I telephoned Tamara to ask how she was feeling. She said she was still dressed and just lying on the bed. I said, "Are you all right?" She answered, "Yes, quite all right but no one in Europe ever told me that American hotel rooms spin round."

One night I went with a friend to another Russian restaurant, a sort of cabaret called The Club Petruschka. Among the singers I noticed a very interesting woman. She was small in height, with straight dark hair parted in the middle and twisted in a bun at the back of her head. She had large, sorrowful eyes and she looked extremely thin and ill. I asked the manager her name. He told me she was a Russian lady who had fled before the Revolution with her young husband. They had come to America with *The Chauve Souris,* a theatrical troop which became world famous and was developed by the amazing Balieff. He said the young woman's name was Lucia Davidova.

I went home that night and told Abram I had discovered a charming young woman whom I thought he should try to persuade to pose for him. The next night he went to the cabaret and invited Margaret Case to go with him. They both agreed with my opinion of Lucia Davidova and went back when the singing was over to ask to meet her. Abram introduced Margaret as his wife thinking it would make Lucia more comfortable about accepting his request and this resulted in quite a lot of confusion.

When she came to pose she asked him when she would see his wife again but Abram had forgotten the episode and said, "My wife will be in any day. She's hoping you'll give her Russian lessons." Which was true. I had said to Abram that if I liked Lucia when I met her, I would suggest this as it would help her out financially, and give me an opportunity to learn a language I had always been interested in because of its great literature. Not long after this I went into the studio when she was posing and he presented me to her as his wife. Lucia was surprised and mystified, but she made no comment. I asked her if she would like to teach me Russian. It was only when we began to see each other alone that the mystery was cleared up.

I went this winter for the first time to Mrs. Simeon Ford's poetry dinners. These were dinners at which Mrs. Ford gathered poets, and after feeding them well, invited them, still sitting around the table, to read or recite their latest poems. Here in Mrs. Ford's house I met many of the most important poets in America: Edgar Lee Masters, Vachel Lindsay, Robert Frost, Sara Teasdale, Elinor Wylie and Leonora Speyer were often there, and also Charles Hanson Towne, Edna St. Vincent Millay, Dorothy Parker, Ezra Pound and Kahlil Gibran, all of whom I already knew.

I enjoyed these dinners enormously, as I believe all the others did. I also dreaded them because there was the ever-impending danger that I might be asked to recite, and this was a request which could not be refused. Mrs. Ford used to say laughingly, "Everyone must sing for his supper." I suffered agonies when I had to recite before any one of these fine poets, but I especially suffered when I had to recite in the presence of Elinor Wylie. She had all of her own poems at the tip of her tongue and could recite them with great charm and a fine delivery. It was a joy to hear her and they were all first-rate.

In March Michael Strange rented a house in Silver Lake, not far from New York. One day she called and asked me to spend the night with her, because, after a row, Jack had disappeared and left her alone. I took the train to Silver Lake where there was deep snow. The branches of the stark trees were laden with icicles glistening in the pale setting sun, which suddenly shone feebly forth again as we coaxed the car up the drive to the house. Michael looked radiantly healthy and handsome. She was in wonderful spirits and laughed; she was sure Jack had gone to New York "to pour out his woes to his nanny—Ned Sheldon."

After dinner we sat before the hearth in front of a great blazing fire and she began to read me a version of L'Aiglon she had been working on. Outside there was the dead silence of falling snow.

Michael read for about an hour. Suddenly we both heard a strange groaning noise. We listened. She said it might be a wounded animal. I went to the window but I heard only the almost imperceptible sound of the snow as it fell on the ground. I closed the window and the groaning began again. Michael rose and in a frightened voice said, "It's coming from the cellar." We went to the cellar door which gave into the dining room and was closed. The weird sound was unmistakably coming from it. We thought of calling the police or a neighbor, rejected both ideas and decided to look for ourselves. Michael said, "It's probably a wounded cat or a skunk." "Cat or skunk, he must be a baritone," I said. "He sounds more like a bear."

I armed myself with a poker while Michael snatched up a carving knife and together we opened the door. There was no electricity in the cellar so Michael held a candle aloft. As I advanced slowly down the steps with Michael and the candle behind me, the sound grew louder. All at once I knew it was neither cat, skunk or bear, but a dark human figure lying huddled in a corner. Seizing the candle from Michael I approached the spot. There lay poor Jack with several empty bottles of gin strewn around him. We managed to pull him up the stairs and sent for the local doctor. When he arrived and Jack came around enough to make some sense, he said that he had been so upset by the row with Michael that he had pretended to leave the house by slamming the front door when she was upstairs. He said he had not meant to drink so much in the cellar—only just enough to get "a few hours of forgetfulness from his unhappy state."

It took a little coaxing, but I persuaded Michael to forgive him. The next day when I left the house in a taxi to return to New York they stood together, happily holding hands at the front door, blowing me kisses.

Eva's tour in *Liliom* ended in June. The play was to open again in the autumn and finally close after playing Brooklyn and New York. This, fortunately, gave Eva a free summer. Ferenc Molnar was grateful to her for so beautifully interpreting his play and he invited her to come to Budapest. She asked me to go with her. We planned it so that when she had to leave me in Budapest to meet her mother, Abram would meet me, and we would go on to Constantinople, a city I had always longed to see.

At the end of June, Eva and I started for Budapest by way of Paris, Genoa, Venice, Munich and Vienna. We were met at the airport by Molnar, a brass band, and some of his friends carrying banners with *Welcome Julie* printed on them in Hungarian. (Julie was the name of the character Eva had played in *Liliom*.) When we got out of the plane Eva was handed bunches of flowers and embraced by people she had never laid eyes on, and, while the band played on, she was photographed with Molnar. After this we were driven to our hotel, the Dunapalata, where masses of people came, uninvited, into our suite. They were writers, actors and actresses, all friends of Molnar's, and evidently well aware that soon brandy would be flowing. Molnar was famous for his generous heart. If I remember anything about this visit to Budapest it must be because I have a remarkably strong head. Brandy was poured down our throats every minute until the small hours of the morning. Sleep was evidently not for Hungarians, at least not at night. We were taken to the famous club with a tree in one of the rooms where everyone sits and drinks. We were presented to every person of note, toasted and sung to. The Gypsy orchestra which Molnar had hired to dog our footsteps tore our hearts out and reduced us to tears. Out of a dim haze I remember Molnar saying, "And now I wish to serve you a rare fruit known only in Hungary." He then presented us with nothing less than—watermelon! We pretended we had never seen one before and, after what seemed like the hundredth brandy, we believed it. In a stupor the following day, I said good-bye to Eva and boarded the Orient Express. Abram joined me and we went on our way to Constantinople.

I have a vivid recollection of Constantinople. That visit left me with a haunting and poignant memory, perhaps because at this time there were masses of Russian refugees there who thronged the streets or huddled in holes or internment camps. They all seemed to be starving, diseased, and dying.

I often walked the streets at night. Here in this jumbled chaos of sweating humanity the supreme pattern of God seemed put to a test. In this confused labyrinth of beauty, vice and ugliness, I groped for the spiritual answer to life. Many evenings I climbed a quiet hill near a minaret and listened to the strange song of the minaret singers, which held all the nostalgia of the East.

The Sultan was still ruling at this time and in his palace. Abram and I went with Admiral Bristol (who was acting as American Ambassador then) to lunch with him. He showed us some of the rooms of the palace. He was a very old man and seemed a little vague in all he said. When we were leaving he seemed to want me to take his photograph. As I had no camera and nothing was further from my mind than photographing anyone who had asked me to lunch, I had to borrow one from Admiral Bristol's aide to satisfy the old gentleman's wish. As a parting gift he gave me some of his specially blended cigarettes with his coat of arms marked in gold on each one.

One day in the lobby of the Pera Palace Hotel I saw one of the most hauntingly beautiful women I had ever beheld. Her features and her movements were so distinguished and aristocratic-looking that I decided she must be a refugee Russian princess. The porter said he did not know her name but he thought she was a Swedish actress who had come to Constantinople with the great Swedish film director, Maurice Stiller.

Several times after this I saw her in the street. I was terribly troubled by her eyes and I longed to speak to her, but I did not have the courage. Also I did not even know what language to use. She gave me the impression of great loneliness which only added to my own already melancholy state of mind. I hated to leave Constantinople without speaking to her, but sometimes destiny is kinder than we think, or maybe it is just that we cannot escape our destiny. Strangely enough, as the train pulled out of the station which carried me away from Constantinople I had a strong premonition that I might again see that beautiful and haunting face on some other shore.

Twenty-Two

On my return from Europe I met Natacha Rambova again. She has had such a full and unusual life with so many varied careers that it is difficult in a circumscribed space to do justice to it and to her. I must first say that she is physically very beautiful—a fact which is well known. She was born in Salt Lake City with a most interesting inheritance and background. Her great grandfather on her mother's side of the family—Heber C. Kimball (of Scotch ancestry, the name was originally Campbell)—was the closest friend of Brigham Young. They were the first two followers of Joseph Smith, who was the founder of the Mormon Religion.

This, however, is Natacha's inheritance from her mother. An inheritance filled with religious fervor and beliefs—violent in the right to defend these beliefs. She is a descendant of a people courageous, zealous, fanatical, long-suffering, who were willing to undergo persecution while stubbornly holding to what they conceived to be right. They were a people who were pioneers.

Her father, Michael O'Shaughnessy, was of Irish descent, and a Roman Catholic. He was a colonel in the United States Union Army and fought in the Civil War. Dashing, handsome, and a daredevil, he was sent out at the head of the United States forces to Utah to keep an eye on the Mormons and hold them in hand and, principally, to stamp out polygamy—which the Mormons claimed was part of their religion.

Fate is a strange thing. He married a Mormon—Natacha's mother. Natacha was christened Winifred O'Shaughnessy and baptized in the Roman Catholic Church. The Mormons never forgave Michael O'Shaughnessy these two events and remained antagonistic to him, despite the fact that as soon as Utah was admitted into the Union and became a state, he was elected and took office as its first governor.

At the age of seven, Natacha was taken to Paris by her mother, who in the meantime had divorced O'Shaughnessy and married Elsie de Wolfe's brother, Edgar de Wolfe. At nine years of age Natacha began studying ballet with the famous ballet dancer of the Paris opera, Rosita Meuri. She continued this study until she was sixteen, in the meantime also studying architecture at the Beaux Arts. She lived most of this time in Versailles in Elsie's house where the trio, Elsie, Anne Morgan, and Anne Vanderbilt, entertained frequently and, in a manner of speaking, held court. But Natacha did not like this social way of life and as soon as it was possible she broke away from it and returned to New York.

On her return to New York she joined Alexis Kosloff's Ballet Company and danced with him in a ballet the Shuberts produced. As she was not yet of age and had heard that her mother intended to stop her dancing, she ran away to Canada and then to England. She changed her name to Natacha Rambova and when Kosloff's company came to London, she again joined him and became his première ballerina.

She returned to America with Kosloff and toured the United States with his ballet. In Los Angeles they formed a school and together they taught ballet dancing. Alla Nazimova came to this school for lessons and met Rambova. Nazimova was at this time about to act with Rudolf Valentino in *Camille,* a film that Cecil B. de Mille was producing. Being dissatisfied with the sets and costumes of this film and hearing that Rambova could design, she asked her to make some sketches for the film. These were so successful that Nazimova showed them to De Mille, who instantly put Rambova under contract to execute both sets and costumes. While working on this film she met Valentino. Not long after this she and Valentino were married. While married to him she designed many productions in Hollywood. (One of the most notable was *Salomé,* in which Nazimova played the title role. This film is still shown in the Museum of Modern Art in New York.) When Natacha's marriage ended in divorce she returned to New York and opened a dress shop, designing all the clothes herself. She designed a number of beautiful things for me in this shop. But this métier was not profoundly hers.

During all those years her secret and real interest lay in Eastern and ancient religions. She told me that even as a small child it was always oriental religious art which attracted her when she was taken to museums. She has continually done research in Eastern religions. After returning from Europe she came, so to speak, into her spiritual own. She began lecturing on Eastern religions and religious subjects and she taught astrology and yoga. During the war she had a book published, *Technique for Living,* and she wrote at this time a text on judo which was used in the training camps of the United States Army. Recently the Bollingen Foundation published a prodigious series of works on Egyptian religious texts and representations. Natacha was instrumental in organizing this publication. She edited the three volumes and contributed to the text.

She no longer lectures and has retired into a life of study. The contrasts in her life have been enormous. Had she wished, she could have successfully lived a social or an artistic life, but she chose a more difficult way. She has chosen The Way that all adepts and sincere seekers of Truth must, sooner or later, follow. The Way of anonymity and seclusion.

I have studied astrology, cosmic-astrology, mythology and yoga with Natacha, but these are only a few of the many things she has taught me.

At this particular time I was studying astrology with her. This is a science of which she has an amazing knowledge. When I use the term "astrology" I do not mean the ordinary mundane and accepted, so-called astrology which one reads about in every twenty-five cent astrological publication, or the kind of astrology for which one pays fifty dollars to some commercial prognosticator to discover how to invest money or whether to marry a blonde or a brunette. When I speak of astrology I mean a serious science which was used by the priests of all ancient Eastern religions to make Man aware of his own soul pattern which he could discover by studying his astrological chart. This chart is his soul's blueprint, his own particular life path on this planet. Astrology, as such, was practiced by the early founders of the United States: Washington, Jefferson, and Franklin among them.

Benjamin Franklin compiled and printed an Ephemeris—an astronomical index of the positions of the planets over a given number of years, months, hours, minutes and even seconds, used for the setting up and casting of charts.

At this same period, Natacha and I were also interested in psychic phenomena. I believe that most people who are seeking inner truth go through this stage of investigating psychic manifestations even if they depart from it later on. I do not regret the experience I gathered from it.

I have worked with a number of fine and honest mediums. I have seen demonstrated much so-called "phenomenon." I have seen mediums materialize ectoplasm, flowers, fish, and all sorts of things. I have never for one second doubted that these materializations were anything but genuine. I have assisted at trumpet sessions and heard voices speak out of trumpets. I have had voices speak to me, through a medium, claiming to be the voices of people I had known when they were living. This claim I have always doubted. I did not doubt, nor do I now doubt, that it is possible for entities on the astral plane to speak to us through a medium, but I doubted that the voices I heard were those of the people they purported to be.

To go into this subject is a very complicated matter. It is impossible to explore thoroughly such a vast and generally misunderstood subject without writing a whole book about it, and certainly I can come nowhere near evaluating it on a page.

I can only say the following, which anyone can take or leave. In my opinion to disclaim psychic phenomena is sheer ignorance; of course it exists, and people who are looking for phenomena and miracles forget that these occur every day right under their noses. They occur in what we incorrectly call the "rising" and "setting" of the sun. They also occur in the bursting open of a blossom, or in the emerging of a seed from the earth, and in a hundred other ways. People say that these are just natural phenomena. But what in the final analysis *is* natural or unnatural? Is not one or the other only that which we have accepted as "natural" or "unnatural"?

During the last week before *Liliom* closed, Eva gave me a beautifully bound book in which she had copied the entire play in her own handwriting on parchment. She said, "Now I must do your *Jehanne d'Arc.*" It was easier said than done. We approached Sam Harris about it and at first he seemed interested. Then he said it required too expensive a production for him to consider at that particular time.

I had been working on another play about Simonetta Vespucci, who is reputed to have been in love with Sandro Botticelli and was the inspiration for his great masterpiece, "The Birth of Venus." She even posed for this painting. The play was far from finished.

One day when I went with Eva to see Sam Harris, he turned to me and said, "If we cannot do *Jehanne d'Arc,* have you any other play I could more easily produce for Eva?" I told him about *Sandro Botticelli* and when he asked how soon I could let him have the manuscript, I promised it within a week's time. Eva looked startled, but she said nothing. Once outside, I started off in a rush and when Eva asked me where I was going, I said I was going home "to finish the play."

Like all theatrical ventures which are complicated and tiresome this one was no exception. To be brief, the play went into rehearsal with Harrison Fiske (Mrs. Fiske's husband) directing it. We had a good cast with fine actors and actresses such as Basil Sydney, Ian Keith, Philip Leigh, Merle Maddern. Basil Sydney played Botticelli, and, of course, Eva played Simonetta. Ernest de Weerth, who had been Reinhardt's assistant in *The Miracle,* designed the décor and the costumes, and he did a lovely job of it. Nothing, or no one, was at fault except the play itself. It was a good idea and already well worked out as a sketch, but it needed a great deal more work and it was a pity that I was so stupid as to sacrifice good material in order to hasten production.

When it opened it was thoroughly panned by all the critics, as it deserved to be. Eva, Basil and all the company did the best they could with thin material. Gilbert Miller said, "I could spank you for not having brought this play to me. I would have made you work on it and you would have had a good play."

After it closed, Gilbert Miller offered Eva an engagement for the following season in *The Swan,* another Molnar play. She needed very beautiful costumes for it and Marie Doro suggested that Edward Molyneux should make them. I agreed to go to Paris with Eva to help select them.

We sailed off in high spirits, as I had heard from Gabrielle Enthoven that Duse had accepted an engagement to appear in London that summer under Charles Cochran's management for a series of matinees. Gabrielle wrote that Duse was to be in Paris, on her way to London, at about the same time as Eva and I, and would be staying at the Hotel Regina.

The morning after Eva and I arrived in Paris was beautiful and sunny. We started off at once for the Tuileries Gardens and stood opposite the Hotel Regina. We looked up at the windows of the hotel, and the miracle occurred. Sitting there, wrapped in a blanket, on a balcony in front of one of the windows was—Eleonora Duse. How wonderful and ridiculous it is to be able to remember now that anything mattered as much as this did to us then. How sorry I am for people who have never been as emotionally foolish. Tears poured down our faces. I said to Eva, "We should kneel." But the physical act of kneeling was unnecessary. We had been kneeling in spirit from the second we had perceived her on the balcony.

Soon afterward, after a good deal of conniving, we were lucky enough to be present at Duse's first performance in London. This performance of *Così Sia* was the deepest experience of my life in the theatre. What mystic magic there was in that frail woman that lifted the spirit beyond time and enveloped it in eternal values! When the curtain descended on the final act, no one applauded. Many people were weeping and the audience filed silently out.

When *The Swan* opened in New York both Eva and the play were an instantaneous success. In the meantime Duse had arrived to begin her ill-fated tour throughout the United States and was living at the Hotel Majestic, just off the Park on the west side of Seventy-second Street. Eva met her and even had the wonderful privilege of acting for her.

After Duse herself had begun her performances in New York, Gabrielle Enthoven wrote her about me and told me to ring up Desirée and ask for an appointment. I rang up one day and in a shaking voice gave my name to Desirée. She put me at ease by saying that "Madame," as she always called Duse, had been waiting for me to call.

When I went to see her, faint with excitement, I observed—not only this time, but the comparatively few times I saw her—that she always started speaking from another room before she actually reached the room in which she received me. This impatient manner of speaking was, I felt, her spirit and mind traveling so much faster than her body. It often seemed to me that she was impatient with such things as gravitation, space and time. She was especially impatient with time. This, I believe, is why she dashed off so many letters. She wrote to anyone and everyone. Desirée said that whenever she had anything to say, no matter how trivial in essence, if the person was not on the spot at the time, she simply could not contain herself and would dash off some exalted phrase and dispatch it. Even if someone were in the next room she would write to that person if the mood moved her. Desirée told me that she often wrote her four or five notes during the night when she could not sleep. She simply could not wait till morning to say what was in her mind.

I wrote a play for Duse while she was in New York—*The Mother of Christ*. I worked over it feverishly and finished it in a remarkably short time. An Italian friend of mine, the Princess Santa Borghese, who was studying at Columbia, translated it for me into Italian. Eva translated it into French. Duse read it and said, "I will tour the whole world with this play. After playing it I will never act again." Unhappily, death had other plans for her.

When she had her première in New York in Ibsen's *Lady from the Sea* at the Metropolitan Opera House, Eva and I went together. I saw every performance after this when she played at the old Century Theatre.

At this time I wrote an article about her which was published in the Boston *Evening Transcript*. After Duse died, Desirée found this article in her prayer book.

This same winter Rita broke her engagement to Dr. Grant. It was a blow to her heart and pride. Dr. Grant was not capable of sustaining her idealistic dream of him. He did not have the courage to break with Bishop Manning or the Church. It was not entirely his fault. Rita had tried to impose upon him a grandeur of spirit and a lofty vision which he simply did not have.

He went into retirement. Rita was completely broken up in spirit and in health. But with that pathetically fantastic pride she had, she was not going to let anyone know it. She held her head high, and except to me, she never mentioned Dr. Grant to anyone.

People take to various things when they are unhappy: drink, drugs, silence, suicide, to name a few of them. Rita took to extravagance. To her, spending money became a form of escape. When Dr. Grant went out of her life she spent money in a way that, as I see now, bordered on madness. I once went into a rug shop with her in New York. She asked the price of a certain rug and the clerk quoted it at sixty thousand dollars. She didn't really want this rug and had no place to put it, even though it was beautiful. But she turned to the clerk and said, "I'll take it home with me. Call my footman and tell him to throw it in the back of the car." I could do nothing with her. With great delight the clerk called the footman and the rug was carried out. Whatever happened to it, I never knew.

At this time, with priceless things in her house in Washington Square, Rita insisted on sleeping alone in it with the front door unlocked. The servants all slept over the garage and she could not have called them very quickly if she had wanted to. If anyone protested, she merely remarked indifferently, "These things which you call priceless are merely mine by an accident of wealth. An accident of poverty has as much right to them. Let any poor person come in and take them if he wants to. I would not lift my finger to prevent it." Yet I never remember Rita having even the smallest thing stolen.

After the New Year, Duse's engagement in New York was coming to an end. At this time she was already very frail and ill; her attacks of asthma came frequently. Nevertheless, there was a curious vitality about her which seemed in some way to pertain essentially to the spirit rather than the body.

Even when she was not well, contrary to the established idea of her, she could be very lively and full of humor. She laughed at many things one would not have thought she would appreciate. Once when she was standing off-stage hidden by the wings while the curtain was being held for her, she overheard an Irish stagehand exclaim impatiently, "Dooze Dooze go on or doozn't she?" This amused her very much in spite of the fact that she spoke and understood very little English.

Always tired after a performance, she was in the habit of having a glass of champagne in her dressing room immediately after the final curtain. She told a story about one occasion in New York when Morris Gest came back to see her just as she was having this one little glass of wine. It was during prohibition and he himself had visibly gone far beyond the law. Swaying gently on his feet, he said, "Madame, you must hide that glass. We can't have it known that anyone drinks in this theatre."

Shortly after this she embarked on her American Tour. That she, a woman of sixty-six, was sent on this tour is one of the most deplorable episodes in theatrical history. She was already ailing, and could hardly breathe from asthma. Desirée told me how she suffered in the trains because of the dust in her throat as this was, of course, before the days of air conditioning. She suffered from the drafty theatres, the steam-heated hotels, and American food which she was not used to. In California she recovered a little health and peace. She said, "I feel better here, in the warmth of the Pacific." In San Francisco she could have given many more performances and stayed in a place where she felt stronger. She begged to stay on a little longer, but the fixed itinerary throughout the country could not be changed. This, and the box office, were put before the needs of a dying woman.

One can imagine how she suffered during the journey across the desert in Arizona when the dust crept through the windows and entered her lungs. At Detroit she was met by a blizzard, intense cold, and wind. In Pittsburgh by a downpour of icy rain.

Here in Pittsburgh she went to the theatre to play *La Porta Chuisa*. She had not left her hotel for four days because of ill health. On that dark, fatal evening the chauffeur, instead of stopping at the stage door, deposited her in front of a fire exit and drove away. She waited for five interminable minutes in the pouring rain, before a closed door. Posters all over the city were announcing:

ELEONORA DUSE
and her company from Rome
in
THE CLOSED DOOR

What a sinister omen!

That evening on the stage, hardly able to stand from the chill she had contracted, she said the last words at the final curtain that she was ever to say on any stage. *"Sola! Sola!"* she whispered. These were the words of Bianca Querete in the play, but strangely enough, they were the cry of Duse herself, which she had echoed through her whole life. As the curtain fell, both Bianca Querete and she herself stood alone and awaited death.

Maria, who, with Desirée, watched over her untiringly during those last days and nights, told how La Signora said over and over again, "I will not die." Then finally she said, "I have no more strength left in me to undertake this horrible life."

At two o'clock in the morning of April the 21st she lifted herself up in her bed with extraordinary vitality and said to these two women, *"Il faut se bouger! Il faut partir! Agir! Agir!"* Suddenly she was seized with a chill. She could not feel warm or stop shaking, and cried out, *"Couvrez moi!"* Then again she said, *"Partir! Agir! Agir!"* These were her last words.

Bathsheba Askowith, who taught acting and whom Duse called La Russa, and who loved Duse so much that she gave up her job and went with her on the road, wrote me the following account:

> Thirty-five minutes after her death, in compliance with the American law, the body of our beloved Duse—covered with a sheet—was carried down in the baggage lift of the hotel, and out through the service hallway, and deposited in a gruesome and horrible funeral parlor. No one in the company—not even Desirée—was consulted about this ghastly place. It was chosen by the manager of the hotel and Duse was shipped off to it like another piece of luggage.

Certain things which followed are difficult now to believe. The Italian Embassy, having been informed immediately of Duse's death, did not want it given out to the press that day because a state dinner was being held that night. It was only when the Embassy realized that if a representative did not go to Pittsburgh the negligence would be reported in the *Journal American,* that the Ambassador rushed there.

Not a single Italian in the city of New York opened his house to receive the body of Duse, and the Italian Ambassador made no arrangements for its reception.

Fortunately Eva and I were able to arrange with the head Father in the Dominican Catholic Church on Lexington Avenue at Sixty-sixth Street for her body to lie in Saint Joseph's Chapel—a little side chapel of the church. This wonderful man had never heard of Duse, but when we told him that she had died a stranger in this country and that she had no home, he said at once, "Bring her here to this church. This is God's home and also her home."

That night when the doors of the church were closed to the public, the priest allowed Eva and me to go into the small chapel where Duse's coffin had been placed and remain there until the early hours of the morning. Desirée and Maria and the rest of the troupe were worn out from their vigil in Pittsburgh and went to bed.

The following night Desirée, Maria, Bathsheba and all of the actors and actresses, as well as Eva and I, kept vigil and prayed beside the little coffin. There in the church in the candlelight, Desirée gave me the newspaper clipping of my article which Duse had kept in her prayer book. She also gave me the copy of my play, *The Mother of Christ.* She told me that "Madame" had read and reread it, and many nights when they were on tour she had tucked it under her pillow and slept on it. The manuscript was written all over with notes in Duse's handwriting.

Since the coffin was already closed, I asked Desirée that night in the church to keep the manuscript and drop it into the grave when Duse was buried in Asolo. This was where she had lived, and where her body would return to the soil under the shadow of the hills she had loved. I had written this play for her and although I was tempted to keep it for all she had written on it, I felt that it was her play and should be buried with her. Desirée told me, a year and a half later in Asolo, that she had fulfilled my wish.

The day of the funeral, huge masses of flowers and wreathes were sent to this same Dominican church. Thousands of dollars were spent on flowers for her funeral, but no one, when she was living, had made life financially easier for her.

At the funeral people who had not known her sat in the front pews, while Desirée and Maria, the only people in the church whom she had really loved, were given places on the side aisle. All these arrangements were made by the Italian Embassy, which when Duse was alive had not lifted a finger to help her. Probably it was known that she did not admire Mussolini. She made no secret of that.

The Duce, however, sent a battleship to take her body back to Italy. That afternoon after the funeral, the same little group that had watched beside the bier followed the black-covered coffin down into the hold of the ship. A corner had been squared off with Italian flags and depressing black draperies, and here Duse's body was to rest in the darkness as the ship plowed its way through the waters from the New World back to the Old. We stood there mute and forlorn. I remember the whistle warning us to go ashore. I remember, too, the sound of a steel door closing. Then I found myself standing on the pier as in a nightmare. I stood there and watched the great ship glide out into midstream bearing Duse away. As I watched, for a fleeting second, the gray battleship brought to my mind a black gondola. The sea had brought Eleonora Duse to me and the sea had carried her away . . . La Donna del Mare!

Twenty-Three

Through my friendship with Duse, I met Amy Lowell. I did not know her, but one day after Duse's death she called me on the telephone and asked if she could come to see me. She had an idea for starting a memorial foundation in Duse's name. In the end it came to nothing, but I gained a valued friend.

She lived just outside Boston, and when she went home the next day I wrote her a letter. I am a very bad speller and no sooner had I mailed it than I realized I had misspelled a word. I thought she would think me an ignoramus and was extremely upset. Like a first-class idiot, I sent her a telegram, saying, PLEASE EXCUSE ME FOR MISSPELLING A WORD IN MY LETTER. A few hours later I got one back, saying: WHICH ONE? It seemed that Miss Lowell was just as bad a speller as I was. She then asked me to visit her so that she could show me her collection of Keats' letters. *I will show you many of Keats' letters in which you will see that he is even a worse speller than you and I,* she wrote. *This should console us.*

Amy Lowell regulated her life in the most sensible manner for a writer. She slept all day until four in the afternoon. She had breakfast at five in the afternoon, lunch at seven-thirty in the evening and dinner at midnight. This was the meal to which she invited her guests. She generally started to work soon after one in the morning and wrote until eight o'clock. Working through the night saved her from the annoyances and noises of the day and gave her the peace and silence of the still hours.

The last time I visited her, I arrived at her house at about five in the evening. It was winter and there was snow on the ground. It was already dark. I was told that Miss Lowell would soon be down for breakfast. Her breakfast fitted in neatly with my tea hour. We both had tea and toast. She was an enchanting talker and the two hours and a half sped fast until seven-thirty—her lunch hour and my dinner. After this we went for a walk. It was a brilliant star-light night and the snow-weighted branches of the trees hung low and glistened like frosted lilies. She was a large woman but she walked lightly and I was aware that her steps made practically no sound on the ice-covered ground. I told her she walked like an American Indian, which pleased her.

After our walk we moved into a room warm with many-colored books on its shelves and a great crackling fire on the hearth. Miss Lowell produced two large black cigars and handed one of them to me. She did not ask me if I wanted it, but I accepted it. I had smoked cigars before but never such a large one. I hoped I would not be violently sick. I decided to engulf myself in its aroma and hope for the best.

Miss Lowell stood surprisingly far from the fireplace, bit off the end of her cigar and spat it directly into the fireplace—a bull's-eye. I bit off the end of mine and hesitated. I was not nearly so far from the fireplace as she was, but somehow I knew I would fail. So I took the end of my cigar out of my mouth and in the most ladylike way imaginable laid it gently on a highly polished silver ashtray. I detected a slight look of disdain on Miss Lowell's face, but she made no comment.

It was really a memorable night. I saw many of Keats' letters and manuscripts which Miss Lowell had not shown me before. These were the gems of her collection. One could almost feel Keats' presence in the room. If Amy Lowell sometimes fell short of her own standards as a great poet, we can at least be grateful to her for her fine *Life of Keats*. I do not know any life of this poet which is more comprehensive than the biography of this strange, large New England woman, who loved him so passionately that she seemed, in some curious way, to evoke his spirit wherever she was.

During the winter of 1925 Firmin Gémier, who was at that time director of the Odéon Theatre in Paris, came to New York. He came at a moment when Norman Bel-Geddes had just finished designs for both my *Jehanne d'Arc* and *The Mother of Christ*. Gémier saw these designs and was enthusiastic about them. He read my manuscript of *Jehanne d'Arc,* and then invited Eva, Norman and me to produce it at the Odéon in Paris. He felt that Eva would make a beautiful Jehanne d'Arc and he was especially happy when he found she could speak French perfectly. The cast was to be entirely French with the exeception of Eva.

Gémier arranged for us to be invited to Paris under the auspices of the Ministry of Beaux-Arts. So the three of us, including Eva's dog Tosca, sailed off on the *Mauretania.*

A friend of Eva's and mine, Margaret St. John, followed us to Paris. She was a great help to us in many ways. St. John is as British as she can be in spite of the fact that she has lived in America forty years. She has all the best qualities of her people and a good many of their eccentricities. She is a poet—a metaphysical, mathematical poet, if I may be allowed to string these words together. She is also loyal, extremely intelligent, full of humor, and utterly reliable. I can call on her, and always could, at any hour of the day or night. If I do, she asks no questions but is by my side at the drop of her hat which, in those early days, was a flat one with a very sad-looking dead bird on the top of it. She also wore then an Inverness cape and, of course, low-heeled shoes. She looked every bit the character she was. Now, unfortunately, she dresses more conventionally but her mind still works in complex geometrical and poetic images.

In Paris we received our first blow. The Odéon stage was far too small in scale for Norman's sets. The electric voltage was too weak to sustain the modern equipment he had brought with us. It would have blown out all the fuses on the Left Bank.

From this moment on, troubles poured down on our young heads like sheets of tropical rain. The Sarah Bernhardt, the Champs Élysées, and the Porte Saint Martin theatres were the only ones in Paris with stages large enough for Norman's décor and electrical equipment, and all three of them were engaged.

At this point we thought of giving up the whole venture, but Mr. Herrick, the charming and kind American Ambassador, requested us not to. Since our arrival we had had a great deal of publicity in the French press which had welcomed the idea of an American actress playing in perfect French in an American play about a French heroine as well as a French saint. They also welcomed the idea of a celebrated American designer presenting his décor and costumes in Paris. Because of the sets he had done for *The Miracle,* Norman's reputation was by then well known in Europe. Considering all this, Mr. Herrick felt it would create ill-feeling if we returned to America without doing what we had said we would when he accepted the Beaux Arts' invitation. Added to this we had, by implication, committed ourselves to employ French people in various capacities—making costumes and scenery, acting and so forth.

We had arrived in March and now it was already April. I would like to be able to say that we cooled our heels until we could get the Porte Saint Martin Theatre in June. But actually we burned them running about attending to a thousand things. Norman set up an atelier with his two assistants, Thomas Farrar and Gerstle Mack, where Romanian, Russian, and French women cut and sewed costumes, while men of a dozen nationalities hammered and painted scenery.

The Odéon Theatre had been promised us for nothing and rent had not been included in our budget. Now that we had to use another theatre, all our money calculations were thrown out of kilter. The Porte Saint Martin Theatre, which we were forced to take, no other being available, held us up for what was then the large sum of $7000 for thirty days, and the contract that went with it obliged us to use the permanent company of actors and actresses employed there. It was a form of blackmail but there was nothing we could do about it.

A hundred other expenses we had not foreseen when we had so cheerfully accepted Gémier's invitation in America cropped up and, with our budget crippled by the high rent, we had to collect more backing. Gémier himself faded out of sight when he saw our increasing financial difficulties, and we could not even reach him on the telephone. As Norman and I were not very good at collecting money, the task fell to Eva. She did it bravely and courageously. It was no small job for her. It was she too who had to engage the actors and actresses, and in the meantime start rehearsing her own role.

We had to engage 150 supers, mostly Russians, because we needed large-sized men. Our difficulties were increased by the fact that Norman couldn't speak a single word of any known language except English and, his English being what they called American, most of the French and Russians who claimed they could speak English said they couldn't understand a word he said. The rehearsals, with every language being translated into another one, resembled a committee meeting among the inmates of an insane asylum.

Eva translated my play into French and for our first reading rehearsal the Ministre des Beaux Arts kindly offered us the big Trocadéro Hall for nothing. At least we all thought it nice of him at the time and praised his generosity to the skies. We did not know there was a trap in it—babes in the wood that we were! A few days after the reading we were presented with a bill for "destruction" of the hall. We had done nothing but read the play in it but the shrewd minister saw a chance to gather a little money from three innocent Americans to renovate the already collapsing Trocadéro. Luckily for us, Mr. Herrick took the matter up and we didn't have to pay anything in the end.

Our expenses increased daily, partly because we were constantly being cheated, and partly because Norman had no idea how to control a budget, and even less idea about the value of the franc. This was painful to Eva, who had to run around humiliating herself to get funds; and it was anguish for me to see her using up her vitality in this way when she should have been conserving it for the tremendous task of acting the difficult role of Jehanne d'Arc, a role that needed not only spiritual inspiration, but also great physical strength. Added to this, she had to speak in a foreign language, and no matter how well she spoke it, it was still not her own. In addition, she would be playing in a foreign country and before a French audience, which is probably the most critical in the world.

The opening night took place on schedule, believe it or not. A brilliant audience of the highest intellectual level gathered and the play was presented:

Sous le haut patronage
de M. l'Ambassadeur des États Unis d'Amerique
et
de M. le Ministre des Beaux Arts de France

In one stage box, with the American flag draped, sat kind and encouraging Mr. Herrick and his staff. In the other stage box sat old Joffre and M. le Ministre des Beaux Arts, with another gentleman representing the President of France, and over this box was draped the French flag. All the most interesting artists were there and the house was also filled with the social élite of Paris. Constance Collier and Ivor Novello, with a number of other English artists, flew over from London. The house was sold out, packed tight and—expectant.

That Eva was able to act at all was nothing short of a miracle. She had not been to bed for three nights and every responsibility had been heaped on her weary shoulders. One hour before the curtain rang up the hundred and fifty pairs of shoes for the supers had not yet been delivered. When they came, at almost the last minute, the manufacturers would not leave them until we paid the bill, which came to $500 in American money. Neither Eva nor I had it. The supers were playing soldiers and could not go on in stocking feet. Nothing would move the man to leave the shoes without the money. Just when all seemed lost, Felix Rosen came backstage to bring me some flowers. He saw our terrible predicament, produced a book of traveler's checks and generously paid off the shoe manufacturer. Thanks to him the curtain went up.

We had other troubles too. The French stagehands were jealous of our modern electrical equipment and someone tampered with it and put it out of order. Tommy Farrar and Gerstle Mack had to stand guard constantly over the switches and cables and watch the lamps and spots like hawks. It was an unhappy feeling to know that there were people who wished us ill and wanted to ruin our opening.

At the final curtain on the opening night I was thankful that Eva had been able to get through the performance. It was a real feat, compounded of guts, inspiration, and artistry. She well deserved the rounds of applause which called her before the curtain over and over again. Few actresses have ever had to cope with so much stress right up to the last second before the rise of the curtain. In spite of everything, she gave an inspired, moving and magnificent performance. In my opinion no actress I have seen in the role has ever remotely touched her conception of Jehanne.

Generally speaking, the French notices were good for all three of us. The American press praised only Norman's décor, but had not a kind word for Eva or the play. Nevertheless, many French artists, whose opinion I valued more than the American press, were greatly impressed by the whole production and thought that the entire play—décor, Eva's conception of Jehanne, and the play itself, were ahead of their time. I still think so, too. It was a production that would be more readily appreciated today.

Shortly before his death Norman said to me, "Your *Jehanne d'Arc* was the best piece of work I have ever done. I would give anything to be able to produce that play over again now."

During the four weeks' run there were a number of people I remember in Paris. Scott Fitzgerald, for one. In those days he looked like a golden archangel—but he didn't always act like one. One evening after a party at Alfredo Sides', Scott said he would take Eva and me home.

In the street was a little car that belonged to Alice de Lamar. Scott said that Alice had given him permission to drive it, so we got in it not realizing how drunk he was. He suddenly threw the gears into high speed and, like a madman, drove the car along the Quai, across the Concorde Bridge and up the Champs Élysées, missing cars by a hair's breadth and never once slowing down for traffic. Eva and I shouted at him but the sound of our voices was lost as the car swerved from left to right and right to left. It was open and we had to hang onto the sides or be thrown out. At the same speed, he drove us around the Bois, sometimes shouting and yelling and taking one hand off the wheel. It is said that God takes care of fools, babes and drunks. He must have that night.

At six in the morning he landed us in front of the Ritz, where he said he intended to have another drink. Eva and I crawled into a taxi and went home, leaving him to his own devices.

No one could have been more full of charm than Scott when he wanted to be. But he was one of those violent people who always create confusion for themselves and everyone around them. There was something in him that needed violence at any cost. I once saw him, quite sober, deliberately hurl himself down a whole flight of stairs, ending in a heap at the bottom with his head badly bruised. I asked him later why he had done such an idiotic thing; he might easily have been killed. He answered that everything had been going too calmly that day and he felt he needed a little excitement.

After the performance Eva and I often went to a little supper bôite called Chez Fischer. It was an informal place where it was fun to have supper and at the same time listen to various fine artists who sang or in some way performed. It was a famous place in the twenties and was generally crowded with people of note. It was here that Yvonne George first sang "Pars," and Dora Stroeva sang, accompanied by her guitar, *"Tu sais les mots calins et tendres."* Dora was a perfect product of this era. She was dark, handsome and Russian. When she sang, she wore a man's dinner coat with a scarlet scarf round her throat, and her sleek black hair was cut short like a man's. Her voice, too, was like a man's— deep and powerful. She was a most arresting and unique personality.

This was a period when it was greatly in vogue for women to wear strictly and severely tailored suits and evening jackets cut like men's. Women had been so used to wearing uniforms and trench coats during the war that it seemed only natural that they should continue wearing masculine-cut clothes after the war. Often the evening jackets of black cloth were exactly like men's but more often they were made of various-colored satins or gold lamé. The skirts were straight, tight and short.

Young women with slender figures, their hair cut short and wearing a man's evening jacket, could have easily passed for young men or young boys. It was the era when many young women wanted to look masculine and many young men wanted to look feminine. Which after all only proves once again that there is nothing new under the sun. Young women and young men were doing just this in Greece two thousand years ago.

Eva and I sailed for New York on the *Majestic* later that summer. On board were several friends; among them, Ruth Chatterton, Gladys Calthrop, Eugene Goosens and his wife, Boonie, and Noel Coward, who was going for his first production in New York—*The Vortex*. I had been home only a few days when that talented photographer, Arnold Genthe, rang up on the telephone to say that he was photographing the most beautiful young woman he had ever seen in his whole life, and he would like me to come to his studio to meet her. I had to refuse as Eva and I were leaving that afternoon to spend the weekend with Richard Le Gallienne in Woodstock.

Although I had read many of his poems, I had never met Richard Le Gallienne. He was charming. In beautiful writing, very much like Eva's, he copied for me the lovely passage from Pater's "Renascence":

> While all melts under our feet, we may well grasp at any exqui- site passion, or any contribution to knowledge that seems by a lifted horizon to set the spirit free for a moment, or any stirring of the senses, strange dyes, strange colors, or work of the artist's hands, or the face of one's friend. . . . Not to discriminate every moment some passionate attitude in those about us, and in the very brilliancy of their gifts some tragic dividing forces on their ways, is, on this short day of frost and sun, to sleep before evening.

I had this quotation framed and have always kept it on my desk.

Back in New York, I found a package with a letter from Arnold Genthe. In the letter he said: *I am sorry you could not come to my studio to meet my beautiful Swedish friend who has now, unfortunately, gone to Hollywood with the great Swedish film producer, Maurice Stiller. I am enclosing a photograph I took to make you regret that you did not meet Greta Garbo.*

I opened the package and took out a large photograph. There before me, in profile, was the beguiling face of the haunting person I had seen in Constantinople.

Twenty-Four

The following winter was a sad one for me, mainly because of Rita's unhappiness. Dr. Grant died. She had not seen him for some time before his death, but when she heard of it she was profoundly affected. She loved life more than anyone I have ever known and she was able to stand its blows in a most courageous way, but when this news was broken to her, she became very melancholy and completely lost the radiant grip she had always had on it. I did not know what to do to help her.

That same winter she went to a hospital in New York for an operation. When she was about to be wheeled into the operating room, I had a remarkable presentiment. I did not know then, and I do not know now, whether it is customary to put patients on an electric pad during an operation. I only know that, just in that second, I saw in my inner eye Rita burned on an electric pad.

I rushed after the nurses as they wheeled her down the hall and cried out, "Don't put my sister on an electric pad!" Rita heard the fear in my voice. She put her hand out to mine from under the blanket and said, "Don't worry so, darling. Everything will be all right." I persisted and cried out again, "Don't put her on an electric pad!" A nurse half nodded to me as one would to a tiresome child, and the doors of the operating room closed. I stood alone in the hallway. A cold sweat broke out all over me and I began to cry. Another nurse came and led me back to

Rita's room where I waited in a dreadful state of mind until the operation was over.

I waited so long that I knew something had gone wrong. I walked up and down that room and wrung my hands. I fell on my knees and prayed. Suddenly a nurse came in looking very disturbed. She said, "There has been an unfortunate accident. They put Mrs. Lydig on an electric pad during the operation. It short-circuited and deeply burned the base of her spine. I am afraid it is a very bad burn."

It was indeed. Rita recovered from the operation, but she never recovered from the burn. For two and a half years after this, until her death, which was ultimately caused by this burn, she had either to stand or lie down. Every day she had to have this area of her spine dressed. She suffered not only great physical but moral pain. She had always had a beautiful body and to have it so scarred was not easy for her to accept. She had a strong case against the hospital, especially as I had warned them before witnesses not to use an electric pad. She undoubtedly could have brought suit and recovered very high damages. But Rita was too generous to do this. She did not wish to hurt the surgeon's reputation.

Apart from worrying about Rita, I had a disappointment that winter when the plans for producing *Jehanne d'Arc* in New York fell through.

Otto Kahn had given Norman Bel-Geddes a certain sum of money to produce three plays that season. One of them was to have been my *Jehanne d'Arc*. The scenery, props, and costumes had been sent back to New York and were stored in a warehouse. Had Eva and I been wise, we would have seen to it that Norman put on our play first. As a matter of fact, he would have been quite willing to have done so, but for some reason or other we let the matter slide. So he went into production with a play called *Arabesque*. As we might have known, had we been any kind of realists, the inevitable happened. He spent all the money Mr. Kahn had given him on this first play. He thought that *Arabesque* would make money which he would then use to produce my play. *Arabesque* did not make money. It was a total failure. Mr. Kahn was angry about the whole matter and refused to finance him any longer, so my play was never produced.

Just how unwise people can be who work in the theatre is always a source of amazement to me. Even a man like Otto Kahn, with all his business ability, seemed to lose his sense of judgment when he did anything in the theatre. He should have controlled the money he gave Norman and limited him to a specific amount for each play, especially as

Norman was known for his "largesse"; and Eva and I, after our experience with his extravagance in Paris, should have seen to it that my play was done while the money was still actually in the bank. Probably neither of us thought about it at all. We just went on living in that dream state one enters and remains in while working in the theatre.

It is just this state which makes it so irresistible. It is, in a way, a "dream" state, even an escape state. It is a realm of unreality in which the actors and actresses must necessarily live, but this unreality also touches every other person starting at the top and descending to the most humble participant in it. It seems to touch the "angel" as well as the most obscure stagehand. Everyone who works in the theatre seems to live in a sort of twilight dream—a world of illusion.

One alternates between hope and despair. At one moment one feels sure of capturing success; the next, one is equally sure of losing it. The entire venture of producing a play is illusive, furtive, unsure and unpredictable. It is like building on sand and then breathlessly waiting for the sand to solidify. Most times it doesn't. It is an enchanted domain where there is always the possibility of a miracle, and people of the theatre, unconsciously living by faith, are always waiting, like expectant children, for this miracle to occur.

About this time I found that Eva and I for a variety of reasons were growing apart. We had often discussed founding a theatre together, one with a permanent company. I had hoped it would be along experimental lines with only new plays being produced and in that way we could encourage dramatists all over the world—especially young dramatists—to write for it. We had even planned to call it the Eleonora Duse Theatre. But this was not to be. Eva started her own Civic Repertory Theatre with the idea of producing plays that had already been produced, mostly classics. I did not see her again until she was acting out in Hollywood in the thirties.

At this time Noel Coward opened in *The Vortex*. I went to the opening night and it was an instantaneous and sensational success. It was the beginning of Noel's career in New York as an actor, as well as a dramatist.

Often during this season he came to my house on matinée days and had dinner with me between performances on a tray in my study. These little dinners were always an event for me as I so much enjoyed Noel's keen mind, his witty humor, and quick response to any subject we discussed.

He introduced me to Joseph Bickerton, who backed *The Vortex* in New York. Joe was a sweet and extremely sensitive man and I saw a great deal of him that winter. I felt sorry for him, especially when I discovered that about every six months he drank himself into such a state that he would disappear for days and forget his name. Then suddenly, at any hour of the night, he would call me from a speak-easy and, in a shaky, weak voice, ask me to come and take him to his sanitarium. I say "his sanitarium" because I found that he paid a yearly sum to a private sanitarium so that he could go there whenever he felt the need to.

That winter I was inundated with the problems of my friends. John Colton, like Joe Bickerton, took to calling me at any hour of the day or night. He called me a number of times from dives in Brooklyn. In the dead of night I would get out of bed, take a taxi and go over to find him. I walked where angels fear to tread and sometimes I had to argue with gangsters to persuade them to let me take John home.

I saw a lot of Jeanne Eagels and always had a battle with her, too, because I was very fond of her and couldn't bear to see her destroying herself. I spent many weekends at her place in Ossining-on-the-Hudson and there I was able to help her control her sad habits. We used to take long walks in the country and Jeanne would revive and swear she was going to reform. But the city was too much for her. As soon as she returned to New York she would fall back into her old weaknesses.

Yvonne George, another drink and drug sufferer, was in New York this season, singing in a theatre and under contract to the Shuberts. Lee Shubert used to beg me to see that she got to the theatre every night on time. A French actor and friend of mine, Marcel Herrand, was in New York then, and together we went every afternoon to pull Yvonne into shape. When she was actually on-stage with the curtain up, in some miraculous way she always managed to give an inspired performance. Back in her dressing room, she would collapse completely.

These appalling experiences with so many of my friends took up a great deal of time and energy, and I became very discouraged and did not feel like writing. But Marie Doro encouraged me to finish a play I had started called *The Dark Light,* and a friend of mine, Gertrude Newell, who had just designed the décor for *Peter Ibbetson,* with Constance Collier and Jack Barrymore, became interested and wanted to produce it. We had readings in her house with various actors and actresses. Unfortunately none of the actresses we wanted for the leading role were available and it ended up, like so many plays, on the shelf.

When spring came, Nazimova asked me to go to Paris with her. Abram had been given a commission by Marshall Field to paint murals in the large entrance hall of his Long Island house and he expected to be working there all summer. Rita wanted to go to Vichy for six weeks, so I decided to go with Nazimova and be in Paris when she arrived.

Alla and I went to a small hotel on the Left Bank, the Hotel Montalembert. Rita arrived a few weeks later and I went to meet the boat train at the Gare St. Lazare. She stepped off it followed by her female doctor, her maid, her masseuse, her chauffeur, her secretary, and her valet. She had with her forty large Louis Vuitton trunks, not to speak of innumerable suitcases and all the luggage belonging to the persons of her entourage. She had promised me before I left New York that she would, for once, travel as inexpensively as possible. I should have realized that she simply did not know how to.

She had engaged an entire floor in the Ritz, including a pressing room and a trunk room. Of course each member of her entourage had a room and she had a bedroom, a living room, and a dining room. She had brought all her own linen with her, books, and silver. The entourage scampered wildly about unpacking the forty trunks, and in less than half an hour the rooms were miraculously transformed as nearly as possible into the rooms of her own house. She had brought her own vases, and while the servants were unpacking, masses of white lilies appeared from the florist. Rita could not be without white flowers and she had cabled the florist to provide them on her arrival.

A few years ago in Paris I saw in the *Herald Tribune* that Clare Boothe Luce had arrived, unaccompanied, by plane. The article said she had arrived with the exact limited weight of sixty-five pounds. It went on to say that she had with her only two changes of nylon underclothes, one evening dress, one suit, two pairs of shoes, and that all her toilet things and toilet bottles were plastic. I thought of Rita in 1926. It was interesting to compare this streamlined arrival with Rita's.

That spring in Paris I tried to keep her within bounds. She had a habit of carrying unset emeralds and sapphires in her pockets to give away when she left a shop, or when a vendeuse came to the Ritz to discuss a fitting. I talked it over with her and said that I felt she could not afford to go on doing it. It seemed wildly extravagant and uncalled for. She was very angry with me and said, "What do you expect me to give these wonderful women if I don't give them emeralds? Surely you don't expect me to insult them with money?"

There was nothing I could do. I saw her off to Vichy with the entire entourage and only ten trunks instead of forty. "Only ten trunks and they are a concession to you," she sweetly said. She left in her car with the doctor. Another car followed with the masseuse and the servants. The trunks were sent by rail. "This is another concession to you. *I* would have sent them by car," she added, blowing me a kiss as she drove off.

After this I went over to London to be with my friends Mary and Jim Fagan. Jim came from Dublin and was the first producer ever to put on a play by George Bernard Shaw. He and Shaw were great friends.

They introduced me to Dunsany, Synge, and John Drinkwater. They also introduced me to Shaw, whom I saw several times with them over the following years. Shaw took me to a matinée of Strindberg's *Spook Sonata,* carrying a steamer rug, and when we were in our seats he insisted that I share it with him, leaning over to carefully tuck it around my feet. We had great fun that afternoon pulling each other's leg about Jehanne d'Arc. He said it was the first time in the world that two people who had written a play about Jehanne d'Arc had met and had even sat together at another play. "Not only met, but liked each other into the bargain and actually been amiable to each other. Why, we might have fought about the color of Jehanne's hair and ended by murdering one another," he said.

When I returned to France Jack Barrymore invited me to visit them in a place they had taken in Normandy near Honfleur. Jack met me at the station looking tanned and well, and he and Michael and I had a wonderful first evening together. They had no servants so we all cooked dinner and had great fun. Their room was upstairs and mine was on the ground floor with French windows opening onto a small garden.

That night I was awakened by Michael's voice yelling "Help! Help! Mercedes help!" I rushed out of bed and ran upstairs. Michael and Jack were rolling on the floor and Jack had a knife in his hand which he was waving over Michael's head. I threw myself into the fray, managed to seize the knife and throw my weight between them. Jack jumped to his feet, lifted a kerosene lamp high over his head and hurled it at Michael and me. We both managed to dodge it and it smashed to pieces against the wall. At the same time I realized I had cut my hand on the knife and blood was pouring from it. This turned out to be a fortunate thing because both Jack and Michael paused when they saw the blood and forgot to attack each other.

Jack flew for a bandage and tore one of his best linen handkerchiefs in strips. Michael rushed for iodine, and I put on a great act about the pain of the wound. They became so sympathetic with me that we all ended by kissing each other. Jack ran for a broom and swept up all the pieces of the broken lamp. Michael remade the bed. Sweetness and love reigned everywhere. Michael called Jack her "honey bun." Jack called Michael his "beautiful fig." They both called me their "wingéd meadow lark," and I just called them my favorite pair of "nuts."

We all went to bed. I was hoping to get a few winks of sleep before daybreak. I had no sooner fallen into a deep sleep than I was awakened by an unearthly and blood-freezing cry. I lay there petrified with fear and so thoroughly shaken that I could not have moved if I'd wanted to. It came from outside my window. I heard not a sound from Michael and Jack. I just lay there in the bed until the sun rose. Then I crept to the window. There lay a cow licking the tiny and beguiling calf she had given birth to that night. It was the mother's anguished cry that I had heard. Jack and Michael said they had heard it too, and they were just as scared as I was. I could have been murdered in my bed and they would not have raised a finger.

Twenty-Five

The night I returned to Paris I ran into a man I knew who said, "I know you are a friend of Isadora Duncan's. I hear she has behaved so badly that everyone has abandoned her. I am told that she is in a hotel on the Left Bank, practically starving." I had not heard any of this and I hoped it was only gossip, but when I went to bed I couldn't sleep. Around two o'clock in the morning I could stand it no longer. I got up and dressed, hailed a taxi, and explained rather hopelessly to the driver that I was looking for someone in a small hotel. We began with the Hotel du Quai Voltaire, tried the Saints Pères, Foyot, L'Université and in all, sixteen inexpensive others. At three in the morning I gave up and we started back, but driving along the Boulevard Raspail we came to the Lutetia. I had not thought of it before because it was large and expensive. (Little did I know Isadora in those days—nothing was too large or expensive for her at any time.) A porter was washing the sidewalk and as a last effort I stopped the taxi and asked him if by any chance Madame Isadora Duncan might be staying there. To my intense delight he assured me that she was and I leapt from the taxi.

"Room sixty-seven," the porter said. "Shall I announce you?" But I was already halfway up the stairs. I knocked timidly and hearing *"Entrez!"* I opened the door. Facing me and sitting up in bed was Isadora. A small lamp was lighted on the table beside her, but a scarf (the eternal scarf) was thrown over it, and the room was in semidarkness. "Archangel!" exclaimed Isadora.

(I was dressed in a white cape without a hat and she afterwards told me she had been lying there praying for help at that moment. As I stood in the doorway the light from the ceiling in the hallway fell on my head in rays, and for a moment she really thought I was a celestial being.)

"I thought you were an archangel from another world come to help me in answer to my prayers," she said. "I think you are an archangel. I shall always call you that from now on. How did you find me?"

I told her what I had heard about her and how I had found her. I discovered that she owed the hotel a large bill and that the management had refused her any further service. They would bring her no food and would not even allow her to make an outgoing telephone call. She did not have a sou and was staying in bed because she had been living on biscuits for nearly a week and was too tired to get up. I asked her why her friends hadn't helped her.

"I have spent their money and not repaid them," she said, in that childlike voice she often assumed.

"Did they ever think you would repay them?" I asked, laughing.

"That's just it. I spent their money which is just what they should have expected me to do. What else is money for but spending?"

I had heard this argument before from Rita, and in fact, I had often advanced it myself to Abram.

"Yes," I said. "I suppose money is to be spent—at least if it's your own money."

"Money is only dirty paper and dirty silver and dirty copper. Everyone knows that money is full of germs. People should be glad to have those horrid germs taken from them," she said.

I was forced to laugh at this. Then she plaintively added, "Please don't scold me. I am hungry."

I called the porter and, tipping him well, told him to go to the nearest café and bring us a roast chicken, bread, butter, and a bottle of wine. "Two bottles!" Isadora called out. "Two bottles," I repeated to the porter. "And some strawberries," Isadora added. "And some strawberries," I echoed. "*Et vite, vite!*" Isadora shouted with a great deal of vitality in her voice. "Not at all like a starving woman," I remarked.

As a matter of fact, I took Isadora's starving saga with a pinch of salt. I knew only too well how many loyal and true friends she had. None of them would have let her starve. The truth was that Isadora's feelings were very easily hurt. Probably someone spoke severely about her continually asking friends for money and always spending it recklessly, and she had just retired to bed without communicating with any of her real friends. That she owed a large hotel bill which had run over a period of many months was certainly true.

When the food arrived, I pulled open the curtains. It was almost daylight. I spread the chicken and the strawberries on the bed and opened the bottle of wine. Isadora clapped her hands wildly and fell on the food. We had a wonderful picnic.

When the last scrap had disappeared I suggested a drive in the Bois. She jumped out of bed gleefully and put on her sandals and her Greek dress. Within a few minutes we were downstairs in the street. There was my taxi driver sound asleep. I had forgotten about him. The sun had just risen and Isadora cried out to him, *"Au soleil! Allons au soleil!"* He opened the roof of the car and off we went.

As we drove around the race course at Longchamps, Isadora said, "Life is a continual miracle. A few hours ago I was hungry and in despair, and then suddenly God sent me an Archangel!" And she began singing snatches of Scriabine.

We drove around for hours, stopped at a little café for coffee, and ended up at nine o'clock before the Guaranty Trust Company. Isadora waited in the taxi while I went into the bank and drew out the money for her hotel bill. When she realized I had given her more than just the amount of the bill, she was very pleased.

I said, "There will be food to be paid for this week and another hotel bill, so don't spend this extra money on other things." I should have known she would. The next day she sent me an enormous amount of flowers! But this was Isadora and there was nothing to be done about it.

All that first day she begged me not to leave her. She came back to my hotel and I talked to her about her life, and said that she absolutely must stop squandering it and pull herself together and begin to dance again.

"I am no longer believed in. No one believes I can still dance. I could be saved if someone would organize a recital for me. I only drink and waste my life to forget my little dead children and that no one will let me dance any more."

An inspiration came to me.

"Isadora, if you will behave and concentrate on writing your life, I promise you on my solemn word of honor that somehow I will arrange a dance recital for you, and I will help you get the book published."

She did not react to this suggestion.

"I am not a writer and I would not have the energy to write, and perhaps now, after so many years, I cannot even dance."

"Nonsense," I said. "You will be helped to do both."

"Who will help but you, my Archangel?"

"You will be given Divine Energy, if you will only call upon it," I said.

She took my hands and said, "Your hands are so strong. You are strong. Do you know that you are giving me new life? The strangest part of it is that, foolish as what you say may seem, I believe you. Deep down in the inmost part of my soul, I believe every word you say. I believe a Divine Source *will* help me and I believe that I will write my life. I have never thought of it before but I know now, just in these few minutes, that I *will* write it. I will also dance again."

The following day she actually started writing. When I told people about it no one believed me. If they did they predicted that she wouldn't stick to it. But I never doubted for a minute that she would. I wrote to Tommy Smith, one of the editors of the publishing house of Boni and Liveright in New York, to tell him the good news, and asked him to give her an advance on it. It seemed a reasonable request to make with the prospect in view for him of a book from such a great name and such a great artist. Tommy answered:

> Isadora Duncan will not mind my saying, I am sure, that her temperamental reputation is rather well known, and it is this which causes us, as it will certainly cause any editor, to be certain of all the manuscript, or a greater part of it, before entering into, or paying any substantial sum of money for its publication.

This made me drive Isadora even more forcibly on. After trying nine publishers, nearly a year later, I returned to Tommy Smith and fairly browbeat him into accepting the book. He gave Isadora a two-thousand-dollar advance. When it was published it sold millions of copies but she never saw a penny of it. She was already dead.

Poor Isadora! How she struggled and suffered over that book. Many days I locked her in her room and only let her out when she slid a number of finished pages under the door. The fact that she wrote it absolutely unaided, with every condition against her, is another proof of her great talent. It was also proof of her great will power and shows that the so-called "temperamental reputation" stupid people glued upon her to have been completely false. Isadora simply saw life in a dimension that ordinary people were unable to see. Incapable to comprehend her, they put it down as her fault, her temperamental character.

I had a little car of my own in Paris at this time and often, just after sunrise, I drove her out to the Forest of Fontainebleau, or the Forest of St. Denis, or the Valley of La Chevreuse. When we came to a beautiful field or wood we got out of the car and walked. It was always at these moments that Isadora was most inspired. She was always inspired by nature—by trees or by the sea. It was then, when she was close to nature, that she talked to me of art, of her own personal experience, of her ambitions, and of her dream of a great universal school for children.

One day, walking at sunrise over a hill, she stopped and turned toward me. She was facing the wind and I shall never forget her standing there with her flowing draperies sweeping back like wings. She placed her hands below her breasts, and said, "Here dwells the seat of man's spirit. When I dance or am creative, I am aware of a glowing light beneath my breasts. It is here where dwells all inspiration, power, and magic. It is here, just somewhere in the area of the heart."

Closing her eyes and extending wide her arms, she said, "Do you see a light shining from me?"

Gazing at her extraordinary grace, I answered, "Isadora, you yourself are light. I see you as all light."

She was pleased with this answer and ran laughing on. Going home in the car she wrapped her cloak partly about herself and partly about me, and laughed again and hummed in snatches. She hummed like a cat purring as we bumped over the country road.

One early morning we stopped at a small farmhouse and asked the peasants if they would give us some eggs and coffee. They were surprised to see us, but they gladly made us an omelet. After drinking a cup of coffee, Isadora rose and disappeared into a back room. She didn't return for a considerable time and I went to see what she was doing. I found her stretched out on an enormous bed (large enough for the whole family to sleep in) with her arms over her head, her sandals off, and as sound asleep as a newborn puppy. I covered her with the quilt and tiptoed out. For half an hour I walked about the field behind the house. When I went in again she was awake.

"What good are you as an archangel if you don't watch over me when I'm asleep?" she complained.

The kindly old peasant lady, not understanding English or Isadora's relish for this kind of pretend game, but sensing that I was being scolded, started to make excuses for me. Isadora broke in and explained.

"This is my Archangel," she said in French, "and she should not neglect me. How can anyone expect me to sleep well if I have not my Archangel watching over me?"

The woman, somewhat bewildered by all this, said that I had only been out walking in the field.

"That's just it," Isadora answered. "The idea of an archangel walking! If she went out at all she should at least have been flying."

I cannot imagine what those poor peasants thought of us. Isadora dressed as she always was in flowing Greek costume, wearing no hat, her hair blown, and I in a gray or white cape—we must have made a strange appearance at that hour of the morning. And on this particular day, when I went to pay the bill I found I had forgotten my money. I gave them my wrist watch as a guarantee that we would return soon. They didn't want to take it, but I insisted. When we drove off, Isadora laughed, patted my wrist and said, "Sweet, generous Archangel, to have given up your watch! Promise you will not go back for it, for now, once and for all, without a watch it will be an excuse for us to forget the tiresome illusion of time."

Although she spoke this way about time, one of Isadora's most charming traits was her impatience when anyone she loved was coming to see her. If I had promised to come at eight o'clock, the telephone would ring at half past seven, and I would hear her voice asking, "Are you on your way?"

When I arrived she would be waiting impatiently at the top of the stairs. She would stretch her arms wide when she saw me. I always think of her like this, with her arms outstretched in the form of a cross. I think of the words she once wrote: Perhaps I am *La Madonne qui monte le Calvaire en dansant.*

Some women can cry easily. For me it is difficult. There are only a few people before whom I would let myself go. Isadora was one of them. She used to laugh and say that she was the only person before whom I could enjoy a good, comfortable cry.

She was so maternal in a large sense that I believe she wished to regard all the people she loved as children. What unbelievable agony it must have been for her when her own Patrick and Deidre plunged into the Seine and drowned. I could not bear to walk in the Bois with her and see her watch little children playing. Sometimes when I saw her eyes following a little blond child, the suffering I saw in her face was so terrible I had to turn away.

She wrote me how much America had hurt her. She wrote:

People are forever talking about my Greek art. This always makes me laugh. For I count its origin in the stories my Irish grandmother often told us of crossing the plains of America in '49 in a covered wagon. She told me of the heroic spirit of the early pioneers, of which she and my grandfather were two, and she told me stories of battles with Redskins. Thrown in with these stories were Irish songs and legends, and she taught me Irish jigs. When I grew older, to all of this I added the poems of Walt Whitman and fused them into my being and into the dance, for Whitman has been a bible to me and I consider him the greatest American my country has ever produced. And this is what people call Greek. I am an American. My ancestors have lived in America for two hundred years. My Art is Life. My dances are of the woods, the fields, the lakes, the rivers, the mountains, the prairies, of my native land, and the sea.

But my country has rejected me. They prefer jazz dancing to mine. When I asked them to give me a great international school so that I could train children, not only in the spirit of the dance, but in all art—in Life itself—no one came forward to help me. So confident am I that one can awaken the souls of children, which can then completely possess their bodies, that I have aimed above all else to bring them a consciousness of this great power within themselves and their relationship to a universal rhythm.

She told me that when America refused her this school, Russia, a few years after the Revolution, offered it to her. Unfortunately, she was no better able to realize her ideals there than in her own country. But she did have the satisfaction of teaching the dance to a thousand children. As it developed, she had to concern herself with finding food and clothing for them instead of teaching them. She wrote Lenin asking for clothes and when he answered that there was no material, she wrote him another letter saying:

> I have seen vast quantities of red flannel in store houses during one of my tours of inspection. I know this flannel is reserved for Soviet flags. Why do you not give me enough of this flannel to make clothes for my thousand children? What could be more wonderful than to keep your children warm, wrapped in their own flag?

She received the material the following day. Shortly afterwards a thousand red-clad children were following Isadora's movements in a snow-covered field outside Leningrad.

There has been much confusion about the personality of Isadora, about her private life, and her political views, of which she had none for she was only universally minded. There have been many exaggerated myths; according to one version her behavior was sublime, according to another, outrageous. Finally, there has been so much misrepresentation as to what she stood for in her art, that it will be many years before these absurd fabrications are submerged and the real Isadora comes forth—the true Isadora, who was the spirit of true artistic values, and who more than most artists of her time understood these values and tried to interpret them.

Just as her art, any more than her life, cannot be explained, so too, in mere words, Isadora herself cannot be explained. Her violence could not be understood unless one knew her personally and intimately, as I did. Although many of her actions made her appear just the opposite in the eyes of the world, she was extremely pure and religious at heart. She said over and over again, "All art should have its foundation in religion, for without that it becomes ignoble. Art which is not religious is not art at all, it is mere merchandise and should only be regarded as such." When all the confused legends have drifted away, dissipated by time, which is the only test of an artist, Isadora will reveal herself.

Rodin made many great drawings of her. He once said to me, "I consider myself fortunate to have known Isadora. She has also been a great sculptor. She has sculptured Life with a feeling and vision which will live long after this generation has faded away. It will be a hundred years before she is understood."

In France, where I mostly knew her, I had a deep appreciation and love for her, but it was not until I went to California, after her death that I truly understood her. In spite of her great passion for France (the only free country in the world, she used to call it) there were certain things about her that had a deep affinity with California. The vastness of this state, with its gigantic trees, huge rocks, canyons, and deserts is like Isadora. Like her gestures when she raised her arms and seemed to encompass all the vastness of Eternity.

Today, on all the beaches of the world, one can see the fruit of her influence and the spirit of her words made manifest. It was her words and her example which freed youth and all the people of our time from the harness and stupidity of layers of clothes. It was her spirit which liberated women from corsets and stockings, and taught them to wear sandals.

Walking on the beaches of her native California and marveling at the beauty and freedom of the sun-tanned bodies of the boys and girls, I moved among them with a sense of tenderness for Isadora's sake. Perhaps few of them had ever heard of her nor did they have the slightest idea that she had dreamed a dream for them. By their very relation to that dream I felt they were a part of her. She had said to me:

"I have a dream of uniting all the children of the world in one great international spirit of art. I want children of every country to unite. I will teach them one common understanding, one language—beauty. In beauty they will have a vision of love, truth and companionship. I will teach them to dance, not only with their bodies but with their whole hearts and souls. Across the entire world children of every country will join hands in a great and glorious international dance of joy, peace and brotherhood. The spirit of the children will abolish war. I dream of an idealistic exchange of children throughout the world. By sending children into foreign countries and teaching them the language and customs of others, they will learn to become universalists rather than nationalists, so that they could never entertain the thought of war."

Isadora had a vision of merging art with life—of merging art *into* life through the medium of the child. She dreamed of millions of children breaking down the barriers of internationalism by a common interest in the dance. She longed to combine the dance with every other art in the education of the child. Because she felt it was the mission of art to express the highest ideals possible, she believed first and foremost in teaching it to children so that these ideals would surely flourish in the race. She dreamed of the "exaltation of life in movement"—a phrase she often used to me. A movement that would awaken the soul, and by its awakening in beauty and truth completely possess the body. She had a vision of the soul's awakening within perfect bodies—strong, vital, free bodies. She said, "The noblest in art is the nude. The child must learn to recognize this and glory in the beauty of its own naked body."

Many nights Isadora danced for me. She danced for me three and four hours at a time. She would completely lose herself as she moved about, and became utterly unconscious of anything but the rhythm of her own body and the exaltation of her own spirit. She accompanied herself by singing or humming in a curiously low tone that often gave me the illusion that the sound was coming from somewhere far away and not from her at all. I was constantly amazed by her extraordinary ear for music. She could hum the most difficult passages without missing a note —Mozart, Brahms, Bach, Scriabine, and many others whom she loved. Often she danced until the first light of the morning began to creep in, then suddenly she would stop and look about, bewildered, like someone returning from a long journey.

The rue du Bac at this time was a small world of its own. Everyone in it seemed to know everyone else. It was more like a little provincial town than a street. Mary Garden and the celebrated French actress, Madame Simone, lived in Number 46—the apartment house next to Dorothy Ireland's, a friend of mine who lived most of her life between Paris and Capri, although her home was actually in London with her adopted parents Lord and Lady Rothermere. Gerald Kelly, sensitive, feminine and amusing, lived not many doors away. His job in Paris was buying paintings for Duveen.

Many people I knew had small apartments in the Hotel Montalembert and the Hotel Pont Royal, both of which were situated where the street forks into the rue Montalembert just opposite Number 44 rue du Bac. It seemed, too, that there was no one who didn't at some time live at Number 44 during these years, or who at least didn't come to see someone who did live there, or know someone who knew someone who lived there. I lived there, too, for some months when I rented Dorothy Ireland's flat. Number 44 was famous in the twenties because of the many celebrated characters who tripped in and out of its courtyard for one reason or another. Such characters as Étienne de Beaumont, Mimi Franchetti, Mary Garden, Teddie Gerrard, Natalie Barney and many others.

At this time I discovered that Isadora had posed for Bourdelle. He had done a Bacchanale of her and given her a plaster cast of it, signed and dedicated to her. She needed money so badly that I conceived the idea of auctioning this piece off. Dorothy Ireland very kindly agreed to have the auction in her apartment and to invite all her friends and give a cocktail party for the occasion.

A few hours before the arrival of the guests Dorothy rang me, weeping over the telephone. While arranging the statue for the auction she had knocked it over and it had broken into small pieces on the floor. She was in a dreadful state about it and I tried to calm her. I said that bad as the news was, we should go at once and break it to Isadora.

We found her in bed. She listened, then very quietly she remarked, "It doesn't matter. I have always said that life is more exciting than art."

Twenty-Six

Later this summer I went with Marcel Herrand and Walter Shaw to the South of France to visit Marie Laurencin in a small place by the sea near Toulon.

Marcel and Walter were friends of Isadora's, who called them her two pigeons. They were both young and remarkably handsome. Marcel became famous in France as an actor both on the stage and on the screen. With Jean Marchat, he ran the Théatre des Mathurins and produced, directed, and acted in many of the most interesting and progressive plays seen in Paris during the thirties and the years following the war.

On this trip the two pigeons and I sat up all night in a second-class coach drinking red wine and eating cheese while Marcel impersonated the Count Étienne de Beaumont, the famous patron of the arts. He even succeeding in deluding the conductor.

We arrived early in the morning in high spirits and took a taxi to the hotel on the little *plage* where Marie was staying with Suzanne, who was a combination of devoted friend, confidante, companion and jack-of-all-trades on every level of her life. Suzanne Morand had begun her career with Marie as a maid, but through her devotion, intelligence, and extreme discernment concerning any problem relating to her mistress, she had moved out of this category and become a powerful influence in Marie's life. Just before Marie's death in 1955 she legally adopted

180

Suzanne, who inherited at her death not only her money and apartment on the Champs de Mars but also all her paintings.

This was my first real meeting with Marie Laurencin. Marcel, with his enthusiasm for introducing people he liked to each other, brought it about. It was the French national holiday—the Fourteenth of July—and it was exceptionally warm. As we walked into the garden of the hotel, Marie was waiting for us in the sunlight. I was enchanted to see her screw up her very beautiful eyes to peer at us, and then whisk out a pair of glasses to see us better. I had not realized when I had met her briefly some years before how very nearsighted she was. Myopia in women has a great charm for me. There seems to be a troubled, unde-fined look in their eyes which touches and amuses me.

When we had exchanged greetings and she had looked me over thoroughly through large tortoise-shell rims, we sat down and I told her my theory about Emily Brontë—that she had been extremely myopic and that because of this cutting off from the visual world she had been forced to rely solely upon her imagination in a world of fantasy. Marie grew tremendously excited. All unknown to me, Emily Brontë was a great passion of hers, and the mere mention of her name began a lasting friendship between us.

As a woman, Marie has always been for me a most original and fasci-nating person. As a painter I regard her very highly. The average person who thinks of her only as the interior decorator's delight, because of the many reproductions of her more seemingly facile paintings used in house décor and because of the number of bad imitations done in her name, is misguided. She has done great and important work, but most of it is owned by private collectors and seldom seen.

On this visit I had brought Bambina, my beloved Bedlington terrier, with me. Marie took a great fancy to her. She said Bambina looked like a gray mist, and made a number of drawings and several water colors of her. After this trip, Bambina appeared continually in her paintings and became quite famous.

A few weeks later I booked passage home on the *Homeric* sailing from Cherbourg. Marie Doro and her mother, who were then in Paris, decided to motor me down. I sent all my luggage except one small suit-case on ahead by train and we left several days before my sailing date to make a leisurely, sauntering trip, stopping nights in Normandy in various places and hotels. We thought we had plenty of time and so we lost track of it. As we arrived near the beach in Cherbourg the *Homeric* was put-ting out to sea. It was a frustrating feeling and I have known all my life since then what it means literally as well as figuratively to miss the boat.

As I had already said all my farewells, I decided to remain alone. My luggage had gone off on the *Homeric,* so possessions were not a problem to me. I had a delightfully free feeling all that week as I wandered through the streets on the Left Bank watching the children sail their boats on the pond in the Luxembourg Gardens, observing the various types passing by as I sat at sidewalk tables in small cafés. I poked in old bookshops and moved lazily through the rooms of the Cluny Museum. I literally had time on my hands and I found it a great mental as well as a physical rest. Bambina, who was most of the time by my side, seemed delighted that for once we weren't rushing somewhere.

Taking no chances the following week, I went to Cherbourg on the boat train and found I had been fortunate in missing the *Homeric.* That enchanting and beautiful person, Gladys Calthrop, had boarded the *Majestic* at Southampton. We spent most of the trip together and had a very pleasant crossing. Gladys is a fine artist who through the years has done most of the décors for Noel Coward's plays. Her stage designs are well known in London and New York.

That winter Lee Shubert produced a play of mine, *Jacob Slovak.* Curiously enough, although I was not aware of it at the time, it was a prophetic play because it dealt with the persecution of the Jews and was, in a far milder form, the writing on the wall for what took place later in Germany.

It was tried out first in Brooklyn with José Ruben and Florence Eldridge in the leading roles and with James Light directing. It opened in New York before Christmas at the Cherry Lane with Miriam Doyle in place of Florence Eldridge. The press gave it good notices, although many people called it unrealistic. Nevertheless, it seemd to have vitality and played every night to a crowded house which, of course, was a small one. Unfortunately Lee Shubert, not content with a full small house, decided it was good enough for a large one and right after New Year's, in a blinding snowstorm which kept many theatregoers at home, moved it to the Ambassador, a theatre far too large for such an intimate drama. In spite of these obstacles I believe the play would have survived had not Mr. Shubert taken it into his head to change the title of it. He had never liked mine and he took this opportunity to change it to *Conflict* without even advertising the change, so that many people who had intended to go to *Jacob Slovak* thought it had closed.

This was the sort of thing that could happen to dramatists before they were protected by the Dramatists Guild. Mr. Shubert had never even consulted me about changing the title and I first heard of it when Rabbi Wise, who had written a beautiful piece in the paper about the play, called me in dismay to ask what had become of it.

It was not encouraging when soon after this Mr. Shubert was sued by an author who claimed the title *Conflict* belonged to him, and Mr. Shubert was forced to withdraw it. I wanted him to resume the original title, but he was angry and bit off his own nose by closing a play which had the possibility of making money. It was a great shock to the cast and a severe one to me. I had counted on *Jacob Slovak* running all season.

In the meantime I began writing a novel and helping Abram find interesting types to paint. He had done so many murals and decorative paintings that I thought now he ought to concentrate on portraits. That winter he painted a variety of interesting people, among them many actresses, and we had great fun working out the compositions together.

He painted a fine and sensitive portrait of Katharine Cornell, and an interesting one of Helen Menken in her famous role in *Seventh Heaven*. Hope Williams posed for him and he painted a striking portrait of Carlotta Monterey, who later married Eugene O'Neill. In painting Ruth Gordon in her wonderful role of Serena Blandish, he wanted to paint her in a *sucré* manner, but I saw her quite differently—a character of brain, and I convinced him to paint her as such. His portrait of Greta Kemble Cooper, who looked anyway like a Greek goddess of Olympian times, won the Walter Lippincott Prize at the Pennsylvania Academy.

He had two other interesting models at this time—Jeanne Karolyi and Valentina Sanina. Since those early days Valentina had become well known through her talent in dress designing. I met her and her husband—George Schlee—almost immediately after they arrived in America at Tom Powers' house in Gracie Square. Tom is a well-known actor and, at this time, Valentina came to New York with a theatrical company and before becoming a designer acted in one play with Katharine Cornell. But fate changed the course of her career. Unknown at this time in the fashion world, she opened a small dress shop on Madison Avenue where she made dresses stitched with Russian embroidery. At this time she had thick golden hair that trailed the floor when she loosened it.

That winter, among the stream of artists who came to our house from Europe, Augustus John appeared and we gave a large dinner for him. He sat at my right and next to him, Greta Cooper. It is curious how small incidents click in one's mind. I remember how at the beginning of the dinner grapefruits were served and as Augustus John's was placed before him, he plunged his cigarette into it and whirled it round. Greta and I saw him do it and held our breaths. We then beheld him swallow down the entire cigarette with a piece of grapefruit.

This same winter Bessie Marbury introduced me to Angna Enters, who dressed herself like a Manet and gazed slyly at me across Bessie's table from beneath a fringe which, in turn, was beneath a hat placed on the back of her head, which, in turn, was beneath a large bow. I at first thought it all a little too posed, but I finally broke down under her smile and admitted to myself her great charm. We became friends and it then became apparent to me that she had much more than charm—she is a versatile artist who mimes, dances, writes, designs, makes her own costumes and clothes, paints, plays the violin and the piano, cooks like a chef, and (most enviable to me of all her talents) can sit in the lotus position! There being almost nothing she can't do, I'm not at all sure she doesn't walk the tightrope while balancing sixteen swords on the tip of her nose in the privacy of her own room.

Although Rita entertained a lot this winter she was not at all well, and had I not been so detestably engrossed in myself, I would have noticed how she was failing. Actually, I realized later, she was always in pain, but with her great courage she managed often to keep even me from knowing it. I should have noticed, also, how much money she was spending. I believe I was not only stupid at this time but also thoughtless, and unaware of what was going on around me. I lived in a world of my own. A world of half fantasy and half pain, and one was an escape from the other.

One evening during this time I saw Greta Garbo in *The Torrent,* her first film in this country. Louis B. Mayer and Metro-Goldwyn-Mayer had led the public to believe that Greta was their discovery, and that she had never before been on the screen. This, of course, was completely untrue. She was already widely known in the cinema world in Europe. Under the direction of the great artist, Maurice Stiller, she had given a beautiful performance in Sweden in *Gosta Berling.* Following this she had played in *Street Without Joy* in Berlin. When I saw her for the first time in *The Torrent* she already seemed to me a finished artist no matter how much experience she still had to gain through the years. Already she was not only a finished artist, but she seemed to me to have the same mediumistic quality that Duse had. I felt that the character she was playing entered *into* her and possessed her, guiding and directing her actions. The character *took hold of her* and not she of it.

Sitting there alone in the darkness of that cinema house I was deeply moved. I sat through the film twice and when I went out into the street I felt a great loneliness. I did not know then, as I know now, that there is such a thing as spiritually getting "on the beam." That there is a secret area of the soul which, when kept pure, can act as a magnet and draw to itself a desire—even an unconscious one. Had I been aware of this then, I would have felt secure in that secret area, and given myself over with confidence to the miracle of its manifestation.

Twenty-Seven

In the spring of 1927 I went to Paris early and solely with the idea of arranging a recital for Isadora. She had kept her promise and written a great part of her book. Now it was time for me to keep mine.

Arriving in Paris I found Isadora living with a young and attractive Russian pianist, Victor Seroff, in an apartment on the Boulevard Raspail. With almost childish excitement she showed me her manuscript and promised me I could read it in a few days. We opened a bottle of champagne and I toasted her: "To wonderful Isadora! Long life to you and to your book." How curiously unintuitive and blind we are in moments such as these. She had before her only a few more months to live.

A few days after this, when I had begun my attempt to raise money for the promised recital, a friend of mine introduced me to a fabulously rich South American lady. This lady had a daughter who aspired to become a dancer and my friend believed the mother might finance us if Isadora would teach the girl. A dinner was arranged at her house and Isadora was delighted. All the day before the dinner she danced around the house singing, "We are going to have dinner with a *very* rich woman who is going to give us money." I looked upon this with a certain amount of doubt. "You will spoil everything with your pranks," I said. "Probably this lady is extremely conventional and you must not shock her."

Victor, whom we called Vitya, agreed with me. It was bad luck, he said, to sing about the money before you had it. Isadora snapped her fingers at us and exclaimed, "Who could be more alike than a Spaniard and a Russian? Both of you filled with superstition."

That evening on the rich woman's doorstep she sang again, "We are going to have dinner with a *very* rich woman who is going to give us money." She couldn't have behaved more sweetly at first. She acted like a demure little schoolgirl, smiling and agreeing with everything the lady said. But I knew from experience that Isadora always made fun of rich people and even more fun of rich, dull people, and with every word she uttered this poor lady certainly gave evidence that she was as dull as she was rich. As the conversation progressed a great uneasiness crept over me. We had just been served cold artichokes on gold plates when our hostess began boring us with a long tale about her objets d'art.

"You have bought all these things for yourself, but what do you do for the poor?" Isadora interrupted her.

"At one time I tried to help the poor but I had so many ungrateful experiences, especially with artists," she guilelessly injected, "that I decided to help only myself and my daughter."

"Indeed," said Isadora. I tried to catch her eye.

"Besides," continued the lady, "I cannot afford to give to the poor now that my daughter is growing up. I must save everything for her dowry."

With that Isadora picked up the gold plate at her place. "Perhaps you will let me sell this. The money I could get for it would feed a lot of hungry people."

Our hostess flushed. "I have already said I am no longer interested in the poor."

Isadora rose. "Then you cannot be interested in me because I am poor," she said, in a dark and menacing voice. "My Archangel has a little money, but she always gives it away, so she too, is poor." She beckoned to me and marched out of the room. There was nothing for me to do but follow.

"We are going to have dinner with a very rich woman who is going to give us money," I sang, mimicking Isadora's voice as the door closed behind us. "You spoiled everything," I added. "We got nothing but boredom from this dinner."

"*I* got something," said Isadora, and produced the artichoke from the folds of her tunic. She placed it on her head and held it there with one hand and waltzed me down the street with the other. Out of breath, she stopped and began to pull the petals off the artichoke.

"I am going to see whether you love me or not. *Aimez-moi, un peu, beaucoup, passionnément, rien de tout. Aimez-moi, un peu, beaucoup—* ah," she cried, "*beaucoup*—that's something, but it is not enough. I always suspected you do not love me *passionnément,* as I think I deserve. But we will let it go at *beaucoup.*"

Incorrigible Isadora! Did she ever have a worse enemy than herself?

Finally came the day of the recital. If a miracle was the cause of its fruition, it must have been one of faith—faith and hard work—because *no one* financed it. The performance fell into shape through the efforts of many people who wished Isadora well. Friends and admirers spent sleepless nights working over the details. The gifted conductor, Albert Wolff, volunteered his services, and the musicians followed suit with the understanding that whatever receipts were left over in the box office would be divided among the orchestra. For practically a box of chocolates, I persuaded the manager of the Mogador Theatre to allow us the use of his house for all the rehearsals and one performance. Publicity flew around Paris like wildfire, and was caught up by the papers.

I prayed fervently that day that Isadora would have a triumph. She did. She danced more marvelously than she had ever danced in her life before. She danced as though her spirit were taken over by the dance— as though she were completely lost in it. Every artist in Paris was there as well as every person of note. But what pleased Isadora the most was that all the little people were there. They jammed the top of the house and crowded into standing room and cheered and called for her at the end of each number. It was Friday, July 8, 1927, and the last public performance of her life.

The advance came from Boni and Liveright for her book and although she got no pleasure from it as it all went into paying debts, there was a certain satisfaction in receiving it. Through her great performance, she had again come into prominence in Paris and the art world. A number of managers were discussing future performances in the autumn. She was gay and full of hope.

One day she jokingly complained that no one ever gave her enough caviar, strawberries, asparagus, or champagne. These were the four treats she said she loved the most. So a few days later I invited her to my flat. In the middle of the table were seven great piles of asparagus, already cooked, and surrounded by pyramids of caviar. Circling this was an array of bottles—only the best champagne—and at the four corners of the table were baskets of freshly picked strawberries. Placed around the room on every flat surface were mounds of asparagus, strawberries, and caviar, and more bottles of champagne. Isadora was enchanted. When she left that night I gave her all that was left of the feast to take home.

"If I die tonight," she said, "people will say I drank too much champagne. No one will suspect that I died instead of a strange hash of caviar, asparagus and strawberries."

After a trip with Marie Laurencin, Suzanne and Bambina to Bagnoles-les-Bains in Normandy, I sailed back to New York on a French boat from Le Havre. Isadora and Vitya came on the boat train with me. Bambina sat on Isadora's lap. Ordinarily she didn't like animals, but she loved Bambina—I'm afraid only because Bambina loved brandy. They had this taste in common. The train went so fast we thought it would rock off the track. Isadora said she hoped it would and that we would all be killed together.

"I don't want to live any longer," she said. "I think it would be wonderful to die a sudden and violent death, and I am selfish enough to want to take you and Vitya with me."

On board the ship when we were alone in my cabin, she suddenly begged me to take her to America. I was amazed at this, especially as some years previously because she had mentioned the word *Comrades* on arriving in New York, the immigration officers had sent her to Ellis Island. I did not want to see her exposed again to this kind of rudimentary treatment, and as I also knew she lacked a passport, I turned a deaf ear to her pleading. But it broke my heart to hear her say: "I am homesick. I want to go home. Please take me with you. Hide me here in your room until the boat sails and then we will go to see the Captain. He is French, and civilized. He will understand."

"He possibly will, but without a passport those American immigration officers won't let you land."

"But I am an American. I am an American and I am homesick," she repeated.

Could I have changed the path of her destiny? Or was her terrible death, like the last act of a Greek tragedy, already inevitable? I do not know. But that I did not take her to America with me, risk or no risk, has always haunted me.

As my ship sailed out from the pier she ran along the breakwater, and in the setting sun, with her head thrown back and her arms extended, she waved the same red scarf that some weeks later strangled her to death. This was the last sight I ever had of her. I went sadly down into my cabin and there I found a white rose and a red rose lying on my pillow. A card pinned to them said:

The white reaching toward the sky is YOU, *darling, and the red is the earth*—ME. *I adore you.* ISADORA.

Twenty-Eight

Abram met me at the dock, smiling and good-humored, happy to see me home sooner than expected. This blissful state of mind was discontinued when the porters dragged up a heavy trunk and deposited it with the rest of my luggage.

"Is this the trunk containing one thousand dollars' worth of writing paper?" inquired the customs officer scanning my declaration slip.

"Yes," I answered, "it is."

A dark look came over Abram's face. Today I write letters on cheap, lined pad paper, but in those days I was a perfectionist and cherished such things as exquisitely sharpened pencils and beautiful paper arrayed on my desk. On this particular trip, thinking myself very wise and economical, I had ordered the paper *en gros*. My owl with *Verdad Y Silencio* and my address were inlaid in silver on every sheet and there were hundreds of boxes of it. It did not seem unusual to me to have paid a thousand dollars for it. Many women of this era would have spent ten times the amount on clothes and been welcomed home without a murmur. I had bought no clothes but Abram quite rightly, I suppose, walked angrily off the pier.

When I arrived at the house hours later I found him locked in his studio. Depressed, I began to unpack box after box from the offending trunk, and suddenly I hit on a plan to woo him out of his studio. Sitting down I wrote him endearing words on each size of paper, enclosed each sheet in its envelope and one by one slid them under his door. I did not have to wait long. Within a few minutes he arrived upstairs with all the letters in his hand, and the incident ended happily.

When we moved from this house to Beekman Place two years later, I still had dozens of boxes of the stationery and it was useless at the new address. I put it in the storeroom and when we sold this house during the war, up popped my white elephant. I called the Salvation Army and a charming Major Barbara type, a young Salvationist, came to claim it with delight. What she did with it I'll never know, but I hope it was used for the sole purpose of writing love letters.

That August Bessie Marbury invited me to visit her in Maine. I went up with John Van Druten, who was then a comparatively unknown young dramatist, although he had already written *Young Woodley* in which Glen Hunter gave such an inspired and unforgettable performance. One day while John was dozing on the grass and Bessie and I were sitting on the porch steps, she fixed her gaze on me and said, "I'm glad we have these few days up here undisturbed because there's something I want to advise you about."

"What is it, Granny Pop?"

"I want you to buy yourself a nice, cheap notebook [Bessie did not believe too much in extravagance] and write down all the incidents of your childhood that seem to you of interest. Keep a record, too, of all the people who have impressed or influenced you. In a word I would like you to prepare a sort of fertile ground so that you can eventually write an autobiography."

The idea seemed so foolish that I looked hastily at John to see if he was sound asleep. "What on earth could I say in an autobiography?"

"You could say a lot if you wrote with courage. Anyway, that is what I want you to do and I shall be very angry with you if you don't do it."

Many times after this she brought up the subject again. In New York she often called me early in the morning and our conversations would begin with "Have you started to write *the* book?" When I said no, she would call me an idiot and an imbecile and say, "I don't know why I bother my head about you." Although her pleas and commands rolled lightly off my shoulders at the time, it was she who sowed the idea of this book in mind.

John had to go back to New York, but Bessie had invited some other guests up for a few days: the Eugene O'Neills and Carlotta Monterey. It was a strange house party. I was impressed by Agnes O'Neill, who seemed to me a typical Biblical Martha—a woman willing to serve and efface herself. I had never met Eugene's wife before but I knew she had been through difficult times with him in their early life together when they had no money and he was a hard drinker.

Carlotta was a very charming person—an actress, sophisticated, beautiful, and romantic-looking. She was the kind of woman who would make most men shy, and Gene was no exception. He behaved like a nervous schoolboy whenever she even looked at him.

One afternoon she asked him to take her out on the lake in front of Bessie's house. Agnes was sewing and we were all sitting on the porch as they drifted off in the boat with the sun red and sinking behind them. Agnes followed them with her eyes and I felt embarrassed and depressed. As everyone knows, Gene and Agnes were divorced later on, and Gene married Carlotta.

I was back in New York and it was early in the morning of September the fourteenth when I received a staggering cable:

> ISADORA KILLED YESTERDAY IN NICE
> LOVE RITA

I could not convince myself of the reality of this message until it was followed by a similar one from Vitya, another one from Mary Desti, and the evening papers blazed out the full story. Isadora had been instantly killed driving in a small Bugatti car. As the chauffeur started the car the fringe of her shawl caught and tightly wound around the axle of the wheel. Her head was pulled down as the car moved forward and in one split second her neck was snapped, her larnyx crushed, and her carotid artery opened. Death came in that second, fulfilling her wish to die suddenly and violently.

Shortly after this I had a letter from Vitya. He wrote that he was in Paris when Isadora was killed. Her last days had been troubled and without money. She had been counting on the American serialization of her book but had had no word from her publishers. He quoted the end of a letter to him in which she said: *Perhaps you will be nearer to my spirit when the body with all its material nuisance is not here. There are a few inspired moments in life, and the rest is chipoka.* Chipoka is a Russian word Isadora used frequently, and it means rubbish or a kind of nonsense.

Just before Christmas of that year Boni and Liveright published her book *My Life*. It was proclaimed a great autobiography by the critics, was translated into many languages and has sold millions of copies over the years. The publishers printed these words on its jacket· *Just before her tragic death, Isadora Duncan's book was finished. It is perhaps the supreme affirmation of her courage and her genius and her creative love of life.* Nine publishers had rejected it, but it proved to be a great human document.

When I was in France with Isadora the last summer before her death she said to me, "If anything should happen to me before my book is published I want you to promise me that you will send Gordon Craig a copy."

Before the book appeared on sale, Boni and Liveright presented me with a specially bound advance copy. I sent him one of these. He was living in Genoa at the time and he wrote me a strange letter to the effect that he did not believe Isadora had written the book herself. He said he considered it "vulgar."

I answered that he could not have read it and that when he did he would have only praise for it. I urged him to read it honestly with an open mind and reconsider his criticism. Shortly after this I received a letter from him in which he said that of course it's not vulgar since I had assured him that she wrote every word. Then he added "how wonderful and strange."

I would like to quote a few lines of Isadora's. Lines which I think reveal the deepest essence of her nature, and embody the entire creed of her philosophy:

I believe that in each life there is a spiritual line, an upward curve, and all that adheres to and strengthens this line is our real life—the rest is but chaff falling from us as our souls progress. Such a spiritual line is my art. My life has known but two motives— love and art—and often love destroyed art, and often the imperious call of art put a tragic end to love. For these two have no accord, but only constant battle.

Twenty-Nine

During the winter Jeanne Eagels was filming Somerset Maugham's *The Letter* at the Paramount studios in Astoria. I saw her very often at this time and spent many weekends at her country place at Ossining-on-the-Hudson. She was very mentally alert and stimulating and we always had interesting discussions on a variety of subjects but mostly, of course, on acting and the theatre. She had a natural instinct about great acting. It was just impossible for her to be wrong in the reading of a line or the interpretation of a role and it was always exciting to hear her speak in her rich, warm voice whether off or on the stage.

She had the reputation of being difficult. At times she was. But I believe one can only judge a person from one's own personal experience. She was never remotely difficult with me, perhaps because we were both Spaniards. Her real name was Aguila—Spanish for *eagle*. She did have a violent temper, but then she was violent about everything—her art, her dreams, her likes and dislikes. She could not have been otherwise. She was one of the marked children of nature, marked for tragedy by a kind of genius, a violence of character. And yet she was gentle-looking with a small, charmingly molded face and a tiny beautiful nose.

Walter Wanger was the producer of *The Letter* and, as Jeanne and he often came to a deadlock about various ideas while shooting, he was glad to have me on the set to calm her down and if possible take his side on any disagreement between them.

One day she walked off the set, went into her dressing room and locked the door. I arrived just after the blowup and he begged me to get her before the camera again. He said she was burning up Paramount's money. He made a mistake if he thought Jeanne cared a fig about this. She was as indifferent to burning up Paramount's money as she was to burning up her own energy in a childish row. I knocked and said, "Darling, open the door." Getting no response, I persisted. "Don't be an ass—you're acting like one. Have a little humor and stop playing the tragedy queen. If you are right, come out and stand by your opinion, or throw a vase at Walter if you want to work off some energy, but let's in any case get on with the shooting."

I heard the key turning and then the door opened. Jeanne stood there all smiles, making me feel she had never been otherwise. She threw her arms around me. "All right," she said, "I'll settle for the vase but get me a nice big one." Back she went before the camera as though nothing had happened, and the shooting was resumed. Some time later I was told that she actually did throw a vase at Walter.

I gave a strange dinner party that winter that taught me there can be only one lion on occasions of this sort. What made me give this dinner I will never know! Fearlessly I invited the guests I wanted and the place cards read like the all-star cast of a benefit performance: Mrs. Patrick Campbell, Doris Keane, Jeanne Eagels, Alla Nazimova, Elsie Ferguson, Constance Collier, Laurette Taylor, Helen Hayes, Helen Menken and Katharine Cornell. Needless to say, each one of these marvelous women could glitter and shine in her own right, but together they eyed each other almost dumbly—all except Mrs. Pat Campbell, whom no one could ever silence. She was especially well known for her biting remarks to other women. On this occasion she decided to direct them at Doris Keane.

Doris had been playing with great success for many years in *Romance,* by Edward Sheldon. Actually I believe she had played it for over nine years and she had played with as much applause in London as in New York, and everyone knew it. Mrs. Campbell addressed her across the dinner table. "Doris, darling, why don't you go to London with your little play *Romance?*" Laurette took up Doris's defense with her Irish forthrightness: "Don't play the cat, Mrs. Pat. You know perfectly well that Doris has had a raving success in London—or perhaps you don't read about other actresses' successes? Maybe you just try to forget them." The dinner was definitely *not* the happy event I had hoped it would be.

I had another adventure that winter with a dinner party. I invited Texas Guinan to dinner and came home gaily to tell Abram about it. He put his foot down and said I absolutely could not have her in the house. When I told him that I had already invited several friends to meet her, he began saying, "What will *they* think when *they* hear we have a madam in our house?" I assured him that *they* would not hear a word about it. I told him I would ask all the friends I had invited— Muriel Draper, Greta Cooper, Bertie Eskell, Clifton Webb, John Mosher, Charlie Bracket and Harold Ross—to promise me they would keep the whole evening a secret. Abram was appeased. Looking back on it now, I can understand how he felt. Texas in herself was a unique character and a special product of this era, but there can be no doubt that she was mixed up with gangsters and the underworld. She boasted once to me, half jokingly and half seriously, that she could have anyone she wanted "bumped off."

At nine o'clock Texas looked at her wrist watch and said she would have to leave, as at nine-thirty she was making a coast-to-coast broadcast, then a rare and important event. However, she assured us she would not be away more than forty minutes and would return in time for coffee. She asked us to be sure to listen in to her broadcast.

At nine-thirty we gathered in Abram's studio and he turned on the radio. Suddenly we heard Texas' voice: "I want you all to give the little girl and her man—Mercedes de Acosta and Abram Poole, with whom I have just been having a delightful dinner—a hand." Abram turned deadly pale and switched off the radio. THEY knew it now and they knew it from coast to coast. Of course everyone was convulsed with laughter and to Abram's credit, after his first reaction he laughed too.

I worked that winter on a translation of Alfred Savoir's play *Lui* with Rollo Peters, who was a fine actor and also a gifted stage designer. Unfortunately, I did not have clear rights to the play and the Theatre Guild produced it in another translation.

Rollo had been brought up by a Breton nurse who had retired in her old age to her home in Brittany. He suggested that he and I go to visit her that spring. Abram had a great deal of painting to do and preferred to remain in New York, and I felt happy in my mind about Rita. She had made friends with Harvey O'Higgins, a well-known writer and a charming man who adored her from the minute he saw her. They were constantly together and I knew he would take care of her. He was absolutely fascinated by her and told me he had never met a woman with as remarkable a mind. They began writing a book together about the lives of millionaires to be called *Tragic Mansions,* and I left for Europe feeling that she was occupied.

I had my car in Paris and Rollo, Dolly Wilde, and I started off for Brittany. Dolly was Oscar Wilde's niece. She was very pretty although she much resembled her uncle's photographs and was said to look extremely like him by people who had known him. She was also mentally very like him, witty and alert.

On our return to Paris we stopped at Vanne to lunch with Arnold Bennett, who was a great friend of Rollo's. He showed me one of his numerous manuscripts which very much impressed me as the whole thing was written with great neatness in longhand.

Meeting the remote and beautiful Virginia Woolf at Elinor Wylie's house in London on the way back to New York, I had a premonition that she would at some time kill herself. When I told Elinor about it, she said, "Write this down so as to remember if it ever happens." But I didn't want to write down such a sad thing.

I remember an event during those weeks in London.

Greta Cooper and Bertie Eskell were arriving at Plymouth on a ship from America and I had promised to meet them in my car. Plymouth is nearly a day's motoring from London so I started very early in the morning. When I arrived at the dock I was told that because of storms the ship was late and the pilot was going many miles out to sea to meet it. I asked where he was and found him in his pub. He was a wonderful old seafaring type and he warmed up and embarked on long tales about himself. The result was that he agreed to take me out on his ship although he assured me it was strictly against his company's rules. I did not realize what I had got myself into. There was a heavy sea and the boat not only pitched and rocked but waves broke over her decks. The sailors dressed me up in an oilskin and hat in which I tried, like grim death, not to be sick. After hours of tossing about on the open sea, we saw the big ship and then came an exploit I had not foreseen. My seafaring friend the pilot said that if I wanted to board it I would have to go up on a rope ladder. As we pulled alongside I looked up and nearly fell backward, appalled. It was terrifying. With my heart in my mouth and a sailor standing on the deck below in case I fell, I ascended. I reached the deck and two strong hands pulled me on board. It was only four o'clock in the morning but I went to Greta's and Bertie's cabin and knocked on the door. Greta opened it, dazed and dumfounded. There I stood, as they told the tale for years afterward, dripping wet—my hands covered with blood where the rope ladder had torn and cut them and I had nearly foundered in the oilskin coat and hat.

Flowers have at times moved me the way certain beautiful women have moved me. Once while staying in a historic Elizabethan house in England, I had quite an amusing adventure. My hostess took me out to the greenhouse to show me some of the most remarkable tulips I have ever seen. They stood high and straight as though aware of their strange beauty, and their petals were the deepest black, their stems a violent green. Their fragrance and grace affected me deeply and I was silent before them while my hostess rambled on about importing them from Holland. Then she grabbed five of them in her hand and with a pair of scissors cut their marvelous stems. I said nothing and followed her into the house, hoping she would at least put them in my room. But she put them instead in a vase in the living room.

That night I couldn't sleep. Finally I rose. In bare feet, so as to make less noise, I went out into the hall and down the wide stone stairway into the living room. It was in darkness but I singled out one tulip and lifted it from the vase. A book fell off the table. Lights flooded the hallway and the old butler plunged through the door in his nightshirt. I hid the tulip behind my back. He was relieved to see only me. I mumbled something about walking in my sleep and dashed up the stairs into bed with the tulip.

The next morning there it was crushed in my bed. Where could I put it? I finally chose my traveling case but at breakfast my hostess said, "I am convinced that yesterday I put five tulips in that vase in the living room and today there are only four." I did not look at the butler and after breakfast I rushed upstairs before the maid could begin packing for me, as I was leaving for London that morning. Where could I put it? Down the one and only old-fashioned toilet was out of the question. The gardener would find it if I threw it out the window. I put it in the lining of my hat and returned to London carrying it on my head, faded but, nevertheless, a kind of crowning glory!

Thirty

Rita was finally forced to file a petition for voluntary bankruptcy. It meant selling her furniture and her house and many of her jewels, paintings, and rare books. She had already given away what was left of her fortune to people she had helped and to Dr. Grant during the last years of his life. Always a target of gossip and attention from the newspapers, she preserved through this and many other misfortunes her gallantry, graciousness, and charm. The headlines at this time were very painful, although many articles in the press praised her. I have one before me now which reads: *Mrs. Lydig's household effects have been sold at auction; but no one who knows her doubts that, somehow, she will again create an interior which expresses her perfect taste. She will unquestionably continue to "cut the Gordian knot of fashion's rules."*

Almost simultaneously Boni and Liveright published *Tragic Mansions* —the book Rita and Harvey O'Higgins had written together. On the whole the reviews of the book were surprisingly good. One of them said:

> ... Rita Lydig thinks that the people of the so-called "smart sets" and "fashionable society" among rich Americans are trying to live according to European ideals and customs and are thus destroying all possibility of any creative happiness within their own characters and in their own land. She writes that Americans are becoming expert copyists instead of expert inventors, which, she claims, is their richest talent. She wants to see Americans everywhere guide

their lives by their *own* ideals—ideals of service and kindliness. She says that Americans are in peril of losing their spiritual identity —an identity which Jefferson and Washington fought for. This is a profound book. Too profound for the minds of the "Four Hundred" to whom it is directed.

When the time came to leave Washington Square, Rita came to live with Abram and me. I was tremendously happy to be able to shield her somewhat from the many annoyances she might otherwise have had to face, but I who had always leaned on her and taken advice from her now found her leaning on me and taking my advice. I felt unworthy of the change. I could not be the glorious despot she had been, nor could I give advice with the sweeping assurance she had in her best days. I found myself trying intuitively to discover the thing she really desired and advising her according to what would make her happiest, regardless of what I myself thought, because I loved and admired her for what other people might have called her faults. I often admired her mad extravagances and I certainly understood them. I loved her for her recklessness, her indifference to public opinion, and her courage in doing what she wished to do regardless of convention and established codes. I am afraid I always encouraged her in these so-called "faults," because in her they seemed to me virtues.

When she was staying with me, I tried to help her cut expenses. This was like the blind helping the lame. She also loved white flowers. "You can advise me to cut down on anything except my white flowers," said she. "Don't think of it," said I. "I never would advise you to do a thing like that."

When her affairs were finally straightened out, she took a suite at the Ambassador Hotel.

That winter Abram and I sold our house on Forty-seventh Street but we arranged not to vacate it until the following year. In the meantime we bought a house on Beekman Place and drew up the plans for remodeling with David Adler. During the winter Gladys Calthrop lived on the top floor of this house and I used the floor below as a sort of work place. One day the house caught fire because of a defective furnace. Flames on the ground floor made escape down the stairway impossible. I threw most of Gladys' clothes out the window and into the rain before fireboats came to our rescue on the river. Down extension ladders firemen carried Gladys, Minnie her Siamese cat which I had given her, and me to the ground and safety. Guthrie McClintic was waiting for us at the bottom of the ladder and took us to his house not far away, where he and Kit gave us a strong drink. Gladys closed the episode by saying I and not the fire had ruined her clothes!

Adrienne Morrison was my play and literary agent besides Bessie who, because of her age, was working less. Adrienne had been married to the actor Richard Bennett and was the mother of Barbara, Constance, and Joan, all famous later on in Hollywood. At this time she was married to Eric Pinker, with whom she was associated in her business. She was a warm and wonderful person and I was extremely fond of her. Early in the spring of 1929 she sold my play *Prejudice* for a June opening at the Arts Theatre in London, and I went over for the rehearsals.

I found I was to have a wonderful cast with John Gielgud and Gwen Ffrangçon-Davies taking the leading roles, and Muriel Aked and Ralph Richardson (unknown and unknighted then) in minor parts. John Gielgud wrote later in his *Early Stages* that "Ralph Richardson played a small part beautifully" and "Muriel Aked was brilliant." He himself and Gwen Ffrangçon-Davies gave inspired performances. Leslie Banks produced the play, and Gladys Calthrop designed perfect sets and costumes. Those weeks of rehearsals were great fun and not at all the agony I had experienced in the American and French theatre. The play was well received and ran to the end of the season. John wrote in his book: *I had great hopes that some enterprising manager might transfer us to another theatre for a regular run, but it was not to be.*

When it closed I went to Paris and joined Clifton Webb, his mother Mabel, and Libby Holman for a motor trip through Bavaria. Before we left, Libby and I went to a fortune teller—an old White Russian who said, "I see you out in Hollywood and living there for a number of years." Hollywood then was a vague place to me and I hadn't the slightest idea of going there. She then made an even more remarkable prediction, asking me how well I knew Libby and if I was fond of her. When I said that I was, she said, "I did not dare tell her but she is in some way going to be mixed up in a violent death scene with a man she will marry." At this time Libby was not married and had not even met young Reynolds, whom she did eventually marry. But long afterwards the fortune teller's prediction came true. Reynolds was shot dead at a party in a crowded room.

We motored through Bavaria and ended up in Munich where I had an invitation to stay with John Becket. John was born in Texas and because of many years abroad had become very Europeanized, although he has never lost his southern drawl. Staying with him there in Munich,

I preached to him a lot about the spiritual meaning of life. He listened patiently and I think tried not to appear bored. He drank heavily in those days and I tried to persuade him not to. Even though he only listened to my monologues with one quarter of an ear, something I said must have impressed him. When the war came he volunteered and was sent out to the Pacific. On his return he went to Hollywood and began to study Science of Mind and was accepted into this group as a practitioner and preacher. It was not long before he was successfully preaching to thousands of people twenty years after I had preached to him.

When I returned to Paris in August, I expected to find letters and cables from Rita. Instead I found a letter from Abram telling me that her close friend Harvey O'Higgins had died of pneumonia and that Rita had locked herself up and refused to see anyone. Fortunately, there was a ship sailing from Le Havre the next day and I got a passage on it.

The night before sailing I had dinner with Prince Agoutinsky and Tamara Karsavina. We went up to Montmartre and sat talking in a little café far into the night. We were all terribly depressed and talked only of the past. Diaghilev had just died in Venice. Nijinsky was in an insane asylum in Switzerland where Tamara had recently been to see him. He did not know her and the visit had saddened her greatly. She talked a lot about him and about his early days with Diaghilev. Agoutinsky listened and sipped brandy, looking like a melancholy Buddha. I listened too, but I could not get Rita out of my mind. It was nearly dawn when we rose to leave the café. Tamara said: "The wonderful days are over. Everything has been taken from us."

We stepped out onto the street. The sun was rising and Paris lay at our feet.

"Look, Tamara," I said. "We still have Paris!"

The trip back to New York seemed endless and agonizing. How I would have blessed a plane at this time. I knew what Harvey's death meant to Rita and I had no illusions that she would long survive him. I blamed myself for wandering selfishly around Europe instead of returning to New York after my play closed.

As I expected, I found her desperately ill. Harvey's death had added the last blow to the many she had already endured. There was no more fight in her. I knew that she would die soon.

The last morning of her life she seemed much better. She had had a birthday two days before and she had seen Aida and my brother Dick, and from then on she had seemed to improve. On this particular day I was very encouraged. Rollo Peters called and urged me to go out to dinner and the theatre with him, insisting that it would do me good. I would only be away a few hours. Rita wanted me to accept and the doctor came and promised me that she was in no danger, saying, "At the exhausting rate you're going on, it will be Rita who will bury *you*." I gave in. In the middle of dinner I distinctly heard Rita's voice calling me, and I told Rollo I had to go back to the hotel. He said I must be overtired. Without answering, I rushed out of the restaurant and jumped into a taxi. The nurse met me at the door. Rita had had a relapse and was calling for me. The doctor could not be reached. As I went into the room Rita's face lighted up. She said she knew I would come because she had been calling me. I held her in my arms. She asked me to fan her. She closed her eyes and said her last words: "Is it a Spanish fan?" Happily it was.

People cabled and wrote me from all over the world sympathizing and sorrowing over Rita's death. I heard from many of the little people she had helped as well as the great. Newspapers in every country, especially in France and Spain, carried editorials about her. In the Paris *Herald,* Constant Lounsbery, herself a patroness of art, wrote:

> A word should be said about Rita de Acosta Lydig, the magnificent patroness of art, and her service to French artists. I have at hand a dossier with letters from Mm. Tardieu, Brieux, Jouvet, Copeau, and Mmes. Georgette Leblanc, Yvette Guilbert and many others, expressing their desire that she should receive the Legion of Honor in recognition of the great services she has rendered to French culture.
>
> She was a free, a valiant and a kindly spirit, a woman of culture and of beauty.

Frederick MacMonnies, the celebrated sculptor, wrote at this time in a leading New York newspaper:

> Rita Lydig's quality was so unusual in type, that it is difficult for us, in our habitual acceptance of standardized forms of service, to recognize its greatness. . . .
>
> This great lady, courageous, free and triumphant, lived her own life in her own beneficent way, heedless of criticism.
>
> A fiery champion of every beautiful thing, she jeered at pretense and no hypocrisy escaped her fleet mocking wit—her slogan must have been not unlike Whistler's: "Why put up with anything?"

Rita Lydig, marvelously made up by nature for the part she was to play by her gifts and great natural beauty, had a magnificent start in life, but the final product, the result of years of infinite patience and study, enhancing, correcting, eliminating, was as different from the original as a work of art from the raw material.

She became a perfected personality, radiant, individual, of consummate style and judgment . . . in fact a masterpiece of civilization.

It is true we were sisters. But by choice, foremost we were friends and after nearly a lifetime of evaluating her, I think I can say without any kind of prejudice that I have never met any other woman of her quality.

She still stirs and holds the imagination. In many cases, the imagination of people who have never even known or seen her has been stirred, and I still receive many letters from young people about her. Only the other day I got one postmarked Ceylon from a young man who had read Cecil Beaton's book *The Glass of Fashion.* From time to time things appear about her in the newspapers and last winter a few simple lines written by a columnist in a New York newspaper moved me very much: *The righthand stage box in the Metropolitan Opera House remains eternally lonely without the magic presence of Rita Lydig who once owned it and adorned it on the glamorous Monday nights during the Diamond Horse Shoe period of the twenties.*

That fine writer and designer, Robsjohn-Gibbings, recently said to me: "Your sister still tops the list of the most arresting women of our lifetime. There is no woman today who can remotely fire the imagination as she did and still does."

After over a quarter of a century of missing Rita's actual presence, it is good to hear these things about her and to know that, above and beyond the legend already created about her, it is her *spirit,* and not solely the legend, which lives.

Thirty-One

I could not recover from Rita's loss and I believe it is a fallacy to contend that time heals a great loss.

Friends were kind to me, especially my theatre friends including Noel Coward, Greta Cooper, John Wilson, Harold Ross, Alex Woollcott, Alfred Lunt, Lynn Fontanne, Margalo Gilmore, Clifton Webb, Kit Cornell and countless others. Sensing my depression, they came to my house late at night and somehow or other I established a kitchen-supper routine. My kitchen became a sort of club and these informal night parties which generally lasted till dawn were a great solace to me.

Toward spring our Beekman house was finished and Abram and I moved into it. I was glad to move. The distraction was welcome and gave me the sense of a new start, although it was painful to leave our first house, which held so many memories.

Thinking I needed a complete change, Abram suggested we go West that summer. We went to Taos and saw Mabel Dodge and her Navajo husband, Tony. I took a great fancy to him. We also met Dorothy Brett and D. H. Lawrence's wife, Freda. Freda was warm and made me feel secure, as if I were standing with bare feet on the earth.

One day the following winter Granny Pop telephoned and said, "R.K.O. wants a story for Pola Negri. I have suggested you might write it. If they accept you it will mean going to Hollywood. I know you are unhappy over Rita's death. Hollywood will give you new life."

At this particular time Granny Pop was not happy herself. Her close friend, Elsie de Wolfe, had cabled that she had married Sir Charles Mendl. Granny Pop took this news very much to heart and seemed hurt by the fact that Elsie had not consulted her about the marriage. But Sir Charles soon came over to New York for the sole purpose of meeting Bessie. He charmed her at this meeting and she told me that in less than an hour she became completely reconciled to the marriage.

I wrote the brief outline of a story for Pola Negri and called it *East River*. I showed it to John Colton and suggested that he and I write it into a screen play together. He agreed, and when we finished it Bessie sold it to R.K.O. When Pola came to New York, Granny Pop arranged a meeting between us. I think I can say that we "took" to each other at once, and on her recommendation R.K.O. put me under contract. It was arranged that I should go out to Hollywood to start work in June. John was also going at this time so we planned to go together and Marjorie Moss, the exquisite dancer who had become a great friend of mine, decided to go with us.

Marjorie and her partner Georges Fontana were the well-known dance team billed as "Moss and Fontana." This was the period of ballroom and cabaret dancing, and Marjorie and Florence Walton were its most celebrated women artists. Marjorie, fragile and delicate-looking, was so light on her feet that she seemed like a white moth fluttering through the air, and although she was not trained as a ballet dancer, her elevations were as high as any ballerina's I have ever seen.

But just then she and Fontana were out of a job and going through one of the bad periods most artists face from time to time. I told her to come with me, feeling that it might change her luck, and unbeknownst to her I telephoned Ivor Novello in Santa Monica and suggested that he invite her to visit him. Ivor was very fond of Marjorie and, always most generous, he at once invited her to come and stay as long as she wished.

The weekend before I went, Marjorie, Hope Williams, Tallulah Bankhead and I went to the country to stay with Clifton Webb who with his mother had taken a house for the summer on Long Island. One evening Tallulah produced a pack of cards, and asked me to draw one and make a wish. To please her I started to draw a card in an offhand manner. She pulled the pack from me and said, "I won't do it unless you take me seriously. I never make a mistake with the cards. I can always tell whether a person is going to get his wish or not." I tried to appear serious and when she offered me the pack a second time,

I wished. I wished that I would meet Greta Garbo in Hollywood. It was a childish wish and I knew it was. I also felt it was a futile one because it was already widely publicized at this time that Greta never wanted to meet anyone. But I was in a silly mood and secretly made it. I drew a card. Tallulah put it back in the pack, scanned the cards and said, "You will get your wish three days after your arrival in Hollywood." I did not mention to anyone what my wish had been and I promptly forgot about it.

The following day Marjorie, John, and I took the train for Hollywood. The last night on the train a strange thing happened. Marjorie suddenly began to weep and said she had a feeling she would die in California. Four years later she did.

Pola met us at San Bernardino and drove us all to our destinations.

So began my life in Hollywood—that world-publicized place of so many illusions. It began, I think, at a good moment—a period I would call its "Golden Age."

Thirty-Two

When I was in Hollywood—especially my first years there—it was considered a wild and, in a manner of speaking, a morally "lost" place. The whole world thought of it as a place of mad night life, riotous living, orgies, careers which shot up like meteors and crashed down like lead, uncontrolled extavagances, unbridled love affairs and—in a word—SIN.

This may or may not have been true. In any case I do not intend to write a history of Hollywood morals or even try to show its way of living except where it directly—or sometimes indirectly—touched me. Many "goings on," like distant rumbles of thunder, I heard about, but rarely did I encounter the depravity I read of in the newspapers and magazines. Stupidity, vulgarity, and bad taste I encountered often when I went to the studios or brushed against the lives of people who termed themselves "film people." Because of my profession, I was forced to go to the studios. But fortunately, because of my free will, I never associated with anyone who called himself or herself a "film person" no matter what they might have been called by other people behind their backs. The true artists there were artists. They would have been so anywhere else in the world. The rest have already been judged by time. Where are they now? Only a handful who flourished there will be remembered when Hollywood is forgotten.

Oddly enough, my own life out there passed as though I were living in a monastery. I am grateful to Hollywood for many things. I was more tortured within myself during those years than at any other time in my life, but this suffering taught me much.

For me Hollywood was divided into four categories: first, the Hollywood of the studios and so-called "film world" with which I associated as little as possible; secondly, the Hollywood of my own distinct friends, people who also would have been my friends had I met them anywhere else in the world; thirdly, the Hollywood of the beautiful land itself— the actual soil of which a geologist said to me, "It is the most ancient ground in the world. When the molten lava in·its first stages of this planet began to cool off, the terrain of Colorado, New Mexico and California were the first to harden"; fourthly, the Hollywood which held true spiritual teachings as taught by Krishnamurti. Unfortunately there was also the opposite side of the coin—dozens of phony teachings, quack fortunetellers, and commercial astrologers.

As I advance in this book and finally reach this period in which I must write about Hollywood, I realize more and more the impossibility of writing about myself, for indeed I am not writing about one life and one person but of many lives and many people rolled into one. I, like everyone else, am composed of hundreds of lives. Then too, I believe that each person with whom we come in contact unconsciously imposes a new role upon us. We become melancholy, gay, saintly, devilish, childish or wise according to the role we have assumed to play. Thus, it is impossible for any two people to see us in the same light.

Another problem arises in writing this book. Incidents which seemed to me to last a lifetime have taken only a few lines for me to write, and intervals that seemed centuries of suffering and anguish do not appear at all long in these pages. I desperately asked myself, Where is the truth? Which person in me am I writing about? Am I writing only of what my eyes have perceived or am I writing of the things my spirit has revealed? I know we perceive with the eye but we do not *see* with the eye. What then is the truth to me? Shall I write this book as the artist in me, or as the potential saint in me, or as a vagabond who longs to throw my cap over the windmill and once having started out on the symbolic "open road" of life inclines, so to speak, to let everything rip? How am I to convey to the reader the diverse people I feel within me?

My first evening in Hollywood was a unique experience and a curious initiation to "Follywood," as many people then called it.

Pola took me to dine with a Mrs. Blanche Sewall who was, before her marriage, a Guggenheim and a member of the wealthy family of that name in New York. In telling about this evening I do not wish to depreciate Blanche Sewall. She is now dead and anything I recount about her I only do as a sort of humorous recording of Hollywood history. What seemed startling to me then I would most likely today take easily in my stride. I have learned now to discriminate eccentric people from vulgar people, which I perhaps did not do so well then. Blanche Sewall was eccentric rather than vulgar. According to my taste she had absolutely none. According to her taste mine was too conventional.

When Pola called for me to take me to dinner she said, "You will like Blanche Sewall. She is a sweet person." She was right in the first statement but wrong in the second. *Sweet* was too characterless a word for Blanche.

When we rang the doorbell of her very grand house on Benedict Canyon in Beverly Hills, she opened the door herself. I was amazed at her appearance. She was tiny and barely came to my shoulder although she wore shoes with heels at least four inches high. They were sandals and it was a miracle that she could walk on them at all. Her hair was frizzed and stood out from her head like the hair of a Fiji Islander. Her cheeks were caked with rouge, her mouth smeared and brimming over with brilliant red lipstick, and her eyelids and eyes were smudged with black as though she had made them up in the dark. She wore a red low-necked blouse and Turkish trousers. On her arms and ankles dozens of gold bracelets dangled and clanked as she mincingly took one tiny step after the other. Her voice was high and shrill and her fingernails extremely long and the color of blood.

Automatically I recoiled when I saw her in the doorway. She seized my hand in a gesture of greeting and screamed, "Would you like to see my bathroom?" I wondered if I looked in pain or needed to wash my face. "I always get the bathroom over before anything else," she added. "Follow me." There was nothing to do but obey and we proceeded through one room after another over shining multicolored pseudo-Arabian floors. A Roman emperor might have envied the bathroom. It was more than a room. I would have called it a hall. The walls and floor were white marble and in the center was a sunken black marble swimming pool. Blanche called it her "tub" but it was certainly fifteen feet long and as many wide. At either end water gushed from great gold dolphins. At the windows, which opened out onto a garden where blackbirds hung in white cages, there were black patent leather curtains. I stood a little aghast but my hostess allowed me no time for comment.

The Cook's Tour was on and I followed her from one bedroom to another. Over the doors were painted such beguiling names as *Nid d'Amour, Une Nuit d'Amour, or just plain 'Amour*.

When we arrived a trifle breathless in the drawing room, where an array of cocktails were awaiting us, Mrs. Sewall proclaimed in a childish voice, "We are going to have absolutely *nothing* for dinner—only a few bits." I watched Pola and our hostess toss off quite a number of cocktails and did pretty well myself in that respect, then we went out into the patio where the "bits" were going to be served under the open sky. I was surprised to see it was full moon. I am very moonconscious and had not realized it was full moon. Nor was it. The moon I saw was an electric one hung from an invisible wire over the patio, shedding sweetness and light down on us.

The "bits" turned out to be an eight-course dinner with six different kinds of wine including champagne. All this was served by a jolly Negro butler wearing white cotton gloves two sizes too large for him. When he served the soup, both of his thumbs went into it. When the evening was over Mrs. Sewall, in high spirits greatly aided by the real thing itself, led us to the front door and screamed good-by. "Come again and the next time you will have a proper dinner," she yelled.

The following day held further surprises. I went to the R.K.O. studios, then called Pathé. Pola's dressing room was a bungalow as sumptuous as a palace, but the studio executives looked at both Pola and me as if they were gazing at a flight of birds over our heads. I learned then and kept on learning all the years afterwards in Hollywood that rudeness was the byword of most studio executives. Eventually my contract was signed and I was ordered to start work the following Monday on *East River*. In the meantime Pola was to begin shooting on a picture called *A Woman Commands* which was to take about eight weeks. *East River* would be her next picture after that.

My second day in Hollywood Mary Pickford asked John Colton and me to lunch. I went to Pickfair dressed in a white sweater and white trousers and inadvertently became a pioneer. In Hollywood, Greta sometimes wore sailor pants but she had not as yet worn trousers or what afterwards came to be popularly called *slacks*. I was surprised when Elsie Janis drew me aside and said: "You'll get a bad reputation if you dress this way out here." But before long every one else was dressing that way too including Elsie herself and Mary Pickford.

I woke up the third day with a feeling in my bones that something out of the ordinary was going to happen. The telephone rang. It was an invitation to tea that day at Salka Viertel's. I had heard of her vaguely through a friend of Hope Williams' and it was she who called me. She remarked that if I went to tea I might have a "surprise." Feeling a bit lost alone in my hotel, I accepted.

That afternoon while dressing for tea I noticed a bracelet in a box where I kept a few odd pieces of jewelry. It was a bracelet that I had bought in Berlin. It was streamlined, heavy and modern and made of steel—a material that was for a time in vogue in Germany then. I had bought it partly because I had read an article in a German magazine which said that Greta Garbo liked heavy bracelets. When my eye fell on this one in the shop window I thought of her and to amuse myself I went into the shop with a great deal of gusto and pretended that I was buying it for her.

Salka Viertel lived on Maberry Road in Santa Monica. I had no idea where that was but I gave the address to the taxi driver and we proceeded toward the sea. Salka and I had a great mutual friend in Eleanora von Mendelssohn, which started us off well. In fact, it was because of Eleanora that she had invited me to her house. She also said that a friend was coming who had expressed a desire to meet me. She made an attempt to speak naturally and as though the name was commonplace: "Greta Garbo," she said. At this moment Mrs. Viertel's husband, Berthold, came into the room with their young son Tommy. Berthold was a writer, but he looked more like a musician with thick, wavy white hair which he wore quite long. He was gentle and sympathetic, also extremely European and poetic. I always felt he was like a fish out of water in Hollywood.

We discussed various subjects and in true German fashion drank coffee although I had been invited to tea. Suddenly the doorbell rang. Salka went to open it. I heard a very low voice speaking in German. Of course it was unmistakable although I had only heard it once before —in *Anna Christie,* the only talking film Greta had made up to that time. Salka brought her into the room and introduced me.

It is strange how something that in imagination seems extraordinary can suddenly become very natural when it really happens. To have Greta in the flesh before me instantly seemed the most natural thing in the world. As we shook hands and she smiled at me I felt that I had known her all my life; in fact, in many previous incarnations.

As I had expected she was remarkably beautiful, far more so than she seemed in her films then. She was dressed in a white jumper and dark blue sailor pants. Her feet were bare and like her hands, slender and sensitive. Her beautifully straight hair hung to her shoulders and she wore a white tennis visor pulled well down over her face in an effort to hide her extraordinary eyes which held in them a look of eternity. When she spoke I was not only charmed by the tone and quality of her voice but also by her accent. At this time she spoke English quite incorrectly with a strong Swedish accent and her mispro-nunciations were enchanting. That afternoon I heard her say to Salka, "I trotteled down to see you." Oddly enough, the words that she said were often more expressive than the correct ones.

Greta has never at any time used slang, although it would have been very easy for her to have picked up slang phrases in the studio. It would also have been easy for her to have picked up an American way of speaking because at this time she never heard anything else. Yet she has never spoken with an American accent. George Cukor used to say in Hollywood that I taught Greta her beautiful English and it was generally accredited to me that I did. But this was not really true. It is possible that her English was in some small way influenced by mine, but she has such innate taste that she could never speak any language other than beautifully. I have been told by Swedes that her Swedish is flawless and by Germans that her German is most engaging and, although she speaks little French, whatever she says in this language is charmingly and correctly pronounced.

I do not recall too well what we talked about that day. I was too overwhelmed to record the conversation. I remember discussing Duse with Greta and Salka, and then Salka went upstairs to telephone. Berthold had gone out to the garden to read to Tommy. Greta and I were left on our own. There was a silence, a silence which she could manage with great ease. Greta can always manage a silence. But I felt awkward. Then suddenly she looked at my bracelet and said, "What a nice brace-let." I took it off my wrist and handed it to her. "I bought it for you in Berlin," I said.

She didn't stay long. She explained that she was still shooting *Susan Lennox* and had made this visit as an exception. "I never go out when I'm shooting. Or perhaps, I just never go out," she said, adding with a laugh, "Now I will go home to dinner which I will have in bed. I am indeed an example of the gay Hollywood night life!"

I wanted to ask her if I might see her again but I did not have the courage. Salka took her out to her car and when she came back said, "Greta liked you and she likes few people."

Thirty-Three

Two days later, on Sunday, Salka rang me on the telephone. She asked me to breakfast at nine-thirty that morning. She said Greta would be there and that it was she who had suggested calling me.

I scrambled into my clothes and arrived at nine-thirty to the minute. Greta was already there, in white shorts this time, and again the visor. I noticed what an exquisite color her legs had become from the sun. At this second meeting she was more beautiful than I had ever dreamed she could be. Her face was fresh and glowing. She was in high spirits and full of mischief.

We sat down to breakfast with Salka, Berthold, and their three sons, Hans, Peter and Tommy. As Berthold was expecting a producer at the house afterwards, Salka suggested that Greta and I go to Oliver Garrett's. Oliver was a close friend of Salka's and his house was just on the corner overlooking the sea. He was away on "location" and she told us we would find the door unlocked.

It was a brilliantly sunny day. From the window we could see the blue Pacific with the colored sails of little Japanese fishing boats standing out on it. (When the war came it was said that these Japanese fishermen were spies who reported all the ships that sailed from the harbor at San Pedro.) We put records on the phonograph, pushed back the rug in the living room and danced. "Daisy, You're Driving Me Crazy" we sang and danced over and over again. I loved Greta's deep voice, and

I made her repeat and repeat it, until she said, "We will wear the record out, not to mention my poor throat." For waltz time we put on "Ramona" and "Goodnight Sweetheart." Finally for a tango we wound up with "Schöne Gigolo"—which was all the rage at this time. I mention these tunes because they, to me, are nostalgic and part of this period.

"I will take you home to lunch with me," Greta said, but I had already promised Pola I would lunch with her.

"What of it? Just telephone Pola and say you can't come."

"How can I at the last moment without being very rude? Pola said she was just having a little lunch for six."

Greta roared with laughter. "A little lunch for six! Don't be silly. More likely six hundred. I know these little lunch for six parties." She shook her head sadly. "I see you don't know Hollywood, but go to Pola's today and learn your lesson. You will see for yourself."

Of course, I did not quite believe her. I felt that since Pola had said there would be six for lunch that was the way it would be, and I must stick to my promise. I happened to mention a Russian word to Greta—*toscar,* which means "yearning." She seized upon this word and repeated it many times, pronouncing it richly and turning it, as it were, round her tongue like someone who might be speaking a beloved name. She told me the equivalent of the word in Swedish.

When the time came for me to leave I got into the car and as the chauffeur started it moving, Greta plucked a flower from a bed in front of the house and gave it to me. Gaily she said, "Don't say I never gave you a flower," and stood there laughing and waving as I drove away.

As predicted, at Pola's I was caught up in a crowd of about a hundred, all pushing and edging their way onto the terrace where lunch was to be served overlooking the sea. Just when I had made up my mind to turn and flee, Basil Rathbone seized my hand and said, "You are sitting next to me at lunch. I have already looked at the tables and seen the place cards." There was nothing else for me to do but say politely, "How nice." Fortunately I liked Basil very much.

Pola came over breathlessly to greet me, bringing Ramon Navarro who, she said, was also sitting next to me at lunch. I looked around and saw a few familiar faces. Still bewildered, I had to say it: "I expected six people." She shrugged her shoulders and laughed. "Don't be silly," she said—Greta's exact words. I had learned my first Hollywood lesson.

In the middle of lunch a butler leaned over my shoulder and said, "Miss de Acosta, you are wanted on the telephone." He pulled out my chair and beckoned me to follow him. "Who is it?" I inquired. "A Mr. Toscar," he said. "The gentleman spelled his name for me." Picking up the receiver I heard the gentleman's voice: "Well, are there six people or six hundred?"

"I should say six thousand," I answered.

Greta laughed. "Let this be a lesson to you. Now, make for your car and come to my house and no more nonsense about being polite to Pola."

I did not need a second lesson. I rushed from the house without even telling the butler to make my excuses. Finding my car I shouted to the chauffeur, "1717 San Vincente Boulevard!" No doubt he thought me a little mad as I added, "And drive as fast as the wind or I will push you out of the car and drive myself!"

Greta was waiting for me on the driveway near the house. She motioned to the chauffeur to stop. She did not want him to drive up to the house. She was wearing a Chinese black silk dressing gown and men's bedroom slippers. She looked tired and depressed. Only a few hours ago I had seen her radiant. When I came to know her well, I realized how easily her moods and looks could change. She could be gay and look well and within five minutes she would be desperately depressed and apparently terribly ill.

Leading me around the house into a garden enclosed by high box hedges, she drew me to a stone bench at the end of the garden facing the house and we sat down. She explained to me that she was alone in the house because on Sunday her only maid, Whistler, was out for the day. When she was in a happier mood she used to whistle instead of saying Whistler's name, but that afternoon she was not in a happy mood.

"I am not going to take you into the house and you will have to leave soon. I am very tired and I have to shoot again tomorrow very early on that ghastly *Susan Lennox,*" she said.

"Aren't you happy about the film?" I asked innocently.

"Happy? *Who* is happy? No one making films can be happy."

"I'm sorry. I hoped you were. You were happy this morning, weren't you, when we were dancing and singing?"

"Yes, thanks to you I had a few minutes' gaiety this morning. But now it is nearly evening. Soon it will be night, and I will not sleep, and then it will be morning, and I will have to go again to that terrible studio. Let's not talk. It is so useless talking and trying to explain things. Let's just sit and not speak at all."

And so we sat silently as the shadows of the eucalyptus trees began to stretch out across the lawn and finally the sun grew fiery red and slowly sank behind the hedge.

Greta sighed and broke the silence. "Now you must go home," she said.

This day she created a pattern between us that we have ever since carried out. Whenever I go to see her and it becomes time to leave, she asks me to go home as she did this day. It is a joke between us. She always has to remind me to go home.

The next day I went to the studio and reported to begin work on *East River*. That evening when I got back to the hotel, John Colton came to my room to say he had seen a house he wanted to rent. He hated living in a hotel and suggested that we share it. I no less hated living in a hotel and was delighted with the idea. It never occurred to me that it was an unconventional thing to do. The next morning we went to look at the house—Number 12842 on the corner of Sunset and Bristol Avenue. It had four master bedrooms, a sleeping porch, a big living room, a study, dining room, kitchen, two servants' rooms, large grounds and no charm at all. But John liked it and I said it was all right with me. We moved in that afternoon and that evening John appeared with a Chinese cook he had hired in Chinatown. I was too innocent to realize that a Chinaman might spell trouble for us. The next day I hired a maid by the name of Daisy. Considering the song "Daisy, You're Driving Me Crazy," I was not sure whether her name was a good omen or not.

One day when I was at the studio the story editor warned me not to break my neck trying to finish the scenario quickly. "Take your time," said he. "Since you're being paid by the week, get as many weeks pay out of it as possible. I don't think the studio has the slightest idea of filming your story anyway."

I was horrified by this remark and asked him what he meant. "Well you see, the studio just wants to keep Pola quiet by letting her believe they have another story for her after the one she's shooting. But in my opinion they won't take up her option."

"You mean that after I do all the work on *East River* they won't shoot it?"

"Why should you care? You'll get your money anyway."

I was dismayed. "But I *do* care. Of course I want the money but that isn't *all* I'm working for. I want to do a good job and I want to get credit for it."

This brought a big laugh. "You'll get over all that when you've worked a while in a studio. Hollywood is stronger than any writer. It can always break a writer down. You're green and enthusiastic. Take my advice and don't fight Hollywood, and by 'Hollywood' I mean the studios. Just take it easy and make as much money as you can. Forget about good work. That's only a dream here. I like you, so I am giving you rare advice. I can see you are the artistic type but take a tip from me and forget about art—especially art with a large A." (This was, of course, before the Screen Writers' Guild was formed and when writers had no rights.)

I went home and wept. John came into my room and found me crying. "Hollywood is not going to break *me* down," I boasted through my tears.

I had telephoned Greta at Metro-Goldwyn-Mayer to give her my new number, and she had promised to call me when the shooting on *Susan Lennox* was over. The following Sunday she rang up to ask me again to her house in the late afternoon. "My present prison term is over," she said. "I have finished shooting." Her voice sounded light and relieved.

It had been a very hot day and that evening it was still extremely warm even for the month of July. She was again waiting for me in the driveway, but this time she led me to the door. She paused a minute before speaking as though to give her words importance, then with a pretense of pomp, as if a ruler were conferring an honor upon a subject, she said, "I never invite anyone to my house but today, as a great exception, I am inviting you. Will you come in?"

We entered directly into the living room. It seemed gloomy and unlived in. Greta caught my thought. "I never use this room. I live in my bedroom," she said, and we went on upstairs. It was a simple and rather empty room. It had a bed, a desk, a dressing table and a few uncomfortable straight-backed chairs, all in heavy oak. There was not a single personal thing in it. Greta moved toward the window. She pointed to a slim, leafless, dead tree. "This tree is my one joy in Hollywood. I call it 'my winter tree.' When my loneliness for Sweden gets unbearable I look at it and it comforts me. I imagine that the cold has made it leafless and that soon there will be snow on its branches." She turned sadly from the window. "I have never told anyone before about this tree."

She looked at me and saw there were tears in my eyes. "Oh, I have made you cry," she said.

"Yes, that is such a sad story," I answered. "Tell me about your childhood—about your life."

She hesitated, then quietly in her low, rich voice, sometimes pausing, as though she were groping her way, she began to speak. She told me in snatches, stopping and then continuing, many little things about her childhood, seemingly unimportant things. Yet each revealed much to me. She spoke of her dreams, of many things she had done and had wished to do. She spoke with great love of her sister who was dead and said she had been very beautiful. Her name was Alva. This gave me a great surprise.

"It is the same as my mother's family name—de Alba—but the *v* is a *b* in Spanish. And Garbo is a Spanish word. It means chic or stylish."

The room grew dark. We sat silently. After a little she said, "I have never spoken like this before." She rose. "I'm hungry. Let's go down to the kitchen and eat something—no, I'll bring it here because Whistler may be home soon."

She ran downstairs and returned with a tray of cheese, milk, and bread. The moon came up and shone into the room. We ate the food by its light. When we had finished I said, "Let's go out to the beach."

We went out and found the "bus," as Greta called her old black Packard limousine. It was sedate and conventional. "Every inch a car Queen Mary would drive in," I said.

I drove and Greta sat beside me. "A perfect footman," I said to her. We started off gaily toward the beach, following the coast to Casa del Mare where we parked the car and walked up the mountain until we reached the top and looked out over the coast. The sea had a silver gloss in the moonlight and back in the trees, nightingales sang.

"What do you believe about God?" Greta asked.

"I wish there were no such word. How can anyone express God by using a word like *God*? I just think of God as all creation. Everything is God on its own level. Those nightingales singing are God. If God is God, then there can be no separation between any of his creatures. And by 'creatures' I mean trees, rocks, animals, insects, as well as people. Perhaps I am right or wrong. I don't know."

We talked of other things, profound and trivial. Then finally, as the moon sank and disappeared and a tiny streak of light fell across the sky in the east, we were silent. Slowly the dawn came. As the sun rose we walked down the mountain and picked rambler roses as we went along. At the bottom there was the beloved "bus" waiting. It seemed like something alive—faithful and patient. We got in it and drove away.

Thirty-Four

That evening Greta telephoned to ask me to come to see her early the next morning. She said she had something to tell me.

About eight o'clock I went to her house and found her car with James in it in the driveway. James was her Negro chauffeur and he was a character if ever there was one. He had originally come to Greta as a window cleaner, and finding him very quiet, she asked him to become her chauffeur. Of course he was delighted and started in that very day, working faithfully for her for many years. As the Hollywood saying goes, he was "dumb like a fox." He was tall and very thin and he looked at you slyly out of the corner of his eye. He never made the slightest comment about anything and he never moved faster than a snail. Besides chauffeuring, he was also supposed to clean the house. This he would do in slow motion, taking at least half an hour to polish one doorknob, and when Greta would say to him, "James, you are very lazy," far from disagreeing with her he would answer, "Yes, ma'am" in a soft drawling voice.

I would say to Greta in front of him, "You know, James has charm, so you can't expect much of anything else." This made him roar with laughter. He never drove faster than twenty miles an hour. Luckily Greta liked this pace. When we got in the car he never asked where we were going. He would start off in a straight line and follow it indefinitely unless we told him otherwise. Greta would say to me in an undertone, "Let's just see how long he will drive without asking where we are going." Finally, as we were about to drive into the ocean or up some mountain, she would say, "James, do you know where we are going?" "No, ma'am," he would answer. He had one unfortunate weakness and this was that he did not know his right hand from his left. If we said, "James, drive right," he usually turned left. But if we tried to even things off by saying left when we meant right, or right when we meant left, he still went in the opposite direction.

By this time I had had my own car sent out from New York. It was a roadster with a rumble seat. When I drove it up Greta's drive that day and saw James' slantwise look, I knew something was up.

She came out of the house and called me in. I followed her upstairs to her room. She looked white and tired. "I asked you to come," she said, "so that I could tell you I am going away today for six weeks."

"Six weeks? What for?" I asked.

"I am terribly tired. I must go away and be utterly alone. I have taken a little house on an island in a lake in the Sierra Nevadas. No one will know where I am and no one can reach me. I am only telling you because I know you would wonder where I was. I ask you not to tell anyone where I have gone or even to say I have gone," she said.

We went down the stairs together and stood silently on the driveway while Whistler put the last things in the car. She took my hand and said, "Forgive me. I am just so terribly tired." She put on her dark glasses and got into the car. James backed it down the drive and then I saw it turn and drive away. I stood there so long that Whistler, who was like a kindly mother, came out of the house and asked me if I would like a cup of coffee. When I shook my head, she said, "Don't worry. She will be back sooner than you think." I did not believe her and I got into my own car and drove back to my house.

Ironically enough, when I got home I found a message to call the story editor at my studio. He informed me that the studio was not going to follow Pola's present picture with a second one and that in all probability they would shelve *East River*. He said the studio would keep me on the payroll for the present, or in any case, until my contract expired, but that I did not need to do any further work on the scenario.

This news just about sank me. Fortunately, Ivor came for me that night and distracted me by taking me to dine with Joan Crawford and young Douglas Fairbanks, to whom she was married at this time.

We were just four at dinner and I was amused to see place cards at the table for so few people. Joan was charming and very much the hostess. I liked her and found her forthright and easy to get on with.

Two nights later the telephone rang. Greta's voice said, "I am on the way back. I have been to the island but I am returning for you. I am about three hundred miles away and I am motoring steadily, so I will get to your house sometime late this afternoon. Can you come to the island?"

I was so excited that I jumped up and thought, I must begin to pack. Pack what? What would I need on an island in the Sierra Nevadas? I decided practically nothing but slacks, sweaters, shorts and a bathing suit. Early in the morning I woke John up and told him that Greta was coming for me. Darling John was almost as excited as I was. He said we must have some delicious food and champagne ready for her and he fussed in the kitchen all day.

Toward midnight of the following evening the big black limousine came slowly up the drive. Then I heard James blowing the horn and I rushed out of the house. Wearily Greta stepped out of the car. They had motored for three days without stopping except for food. The heat crossing the Mojave desert had been 120°. James was "all in" too, but when I praised his driving he just said "Yes, ma'am," and I knew he was still himself.

John came out and we took Greta into the house. Then he opened the dining room door and there was a feast of roast chicken and delicate Chinese dishes. Before Greta had even washed her face we drank one another's health in champagne, and revived James with a few glasses. Greta said that the scenery and lake were beautiful beyond words. "I had to come back for you because I could not be such a pig as to enjoy all that beauty alone," she said.

We started off late that afternoon in my car, Greta and I in the rumble seat and James driving. Greta asked him if he was too tired to go that day and when he answered "No, ma'am," we knew that all was well. We planned to cross the desert at night to avoid the heat as much as possible. We were heading for Nevada which lay the other side of the Mojave desert but when we reached the desert the temperature had gone up to nearly 140°. The hot wind and blowing sand cut into our faces and each time we stopped to refuel the car, we smeared them with oil.

But we were very happy. Even James seemed gay and happy, and once he actually knew his right hand from his left when we gave him directions. We stopped two nights at small hotels along the road, once on the desert and once beyond it. The third day we saw the Sierra Nevadas and began to climb. The air cooled near the top and then the whole magnificent range stretched before us.

Suddenly from a great height we looked down and saw Silver Lake in the distance between two mountain peaks. Greta grew very excited. "There is our lake and there, that little island in the center, is our island!" We began to descend and as we drew nearer we could see the little house on the island. It was really only a shack but we were as thrilled about it as though it were a castle. It belonged to Wallace Beery and he had said Greta could have it for these weeks and had given her the keys.

The lake was about fourteen miles long and three miles wide and the island was about half a mile out from the west shore. We stopped at a small boathouse where James helped us carry the provisions on the boat, then Greta sent him off, telling him not to come back until the last second of six weeks. "If you turn up one second earlier I will throw you into the lake. And mind you, absolutely *no one* is to know where we are. Not even Whistler, and certainly *not* Louis B. Mayer!"

"No, ma'am," James answered solemnly and climbed into the car to begin the long trek back to Hollywood at twenty miles an hour. We clambered into the boat and Greta took up the oars.

I was amazed to see how well she rowed. Her stroke was quite superb. "Have you been training with the Oxford crew?" I asked. She rowed steadily and smoothly into the shadow of the mountain which lay reflected on the water. The sun had dropped behind it, although it was not yet five o'clock, and its reflection glowed on the mountains to the east, many of which were still covered with snow.

With Greta's steady stroke we soon reached our island.

All around us, like peaks of a crown, stood the snow-covered mountains. Majestic and serene they stood, making us feel like the merest specks in the Divine Cosmos. With the exception of the water lapping against the pier there was an intense silence. Then far away on the farthest shore we heard the cry of an owl. Greta paused and listened. Knowing how superstitious Scandinavians are, I said, "There can be no bad luck up here. That owl is merely politely welcoming us." She looked relieved and the incident passed.

How to describe the next six enchanted weeks? Even recapturing them in memory makes me realize how lucky I am to have had them. Six perfect weeks out of a lifetime. This is indeed much. In all this time there was not a second of disharmony between Greta and me or in nature around us. Not once did it rain and we had brilliant sunshine every day. We saw a new moon and watched it grow to fullness, making the mountains and the water shine like silver and the snow on the far-off peaks glisten like polished crystal.

The little house could not have been simpler. It was only a log cabin but neat and clean with windows all around it.

Greta said, "We must be baptized at once." Throwing off her clothes she made a magnificent dive into the water and followed it with the long, powerful strokes of an expert swimmer. "First I find you training for the Oxford crew and now I find you training for a swim across the Channel. Isn't there anything you do badly?" I called out to her. She waved her hand from far out in the lake and I heard her happy laugh across the water. I plunged in myself—no expert dive, no cross-channel stroke. The water was icy cold and I had to keep going or freeze. Greta swam beside me. "I never knew Spaniards could stand cold water—bravo," she said.

That evening she cooked dinner. Along the way we had bought mountain trout. She poached it and made the wonderful strong coffee that Spaniards and Swedes like to drink. "None of this American coffee, just hot-water business," she said, adding proudly, "I make *good* coffee." And indeed she did. Once again within a few hours she hit the bull's-eye and surprised me.

The days and hours flew past far too quickly. They did more than that. They evaporated. There was no sense of time at all.

It is generally accepted that Greta is morose and serious. This is one of the things said of her in the legend that has been built up around her. All legends are built on rumors and hearsay. Of course she is serious if there is something to be serious about and she does not run around with a broad grin on her face like most American executives, but that does not mean that she is morose and lacks humor. As a matter of fact she has *real* humor and a remarkable sense of it. During those six weeks in Silver Lake, as well as many times since, she has shown her sense of fun to me.

Metro-Goldwyn-Mayer employed her from 1925 to 1938 before they discovered she could play comedy, and upon this discovery they cast her with great success in *Ninotchka*. But Greta can play more than just comedy. She can play high comedy and low comedy and she can play the clown when she wishes. It is a sad commentary on the stupidity of the studio that they did not discover this until it was too late. It is a pity that all those years Greta was cast always in tragic parts. Had they given her happy and fun-making roles, she might still be in pictures. Who can stand forever playing tortured, depressed, sad roles? Certainly not a sensitive artist like Greta who does not play her roles but who, I believe, *becomes* them and actually *lives* every second of them.

There on Silver Lake I laughed more than ever before in my life and it was Greta who made me laugh. She told me amusing stories of her childhood, of her adolescence, and of her life in Hollywood.

No one can really know Greta unless they have seen her as I saw her there in Silver Lake. She is a creature of the elements. A creature of wind and storms and rocks and trees and water. A spirit such as hers cooped up in a city is a tragic sight.

There in the Sierra Nevadas she used to climb ahead of me, and with her hair blown back, her face turned to the wind and sun, she would leap from rock to rock on her bare Hellenic feet. I would see her above me, her face and body outlined against the sky, looking like some radiant, elemental, glorious god and goddess melted into one.

Often she rowed me across the lake to a lumber camp a few miles away. Here we bought milk and eggs and talked to the lumbermen, who thought we were schoolgirls on a holiday. And at night in a fantastic silence and with dark mountains towering around us we would go out in the boat and just drift.

To write of Greta and these things connected with her is the most difficult task I have had in this book. No one knows better than I how much she dislikes being discussed but I cannot write my life and leave her out of it. I have deeply considered and weighed the problem and it has caused me untold anguish and anxiety, but I came to believe that, in spite of this I must, nevertheless, write the book and stand by myself in so doing. No one can write an autobiography without bringing back on the stage of her life people who have played major roles in it. And so Greta must also, like other people I have written about, play her role in this book as I, too, must play my role in writing it.

Somehow, six weeks that seemed only six minutes wound itself round and came to an end. We had forgotten time and date. We had almost come to believe that we would never return to civilization. Then one day across the lake we heard James' horn. Greta turned deadly white and fled into the house. "I can't—I *can't* go back to Hollywood and that studio life!" she cried.

But we packed our things and, without a word between us, got into the boat. Slowly, and as though a great sadness had befallen her, she rowed to the other shore.

Thirty-Five

Soon after this, Greta moved from San Vincente Boulevard to North Rockingham Road in Brentwood. I encouraged her to move as I thought the San Vincente house far too gloomy for her. The new one was only half a block from John's and mine. It was a large house with a lovely garden and a fine view overlooking the Canyon and the hills. Greta also had a tennis court at her new place, which we found very pleasant. I played quite a good game at this time but she always managed to beat me in the end. She had a natural talent for any kind of sport. At this period we used to ride. We hired horses from the Bel Air Riding School and rode into the hills. She had never ridden before she came to Hollywood, but she sat her horse as if she had ridden all her life.

Greta had not yet started shooting on her next picture, *Mata Hari,* which was in preparation, so neither of us was working and we used to exercise so much that looking back on it now, I wonder why we didn't kill ourselves—especially as I weighed under a hundred pounds and Greta was as slim as a pin. The end of Rockingham Road went right into the hills. Over them through wild country to the San Fernando Valley was over ten miles. Several times we walked this distance and James would meet us with the car at the other side in the Valley. We thought very little of such a walk and most days we did at least six or seven miles, played several sets of tennis, swam in the sea and sometimes rode. Our day started very often at five or five-thirty in the morning and never later than six. Greta would come down to my house a little while after the sun was up and whistle under my window. I would dash into my clothes and we would be off over the hills. Sometimes we took picnic lunches and spent the whole day on the beach far up toward Malibu. We went to bed very early. When Greta was shooting she went to bed at seven, otherwise about eight, or nine. I never went to bed much later than nine. We used to laugh when we read and heard about the so-called "night life" of Hollywood.

Greta often came to our house and she used to sing "Daisy, You're Driving Me Crazy" to our maid. John adored her and was forever asking her to dinner and making her little specialties. She ate corn on the cob for the first time in our house. She loved my Bambina and at this time I had another little dog—a tiny white Maltese puppy some horrible people had thrown out of their car onto my lawn as they passed. When I picked her up I found she had a hernia and took her to the veterinary to be operated on. Greta came with me and after the operation we tenderly carried her home. I wanted Greta to take her and she did for several days, but in the end Chotzie came back to me. Curiously, Greta has little talent with animals and very little understanding of them.

In the meantime things were not going so well in my house. John had begun inviting in people whom I did not like. I would come home and find speak-easy proprietors and various underworld characters sitting around and I felt the house was not safe and that I had no privacy in it. I told Greta not to come there any longer and I decided to move, but I didn't want to hurt John's feelings. He was a kind and gentle person and I would not have wounded him for anything in the world. He was a writer of great talent, as *Rain* and *The Shanghai Gesture* proved, but I soon discovered that he simply could not resist strange underworld characters. He was a man full of humor, intelligence, and charm. Everyone loved him and he could have had any friends he wanted, and yet he told me he was not interested in anything but an underworld life.

Fortunately, I had already looked at a house for rent on Rockingham Road next to Greta's. I telephoned the agent and said I wanted to move into it at once. By one o'clock I had packed and moved in. I left John with Daisy, the Chinese cook, and several cowboy friends, so I knew he was in sympathetic hands.

When I had known Greta a little while I got her to exchange her sailor pants for slacks. Looking back it seems difficult to believe that at this time people were still shocked to see women in trousers. Once we were photographed in them on Hollywood Boulevard without our knowing it. The photograph came out in the newspaper with the caption under it: GARBO IN PANTS! *Innocent bystanders gasped in amazement to see Mercedes de Acosta and Greta Garbo striding swiftly along Hollywood Boulevard dressed in men's clothes.* Considering what walks down Hollywood Boulevard now, it seems strange that Greta and I should have caused a sensation such a comparatively short time ago.

The day after I moved into the house I engaged two maids. One was a Swiss girl by the name of Rose Fleury, and the other a German girl named Anna Nehler. Anna remained with me all the time I lived in California. She was a faithful friend and played an important part in my life out there.

My contract at the studio was terminated. They paid me for ten weeks, but this was not all I wanted. I was extremely disillusioned with the whole assignment. The story editor had been right. The studio did not take up Pola's option. She had given a fine performance in *A Woman Commands* but the studio had other plans. They shelved *East River* because they said there was no other star in the studio who could play it. Not a thought was given to the creative work a writer put into a script. The attitude was: "They have been paid. Why should they kick?"

I was very depressed about it. Now that I was no longer working, what excuse did I have to remain in Hollywood? John advised me to get myself an agent and another contract with a different studio. I turned the possibilities over in my mind. Greta was not working yet on her new film and as we saw each other every day, I was kept busy.

Christmas of that year was very warm. Greta closed all the curtains so that we could have candlelight and pretend it was snowing outside. Anna cooked us a goose and we sat on the floor around the tree and opened our presents. Among other things Greta gave me a raincoat, rubber boots, and sou'wester hat. She said the rains would soon come. They did. Shortly after Christmas it began to pour in such torrents that the drops seemed like eggs. We would put on our raincoats, hats and boots, and make for the hills. Sometimes terrific thunderstorms came up and we would rush out to the highest peak overlooking the sea to watch the lightning break through the sky like great cracks of fire, and hear the thunder crashing down on us. We were always happy and stimulated in a storm.

Thirty-Six

Right after Christmas, Greta began shooting *Mata Hari*. She had been having fittings with Adrian and had taken me to Adrian's house to meet him. I found him extremely sympathetic and I liked his looks. He was tall and slender and looked like an Arab. He was living on Whitley Heights and his house seemed more like a stage set than a residence. It was a Spanish house with oval doors and all sorts of balconies which made it seem romantic and theatrical, but I felt it was as unreal as cardboard. I was not far from wrong about this because one evening a large stone rolled down the mountain, broke through the wall of the house, and calmly sat itself down in the living room with the other guests. This was the kind of thing which could only happen in Hollywood.

The evening I met Adrian we had a lot of fun. We had a delicious dinner in the patio and then he showed me his sketches for Greta's clothes. I suggested that she wear a long black cape for the scene at the end when she is shot, and that she should brush her hair absolutely straight back. This would give a dramatic effect for the ending. Adrian agreed with me and was delighted with the suggestion. It was a balmy night and Greta and I drove home about midnight. She said she did not want to drive fast so just to tease her I drove about two miles an hour. As we went along we laughed a great deal and she got out of the car several times and picked flowers along the roadside.

One day she came straight from the studio to my house very much excited. After trying to make me guess what she had up her sleeve, she finally told me that she had talked to Irving Thalberg about my writing a story for her. She said he wanted to see me the next morning and that if I could think of an idea he would surely put me under contract. All that night I tossed around in bed trying to invent a story that would be right for her. Toward morning I hit on an idea and a title, which was *Desperate*. It was a romantic story in which she played rather a wild character, somewhat like Iris March in the *Green Hat*. Also in this story there was a sequence in which the character had to make an escape in disguise. I had her make this escape dressed as a boy. Greta was delighted with the outline and a few hours later I went to the studio to see Thalberg, whom I had already met at the Selznicks.

Irving Thalberg was young, a small, delicate, and attractive-looking man who wore his clothes neatly and with style. He was quite rightly considered the sole genius in motion pictures and, indeed there never has been one like him since. I was told in Hollywood that he considered himself the Napoleon of the film world. One did not have to be long in his presence to realize this was true.

At our first meeting he came to the door of his office and greeted me cordially. It was the first and last time he ever met me at his door. He then went and sat in a large chair behind a large desk, which was elevated on a platform. On it were a number of telephones and several instruments into which he could speak and be heard on the various stages and sets throughout the studio. His office was large and to approach the desk one had to walk a considerable distance. In front of it were several extremely low and soft armchairs. Anyone sitting in them at once sank down and could get up again only with the greatest difficulty. Mr. Thalberg could look down from his elevated height on these victims—a trick Mussolini also employed as one of his milder forms of intimidation.

This day I made my first mistake with Thalberg. I set my will against his. Instead of sinking into my chair and allowing him to play the Emperor, I sat straight and as high up on the arm of it as I could, bringing myself almost on a level with him. After a while he said, "Why don't you sit properly in the chair and be comfortable?"

I answered, "I'm quite comfortable this way, thank you."

What a mistake! For on an unseen level I had started up a resistance between us which lasted all the time I worked with him, right up until his death. Yet he listened to the outline of my story and, with very little comment, agreed to put me under contract. He spoke on one of the telephones and told the editorial office I was hired. Then he told me to come back and see him with the first sequence in about two weeks. I went away liking him in spite of the fact that his Napoleonic airs seemed childish.

I was given an office at the studio and started writing there. At five o'clock Greta would meet me outside the studio, and we would go to the beach or walk in the hills. Sometimes during these walks she would discuss various scenes she had shot during the day or intended to shoot the next day, or some problem presented by the picture. More often she was silent, either out of sheer physical fatigue or because she had gone into her inner self and was brooding over her part and spiritually working out some situation she had to act.

I observed Greta during the making of all her talking films with the exception of *Anna Christie,* and I noticed that she never *mentally* worked on a film. Unlike other actresses, she did not work on the script or plan ahead what she intended to do in a scene. I think it would be more correct to employ a word I used before and to say she *brooded* on the part or on a scene or particular situation that she had to play. She never thoroughly read a script before the first day of shooting, when she went onto the set and became the part. She used only to scan through the manuscript, yet she knew intuitively the essential meaning of the story. I had a feeling during these times that had she read and studied the manuscript thoroughly, she would actually have lost its vital meaning. Like Duse, in a manner of speaking, she is vibrantly intuitive. Greta was practically never directed in a scene. She would go on the set and, knowing the character she was to play, she would simply and completely *become* that character. She would not act or play at being this character, she would *be it*. Like Duse, she could make the character come alive and *live* before your very eyes.

A thing very few people outside of the studio knew about her is that at no time did she ever go to see her rushes. I think she knew that had she seen herself on the screen she would have broken some dream quality she had created within her own psyche. She never went to previews of her pictures either, and it was only years after their making that she saw them. When she did they caused her great suffering and she always felt she could have done much better. I think all artists feel this way when they see their finished work. Happily for the stage actor, he cannot do this.

I went often at this time to see Thalberg to consult him about *Desperate* and show him various sequences as I wrote them. When I came to the one where Greta was supposed to dress like a boy, he put his foot down and said she absolutely could not wear men's clothes on the screen. "Do you want to put all America and all the women's clubs against her? You must be out of your mind." When I said that Greta knew all about this sequence and wanted it in the script, he said, "She must be out of her mind, too. I simply *won't* have that sequence in. I am in this business to make money on films and I won't have this one ruined." I could do nothing with him and the sequence came out.

This threw out the whole structure of the story. I was very disheartened. What was more, Irving was angry with me and thought me a fool. He told me in no uncertain terms, "We have been building Garbo up for years as a great glamorous actress, and now you come along and try to put her into pants and make a monkey out of her." I tried to make him see that he had missed the whole idea, but he simply slammed down the manuscript and refused to discuss it. He said, "The story is out." I went home feeling miserable.

Greta had a bright idea. She said she would like to play *Dorian Grey* and have me write the scenario. I said, "You go and tell Irving that idea and have him throw *you* out the window—not me!" But she was right. At that time she could have played this role brilliantly.

I was disheartened, but in a strange way Hollywood with all its trials led me toward a spiritual life. I began at this time to fast and meditate. Sometimes I fasted five days and nights at a time and went off for hours up into the hills alone to meditate. Greta used to call me "a crazy mystic Spaniard," but she was always sympathetic with me when I told her I was fasting. She is rather a crazy mystic Swede herself.

Thirty-Seven

When Greta played *Grand Hotel,* Jack Barrymore was her leading man. In all the world I do not think two more beautiful people could have been found to team together. In coloring they were a contrast but in beauty they were equal. I was of course very excited about Greta playing this picture.

Since my arrival in Hollywood I had not seen Jack. I did not even know whether he was aware that I was there. In any case he had made no effort to get in touch with me and I, following our old pattern, did nothing to get in touch with him. Then one night I was in bed reading. I heard a car stop outside my house and then a pebble was thrown against the screen on my window. I looked out and there was Jack. He was full of tales about *Grand Hotel.* He said that he had a great reverence for Greta but he was frightened to death of her. "Not because she is difficult—far from it. But just because she is so perfect as an artist and as a woman," he said, adding at the same time, "Why has no one ever said that she has such a sense of humor? Do you know, she is always telling me some funny joke on the set and she sees little things to laugh at. Little things most people wouldn't notice. She's really most amusing."

Jack brought up the old days and asked me if I had seen Michael, from whom he was now divorced. "How topsy-turvy life can be," he said. "I never thought that you and I would land out here in Hollywood."

When he left he said, "Please don't tell Garbo while we're shooting that I come to see you. It might make her self-conscious with me." I answered, "I never tell anyone that you come to see me, so you don't need to worry."

At this time I had no assignment. Greta suggested I go to see her agent, Harry Edington, who at once got me a contract at Paramount Studios to do the shooting scripts on two screen plays. I went over to the new lot that week but I did not like it nearly as much as Metro-Goldwyn-Mayer. Difficult as Thalberg could be, it was a let-down to work for anyone else.

Shortly after Greta finished *Grand Hotel* I had a strange dream. I dreamed that she came to me in great distress and told me that the bank in which she kept her money had failed. I ran up to the attic and found an old black bag and went with Greta to her bank. The door was closed and a policeman was standing in front of it. We managed to evade him and ran into the bank where we filled the black bag with papers out of a tin box. At this point I woke up. The dream disturbed me. I told Greta about it and asked her if she did not think it advisable to take her money out of the small bank in Beverly Hills where I knew she kept it. At this time many banks all over the country were failing.

But she would not listen to me. She said she was sure her bank was safe. I even had the same dream twice, but she waved the significance of it aside. In fact, she paid no attention to me when I mentioned it again. Within the week the bank actually did fail and the strange part of it was that everything happened more or less as I had seen it in my dream. Greta came to me early in the morning to tell me that Harry Edington had called her to say her bank had failed and would not open its doors that day. She was trembling when she told me the news, but she was remarkably calm. She asked me what I thought she should do. I called a friend of mine, a president of a bank in New York, and asked his advice. He told me to take Greta to the bank at once with a bag and try to save any securities. As in the dream I ran up to the attic and found a black bag and with it Greta and I motored to the bank. A policeman tried to stop us but we managed to evade him and somehow got in. We went down to the safe deposit vaults where Greta was recognized and allowed to open her box. She took out whatever papers were there and put them into the black bag and we left the bank together.

During this time Greta behaved marvelously and showed the greatest courage and calm. She told me that every cent of money she had earned since her arrival in America was in this bank. She said regretfully but not bitterly, "I'm afraid I am wiped out. Today I have not a cent in the world."

The situation was serious, because her contract was about to be renewed. If Metro-Goldwyn-Mayer knew the position she was in, it was quite possible they would reduce their offer, knowing full well that being pressed for money she would have to accept the reduction. It was important that whatever she did she should do quietly and with absolutely no publicity. The lease for her house had nearly terminated. She could not afford to renew it at a thousand dollars a month. Where could she live? I suggested that she move into my house, the rent of which was less and which I had already paid several months in advance. But the main reason for her move to my house was to conceal the fact that she had moved at all. There was a problem, however, if she moved. Where was I to go? My house was not big enough for Greta, Whistler, Rose, Anna and myself. I did not have the slightest idea where I would find one but I relied on an inner guidance which, in times of crisis, rarely failed me.

I walked down the road and rang the bell at a house that Greta and I had often passed on our walks. A woman opened the door and it turned out to be Cornelia Runyon, an artist and a woman of sensitivity, whom I knew slightly. I explained to her that I was looking for a house to move into at once, and without asking her whether she wished to rent her house or not, I plunged into a long discourse on the importance of her moving out that same day and letting me move in. Poor Cornelia was of course quite speechless at this onslaught. She told me later that she had had no intention of renting her house but I had looked so strange and determined that she felt I must have some deep mystic reason for wanting it so much. In spite of herself, she agreed to give it to me. Almost before she was aware of what was happening she moved that same night into a little apartment over the garage and I moved into her house. The following day Greta moved into mine, but she said she was nervous because it had no gates. She was afraid to sleep in a house that could not be closed off by gates. I told her not to worry and I promised her she would wake up in the morning and find gates.

That same evening I went to a carpenter and said I would give him any amount of money if he would build gates for me overnight. He said he would be quite willing to do so but as it was Saturday he could not get the wood. I told him to take me to a lumber yard I knew in San Fernando Valley. We broke in a window, and entering the shop, carried out the necessary wood. I left a note saying I would pay for the broken window and for the wood on Monday. The carpenter worked all that night and when the gates were finished early in the morning, we painted them white.

Not long after this, when my contract had terminated at Paramount, Thalberg rang me early one morning on the telephone. It was unusual for him to call a writer himself and I knew it must be something important. He was extremely nice and said that he intended to film the life of Rasputin and was going to put me on the story. He asked me to come to the studio that day to sign a new contract. Later, when I went to his office, he asked me to prepare a detailed history of the life of the famous monk. He said he was only vaguely familiar with Rasputin's death and the historical events leading up to it and cautioned me to write a very clear and detailed story. It amounted actually to writing an historical biography of Rasputin before I began a scenario or even a mere working script. I was very excited about the whole assignment, especially as I already knew a good deal about the subject.

While in Paris some years previously I had met Prince Yusupov at Agoutinsky's one evening, and late into the night Yusupov had told us the tale of Rasputin's murder and a great deal about his life. Yusupov had been one of the leaders who had laid the trap, and in fact he himself had assisted in the actual killing. It was not a pretty story, no matter how you looked at it, but I was glad to hear the truth of it from someone who had witnessed the whole bloody affair.

I asked for details about the relationship between the Czarina and Rasputin, and how Rasputin had looked, how he had spoken, and what impression his personality made on people. Among other things I asked if his wife, who was a daughter of Grand Duke Alexander, had ever met Rasputin. He said she had not, adding that she had never even seen him and that he had taken good care that she should not, although Rasputin had wanted very much to meet her. I remembered this particular point very clearly. In fact Yusupov had given me a very vivid firsthand picture of the whole amazing story and it had made a great impression on me.

Feeling, however, that Yusupov's detailed account had been related in confidence I did not at first tell Irving about it. In fact I did not tell him I knew anything much about Rasputin at all. He expected that any knowledge I gave him on the subject would come from books. At the beginning of my assignment I let him think this.

Katharine Cornell came to Los Angeles at this time on tour with *The Barretts of Wimpole Street*. One morning Greta and I were taking a sunbath on a balcony in my house which led out from the study. We heard the doorbell ring and with that startled fawn look Greta can assume when anyone appears, she said in a frightened voice, *"Who is that?"*

"Probably a mistake—someone ringing the wrong doorbell," I answered. Anna appeared and in a hushed whisper called me into the room. "Miss Katharine Cornell is downstairs," she said, looking as terrified as a trapped white mouse. Greta called out, "What is that? Who is downstairs?" scrambling at the same time to her feet.

"It's Kit Cornell come to call on me," I told her. "You can stay here but I must go down and see her. She is an old friend of mine, you know, and I want to see her."

"Please tell Anna to send her away," Greta said.

"Don't be foolish. I wouldn't dream of being rude to Kit. You would like her yourself if you knew her. If you don't want to meet her, stay here in the sun." I pulled on a sweater and slacks and ran downstairs.

Kit explained that she was on her way to the beach and decided to drop in to see me.

"I hope I am not disturbing you," she said. I tried to appear as though she were not and asked her to sit down. She sensed that I was not myself and rather uncomfortably she remarked, "I'll only stay a minute." Then, as if a bright idea occurred to her which she believed would please me, she said, "I know you are a friend of Garbo's. I understand she lives near you. Could you take me to see her? Like all the world, I long to meet her."

"I'm afraid I can't take you to see her. She is not home," I said.

"Oh," said Kit, with a note of unbelief in her voice. At that very moment we heard a thud over our heads like a weight falling on the floor. I said nervously, "It's nothing. Don't be alarmed." The words were just out of my mouth when we heard someone coming slowly down the stairs, descending like a child, one step at a time. Kit looked inquiringly at me. And then Greta, completely dressed and with her hair neatly brushed, leaned over the bannister and in the sweetest, most beguilingly low tone, said, "Hello, may I join you?"

I tried my best not to appear as though I had pulled a rabbit out of a hat. Kit, with an air of saying "This is the moment I have waited for all my life," bent low over Greta's hand and shook it warmly.

I heaved an inward sigh of relief and said, "Please sit down." Then I bolted for the pantry to fetch some brandy. Pouring a large drink for all three of us, I said, "I know this is not vodka but you must drink bottoms-up just the same." We tossed it down in one gulp. The tension immediately eased. From that minute on we all proceeded to have a very good time. Greta gave the impression that she had always been longing to meet Kit and Kit was so obviously happy at meeting Greta that she looked like a real kit who had swallowed a canary. Only I appeared a little in the wrong, but after a second round of brandy no one cared very much who was right or who was wrong.

In the meantime Greta had done a film called *As You Desire Me,* taken from a play by Pirandello. Of all the roles she ever played this, in my opinion, was her finest. It is curious that it has been her least discussed picture and many people do not even know of it. In one scene of this film she is intoxicated. Never was a scene more superbly played. It is rare for an actress to play an intoxicated scene without appearing either vulgar or absurd. She was neither of these, but instead, gave a sense of being lost, like a person taking the wrong turning of a road and trying to grope her way back onto the right one.

Greta played this scene for me before acting it in front of the camera. She told me she was worried about giving it a sense of reality. She asked if she could rehearse it for me and suddenly, right there in my room, she became the character of the play and as suddenly too, I felt the influence of drink taking over her whole personality. I became completely lost and absorbed in the character she was acting. All this without make-up, without props, and in a room with her audience not more than three feet away.

One afternoon while walking on the beach of Santa Monica, Greta and I passed the houses of many of the moving picture colony, including Marion Davies and William Randolph Hearst, Anita Loos, the Albert Lewins, Norma Shearer and Thalberg, her husband, Irene and David Selznick, and many others. Presently we passed another house and Greta said, "That's Ernst Lubitsch's house. He is the only great director out here. I would like you to meet him. Let's go and see him." Greta seldom expressed a wish to see anyone, so it made me feel that there must indeed be something special about Lubitsch. We opened the gate and went into his grounds. Greta leapt onto the porch and knocking on the window instead of ringing the bell, said, "Is anyone at home?" The front door was opened and a very attractive young woman looked out. "Ernst is in the kitchen making drinks. I'll call him for you. Won't you come in?" she asked. This was my first meeting with Ona Munson and led to many years of friendship between us until her tragic death some years later.

When Lubitsch entered the living room and saw Greta he let out a great yell of joy. He was a small man with dark hair brushed down straight over his brow. He had a large black cigar in his mouth and one felt at once that he was a man of enormous energy. He spoke English with a terribly strong Jewish-German accent. *"Mein Gott, mein Gott, Greta!"* he cried as he seized her in his arms and kissed her wildly. *"Gott, such a surprise,"* he shouted. "Greta, Greta, sit down and never go avay." He pushed her onto the sofa and sat beside her holding her hand.

Ona said to me, "I have wanted to meet you for a long time. I have heard a lot about you from Alla Nazimova." I remembered then that I had seen her give a beautiful performance with Alla in *Ghosts*. She was very small and slight with blond hair. I thought her extremely pretty but the thing that impressed me most were her eyes. They were very sad, and there was something about them that touched me deeply.

Lubitsch said, "Greta, why don't you tell those idiots in your studio to let us do a picture together? *Gott*, how I vould love to direct a picture for you." Greta answered, "Ernst, you tell them. I am far too tired to have a conversation with any studio executive." She said this very sadly but for some reason we all laughed. Lubitsch shook his head. "What fools they are. How vonderful Greta and I vould be together. Ve vould make a vonderful picture," he said. Greta sighed and rose. "We must go now. It's after six and nearly my bedtime." Lubitsch kissed her warmly once more and we left the house.

Not long after this Greta sailed home to Sweden. She went for a six-month holiday. After she left, Hollywood seemed empty to me.

Thirty-Eight

During this time Cecil Beaton came out to Hollywood and invited me to go with him one evening to see the famous German dancer, Harold Kreutzberg.

As we took our seats I noticed a striking woman directly in front of me. She turned and rather shyly looked at me. For a second I thought I knew her, then I realized I had seen her in two pictures—*The Blue Angel* and *Morocco*. It was Marlene Dietrich.

The following day as I was working on the script of *Rasputin* in my study I heard the doorbell ring. I listened and heard Anna speaking German to someone downstairs in the hall. A few seconds later she came into my room carrying a huge bunch of white roses in her arms and very much excited. "Miss Marlene Dietrich is downstairs. She told me to give you these roses and she asked to see you if it would not disturb you."

"But I don't know Miss Dietrich. She must have mistaken the house. Perhaps she thinks she is calling on someone else," I answered.

"No, she spoke to me in German so I naturally understood her perfectly. There is no mistake. She said your name very clearly."

I took the roses and extremely mystified, told Anna to bring Marlene upstairs. As she entered she hesitated at the doorway and looked at me in the same shy way. I asked her to come into the room and put out my hand. She took it and in an almost military manner bent over it and

241

firmly shook it, saying at the same time, "I hope you will forgive me. I noticed you last night in the theatre and wanted to meet you. I know very few people here in Hollywood and no one who could introduce us, so I just found out where you live and I came myself. I don't want to stay and disturb you. I just wanted to bring you the flowers." I took her out on my sun porch and asked her to sit down. "It's very charming and informal of you to come and see me like this," I said. "I'm glad you did because it gives me a chance to tell you how much I liked you in both *The Blue Angel* and *Morocco.*"

"Oh, let's not talk about pictures. I would like to tell you something if you won't think I am mad. I would like to suggest something," she said. I encouraged her to talk and she continued. "You seem so thin and your face so white that it seems to me you are not well. Last evening when I looked at you I felt you were very sad. I am sad, too. I am sad and lonely. It is not easy to adjust oneself to a new country. You are the first person here to whom I have felt drawn. Unconventional as it may seem, I came to see you because I just could not help myself."

I broke in and said, "I appreciate your coming. It must have been difficult to ring a stranger's bell."

She answered, "No, it's funny, but it was not. It was only at first when I came up here, face to face with you, that I felt shy. But now somehow I feel at my ease. I feel, even, that I would like to tell you something that will make you laugh. I am a wonderful cook."

I did laugh, but paradoxically said at once, "What's funny about that?"

She answered, "I want to ask you if you will let me cook for you. I will cook wonderful things and you will see, you will get well and strong. I live now on Roxbury Drive in Beverly Hills but before coming here I looked at Marion Davies' small house on the beach. It is quite a charming house with a swimming pool. Will you come there and see me?"

I hesitated. "Perhaps on weekends. I am working on a script for Metro, but I could sometimes go to your house for a swim and some wonderful dishes," I said.

"Then that's a bargain," Marlene answered. I invited her for dinner the following evening, and I was charmed by her, by her soft personality, and her radiantly lovely looks; but I was disturbed because she had rouge on her face. I said, "You have exceptional skin texture that makes me think of moonlight. You should not ruin your face by putting color on it." She went into the bathroom and when she came out she said, "I will never put rouge on my cheeks again."

It was during this evening that I suggested she wear slacks. I told her she looked so well in *Morocco* in the sequence where she wore them that I thought she should wear them all the time. She was delighted at the suggestion. The next day I took her to my tailor in Hollywood and in true Dietrich fashion she ordered not one pair but many more, and jackets to go with them. Of course she looked superb in all of them. When they were finished she appeared at the Paramount studio one day dressed in one of them. The following day newspapers throughout the whole country carried photographs of her. From that second on, women all over the world leapt into slacks.

As she had hoped to, Marlene moved into Marion Davies' beach house in Santa Monica. She was childishly happy about the whole thing and started what I called her "gourmet cure" for me. She cooked meals for me that only a chef for the gods could have achieved.

Marlene is extremely generous as everyone who knows her is aware. Her generosity has the same warm out-pouring that Rita had in hers, and it often touched me in the same way that Rita's also touched me even if I sometimes reprimanded her for it. And as it had often occurred with Rita so, too, Marlene's generosity sometimes made us quarrel.

She swamped my house with flowers. Although I love flowers I do not like them in great quantities, and when Marlene sent me flowers sometimes twice a day, ten dozen roses or twelve dozen carnations, I was at a loss to know where to put them. I never came home that Anna and Rose were not wringing their hands in despair. We never had enough vases and when I told Marlene this, as a hint not to send me any more flowers, instead I received a great many Lalique vases and even *more* flowers. The house became a sort of madhouse of flowers.

Finally I rang up Marlene and said, "If you send another flower to this house, I will throw you in your own pool." She was hurt, but the next day instead of flowers she sent me dozens of charming things from the leading Los Angeles store. I came home to find boxes piled in the hallway and living room and Rose and Anna again wringing their hands. Bullock's Wilshire had moved into my house. As I crawled over boxes and waded through tissue paper, I sat down and laughed. Incorrigible, generous Marlene! What was there to do about her? When she came that evening to see me, all excited about the things, I told her I had sent many of them back to the store. Her beautiful face fell. She went in to talk to Anna and I heard them lamenting in German. But in the end we all laughed together.

On the whole we had very happy times at the beach house. Marlene had two German actor friends, Martin Kosleck and Hans von Twardowsky, who often came to swim with us. Martin is very talented, not only as an actor but as a painter.

I remember we discussed at this time a new film star who had just arrived in Hollywood—Katherine Hepburn. She had made her first film, *A Bill of Divorcement*. I had met her in New York some years previously in a box at Carnegie Hall. I was impressed by her personality then. When she became a success in films, I was not surprised.

Somehow the days went by as though one were treading water in slow motion, as they do in that locust-eating place called Hollywood. Nature, however, provided me with a diversion—an earthquake. I was sitting in my room one evening with Kosleck and Twardowsky when suddenly we heard a distant rumbling. The house started to rock to such an extent that I felt sick. We went down the stairs but it was difficult. They were swaying back and forth. As I reached the lawn, the chimney collapsed and the earth began heaving up and down somewhat as a snake moves.

That winter G. B. Stern and Diana Wynyard had a house together in Santa Monica Canyon nearby and I decided to go and see how they were. They were in a great state. Peter—as G.B. is called by her friends —had been taking a bath when the earthquake occurred and had nearly drowned. She had managed to scramble out of the tub and run out of the house dripping wet. When things calmed down a bit we were able to laugh.

At this time I saw some other English friends, Lawrence Olivier and his wife, Jill Esmonde, and Valerie Taylor who was married to Hugh Sinclair. Larry and Jill lived in a flat off Sunset Boulevard and I used to go there and have dinner with them. Larry was very little known then and I don't think he had the slightest idea of the heights he would achieve. Valerie Taylor was preparing to play in "Berkeley Square" with Leslie Howard. They both had a great success in it. Valerie was charming and talented. I used to see her with Hugh quite often but unfortunately they soon went back to London.

When Christmas came I felt very despondent. I missed Greta. I thought of going back to New York for Christmas, but somehow I felt it would be unfair to Abram if I did not mean to stay there. On Christmas evening I went to Adrian's for dinner. He had moved to North Hollywood. With his usual warmth and hospitality he had arranged a charming party. I brought Marlene whom he had never met, and, together with Hedda Hopper and several other friends, we tried to evoke a Christmas spirit though a warm breeze was blowing outside and not a flake of snow was in sight.

When I came home I found a cable from Greta wishing me a happy Christmas and saying she would be back soon.

I had by this time done a lot of work on the story of *Rasputin* and greatly expanded the scenario. Thalberg seemed pleased with the material I was turning in, and I was becoming more and more engrossed and interested in the assignment. The picture was scheduled for production within a very short time.

One day Thalberg sent for me. "I want you to write a sequence into the scenario in which Rasputin tries to seduce Irene Yusupov," he said. "It must be a very violent and terrific scene."

I was amazed. "But Irene Yusupov never even met Rasputin," I said.

"Who cares? Putting this scene in gives strength to the whole plot," he replied.

"But this is history," I insisted. "History in our own time with the people living who enacted it. Such a sequence would be absolutely unauthentic and probably libelous."

Thalberg rose impatiently from his chair. "I don't need you to tell me a lot of nonsense about what is libelous or what is not. I want this sequence in and that is all there is to it." He walked out of the room and slammed the door behind him.

That evening I wrote a long letter to Prince Agoutinsky in Paris. I asked him to tell Prince Yusupov that I was writing this scenario for Metro-Goldwyn-Mayer and I wanted to know how much I could use of the story he had told about Rasputin and his murder. I felt I should do this as I did not want him to feel that I was exploiting a story he had told me in privacy. I also asked Prince Agoutinsky to tell him that Thalberg wanted me to write in a seduction scene between his wife and Rasputin. I said I would wait for an answer before proceeding with the script.

I was very troubled. I knew if I disobeyed Thalberg I would run the risk of losing my job. On the other hand I would be doing something totally against my inner conviction if I wrote in this sensational, vulgar, and untrue sequence. I pondered on who could advise me from the highest level, and remembered hearing that Krishnamurti had come from Ojai where he lived and was in Hollywood for a few days. Fortunately I knew him, so I telephoned and asked him to come to see me.

Krishnamurti is an Indian who in his youth was a Theosophist and a protégé of Annie Besant. He was looked upon by the Theosophists as the New Christ. He, however, would not accept this title or its implication. With great courage he broke away from the Theosophists and has since been actively interested in educating people toward a realization of Truth. Although he does not quote authorities, or expound a specific system of philosophy, or strive to gather followers, his influence on human thought and action all the world over is immense. I considered myself fortunate that he would come to see me. We walked in the hills as I told him my problem.

"As I see it," he said, "you should give up your job rather than write this sequence. I think you should give up your job, anyway. I do not think a person who is striving spiritually as you are should be working in a moving picture studio. You will always be exposed to either compromise or surrender, or, in any case, a continual resistance. The vibrations and influences in such a place are too strong for one person to cope with. It is a commercial level and therefore a low level. You should not expose yourself to this atmosphere."

After this my conflict was even greater. I received a cable from Prince Agoutinsky. It said in effect that Prince Yusupov trusted me completely with any part of his story that I wished to use, but that he absolutely forbade any mention of Irene whatsoever. Yusupov said if she appeared in the film at all, he would bring suit.

I went to the studio with this cable. I thought it only right that I should show it to Thalberg. I handed it to him at his desk. He read it and turned deadly white.

"How dared you consult anyone about this picture!" he yelled.

"I did not consult 'anyone.' I consulted Prince Yusupov, whose interests are involved," I answered.

"You had absolutely no right to do such a thing without my permission," he shouted.

"But I have probably spared you a lawsuit. Besides, I must protect my friends. Prince Agoutinsky is a close friend of mine and Yusupov is a friend of his," I said.

"Friends! How dare you mention friends? The motion picture industry comes first," he said.

"Not with me," I answered. "My friends come first."

He picked up the telephone and gave an order to bring in my contract. A boy appeared with it in his hand.

"Say that again," he said.

I repeated, "My friends come before any industry."

He tore up my contract and threw it into the scrapbasket. I walked out of his room.

Thirty-Nine

After working on a scenario for several months—thinking about it, dreaming about it, planning it—to have it taken away means losing something of oneself. I not only felt as though I had lost something of myself but I myself felt lost. I did not know what to do and my mind kept turning over some new twist or idea that would save the situation.

I asked Harry Edington to come to my house to fetch the scenario and all my notes and deliver them to Thalberg. I had been paid for them so they were not even mine. Harry was furious with Irving. "He is a damn fool," he said. "I only hope that Yusupov sues him for a big sum of money." As I saw him getting into his car with my manuscript in his brief case I felt a little as if he were carrying a coffin out of the house. He tried to be cheerful and said, "Keep a stiff upper lip. Don't worry, I'll get you a better job at another studio."

But this promise was not fulfilled. Harry tried his best but Thalberg was too powerful for him. He had started an underground movement against me. According to the studio executives I had sinned against the sacred INDUSTRY! At first we didn't even realize what was happening, but when Harry encountered dead silence in one studio after another and they all turned me down without a reason, it finally dawned on us. I was just being kept out of a job and there was absolutely nothing I could do about it. There was no court to appeal to, no motion picture justice to evoke.

These were grim days. It was frustrating not to be able to "hit back." I felt angry and hurt. There was no doubt in my mind that Irving had unjustly dismissed me. I considered that I had done him a service by showing him Yusupov's cable. In any case, I did not know what to do with myself. Time hung heavily on my hands.

Luckily there was Marlene, who was an angel to me and tried to cheer me up in every conceivable way. But she had very little time as she had to go to the studio every day to prepare to film *Catherine The Great*. One day to comfort myself I decided to go up the coast to Carmel and see Robinson Jeffers, whom I had met some time before. He was living in a house he had built with his own hands from ocean-worn boulders and gray Santa Lucia granite found in Carmel and, practically unaided, he had also built a thirty-foot tower attached to the house.

Jeffers might be termed a great American poet, but to classify him so simply would tend to diminish the tragic stature of his genius. He has been frequently called the "poet of tragic terror" because of the somberness and majestic quality of his work. Without doubt, he has more nearly approached Greek ideals of artistic expression than any other American poet in contemporary times.

Like Shelley, Keats, and Byron, Jeffers looks physically as one would have a poet look. He is over six feet tall, slender, but powerfully built. His face is beautifully molded. His skin at this time was tanned and marked by wind and storms, weathered by sun and fog. His blue-gray eyes were searching. I do not know how kindly the passage of twenty-odd years sits on his shoulders, but at this time he was a remarkably handsome man.

We sat in his tower. He told me how most of the poems he has written have their settings and background in Monterey and Carmel. He said he loved Carmel passionately and had no desire ever to leave it. I realized then that there, from his isolated tower, he could see the fogs hanging low like menacing warriors over the ocean, and he could hear the screams of the sea gulls and pelicans with their shrill call of death as they swooped down into the sea. What more could a poet wish for? There he lived, indifferent to fame, applause, money.

He asked how much I earned working at Metro. I was ashamed to answer him and I evaded the question. I was ashamed even to mention the studio. Sitting there with him its stains suddenly seemed washed from me.

He opened one of his books—*Roan Stallion*. He read from it.

> "Humanity is the mould to break away from,
> the crust to break through,
> the coal to break into fire,
> the atom to be split."

This was what Krishnamurti had said to me on a different level, different and yet the same. And once again it was inwardly reaffirmed to me that only the poet and the mystic should be relied upon. I returned to Hollywood much happier. The menace of the studio and of Thalberg had fallen from me.

I started to work on a stage play of my own. At other times, to distract myself, I went to Paramount with Marlene. I remember one incident during the shooting of *Catherine The Great* which greatly entertained me and showed an amusing side of her character.

Joseph von Sternberg was the director of this film as he was of nearly all Marlene's films at this time, and he was also a friend of hers, but he was often very difficult and explosive on the set. One day they had a violent quarrel and Joe refused to speak to her except when directing her in front of the camera. After three days of this Marlene hit on a solution. She was shooting a scene in which she had to sit and ride a horse. She decided to fall off and pretend to be badly hurt. I was afraid she would be and begged her to try something less spectacular, but Joe's silence was getting on her nerves. Besides, she thought it would be a good joke for everyone and clear the air in the studio. The horse was a large one, quite some hands high, and I thought it very courageous of her even to dream of it. She rang up my doctor and asked him to be on the alert at a certain hour when she had decided to fall off her horse. He thought she was quite mad but I explained the problem to him and, greatly amused, he agreed to keep himself in readiness at the appointed hour.

The moment came and I saw her, every inch an empress, high up on the horse before the camera. I became extremely nervous. In fact, I was on the verge of spoiling the whole plot when she quietly tumbled off the horse, slipping to the ground as though it were a feat she often performed. The camera stopped grinding and everyone, hands, grips, assistant directors, and Joe, rushed in wild confusion to her side. Marlene lay as though she were dead. Joe picked her up in his arms and screamed for a doctor, who appeared in an unnaturally short time. Luckily, Joe was too beside himself to notice this. He kissed Marlene's hands and begged her to forgive him, as if she were dying and they were parting forever. The doctor had Marlene carried into her dressing room. She had fainted, the doctor shortly announced. "Probably from undue emotional strain," he said, looking darkly at Joe.

Marlene, in an apparently weak condition, was driven home by the repentant Joe and all ended well. The newspapers carried headlines that Marlene Dietrich had had a bad fall but had bravely recovered. I could not agree that she had bravely recovered but I could agree that she had bravely fallen.

Shortly after this Marlene left for Europe. It was her first trip back since she had come to America. The newspapers were full of photographs of her. This was in May, 1933. She wrote me from the *Europa* saying the boat was empty, all reservations having been cancelled by the Americans because of the "great Mr. Hitler." She felt lost and lonely and when people were screaming her name over the black water and waving handkerchiefs, she suddenly realized she was leaving home. Her child said, "Now you have no country any more," but when she saw Marlene crying she added, "You still have the water." In July Marlene wrote me again from Cap d'Antibes saying how much she longed for Hollywood which she knew I would understand.

And I *did* understand it. She was without a country and without a home. It was as though her roots had been pulled up. After the war many people had to adjust to new countries and new homes. But this was only 1933. I think it speaks very well for Marlene that as far back as 1933 she was willing to give up Germany and her home on account of Hitler. Luckily, she was happy to become an United States citizen and in the war she proved it. She did a magnificent job overseas. Many times, in order to be with the boys who were right up at the front, she was actually in danger. Hitler would certainly have loved to make her a prisoner.

All my life I have had what might be called psychic experiences. To me they have not seemed psychic but on the contrary altogether natural. In my friendship with Greta these so-called psychic forces have been particularly active. This might be explained because my great affection for her has possibly opened a channel, on an unseen level, between us. Or it might be explained because we have known each other in a previous incarnation—perhaps even many. Whatever the explanation, the facts have remained. While she was in Sweden I really believe that, lying on my bed in Brentwood, I was sometimes able to project myself into her room in Stockholm. I later checked up on everything I saw in her room and the details were correct. When Greta came from Sweden on this particular trip she sailed on a slow ship—the S.S. *Annie Johnson*—to San Diego, to avoid the newspaper reporters she would have encountered in New York. I knew she was on this boat because she had written to me, but it was not generally known and the press had not discovered it.

One day while she was at sea, quite suddenly and almost within a second I got a marked swelling on the outside of my throat. It was so noticeable that Anna saw it and asked what it was and what I thought was causing it. I said, "I have a distinct feeling that Miss Garbo has had this same swelling and now, from the second I got this, I have taken it from her and she no longer has it." This proved to be the case. When Greta arrived she told me she had had a swelling on her throat in precisely the same spot and that suddenly it had disappeared. On checking, and allowing for the difference in time, the swelling had come on my throat just at the moment when it had disappeared from hers.

Shortly after Greta's return, I helped her find another house. This one was again on San Vincente Boulevard in Santa Monica not far from the one in which I had originally met her. I helped her arrange it and the evening she moved in I had it filled with flowers and, although it was warm, I lighted all the fires to make it bright and gay.

I had for some time thought of an idea for a film for her—the role of Queen Christina of Sweden. I had made many notes about it and had written an outline of a story. When she arrived I told her about it. But as things often go in the film world in Hollywood, the idea was taken from me. Before I knew it, two other people were working on the story. The scenario had no relation to the actual historical life of Queen Christina and the studio had seen to it that very little of the real life of Christina crept into the film. With a few flourishes of the pen, or more likely with a few taps on the typewriter, history was transformed. Nevertheless, Greta was beautiful in it and if she did not record Christina's history she made it herself a breathtaking and memorable performance.

While this film was in the making I had a very serious automobile accident. One afternoon I was feeling extremely depressed and just lying on my bed doing nothing. Rose and Anna, who were always concerned about me, suggested I go for a ride over to San Fernando Valley. To please them I agreed and Rose and I got in my car and started off. I was in a morose frame of mind and did not speak to Rose all the way over to the Valley, but when we reached there and just at a crossroad when I was slowing the car down, I said, "I wish to God a car would hit us and kill me."

My car moved forward across the road and, as the words were barely out of my mouth, another car which had not slowed down at the cross-roads hit us at the speed of seventy miles an hour. The impact was on my side. Rose, with her leg badly cut from the glass in the windshield, landed in a soft field. I was hurled sixty feet out of the car and landed on my head on the macadamized road. The people in the crowd that gathered by the roadside thought I was dead. They covered me with a blanket and waited for the police to arrive. Perhaps I was dead, for I have always felt that my spirit traveled far in those strange suspended minutes out of time. When I opened my eyes in the police station a policeman was bending over me. I heard him say, "My God, she's alive." I asked to be taken to the Santa Monica Hospital. There I was rushed to the operating room. My whole face was mangled, cut and bruised. Just as the surgeon was about to sew up my face, which would have utterly disfigured me for life, I heard a voice cry out, "Don't let him touch your face." I was able to hear because, it being a head injury, I was given only a local anesthetic. I put my hand up and prevented the surgeon from proceeding. A hand took mine. I heard the voice of a director I knew—Ned Griffith. He said, "This is a job for a plastic surgeon. For God's sake, don't let an ordinary surgeon touch your face. I've brought Doctor Updegraff, a wonderful plastic surgeon, with me." Doctor Updegraff moved forward, and so my face was saved. Afterwards I learned that a friend of Ned's had seen the accident. He had telephoned Ned who had telephoned the police station.

Lying in my bed in the hospital after the operation I realized that I had called this accident upon myself and selfishly enough I had included Rose in it. I trembled at the thought that she might have been killed. The whole thing took on the aspect of a lesson to me—a lesson showing me the great power of a wish when strongly channeled. That I was not killed made me feel that I still had something to do, some pattern to work out. I lay in bed with gratitude in my heart that not only my life had been spared but that I was not to be disfigured.

Marlene's husband, Rudy Sieber, was at this time in Hollywood. He cabled Marlene who was then in Paris about my accident. She immediately telephoned me from Paris to the hospital and said that if I lacked money she would pay for any expense which I incurred there. She said she wanted me to have the best room and the best care. She also called my doctor and told him the same thing. At this moment when I was suffering and down in my luck Marlene's thoughtfulness helped my morale a great deal.

When I left the hospital some weeks later I was in bad shape. Having no job, I was unoccupied and very much alone. The unhappy "spells" I used to have began again to attack me. I resurrected my revolver and went up to the hills and shot at targets that hung on trees. As I held it in my hand I felt again the old sense that it was a way of escape.

Then one day Princess Norina Matchabelli rang me on the telephone. She said there was someone in Hollywood she wanted me to meet. I did not want to meet anyone and I told her so. She said I would not regret meeting this person. "Who is it?" I asked. She would not tell me.

"I want it to be a surprise," she said.

Finally, she prevailed upon me to go into Hollywood to an address she gave me. Norina was waiting at the door and there seemed to be no one else on the ground floor. She told me to go upstairs to a room on the left. Responding to the sense of excitement and mystery I heard in her voice, I rushed up the stairs.

In the room she had directed me to an extraordinary man was sitting in the Buddha position, wth his legs drawn under him. He was dressed in white in an Indian costume. His hair was long and black and he wore a thick black moustache. His dark eyes gave the impression of extreme brightness. I noticed at once his amazing hands which gave the feeling of great strength. All this was impressed upon me in one second but what I felt overwhelmingly was the warmth that radiated from him and seemed to flood the whole room. He stretched out his arms to me and without a moment's hesitation I moved forward into their embrace.

"Who are you?" I said. For answer he made a gesture toward his lips. I understood that he did not speak. Then, confirming my thought, he spelled out on an alphabetical board, "I do not speak. I have taken a vow of silence and have been silent for years." Again I repeated, "Who are you?" He answered, "I am You."

I understood his meaning so I did not persist in the question. Suddenly, he spelled out on the board, "Go, fetch me your revolver." I was amazed, for indeed my revolver was in my car and loaded. How did he know this? I had told absolutely no one of its existence. I went down to my car and returned with the revolver and handed it to him. He opened the barrel and one by one took out the cartridges. He handed them to me with the revolver. He spelled out on the board, "Suicide is not the solution. It only entails rebirth with the same problems all over again. The only solution is God Realization—to see God in everything. Then, everything is easy. Promise me you will put this revolver away and never again think of suicide." I promised this with the utmost sincerity. Suicide suddenly seemed absurd to me, a tragic misunderstanding of life.

I learned that this strange man was Sri Meher Baba, who had recently come from India. He had taken a vow of silence a number of years previously which he had not broken. His followers c 'ed him a "Perfect Master" and look upon him as such. Regardless of what he is or his so-called spiritual position, which meant little to me then and less now, I found him at this time very helpful. He only remained in Hollywood a short while after my meeting with him but during this period I saw him several times. He came into my life just at a right moment, greatly lifted my spirits and I have always been grateful to him.

When he left Hollywood he flew to London. I called him there and had an amusing experience. Norina was with him. When I called she put him on the telephone and when I said, "Hello Baba," he responded by just making strange cooing sounds and blowing me kisses. The London operator, in a most British voice, came in on the line and said, "Speak up sir—speak up! Your party can't hear you." Whereupon I said, "It's all right. The gentleman can't speak but I understand his cooing." I heard her gasp and she faded from the line.

Sheilah Hennessy came out at this time to stay with Gloria Swanson who had been married to her cousin—the Marquis de la Falaise. Sheilah was good for me. She is always gay, and an optimist. She is a reader of cards and when I was depressed she ran for the deck of cards and managed to tell me the most extraordinary and encouraging things. She was so charming looking and so eager to cheer me up that I pretended to swallow all her predictions. We often sat on a swing on the Beverly Hotel lawn just opposite Gloria's house. And, as often, Sheilah would assure me that everything she saw in the cards "always comes true."

When I first met her, I asked, "Are you a brandy Hennessy?" She is. When I am annoyed with her, I call her "one star." If I am less annoyed I call her "two stars," and if she is really pleasing me, I call her "three stars."

Greta moved again. She moved to a house in Brentwood very near me on North Carmelina Drive. She had finished her film, so, as it was winter, we decided to go somewhere in the snow. We went to the Yosemite and it turned out to be a trip full of various adventures, humorous and otherwise.

To begin with Greta was most anxious that no one should recognize her. It was the first time, I think, that she used the name Harriet Brown, a name which she often used afterwards. She registered in the hotel under this name. So that no one should know who she was when we went skating, she pulled a lumberman's cap well down over her head to conceal her hair, and tied the flaps under her chin. She wore dark glasses and, because she felt cold, put on a number of heavy sweaters. She wore trousers and under these stockings and woolen socks. When I saw her on the ice I roared with laughter. There was no trace of her beauty. She looked like a Michelin tire. Of course, everyone stared at her and not because they had the slightest idea who she was. But when she saw people laughing and felt she was attracting attention she went off the ice and refused to skate again. I could not make her believe they were not laughing at Garbo but only at the strange creature she had made of herself. She said that we must get away from people, so we went into the forest where there were only trees to stare at us. We went into it just before sunset which occurs very early and rapidly in the Yosemite owing to the high mountains which surround it. Unfortunately, we did not realize the danger of forests after the sun sets.

When we went in the sun was shining through the trees. When we had gone quite far it quickly dropped behind the mountain and in less than a second we were almost in total darkness with the thickness of the trees and underbrush closing in on us. I think I realized the danger we were in before Greta did. I said, "We must turn back." Back? Which way was back? We did not know. "Which way do you think we should go?" I asked, trying to keep the fear out of my voice. "I don't know," she answered. The temperature was falling rapidly. "We *must* keep moving. Let's try this way and don't let go of my hand," I said. I pulled Greta toward me and turned first one way and then another.

We stumbled on, banging against trees, scratching our hands and faces on them, falling over underbrush. Already our hands, feet, and faces were numb. I was hanging onto myself with all the force in me to keep from becoming hysterical. I knew Greta was doing the same.

Suddenly Greta stopped dead and pulled me back. "There's a light!" she cried. I peered through the trees and saw only blackness. Then, as I moved a fraction of an inch, I saw a tiny light flicker through the trees and as quickly disappear again. But we had both seen it. It could not be an hallucination. We pressed forward, seeing the light, then losing it again. "It is a light," she joyously cried. "It is! It is!" The trees parted and there before us stood a small house with a tiny light flickering in a window.

We knocked on the door. It was opened by an old man. We learned from him that we had been walking in the opposite direction from our hotel. In fact we had been walking further and further into the forest and had we not come upon his house we would surely have died from exposure during the night. He said the temperature was falling fast and would soon be below zero. It was already eight o'clock and we had been walking over four hours. He stirred up some rather terrible coffee and handed it to us in tin mugs. Bad as it was we were grateful to get something warm inside us. He suggested that we stretch out on the floor near the stove and he told us the good news that his son would be passing by in a wagon about five o'clock in the morning and would drive us back to the hotel. He had been a woodcutter but now, being too old to cut wood, he just lived in this little house and his son, who was now the woodcutter, came to see him several times a week and brought him his food.

Greta and I were so tired that off and on we fell asleep while the old man dozed in the corner. Just as he had said, his son appeared promptly at five o'clock and drove us, weary and hungry, back to the hotel. But Greta insisted upon our going home that day. She said the Yosemite had brought us bad luck.

Forty

The film of *Rasputin,* starring all three Barrymores, was now finished. The scenario held all the lurid touches that Thalberg wanted, including the seduction of Irene by Rasputin. At the gala première those who remembered history—and only had to remember events of their lifetime—shrugged their shoulders and said, "This is Hollywood." But this was not the answer or an excuse for Prince Yusupov. In the midst of his triumph, the sword fell upon the head of Thalberg. Yusupov brought a suit against Metro-Goldwyn-Mayer for libel to the tune of four million dollars.

The film had already been released all over the country, but as soon as Yusupov sued, the courts put an injunction on it and all the prints had to be recalled until the suit was settled one way or another. Prince Yusupov, who, since the Russian Revolution, had become a British subject, brought his suit in England. Fanny Holzman who was representing him asked if I would go to London and testify for him. As I was still having plastic surgery on my face I could not go, but I said I was willing to testify in writing that Yusupov had cabled me that he did not want Irene impersonated in the film and that Thalberg had seen this cable. This was a strong point in his favor.

As soon as Metro-Goldwyn-Mayer got wind that I had been asked to testify in London, one of the top executives sent for Harry Edington. He said that the studio would like me to go back to work and that my jobless state during the past months had all been a "big mistake."

"We'll make them pay through the nose for keeping you so many months out of a job," Edington said shrewdly. We did. I went back on the payroll with my salary greatly increased.

I reported for work the following day and to my surprise was told to go to Thalberg's office. He greeted me as though nothing unpleasant had ever occurred between us. He was not a big enough man to admit he had been wrong. Even when Yusupov won the case and the courts awarded him one million dollars and said that the film could never again be shown in England, Thalberg remained with closed lips on the subject.

Back at work, instead of telling me what to do, he asked me what I wanted to do. My old dream for Greta rose before my eyes. I decided to tell him about it.

I believed that Greta was worth much more than all the glamour and sex films she had been forced to play in. I had always wanted to see her play a peasant role in which she could brush her hair straight back off her face and wear simple clothes instead of the grand ones she had always been seen in. I wanted her for once to portray a role where beautiful clothes would not stand between her and her great acting. I wanted her to do a picture close to the soil where nature would play a part. Nature is Greta's element and in no picture has she been allowed to express it. I told Thalberg this. I also told him that I thought Greta should play the roles of saints—several of them. I was surprised when he picked up this remark and appeared very interested in it. "What saints?" he asked.

"Of course Jehanne d'Arc. She is a natural for this. But she could also play Saint Francis and the great Spanish saint—Teresa of Avila."

To my surprise, Irving said, "Tell me about Saint Francis. I don't know anything about him." I briefly sketched for him the life of Saint Francis. Then he asked me questions about Teresa of Avila. Finally he questioned me about Jehanne d'Arc. While discussing her I suggested that if he did film the picture for Greta all the scenes should be shot in France and in all of the places where Jehanne d'Arc had actually lived, and fought. He became so excited and interested about this that he assigned me to write a scenario of Jehanne d'Arc.

After nine months' work my whole heart was in the script. I had worked on it passionately and intensely. Greta complained during these months that I was "not there." In a certain way I wasn't and yet in another way, had she but understood, I was never for a second separated from her, as she and Jehanne d'Arc became inseparable in my consciousness. I arrived at a point when I could not tell which was Greta and which was Jehanne. Yet, curiously enough, I could not discuss the script with Greta. She was too much Jehanne to be able to talk it over with her. It would have been like talking over Jehanne with Jehanne. I suffered a strange shyness about the whole matter with her and if she ever mentioned it I changed the subject.

When I presented the finished shooting script to Thalberg he was delighted. He praised it extravagantly and said it was the best "one-man job" he had ever seen. After reading it he actually came out of his office and with his arm around me walked with me to my car. Even his secretary was astonished by this. I was extremely pleased and touched. He said he was going to discuss the film with Greta that day and tell her how wonderful the script was. I went home very happy.

That night when I was already in bed Thalberg rang me. I knew the second I heard his voice that something was wrong. He said at once, "Garbo does not want to do this film." I was too staggered to answer. He continued, "Have you discussed this with her?" I told him I had not. He then said, "I'm as disappointed as you. She may change her mind. Come and see me tomorrow and we will talk about it."

I lay awake all night. It was difficult to believe that what he said was true. The following day I saw Greta. She did not mention the subject to me and for some unaccountable reason I could not bring myself to mention it to her.

I went to see Thalberg. He said, "Greta is being influenced by someone. She would not make this decision on her own. But don't be discouraged. She may still do it, and if she does not I will find someone else who will. She is not the only pebble on the beach."

I answered, "I wish I thought so but in spite of what you say you know damn well she *is* the only pebble that can play Jehanne d'Arc."

I went home depressed and broken. Of all the disappointments I had in Hollywood, this hit me the hardest. Looking back on it now I ask myself why I did not go directly to Greta and thrash the whole situation out with her. But something held me back.

Thalberg was extremely kind at this time. He said, "Don't worry. Your script will be done. Such good work cannot be wasted." But I had lost heart and I did not care what happened to the script if Greta was not going to play it.

For some time after this when I was with Greta a ghost seemed to stand between us—the ghost of Jehanne d'Arc. But I never again mentioned a word to her or to anyone else about it.

During this time a number of my friends appeared in Hollywood. Hope Williams turned up to take tests for a film and Noel Coward came out "just to look around" as he put it. It was the beginning of what I called "the British era" as a great many English actresses and actors began to arrive in Hollywood then. Gladys Cooper, Rex Evans, Herbert Marshall, Heather Thatcher, and a number of others appeared. Isabel Jeans was among this number. She was charming and beautiful and I was delighted she had arrived in Hollywood. We used to meet often. In a way, Hollywood was a restless place—people were always coming and going. When Isabel went back to London I very much missed her. Then Larry Olivier came back. He was divorced from Jill and engaged to Vivien Leigh. Vivien had also arrived in Hollywood to play her unforgettable role in *Gone With The Wind*. Many of us, old friends from years back, met at various parties and particularly at Ivor's house, which became a meeting center.

I used to go constantly to Adrian's. When we came from the studio we often had dinner by ourselves in his house or he would give parties and ask me to help him arrange the table or receive his guests.

At one of these dinners I met Paul Brunton who had written a book called *A Search in Secret India*. When I read this book it had a profound influence on me. In it I learned for the first time about Ramana Maharshi, a great Indian saint and sage. It was as though some emanation of this saint was projected out of the book to me. For days and nights after reading about him I could not think of anything else. I became, as it were, possessed by him. I could not even talk of anything else. So much so, that as a joke, Adrian made a drawing of me peering out from behind a group of Indians and wrote under it A SEARCH IN SECRET INDIA. But nothing could distract me from the idea that I *must* go and meet this saint. From this time on, although I ceased to speak too much about it, the whole direction of my life turned toward India and away from Hollywood. I felt that I would surely go there although there was nothing at this time to indicate that I would. Nevertheless, I felt I would meet the Maharshi and that this meeting would be the greatest experience of my life.

I have always felt that Paul Brunton deserves a lot of credit for introducing Romana Maharshi to England and America. This book was ahead of its time, as at this period there was very little interest in India except among the special few who understood the spiritual significance of the East.

At this time Greta had another fire in her house, or rather, she thought she did. What actually caught on fire was the brush, and dry, high grass all around it. It made a terrific blaze and created a great deal of smoke. When she telephoned I rushed down the road and even from a short distance away I thought the whole house was in flames. Greta was alone as it was her maid's day out. It never occurred to her to telephone the fire department. She only thought of calling me. The house was entirely circled by flames and hidden by smoke. I scarcely realized it was only the dry grass which was burning and rushed through it, unaware until later that I had burned my hands, hair and eyebrows. I found Greta terribly frightened and no wonder, as from where we stood it looked as if we would be engulfed any minute. We could hear the flames crackling. When I heard that she hadn't called for the fire engines I rushed for the telephone, but they were already on their way. A neighbor had turned in the alarm, and they arrived and did their work quickly and efficiently.

A few weeks after this I received a letter from New York from Abram saying that he was considering marrying Janice Fair—the young woman who was his model. I knew she was a sweet person and had nothing against her. The letter, nevertheless, was a great shock to me. It had never occurred to me that Abram and I would ever be divorced. After all, we loved each other. We were friends and had been married fifteen years. That we could no longer make a success of our sexual life seemed to me no reason to separate. I was too European to feel, as Americans do, that the moment the sex relation is over one must fly to the divorce courts. It is more than just this relationship which holds two people together. I did not believe that Abram loved this model. I felt that he had become involved with her and with his conventional viewpoint believed he should marry her. I decided the best thing to do was to go to New York and talk it over with him.

Several months before this I had given up smoking and I had become a vegetarian. I believe it is psychologically interesting to relate what caused me to give up both of these habits although what prompted me to give up smoking was not the same reason which prompted me to give up meat eating.

I gave up smoking because I read an article Gandhi had written against it. He wrote that "apart from being a dirty and undisciplined habit, it utterly prevents spiritual progress. Nicotine in even the smallest quantity thickens the spiritual body and prevents its development." At this time I was a chain smoker, but on reading this article I stopped smoking and I have never smoked since.

It must be quite apparent that I love animals, and that they have always played an important part in my life. I feel lost without them. When I was forced as a child to eat cows, sheep, pigs and other farm animals, I became unhappy and depressed. Many times I became very sick and vomited. But, most serious of all, I developed a guilt complex about eating them. I felt I was as truly eating my friends as though I were eating humans. When I came to Hollywood I was very underweight and had remained so until this time. I went to see a doctor in Pasadena who was a great dietician—Doctor Harold Bieler. He immediately said my lack of weight was psychological. He said he believed that if I became a vegetarian my health would greatly improve.

I was only too happy at last to find someone to back me up about not eating animals. I gained weight, became much stronger, and definitely much happier. Greta also went to Doctor Bieler and began to live only on vegetables and fruit. He is the only person, regardless of what others may claim, who has had the slightest influence on her health and physical manner of living. She has continually consulted him about her diet and her health for many years.

When I arrived in New York I found that what I had surmised was true. Abram actually did not want to marry Janice and he hoped that I would refuse to give him a divorce; in fact he was counting on my doing just this. Curiously enough my reaction was contrary to his expectations. Suddenly, after discussing the matter with him, my sympathy turned in favor of his model. Although it was against my own interest and what I wanted, I insisted that he go through with a divorce and marry her.

Greta was planning at this time to leave very shortly for Sweden. decided to go to Europe too and to stop off first in New York. I aske Thalberg to let me have a holiday. He said, "You need and deserve one and when you return we will talk about the *Jehanne d'Arc* again. I have not given up the idea of doing it or the hope that I will be able to persuade Garbo to change her mind."

I went to Florence with a British actor friend of mine, Quintin Tod, who had acted in New York in a number of Elizabeth Marbury's early productions. He was extremely small and dressed to perfection and was neatness itself. Whenever we traveled together he always packed and unpacked for me and kept everything in my room in order. He kept all the tickets and never lost anything. We were old friends and I was exceedingly fond of him. We had wonderful times together and he constantly made me laugh, although at the same time, he had a very serious side. He was also extremely religious.

From Florence, Quintin and I went to Assisi. In those Umbrian hills, where Saint Francis was born, there is a magic not to be found in any other place. Many times I have walked in Assisi when twilight has faded—when the streets are empty and the shutters of the houses closed —and I have almost believed that I was back in the thirteenth century.

In the Christian world, Francis as well as Jesus has proved himself a true democrat. In fact these two great figures are two of the most perfect democrats in the Christian world. To think of Francis as belonging only to the Middle Ages is not to understand him. He was far in advance of his own age, and is still beyond our modern age. He lived on the fringe of the world—he lived in it, and yet was not of it. There is nothing that modern life can evolve in the attitude of brotherhood or comradeship that has not been borrowed from his teachings.

Not far from Assisi, in a remote and inaccessible spot high up in the mountains, stands a monastery. This monastery was built in the fifth century by a secret order of Buddhist monks who traveled all the way from Tibet. Saint Francis is said to have visited it. After the death of Francis, the Franciscans took over the monastery for their own Order. They remained in it until the seventeenth century, when it was abandoned and left empty. From this time it remained deserted until after the first World War when it was taken over and restored by a remarkable woman who, like Saint Francis, decided she did not wish to be attached to any church or creed. She dropped her family name and is known simply by the name of Sorella Maria.

I had heard of this monastery and having need of a certain solace, I wrote Sorella Maria from Assisi and asked if Quintin and I might visit her. I waited for her answer with impatience and in a few days it arrived. The first gracious words of her letter, *Si, cara, l'aspetto con amore al nostro eremo,* gave me confidence in my welcome.

On arriving at the station the following day, we were met by an ancient peasant driving a dilapidated old car. He drove us about six miles and then stopped at the foot of the mountain. Here we were told to mount sturdy donkeys which were brought forward by a kindly peasant woman. She told us that the narrow pathway up the mountains was too steep for us to attempt on foot. She eyed our luggage with dismay but after much excited conversation another donkey appeared, and the bags were strapped on his back. It had been a warm day and the setting sun made a glorious flaming color in the sky. As we climbed we could see the whole Umbrian valley below and Assisi in the distance. In about an hour we sighted the monastery, and heard the bell ringing in its tower.

"They are ringing the bell to welcome you," the peasant announced.

As we approached the monastery, the door swung back for us to enter. We slid off our donkeys, and found ourselves on a terrace overlooking the valley. Here stood Sorella Maria with the *"piccole sorelle,"* as her twelve nuns called themselves.

I have known many extraordinary women but on seeing Sorella Maria I knew that I was in the presence of one of the rarest. She wore her hair loosely to her shoulders. Her body was frail, and yet from it emanated that peculiar vitality not uncommon to frail people. Her hands were delicate and at the same time strong and arresting. The two most striking things about her were her eyes and voice. Her eyes had a look as though they were blind—the lids drooping as if it pained her to raise them or as though they were too heavy to hold open. I remembered some lines I had once read about the eyes of Saint Francis, written by a contemporary: *His lids were long and heavy. They half closed over his eyes and impregnated his words with gravity. Sometimes his expression was so intense that it would have taken courage to endure it had one not been rescued by the grace of his smile.* These words, in a manner, fitted Sorella Maria.

It is difficult to write about her voice. The nearest description I can offer is that it sounded like the voice of a minaret singer, or of a young choir boy. Yet neither of these is correct, because her voice sounded far more of another world. It was haunting, unearthly, strangely pure, and at moments, downright unpleasant.

Without a word she led me into the garden. There was a long pause. I waited for her to speak but she did not break the silence. In fact I relaxed in it, and I felt that she meant me to relax. It was not an uncomfortable silence. When she finally did break it she began to tell me in her hauntingly sure voice about my life with as much familiarity as though she were speaking of her own. She told me why I had come to see her, what my problems were.

When we left the garden we went onto the terrace overlooking the valley. The summer evening was long and it was still light as we stood there. There was a wonderful stillness. It seemed as if the whole countryside had paused for these few minutes. I was conscious of something in Sorella Maria belonging essentially to this soil, as Francis must have belonged to it. She told me that the countryside needed rain, that it had been parched for months. I said, "I wish it would rain while I am here. It might be a sign that Saint Francis welcomes me."

I said this partly in fun, but a few seconds later we felt a light shower of rain upon our faces. The skeptical would say, "Just a coincidence!" Nevertheless, it made me happy and seemed a good omen.

The youngest sister—a girl from the south of Italy—took me to my room, which was a cell of stone in which many monks during many centuries had slept. It was small and square. The whitewashed stone walls, ceiling and floor contributed to its immaculate appearance. One small, deeply set, square window, cut into the stone wall, allowed me to look far out over the valley. A narrow bed against one wall was covered by a sheet of natural linen made by the sisters themselves on their own looms. In fact, I found they had made almost everything in the monastery. A small washbasin and pitcher of earthen pottery stood in another corner of my room on a carved wood table. This was all, yet in this cell there was a tranquillity—almost a tenderness—that I had never found elsewhere. I slept that night as though a blessing hung over my heart.

Leading from the monastery was a subterranean passage of stone which wound down into a stone cave. It is said that Francis and the Eastern monks used to sit there and converse. The day of my arrival, and every day during my visit there, I went down into this cave and meditated. It seemed to me to have retained the presence of Francis.

Sorella Maria and the sisters asked me where I had been the past years. I told them I had been in Hollywood writing for pictures. None of them had ever seen a moving picture and they knew only vaguely about Hollywood. This cheered and refreshed me enormously.

Gandhi had once been to the monastery to see Sorella Maria. He had taught all the sisters a hymn which they sang for me. Although they were considerably off the tune and the English words were hopelessly mispronounced, I nevertheless recognized "Lead, Kindly Light."

It was evening when the moment came to leave. Sorella Maria and the *piccole sorelle* stood at the doorway. Sorella Maria kissed me farewell. They all sang as we walked down the mountainside.

"We will sing to give you courage to go out and face life," Sorella Maria called after me.

For a long time as we wound down the mountain path, we could hear their voices, sometimes singing, sometimes calling, "*Addio* Mercedes! *Adio* Quintino! *Adio! Adio!*"

When I reached Paris, it seemed almost impossible to take up my old life. People seemed unfeeling, their voices loud and raucous. I felt ashamed to mingle in their worldliness. It took some time to overcome again my old, dull, uninspired self. Alas! The vision of the sublime fades so easily in this commonplace world. We are lucky, indeed, if we can remember the dream of it.

Forty-One

After leaving Sorella Maria I went to Austria to visit Eleanora von Mendelssohn who had a castle in a place called Kammer not far from Salzburg. Eleanora was the granddaughter of the celebrated composer, and she was christened Eleonora after Duse, who was her godmother and an intimate friend of her father's. It was through our mutual love for Duse that our friendship originally came about. She was a charming and beautiful person both physically and spiritually. When I first knew her and until Hitler took over Germany she was immensely wealthy, as her father had been one of the great German bankers, comparable to the Rothschilds in France or J. P. Morgan in the United States. But he was Jewish and, although her mother was not, Eleonora was forced to leave Germany as soon as Hitler came to power. She fled to the United States leaving all her possessions behind her. Not long after the war, from an accumulation of various tragedies, she killed herself in New York.

Her castle in Kammer was filled with art treasures, but she was completely unspoiled by her worldly possessions, and in the midst of them she was always generous and mindful of less fortunate people. Even when she had lost these possessions and was living in an inexpensive flat in New York, she never relinquished her graciousness and thoughtfulness although she was often pressed for money.

At the time of my visit, Alice Astor, who was then married to

Raimund von Hoffmansthal, the famous poet's son, lived in one-half of the castle, and there were many other guests besides myself—Diana Duff Cooper and her husband, Iris Tree, and Marion Hall among them. Many people came over daily from Salzburg to see Eleonora. She was an intimate friend of both Max Reinhardt and Toscanini.

Eleanora had violent "fixations" on both men and women. She also had them on historical characters who were dead. Once when she had one on Napoleon she arrived in Paris and asked me to meet her at the Gare Saint Lazare. When we came out of the station it was pouring rain and we had great difficulty getting a taxi. We were soaking wet, but Eleanora asked if I would mind if she made a little visit to someone she loved before we went to the hotel. Of course I said yes. She leaned forward and whispered an address to the driver which I did not hear and, thinking it kinder to be discreet, did not question. Nevertheless, I was slightly surprised when we drove up to the Invalides and Eleonora jumped out of the taxi saying, "Darling, just wait here a second while I say a few words to the Emperor."

An amusing incident happened in Kammer while I was there. One day Toscanini remarked how much he loved a particular Guardi which was hanging in one of the hallways of the castle. Eleanora ran out of the room. She returned carrying the Guardi and laid it on the floor at Toscanini's feet saying, "It is yours." The Maestro looked startled, then, seeming to pull himself together, he bent down and picked it up and holding tightly onto it disappeared from the room. Within a very short while he reappeared without it and when we asked him where it was he said, "I have locked it in my car. I do not want to take a chance on Eleanora's changing her mind."

After I returned to New York I received a letter from Greta, who was still in Sweden. In her letter she said jokingly, *I will meet you for dinner a week from Tuesday at eight o'clock in the dining room of the Grand Hotel.* I got this letter on a Tuesday morning. I figured that if I could get the necessary ship passage, I could then fly from Bremen to Malmo, Sweden, that same day, take the train from there to Stockholm and arrive late that night. At this time the only airfield in Sweden was at Malmo.

I was staying with Vouletti Proctor (who had married Vernon Brown) and when I told her of my plan to spend one evening with Greta and fly back to Bremen the following day to catch the *Europa's* return trip on Thursday, she encouraged me to do it. Marion Stevenson and Vouletti always encouraged me in all my wild adventures. I loved them for it. I booked my passage on the *Europa* and sailed the following day. In the meantime, I cabled Greta what I hoped would seem a casual wire: WILL MEET YOU FOR DINNER EIGHT O'CLOCK GRAND HOTEL NEXT TUESDAY EVENING AS SUGGESTED.

The trip over was very rough. This was the month of October and the gales kept portholes closed and even boarded up. But the *Europa* was a well-built ship and we made good time in spite of head winds.

Less than a week later I arrived in Stockholm at one o'clock in the morning. It was bitter cold and I was frozen and desperately tired, partly because of the nervous tension and my excitement about the whole adventure. I had wired for a room in the Grand Hotel and when the porter met me at the station and we drove there in a glacial and thick fog, I felt as though I had reached the North Pole. Seized in sudden panic I thought, What if I don't meet Greta? What if she fails to turn up for dinner? Of course, I knew her address, but she might have gone to the country or be hiding in a Viking's lair!

The manager of the hotel had stayed up to meet me and explain that it was so crowded that the only reservation he had been able to keep for me was the Royal Suite. I was too tired to object and followed him upstairs, praying it was not going to cost me all the money I had. When he switched on the lights I saw an enormous room with great ornate gold mirrors, heavy furniture, crystal chandeliers and stuffy red plush curtains. I was delighted. It was all just as it should have been— every inch a royal suite! When I remarked that I could roller skate in the bathroom as it was so large, the manager took me seriously and asked if I was a professional roller skater.

I undressed and climbed into the great bed. It seemed to me I had just gone to sleep when the telephone rang. I groped for the receiver. To my joy I heard Greta's voice. "It is not possible that you are here. You are really wonderful," she said.

"What time is it? Where are you?" I asked. She answered that it was six o'clock in the morning, that she had called the hotel to see if I had arrived and was surprised and yet not surprised when they said I was there and, in her usual way, she added "I'll be right over."

I rang off, jumped out of bed and began to dress. I looked out of the window. It was still pitch dark outside, as indeed I knew it would be for many hours yet. In winter one never sees the sun in Stockholm before ten. In a very few minutes Greta knocked on my door. She came in and burst into laughter. "You are funny. I might have known I'd find you in the Royal Suite," she said. "But hurry up! Put on your coat and heavy shoes—bundle up. Let's get out of this stuffy place." I asked her where she was going to take me. To my astonishment she answered, "To the zoo." Now it was my turn to laugh. "Imagine sane people going to the zoo in the icy cold dark at six o'clock in the morning!" She laughed again. "But who said we were sane?"

Out in the street it was freezing cold but I did not feel it. I was far too excited. Soon we reached the gates of the zoo and as we passed into it she said, "I know how you love animals so I thought you had better come and show yourself to them before going anywhere else."

We went into the zoo restaurant, which I was surprised to find open at such an early hour, and had coffee and a delicious breakfast. After breakfast and in this same mood we went into the monkey house. Moving toward a cage which held a large monkey, Greta put her hand between the bars as if to shake hands with him. At the same time she bent forward putting her face close to the cage and spoke to him. "How are you, Honey Lamb?" she said softly. He stretched out his hand, but instead of taking hers he made a gesture toward her face. If she had not moved I am sure he would only have patted it. Unfortunately, as his hand reached out of the cage she drew back. Startled by her movement he leaned far enough out to contact her face, and changing his gesture from affection to violence, scratched it. To my horror I saw blood trickling down her cheek. All the tales of people dying from monkey scratches sprang to my mind. I was petrified with fear but I tried not to show it.

"Don't touch your cheek. We must try and find a doctor," I said as calmly as I could, but she knew as well as I did the danger of such a scratch. Besides, I knew she was thinking, as I was, that this might scar her face.

Fortunately, not far from the zoo we found a chemist's shop, and he gave us the address of a doctor nearby. The doctor was an old man and very kind. He cleaned the wound and dressed it and, to our great relief, said he felt no ill effect would come of it and that he was sure it would eventually leave no scar. He also recognized Greta, but he seemed such a nice person that I felt she needn't worry about the newspapers. We left his office with a dressing on Greta's cheek and our high spirits somewhat curbed.

At Greta's apartment I tried to recover a little from my trip, the cold, and wayward monkeys. That evening we dined at eight o'clock at the Grand Hotel as planned.

The evening was a sentimental one. We sat at a table in the corner of the room which Greta had reserved and the same one she had described to me so many times in Hollywood. And we did the traditional things, ordering caviar, champagne, and our favorite tunes from the orchestra. It was a charming evening and there, in that rococo room with its pink-shaded lights, its soft string orchestra and its old-world atmosphere, I felt that I was moving in a dream within a dream.

The White Horse Inn was playing in Stockholm at this time and after dinner we went to see it. When we left the theatre a gang of photographers was lined up outside waiting for Greta. She saw them, lost her head, and dodging through the crowd disappeared before I could follow her. Luckily, I had had a great deal of training in Hollywood at this sort of thing and knew that when the crowd thinned out I would find her somewhere. I was right about this. Some time after the theatre was dark I found her in a small shop down the street where she had hidden behind the counter.

It was an unhappy ending to our evening. I wonder if press photographers actually realize what a thoroughly miserable time they have given Greta over all the many years of their relentless and merciless pursuit.

I stayed on in Sweden longer than I had planned. The following day Greta took me to Tistad, some hours away from Stockholm. We went to stay with two friends of hers, Count and Countess Wachtmeister. Their estate was large and they had a beautiful house there besides a model farm where the Count bred bulls and cows and ran a dairy.

It was interesting to see Greta on her native soil. We took long walks across country and through plowed fields of heavy, dark mud, and as in Hollywood we sometimes started out at the crack of dawn. When we tramped past typically Swedish red-painted farmhouses and saw the cones of fir trees piled high in their courtyards, I realized that in some mysterious way she had an affinity with them, which I, as a stranger, never could have. Something of her spirit was in the earth beneath our feet and in the very wind that whistled round us.

I was in Tistad the last days in October and the first days in November and was told it was still too early for the snow, but nevertheless I said, "I *must* see snow here in the country before I leave." To this Greta answered, "Then you had better try and do something about it." Jokingly I answered, "Tonight I will pray for snow and we will have some tomorrow." That night I did pray for snow and the next morning about seven o'clock, while it was still dark, Greta tossed a snowball through the open window at my bed. It had snowed all night.

Seeing snow made me say how much I would love to experience Christmas in Sweden. Soon after, the whole household suddenly took on an air of mystery. The servants whispered and ran to and fro in the hallways. Greta and the Countess disappeared for hours. They said they were going to the village and did not want me with them. I was rather hurt at this and I went for a walk by myself and nursed my feelings.

That evening with a look of mischief in her eyes, Greta told me to dress for dinner and make myself look as nice as possible. She said a distinguished guest was coming. She herself put on a white sweater and white slacks and twined flowers in her hair. Before dinner we went down to the library and in front of a roaring fire had several rounds of schnapps, which made us very gay. When the Count and Countess appeared in full evening dress, I knew that indeed something out of the ordinary was about to take place.

When the butler opened the doors leading into the dining room, there stood a Christmas tree as high as the ceiling, completely decorated, with brightly lighted candles on its boughs. The table was festively arranged and the whole room had a genuine air of Christmas spirit.

After a delicious dinner with many kinds of wines, everyone gave me presents. Greta gave me a pair of rubber boots which I wore all the following day tramping across the fields with her. I was tremendously touched by the whole evening.

Before I left Stockholm, Greta took me to see the house where she was born. She made no comment as we stood looking at it—nor did I. I was very much moved. I was moved because it was her birthplace and also by the fact that she had brought me there to see it. I knew that such a gesture meant much to her. As we moved away neither of us spoke.

Forty-Two

My first day back in Hollywood I went to the studio to report to Thalberg. He told me he was planning to produce *Camille* for Greta and asked me what I thought of the idea. I answered that I thought she would be magnificent in the role, surpassed possibly only by Duse. He seemed pleased and relieved and asked me to reread the play in French and make notes. He asked me to describe how Bernhardt had acted the part. I left the studio stimulated and excited that Greta was to play what seemed to me a perfect role for her, and one that had been done by two such great actresses as Duse and Bernhardt. I felt sure that her performance would be compared to theirs and that her acting of it would create a trio—an unforgettable trio of Camilles—approached differently but, nevertheless, achieving perfection each in its own way.

When Greta returned she decided to move and I was anxious to have her take a better and more gaily furnished house with more grounds and, possibly, a tennis court or a swimming pool. For some time I had had my eye on the one I hoped she would get. Unfortunately it was rented to Jeannette MacDonald and the real estate agents reported that she had no intention of leaving it. We looked at other houses but always returned to this one.

"What's the use of discussing it? I just can't have it. Miss MacDonald obviously intends to remain in it and since she had it first, why shouldn't she?" said Greta, but I did not accept this.

Without consulting her, I finally came to the conclusion that something must be done to get it for her. I decided to work toward this end on an unseen level. Every night I lay in bed and visualized Miss MacDonald moving out of the house and Greta moving into it. I even told the real estate woman that certain things were coming to pass which led me to believe Miss MacDonald would unexpectedly give it up. I advised her to begin looking for another tenant without letting Miss MacDonald know it.

Shortly after this she called me up one day in great excitement and said that I was right—Miss MacDonald had informed them that she wanted to move. When they asked her why, she said she did not know what it was but that "something" was urging her to move.

Whether this "something" was my doing or not, I shall never know. But the result was that Greta got the house, and according to the real estate women, Miss MacDonald was quite content in another one they found for her.

At this time Greta had started shooting *Camille*. Practically all the time she was filming, she was not well and it was a great physical effort for her to make it. This was very unfortunate for her, but her suffering was an undeniable asset to the picture. It gave a reality to the suffering and illness she had to portray in the character of Marguerite Gauthier.

Many times when she was on the set or actually playing before the camera she was in such pain that she could barely stand on her feet. Often she came directly from the studio to my house, looking deadly white and sometimes scarcely able to drag herself up the stairs. I would make her lie down and rest before we went out for a walk in the hills, because no matter how ill she felt, she always said that after a day cooped up in the studio and shooting in the lights she simply had to have air.

There is no doubt that at this time she really was ill, but there was also a psychological factor involved. She had so much identified herself with the character of Marguerite Gauthier that even off the set and out of the studio she was conscious of the illness of this tubercular woman. Sometimes when we walked in the hills or on the beach she would stop and put her hand to her heart as though her breath was coming too fast. I never commented on these spells but immediately tried to tell her something amusing to dissociate her from the character of Marguerite Gauthier.

It was not a happy time and I was glad when the shooting of this film was over. I have seen it many times since it first was released in

1937, but, as each scene brings back to me Greta's personal suffering; I have no fondness for it, although it is regarded by nearly everyone except myself as her greatest film.

At this time I saw quite a lot of Gabriel Pascal, whom I had known when he was producing films in Europe. I was very fond of this dark-eyed, imaginative Hungarian with the so-called Gypsy temperament. During this period he was completely broke—a state not unusual for him! For one reason or another he could not get a job at any studio. He was living in a boardinghouse for which he paid five dollars a week and used to come to my house for nearly all his meals. If he had an engagement so that he could not come for his usual meal, Anna made him up a package of sandwiches.

He was constantly telling me then that he had a dream in which he met Bernard Shaw who told him he could have the rights to all his plays for films. Shaw had so far refused to give the film rights to anyone although many people had tried to get them. Gabriel and I often discussed why he wouldn't do it. One day I said to him, "Why don't you go to England and try to persuade him to give them to you? Your dream may mean something and after all you have as much chance with the old boy as anyone else." To this Gabriel answered, "How could I get there without money?" I suggested hitching from California to New York and working his way over to England on a cargo boat.

Not long after this he accepted my challenge. I did not hear from him for a number of months. Then one day a letter came saying that Shaw had given him the film rights of all his plays and he was planning to begin production with *Pygmalion*. His letter went on to explain that looking very shabby and unshaven he had gone to Shaw's house and rung the bell. The maid had demanded his name. To this Gabriel responded, "Tell Mr. Shaw he will gain more from seeing me than I will lose from not seeing him." Happily Shaw overheard this remark, as he was listening behind the door. The message amused him and he told the maid to show Gabriel into the study. "My good man, what can I do for you?" he said. Undaunted, Gabriel explained his mission. Shaw smiled. "Very interesting. But where is your money and how do you intend to bring this venture about?" Whereupon Gabriel produced a shilling. He laid it on the table and said, "This is my money but add to this shilling your signature on a contract to me and it will turn into millions of pounds." Shaw walked over to his desk and, according to Gabriel, drew up a contract to him that very hour. Gabriel's productions of *Pygmalion* and other Shaw plays have since become film history.

At this time, a young and then little-known Hindu dancer, Ram Gopal, arrived in Hollywood. He was a superb dancer, but he had yet to become the most famous young Indian dancer of our time—a distinction which he achieved after his great success at the Edinburgh Festival in 1956. At first sight we became friends. We share a feeling of timelessness. I, for instance, have no memory of historic dates, which undoubtedly springs from the fact that time as it is commonly regarded has no reality for me.

For this reason I found it a relief that Ram was not concerned with time in its smaller aspect of dates and years. I once asked him if recently there had been any changes in the classical form of Indian dancing.

"Recently?" he mused, looking a little sad. "Yes, quite recently there has been a change."

"When was this change? How long ago?" I asked, expecting him to say during the nineteenth century.

"About a thousand years ago," he answered.

Somewhere during this period, Cornelia Runyan wanted her house back, so I was forced to move. Luckily, I found a charming little house on Carmelina Drive. It was a small Spanish-style house with a patio and it belonged to that very fine actress Aileen MacMahon, who was then acting in New York and was willing to rent it to me for a few months.

It was in this house that I saw for the last time my beautiful friend Greta Kemble Cooper. She came out to California desperately ill, to stay with her sister Violet. In fact, she was dying and to see her saddened me beyond words. I thought, however, that she would live longer than she did, and while under this impression I unfortunately left for Europe.

I had received a cable from Sri Meher Baba, who had returned from India and was in the south of France. He wanted me to come over and see him, as he was soon returning to India. I was at this time seeking some kind of spiritual guidance and I blindly agreed to go and see him as he requested.

After reaching New York I had just time to board the *Normandie*, sailing that night. When the ship had put out to sea, Noel Coward appeared in my cabin. I had not known he was on board and I was delighted to see him. This made the trip start off well and we had a lot of fun the whole way over.

When I arrived in the south of France I found Sri Meher Baba in a large comfortable house in the hills back of Cannes, overlooking the sea. He was in high spirits all the time I visited him. He had brought with him a harmless but insane young Hindu who was mad on the subject of God and used to shout and pray out loud. One day he locked himself in the toilet and prayed at a great rate in there. No one could entice him to open the door and it finally had to be broken in.

One afternoon the Baba asked me to go for a drive with him and the mad Hindu. We drove in an open car, and just as the chauffeur slowed down for the traffic in Nice the Hindu began to shout at the top of his lungs. A policeman stopped the car and asked Baba what the trouble was. Baba put his hand to his mouth and made strange sounds to explain that he did not speak. The Hindu shouted louder and began to sing. At this point I took it upon myself to explain the situation to the policeman. I said that one gentleman had taken a vow of silence and the other one was mad but harmless. He pushed his cap back and scratched his head. He was hot and the whole thing was too much for him. Shrugging his shoulders, he waved his hand and told us to go on.

Staying with Baba at this time was one of his disciples, Ruano Bogislav. She was a remarkable character and I dearly loved her. She had at one time been married to the opera singer Riccardo Martin and she was the mother of Bijie de Wardener who, before the war, ran Mainbocher's *couture* house for him in Paris. Bijie and I were old friends from the *What Next* days.

Ruano was also a singer. She sang folk songs in eighteen languages. She was strikingly handsome and the most fearless person I ever met. She traveled all over the world with absolutely no money but something always miraculously turned up to help her. If it didn't, she didn't care. She slept as comfortably in a field or in a railroad station as in the Ritz and said her only extravagance was her love of cigars. It was one of my greatest pleasures to have a Corona cigar waiting for her when she came to see me.

One day Baba came into my room. He saw my black cape hanging in the cupboard and, by chance, a Spanish hat was on the shelf. He put the hat on, draped himself in the cape and began dancing a Spanish dance. He danced round the room and from one side to the other, snapping his fingers at the same time. He danced gracefully and I marked time by clapping my hands. I began to laugh. He dragged me up and made me dance with him. I was delighted to see him so gay and full of fun but I hoped none of the *gopis* (women disciples) would come in and catch us. This was what I loved about Baba. He was always unpredictable. Before I had been there a week he spelled out on his board that I had to go back to Hollywood. "Move again! But I have only just arrived.

Must I move again?" I complained. He spelled out on the board, "That's the idea—keep moving. Never allow yourself to become static."

So I caught the *Normandie* on her return trip and I was back in Hollywood before anyone knew I had left. No one but Greta was even aware that I had been to Europe and back.

Shortly after my return from Europe, Irving Thalberg died. He had a bad cold but had gone to the Hollywood Bowl to hear some music. His cold turned into pneumonia and within forty-eight hours he was dead.

This was a great blow to Metro-Goldwyn-Mayer and the film world. He was the only man in Hollywood at this time who had vision and a high standard in making pictures. There was no one to take his place, and I knew that no one could take his place as far as producing for Greta was concerned. She was very much affected by his death and I had a premonition then that she would not continue very long in pictures.

As for myself, I was not only saddened by his personal loss but I knew it was the end to any hopes I might have had for my *Jehanne d'Arc*. I also felt there would be many changes in the studio and that a number of people, including myself, would lose their jobs.

I was right about this. A great many people who worked for Thalberg were taken off the payroll and I was one of them.

Forty-Three

During the summer of 1938 I was back again in Europe. My Hindu friend, Ram Gopal, was booked for a series of dance recitals in Warsaw in July. Janta Polczynski, a Polish poet and writer, was managing Ram and he asked me to come over and help him with these recitals. He invited us to stay with him on his family's estate in a place called Komorza, not far from the German border.

As Ram was already in Komorza when I left Paris for Poland I set out by myself, and in Berlin I had a very unpleasant experience. When I boarded the Nord Express from Paris I had several hand pieces of luggage which I saw the porter place in the rack over my seat. When we reached the Belgian border the customs officer marked each piece over my head, but when the train drew into the Potsdamer Bahnhof at eleven o'clock that night and I called a porter, the luggage was not there.

I was completely mystified and in a great state of excitement called the conductor, who spoke French. He was a typical Prussian and when I asked him where my luggage was, he looked me coldly in the eye and said he had seen me board the train in Paris without any.

I jumped from the train and ran to find the station master. I had only twenty-one minutes to make my connection. Unfortunately the station master could speak only German. Mine is extremely bad and in my hurry and fear I could not get a word out. A pale blond student came forward and in French said he would translate for me. I told him about the disappearance of my luggage and he explained it to the station master, who sauntered off to find the conductor as the minutes passed. When he returned with the conductor the villain repeated again that he had seen me board the train without luggage. The station master shrugged his shoulders and merely suggested that I run for the train to Poland.

Frantic with rage, I said I would miss it, spend the night in a hotel and go to the American Embassy the first thing in the morning. By this time it was pouring. The student walked silently with me to a nearby hotel where I spent a restless night with a huge photograph of Hitler over my bed and without even a toothbrush to make me comfortable.

Just before dawn I heard a faint noise outside my door and then the sound of a piece of paper being slipped under it. After a minute I turned on the light and got up. It was from the student and written in French. He wrote that he was in great danger because he was against the Nazi regime and implored me to help him get out of Germany. He added that he knew my luggage had been taken off the train so that it could be searched, and he advised me to leave Germany as soon as I could without even trying to recover it. He signed his name and put down his address.

I tore this hysterical note into little pieces and put it down the toilet. In a very nervous state of mind I waited for the morning, still planning to go to the embassy.

But I did not have to. At seven o'clock my telephone rang and a man spoke to me in English. Without any explanation he said that my luggage had been found. He said a train was leaving for Poland at eight-thirty and he suggested that I take it. And indeed I did. When I reached Poland and finally Komorza, I found Ram and Janta very disturbed at my delay. When I told them my story they decided that because of my Spanish name the Nazis might have thought me a Spanish Loyalist and wanted to discover why I was going to Poland. This may or may not have been the reason.

I stayed several weeks in Komorza with Janta and his mother—"Mamushka," as we called her—on their very beautiful estate. Little did we dream then that within a short time it would be overrun by Nazis, and later by Communists, the family narrowly escaping into the woods while many of the farm hands and servants were murdered.

One of my most pleasant memories of this visit was driving in an ancient carriage, a relic of better days, with the old driver wearing a faded green livery. The carriage was what used to be called a victoria and, with the hood down, we drove through waving golden wheat fields, the horses bending their heads to make an opening through the stalks. The wheat broke and snapped around us as the carriage rolled from one side to the other. We drove in the sunlight, laughing and joking, through miles and miles of wheat, and it seemed to me as though I were taking part in a scene from Chekhov or Turgenev.

I was back in Paris when the crisis came which was only temporarily postponed by the Munich Pact. There were grim hours before the Pact was signed and it was not known whether there would be war or not. Paris was in darkness and there was suddenly a complete disappearance of manpower, as all had gone to report for service. Most Americans rushed for whatever ship they could get and, I regret to say, behaved very badly. My hotel emptied out. All the waiters, valets and menservants had been called to their regiments. Actually, the only guests left were Marlene Dietrich and myself. Several of my American friends, including Malvina Hoffman, had tried to make me sail with them, but I felt that since I had lived in France so much in peacetime I should stand by it in danger. In the stress of the moment, however, one morning, intending to pour eyewash in my eyecup so as to soothe my eyes, I poured in cleaning fluid, and after applying it I was blinded. I shouted for Marlene on the telephone. She rushed down to my room and put cold compresses on my eyes. Luckily, they were not injured.

A blacked-out city was a new experience then. I remember walking in the darkness from my hotel on the Avenue George V to the Place Vendôme where my friend Lady Iya Abdy was living. She too had stayed on and, as she has the courage of a lion, she was a great comfort to me. She is Russian by birth but she became a British subject when she married Lord Abdy. She is a warm, striking-looking, remarkable personality and for many years she was a prominent figure in the artistic and social life of Paris. That night we did not know whether there would be war or not and we sat in the darkness discussing it. Then suddenly we heard over the radio that Daladier and Chamberlain were flying to Munich.

After the Munich Pact was signed, Daladier returned triumphantly to Paris, and I was standing in front of the Guaranty Trust Company on the Place de la Concorde when he drove through on his way to the Senate. The crowds were wild with enthusiasm, the newspapers carried great headlines, PEACE IN OUR TIME, and that night people danced in the streets with joy.

Strangely enough I did not feel easy. I cannot say I foresaw war but I remember feeling that I must hurry to do whatever I wanted to do.

And this time I wanted most of all to go to India to see the great Indian sage and saint, Ramana Maharshi, and I felt that I must go at once.

I had very little money, far too little to risk going to India, but something pushed me toward it. I went to the steamship company and booked myself one of the cheapest cabins on an Indian ship, the S.S. *Victoria,* sailing from Genoa to Bombay toward the beginning of October. In the meantime I flew to Dublin to see my sister Baba and her husband, Freddie Shaw, and their two children Frederick and Mercedes. Like many youngest sons, Freddie had no money, but he was a remarkably good and fine man. They were living in a modest little house and I never saw a family so devoted to each other or so happy together.

Alfredo Sides' wife sailed with me to India. She intended to stay there several years with Sri Meher Baba, but Alfredo, when he came to the station to see us off to Genoa, said, "Don't let Consuelo do anything foolish and please take care of her." Before Alfredo, Consuelo had been married to Charles Nungesser, the aviator who tried to fly west over the Atlantic at the same time that Lindbergh flew east. Nungesser was lost on the flight. But it was not until she married the unmarriageable Alfredo that we became close friends. I will never know what made Alfredo suddenly marry. He was out of character in doing so and was certainly not the husband for Consuelo.

I had booked passage to Ceylon intending from there to cross over to southern India and go directly to Tiruvannamalai where Ramana Maharshi lived. But when the ship called at Bombay, Norina Matchabelli came on board to see me with a message from Meher Baba saying that Consuelo and I must get off the ship and come to see him in Ahmednagar, about two hours from Bombay. I did not want to do this as my real purpose in India was to see the Maharshi, and I was impatient to get to him. But Consuelo was going to Baba and she and Norina pressed me to do the same. It was an appallingly hot day and I had a migraine headache, so I let them pack my things and, in a daze, followed them off the boat. I remember edging my way through masses of people whose dark faces stood out in the brilliant sunlight against the white which the men wore. There was also a great deal of color among the crowds—turbans and saris of brilliant pinks, blues, greens, every imaginable color, and after the incessant black one sees worn in occidental countries, Bombay gave me the impression of a gay festival.

The next day we motored to Baba's ashram in Ahmednagar. This was a place he had built a number of years ago, even before he had European disciples. He had built it for what are called in India "God-mad men and women." These are people who become possessed by God and the spiritual life, and go out of their minds. A great many of them had become insane at an early age. Thousands of them wander all over India, sleep in the fields and are fed by anyone who gives them food. Most of them are harmless, but their physical condition becomes tragic. Although they are considered holy and like the Sacred Cow allowed privileges, down through the ages nothing had been done about them by the government or by individuals.

Meher Baba is the first person in India who has taken care of them and attempted to cure them. He sends his *Mandali* (men disciples) throughout India to bring as many of them as they can to his ashram. Here he puts them in order physically, and then works spiritually and psychologically to cure them. He has cured hundreds of them and many of them, after coming to their senses, have become his Mandali and helped to cure others. When I arrived in Ahmednagar, Baba had a great compound where about five thousand of these mad people lived. I saw him bathe many of them, a technique he uses to work spiritually through water, which seems to calm a great many of them in an extraordinary fashion. I was very much impressed by these sessions.

I was, however, not at all happy my first night in the ashram. Baba had many times spoken to me about it, and he had always promised me that if I ever went there I would have a room or a cabin of my own. This point had been brought up because Norina had told me that all the women slept in dormitories. I am a poor sleeper and I knew that under these conditions I would not be able to sleep. Also I have a horror of a lot of women herded together. This is one of the reasons why I have always hated convents and the life of nuns and any kind of dormitory school life. So I was extremely upset when I was told I would have to sleep in a dormitory. I mentioned this to Norina, who brushed my objections aside and said that I had to be "like everyone else." Looking back on it now I realize that I had no right to expect special treatment. Baba was possibly teaching me a lesson, but I felt that a man who was a spiritual teacher should not break his word.

In any case I spent a miserable night. The heat was terrific, many of the women snored, and all of them had pots under their beds which they used during the night. This was about the last straw for me. I arose at five and I was in no good mood when Norina told me that Baba expected Consuelo and me to stay with him for five years.

"Five years!" I cried. "Are you out of your mind? I came to India to see the Maharshi and I am leaving here today."

I went to Baba's cabin. He was sitting on the floor in the Buddha posture with bare feet and a garland of flowers around his neck. He embraced me warmly and I sat down on the floor before him. He spelled out on his board, "I see you have slept badly." I shrugged my shoulders. I was not going into all that again. He continued. "I want you and Consuelo to stay here with me for five years. I hope you will agree to this."

"I regret terribly to have to refuse you this request. I could not possibly remain here and I must not deceive you, Baba. In case you don't already know it, I must tell you I came to India to see Ramana Maharshi."

He asked on the board, "Do you consider the Maharshi a Perfect Master?"

"I don't know anything about such things. I am no judge of Masters or of the fact that they exist. I only know that I long to see the Maharshi with all my heart, and I must go to him."

"When do you want to leave?"

"I would like to leave today."

"There is no car to take you to Bombay today. You will have to go tomorrow. But Consuelo will remain."

"I hope she will not. Alfredo put her in my care and I think after a few months she should go back to Europe."

Baba made no comment on this and I felt dismissed. Suddenly I knew I was no longer within the inner circle. The European disciples withdrew from me and their attitude strengthened my wish to leave. I did not feel any spirituality in such a lack of understanding.

That night Norina walked up and down with me in the compound. She made one more effort to change my mind and used all her charm and force of personality—and she had an abundance of both—to accomplish this. When Norina spoke of Baba or God she became ferocious. She told me laughingly once that Professor Jung had called her a "God-beast" because, he said, he feared she might devour God. It was a dark night and as we walked she swung a lantern back and forth in her hand. She told me that by refusing Baba's request I would face ten terrible incarnations. I laughed and said, "I'll take my chances." She said, "Surely you are not thinking of going back to that horrible Western world and to that terrible Hollywood!" I told her that after I had seen the Maharshi it was quite likely I would return to Hollywood. She threw her hands up in disgust. "There is nothing to be done with you. You are lost."

The next day I had a battle with Consuelo. Norina had persuaded her to stay. But I won out. As we were leaving, Meher Baba was very gracious to us, which was more than the others were. He kissed us both good-by and enacted a promise from me that I would not go to see either Gandhi or the Maharshi before sightseeing all over India. I afterwards regretted this because it caused me to miss meeting Gandhi.

When we left Bombay, Consuelo and I kept our promise to Baba and went on quite an extensive tour of India. Among the many places we saw I was most charmed, in a worldly sense, by the little city of Jaipur built entirely of pink stone. Here was a fairy tale world—a world from a Bakst ballet. In front of the pink palace with its ornate door of gold stood Indian guards wearing only short white skirts and white jaipurs, and the most beautiful green turbans draped in a very special manner. I saw a string of elephants belonging to the Maharajah sauntering past the palace. Thrown over their backs were blankets of the most exquisite gold material, while on their heads sat naked boys in the Buddha posture wearing brilliantly colored turbans, and directing the elephants with sharp cries.

Because of the paintings and photographs I had seen of the Taj Mahal I had expected to dislike it. But we had the good fortune to arrive in Agra by full moon, and as I stood in front of the Taj I was overcome by its white beauty. It seemed to me a living thing, and when I touched it the stone was warm and lifelike. The heat of the sun on the stone did not cool off at night.

Benares, of course, is an unforgettable experience. There too we were fortunate, as we arrived for an eclipse of the moon, an event considered sacred by the Indians who are tremendously influenced by astrology and the heavens. Millions of people crowded down to the Ganges and plunged into it, many of them carrying their sick and dead. Regardless of the consequences they were determined to submerge in the river at the moment of the eclipse.

We went to Ellora, and Ajanta. Here, in the caves of Ellora, and especially Ajanta, I felt art transcended beyond art. Here was some blending of mysterious forces that went beyond the human. Here was the testimony of the divine heights man can reach. This was an experience for me beyond Greece and beyond the greatest Gothic cathedral.

Meher Baba wired us to go to Poona, and when we got there he sent us a message to go to a certain cave and meditate for several weeks. This I flatly refused to do. I told Consuelo she could do so if she wished, but that I was on my way to southern India and the Maharshi. So she came along with me. We went to Bangalore, Mysore, and Madras and then to Pondicherry, hoping to see Aurobindo Ghose in his ashram.

Oddly enough, we arrived in Pondicherry on November 21 not knowing that Aurobindo always held darshan on the 22. This word, in a sense, means what Christians would call a blessing or benediction. It is derived from the Sanscrit *darshana,* meaning cognition or even sight. And yet it is not exact to say it is a blessing or a benediction because darshan is neither given nor received—it *occurs.* It may appear to be given by a saint or a sage, but it is not. It is really an experience. An experience which may occur at the sight of the river Ganges, or at the sight of a holy temple, or at the sight of a sacred hill such as Arunachala —any one of these may give darshan as well as a person. The thing to understand is that any spiritually-minded Indian will travel hundreds of miles and put up with any discomfort if at the end he is to receive darshan. Thousands of people had already arrived; many of them had been walking for six months from villages in the north to arrive in time for darshan. The town was already crowded and masses of people were sleeping in the fields. Consuelo and I, not knowing what the crowd was about, went to the ashram and rang the bell. A disciple, dressed in a sort of monk's costume, opened the door. I asked if it would be possible for us to see Aurobindo. He could not have been more surprised. He explained that no one ever saw Aurobindo and that he lived in complete seclusion except on the day of the darshan, which happened to be the next day and was the reason for the great crowds in the town.

It would seem now that Consuelo and I should have known all this, but twenty years ago very few people outside of India knew much about the great Indian sages such as Aurobindo and the Maharshi. I had read everything that Aurobindo had written, although it had not always been easy to get his books in Europe or America. But I did not actually know about his habits as I did about Ramana Maharshi's, in whom I was intensely interested and had taken the greatest pains to find out everything about. I do not wish to attempt a comparison between these two sages. Aurobindo was an intellectual and in his early years he had been in politics. In his later years, in his years of seclusion, he had, I believe, allowed himself to be dramatized by the Mother, a Frenchwoman who ran the ashram and had an enormous influence on him and who understood the value of creating the legend around him that he never saw anyone but her, except at darshan, which he gave twice a year—November 22nd and March 22nd.

When I understood that I could not see Aurobindo alone and would have to wait till the next day to see him with thousands of other people, I asked if we might see President Wilson's daughter Margaret, who was living in the ashram and whom Consuelo and I both knew. She was, of course, surprised to see us but immediately said she could arrange for us to go to darshan and would also find a place for us to spend the night, as the ashram and the hotels were already crowded. As we passed through corridors I had an unpleasant sensation. To me it seemed like another convent and I have always wanted to forget my convent experiences. Women in nunlike costumes were whispering in corners and the whole place had a deadly atmosphere as well as a theatrical one. This was not surprising, as the Mother, who was the supreme influence there, had been on the stage in France. She had evidently not lost her sense of theatre over the years.

I asked Margaret Wilson if she was happy. She said she was and that not for anything would she want to leave the ashram. She said she hoped to die there and only a few years later she got her wish.

That night Margaret arranged for us to stay in the house of a French lady—a Madame Yvonne Gaebelé. Darshan was to be at five o'clock in the morning. Madame Gaebelé graciously served us tea and cakes at three o'clock in the morning and around four we went to the ashram with our garlands and fell into line with the many people who had been holding their places all night. Madame Gaebelé was well known at the ashram and because of her and Margaret Wilson we were allowed to go almost to the front of the line. There was great tension and an extraordinary silence as everyone waited for Aurobindo to appear and take his place on a huge chair on a high platform. Everything was in readiness when suddenly a disciple appeared and made the astounding announcement that Aurobindo would not give darshan. He explained that Aurobindo had sprained his ankle and was in too much pain to give it. He said the Mother would give darshan in his place. I could hardly believe my ears. Thousands of poor people who had traveled hundreds of miles, many of whom had been journeying for months, were to be disappointed because of a sprained ankle. There was a hush, and a wave of depression ran through the crowd that was almost staggering. Many people wept, but I was angry. "If a spiritual leader can disappoint so many people how can one find fault with a government leader or a politician?" I asked out loud—but no one answered me.

The Mother appeared and mounted the platform. Made up within an inch of her life, her lips scarlet and her hair brightly dyed, she wore a trailing chiffon dress, and as she took her place on the chair I wondered if anyone in that crowd could experience darshan. But we all filed past her, placing our garlands at her feet. I felt like a first-class hypocrite. Some years later Vincent Sheean told me that when he was in the similar position before the Mother she had slyly winked at him. I was glad to hear this. It at least made me feel better to know she had some humor. But strangely enough, opinions differ. Consuelo was impressed by the Mother and by the whole place. She wanted to stay there. I, however, said good-by to Margaret, and sadly enough it was really a last good-by. As I left the ashram I wondered how such a great man as Aurobindo could have allowed himself to be so exploited. He is now dead, but the Mother still carries on in the ashram even though the Light has gone out.

Forty-Four

I left Pondicherry and spiritually turned my heart toward Tiruvannamalai where the Maharshi lived. To get there, however, I had to return to Madras. On my way to Madras I had an amusing experience. This particular day I traveled third class in order to study the native types, but the only occupants of the coach besides myself were an old Indian (wearing a loincloth) and a well-dressed young Indian barrister. Presently the conductor appeared and began to talk very excitedly to me in the language of southern India—Tamil. I shrugged my shoulders and said in English that I did not understand Tamil, at the same time displaying my ticket and making signs that I hoped there was nothing wrong with it. The old man leaned forward and, in the most scholarly English, asked if he might translate for me and explain what the conductor was saying. I was delighted and asked if anything was wrong with the ticket. "It is not your ticket he is asking about. He is asking if you believe in the unity of the Divine and the individual soul."

Not a little staggered by this question, I tried, however, to appear as though such an inquiry from a railroad conductor was the most natural in the world. I then replied that I was of the opinion that there is no separation between the Divine Source and the individual soul. My interpreter conveyed my sentiments to the conductor who beamed at me and nodded and bowed, making me understand that he, too, held these same views. He then mumbled something and rushed off into the other coach. "He says he is going to collect the tickets," the loinclothed one remarked, "but he will soon return for further conversation." He not only returned, but he settled himself down next to me, peering into my face, and until I reached my destination we four discussed the Vedas, the old man translating from time to time to the conductor.

In Madras I hired a car and, so anxious was I to arrive in Tiruvannamalai that I did not go to bed and traveled by night, arriving about seven o'clock in the morning after driving almost eleven hours. I was very tired as I got out of the car in a small square in front of the temple. The driver explained that he could take me no further as there was no road up the hill where Bhagavan could be found. I learned then to call the Maharshi "Bhagavan," which means Lord and is a title by which he was always addressed. A religious ceremony was in progress, and men wearing bright-colored turbans and women in their festive saris were already surging into the square, carrying garlands of flowers and images of Siva. I did not linger to watch them, but turned toward the hill of Arunachala and hurried in the hot sun along the dust-covered road to the abode about two miles from the town where the Sage dwelt. As I ran those two miles up the hill, deeply within myself I knew that I was running toward the greatest experience of my life. I was no longer tired and I was unaware of the distance and of the heat of the sun on my uncovered head. I ran the whole way and when I reached the ashram I was not even out of breath.

Though only 2,682 feet high, Arunachala dominates the landscape. It looks as though a giant hand had quietly opened and dropped it into place. From the south side of the ashram it is just a symmetrical hill with two almost equal foothills, one on either side. But its aspect changes as the sun moves and the light varies. It has many faces and early in the morning a white cloud often drapes what seems to be its brow—in reality its summit.

The ashram was a small place. I remember only a stone hall where day and night Bhagavan sat on a couch. Not far from this hall, scattered around the hill, were small houses where some of the disciples lived, including his brother. I am told that all this has greatly changed. Once the Sage's great spiritual reputation began to spread, the ashram grew larger. In my time comparatively few people journeyed to see Bhagavan and only a few Western women had ever been there. In 1943 Heinrich Zimmer, the famous authority on Indian spiritual thought, wrote a book about the Maharshi called *The Way of the Self* for which Jung wrote a Preface. In recent years, and especially since his death in 1950, Bhagavan has become widely known all over the world.

The Sage in Somerset Maugham's book *The Razor's Edge* is supposed to be Ramana Maharshi. It is possible that this is so as a few weeks before my visit to the ashram, Somerset Maugham had been there. I was told that an English author had come to see Bhagavan and had fainted when first coming into his presence. I asked his name but they did not know how to pronounce it. One of the disciples retired and came back with *Somerset Maugham* written on a piece of paper. A few years later I saw Mr. Maugham in New York and inquired if he had actually been to see the Maharshi. He said he had, but I did not feel I should trespass on a possible spiritual experience by asking if it was true that he had fainted.

When, dazed and filled with emotion, I first entered the hall, I did not quite know what to do. Coming from strong sunlight into the somewhat darkened hall, it was, at first, difficult to see. Nevertheless, I perceived Bhagavan at once, sitting in the Buddha posture on his couch in the corner. At the same moment I felt overcome by some strong power in the hall as if an invisible wind was pushing violently against me. For a moment I felt dizzy. Then I recovered myself. To my great surprise I suddenly heard an American voice calling out to me, "Hello, come in." It was the voice of an American named Guy Hague, who originally came from Long Beach, California. He told me later that he had been honorably discharged from the American Navy in the Philippines and had then worked his way to India, taking up the study of Yoga when he reached Bombay. Then he heard about Sri Ramana Maharshi and, feeling greatly drawn to him, decided to go to Tiruvannamalai. When I met him he had already been with the Maharshi for a year, sitting uninterruptedly day and night in the hall with the Sage.

He rose from where he was sitting against the wall and came toward me, taking my hand and leading me back to a place beside him against the wall. He did not at first speak to me, allowing me to pull myself together. I was able to look around the hall but my gaze was drawn to Bhagavan, who was sitting absolutely straight in the Buddha posture looking directly in front of him. His eyes did not blink or in any way move. Because they seemed so full of light I had the impression they were gray. I learned later that they were brown, although there have been various opinions as to the color of his eyes. His body was naked except for a loincloth. I discovered soon after that this and his staff were absolutely his only possessions. His body seemed firm and as if tanned by the sun, although I found that the only exercise he ever took was a twenty-minute walk every afternoon at five o'clock when he walked on the hill and sometimes greeted Yogis who came to prostrate themselves at his feet. The rest of the time, day and night, and for over half a century, he had been sitting on his couch. He was a strict vegetarian, but he only ate what was placed before him and he never expressed a desire for any kind of food. As he sat there he seemed like a statue, and yet something extraordinary emanated from him. I had a feeling that on some invisible level I was receiving spiritual shocks from him although his gaze was not directed toward me. He did not seem to be looking at anything, and yet I felt he could see and was conscious of the whole world.

"Bhagavan is in samadhi," Guy Hague said.

Samadhi is a very difficult state to explain. In fact I do not think anyone has ever explained it. Doctors have tried to analyze it from a medical and physical point of view, and have failed. I have heard it described as "a state of spiritual ecstasy in which consciousness leaves the body." But this is not the whole phenomenon, as the breath stops and so does the beating of the heart. But it is not a form of trance as in the trance state both of these continue. It is claimed that samadhi is a state attained only by highly enlightened people—people who have reached Spiritual Illumination. It is a state where the spirit temporarily leaves the body and goes into one of bliss. All the Enlightened Ones who have attained samadhi describe it as Bliss. In the last century the great saint Ramakrishna often went into samadhi. The Maharshi would go into it for hours at a time, and often for days. When I arrived at the ashram he had already been in it seven hours.

I looked around. Squatting on the floor or sitting in the Buddha posture or lying prostrate face down, a number of Indians prayed—some of them reciting their mantras out loud. Several small monkeys came into the hall and approached Bhagavan. They climbed onto his couch and broke the stillness with their gay chatter. He loved animals and any kind was respected and welcomed by him in the ashram. They were treated as the equals of humans and always addressed by their names. Sick animals were brought to Bhagavan and kept by him on his couch or on the floor beside him until they were well. Many animals had died in his arms. When I was there he had a much-beloved cow who wandered in and out of the hall, and often lay down beside him and licked his hand. He loved to tell stories about the goodness of animals. He was very fond, too, of snakes and many came into the hall to pay their respects. He always had a little milk for them. It was remarkable that none of the animals ever fought or attacked each other.

The story of the Bhagavan is a simple but unique one. Born into a poor Brahmin family of South India, at the age of seventeen he asked himself "Who am I?" He said, "I am not this changing body, nor am I these passing thoughts." Then he tried to imagine death. He stretched out and so vividly visualized himself dead that his body became cold and lifeless. This convinced him that the body was not he, but only a cloak that would be cast off at death. He decided that the goal of every life should be to find the Self and that nothing else was important. He had heard of the sacred hill of Arunachala and had long been attracted to it. He decided to go there and start the quest for the Self. He first went to the temple in Tiruvannamalai. There he meditated for several months with such spiritual absorption that the temple priest began to wonder about him. But people, sensing his holiness, became his devotees. Feeling that he was attracting too much attention in the temple, he left it and one night wound his way up the hill of Arunachala. At this early time he took up his abode in a cave and, until his death fifty-four years later, he never left the hill. Devotees found him and asked his help and guidance. Out of compassion he allowed them to live near him and from then until his death he allowed anyone—poor and rich, great and humble—to come freely to see him. He himself, through the quest of the Self, found Enlightenment, living out his long life in the egoless state but subject, nevertheless, to all the conditions of human pain and sickness. Bhagavan was asked many times about his egoless state. He explained it and said, "The Gnani (the Enlightened) continually enjoys uninterrupted, transcendental experience, keeping his inner attention always on the Source, in spite of the *apparent* existence of the ego, which the ignorant *imagine* to be real. This apparent ego is harmless; it is like the skeleton of a burnt rope—though it has form, it is of no use to tie anything with."

After I had been sitting several hours in the hall listening to the mantras of the Indians and the incessant droning of flies, and lost in a sort of inner world, Guy Hague suggested that I go and sit near the Maharshi. He said, "You can never tell when Bhagavan will come out of samadhi. When he does, I am sure he will be pleased to see you, and it will be beneficial for you, at this moment, to be sitting near him."

I moved near Bhagavan, sitting at his feet and facing him. Guy was right. Not long after this Bhagavan opened his eyes. He moved his head and looked directly down at me, his eyes looking into mine. It would be impossible to describe this moment and I am not going to attempt it. I can only say that at this second I felt my inner being raised to a new level—as if, suddenly, my state of consciousness was lifted to a much higher degree. Perhaps in this split second I was no longer my human self but the Self. Then Bhagavan smiled at me. It seemed to me that I had never before known what a smile was. I said, "I have come a long way to see you." He said, "I knew you were coming and I have been guiding your steps." There was a silence. I had stupidly brought a piece of paper on which I had written a number of questions I wanted to ask him. I fumbled for it in my pocket, but the questions were already answered by merely being in his presence. There was no need for questions or answers. Nevertheless, my dull intellect expressed one.

"Tell me, whom shall I follow—what shall I follow? I have been trying to find this out for years by seeking in religions, in philosophies, in teachers and teachings." Again there was a silence. After a few minutes, which seemed to me a long time, he spoke.

"You are not telling the truth. You are just using words—just talking. You know perfectly well whom to follow. Why do you need me to confirm it?"

"You mean I should follow my inner self?" I asked.

"I don't know anything about your inner self. You should follow the Self. There is nothing or no one else to follow."

I asked again, "What about religions, teachers, gurus?"

"If they can help in the quest of the Self. But *can* they help? Can religion, which teaches you to look *outside* yourself, which promises a heaven and a reward outside yourself, can this help you? It is only by diving deep into the Spiritual Heart that one can find the Self." He placed his right hand on my right breast and continued, "Here lies the Heart, the Dynamic, Spiritual Heart. It is called *Hridaya* and is located on the right side of the chest and is clearly visible to the inner eye of an adept on the Spiritual Path. Through meditation you can learn to find the Self in the cave of this Heart."

It is a strange thing but when I was very young, Ignacio Zuloaga said to me, "All great people function with the heart." He placed his hand over my physical heart and continued, "See, here lies the heart. Always remember to think with it, to feel with it, and above all, to judge with it."

But the Enlightened One raised the counsel to a higher level. He said, "Find the Self in the real Heart."

Both, just at the right moment in my life, showed me the Way.

Bhagavan was not a philosopher and he did not set himself up as a teacher, a master or a guru. He made the same statement all through his life—that there is no use knowing anything if one does not know the Self. He said, "Without knowing the Self, of what avail is it to know anything else? And, knowing the Self, what else remains yet to know? All else but the Self is ignorance." He pointed out a path to Liberation through the practice of "Self Enquiry" and the question "Who am I?" If this question is pursued and narrowed down, the questioner will arrive at understanding that there is no "I" because *I* am not my hands, my feet, my body, my so-called personality, or even my brain. I am certainly not my physical sum total, because, when I am dead, *where am I?* Does some success flatter me? I must ask the question *"Who is flattered?"* Am I sad? I ask the question *"Who is sad?"* By remembering that I am not the doer it is possible to understand the illusion of the world. Bhagavan gave as an example a bank clerk who handles money daily, but without agitation because he knows it is not *his* money. So, too, it is not the Real Self that is affected by changes of states or fortunes.

People said to Bhagavan, "I would like to find God." His answer was: "Find the Self first and then you won't have to worry about God." And once a man said to him, "I don't know whether to be a Catholic or a Buddhist." Bhagavan asked him, "What are you now?" The man answered, "I am a Catholic." He then said, "Go home and be a good Catholic and then you will know whether you should be a Buddhist or not."

Bhagavan pointed out to me that the Real Self is timeless. "But," he said, "in spite of ignorance, no man takes seriously the fact of death. He may see death around him, but he still does not believe that *he* will die. He believes, or rather, feels, in some strange way, that death is not *for him.* Only when the body is threatened does he fall a victim to the fear of death. Every man believes himself to be eternal, and this is actually the truth. This truth asserts itself in spite of man's ignorant belief that the body is the Self."

I asked him how to pray for other people. He answered, "If you are abiding within the Self, there are no other people. You and I are the same. When I pray for you I pray for myself and when I pray for myself I pray for you. Real prayer is to abide within the Self. This is the meaning of Tat Twam Asi—I Am Thou. There can be no separation in the Self. There is no need for prayer for yourself or any person other than to abide within the Self."

I said, "Bhagavan, you say that I am to take up the Search for the Self by Atman Vichara, asking myself the question Who Am I? May I ask Who Are You?"

Bhagavan answered, "When you know the Self, the 'I' 'You' 'He' and 'She' disappear. They merge together in pure Consciousness."

I understood then that Bhagavan, being egoless, could not speak for himself in terms of "I" or "We." His nearest approach to a direct answer was "Pure Consciousness" which to a discriminating mind did not answer the question, though it could not be answered in any other way. Bhagavan, abiding in the egoless state, was awake only to Truth and the Real Self. He was asleep to the world, the appearance of which is false, being born out of and sustained by ignorance.

Noticing one time what I thought were some evil-looking priests who had come from the temple, I remarked on them to Bhagavan. He said, "What do you mean by evil? I do not know the difference between what you call good and evil. To me they are both the same thing—just the opposite sides of the coin." I should have known this. Bhagavan was, of course, beyond duality. He was beyond love and hatred, beyond good and evil, and beyond all pairs of opposites.

To write of this experience with Bhagavan, to recapture and record all that he said, or all that his silences implied, is like trying to put the Infinite into an egg cup. One small chapter cannot in any way do him justice or give an impression of his Enlightenment, and I do not think that I am far enough spiritually advanced—if at all—to try to interpret his Supreme Knowledge. On me he had, and still has, a profound influence. I feel it presumptuous to say he changed my life. My life was perhaps not so important as all this. But I definitely saw life differently after I had been in his presence, a presence that just by merely "being" was sufficient spiritual nourishment for a lifetime. It may have been that when I returned from India undiscerning people saw very little change in me. But there was a change—a transformation of my entire consciousness. And how could it have been otherwise? I had been in the atmosphere of an egoless, world-detached, and completely Pure Being.

I sat in the hall with Bhagavan three days and three nights. Sometimes he spoke to me, other times he was silent and I did not interrupt his silence. Often he was in samadhi. I wanted to stay on there with him but finally he told me that I should go back to America. He said, "There will be what will be called a 'war,' but which, in reality, will be a great world revolution. Every country and every person will be touched by it. You must return to America. Your destiny is not in India at this time."

Before leaving the Ashram, Bhagavan gave me some verses he had selected from the Yoga Vasishta. He said they contained the essence for the Path of a Pure Life.

Steady in the state of fullness which shines when all desires are given up, and peaceful in the state of freedom in life, act playfully in the world, O Bhagava!

Inwardly free from all desires, dispassionate and detached, but outwardly active in all directions, act playfully in the world, O Bhagava!

Free from egoism, with mind detached as in sleep, pure like the sky, ever untainted, act playfully in the world, O Bhagava!

Conducting yourself nobly with kindly tenderness, outwardly conforming to conventions but inwardly renouncing all, act playfully in the world, O Bhagava!

Quite unattached at heart but for all appearance acting as with attachment, inwardly cool but outwardly full of fervour, act playfully in the world, O Bhagava!

I sorrowfully said farewell to Bhagavan. As I was leaving he said, "You will return here again." I wonder. Since his physical presence has gone I wonder if I shall. Yet often I feel the pull of Arunachala as though it were drawing me back. I feel the pull of that Sacred Hill of which he was so much a part, and where his mortal body lies buried.

Guy walked with me down the hill into the town. We went to the temple and saw the spot where Bhagavan had first attained samadhi. Then I went by car to see the beautiful temple in Madura, stopping on the way to see other temples in southern India. From Madura I went to Ceylon, stopping first at Colombo. I went, of course, to Kandy and to a number of places and temples throughout the island sacred to Buddhists. In Anuradhapura I had a deeply spiritual experience. I sat beneath the sacred Pipal or Bo-Tree under which Buddha often sat and preached his sermons. It was transplanted from Buddh Gaya, in India, to Anuradhapura by the Princess Sanghamitta around 288 B.C. It is the oldest historical tree existing. To me it was more than a tree. It was the living essence of Buddha himself. It had sheltered the Tathagata and surely drunk into its very roots the Supreme Holiness of the Blessed One. I touched its trunk and leaves and felt purified. And I sat beneath its shade and meditated.

While visiting a Buddhist monastery, a monk asked me if I came from America. When I told him that I did he said there was a monk in the monastery who was an American, but that, unfortunately, she was in India on the road with the begging bowl. In Buddhist monasteries no distinction is made between men and women. They both wear the yellow robe, shave their heads, are considered monks and are known only by the name they take when they enter the order. When I inquired this monk's name, he said he would go and look it up in the book. He came back with it written on a slip of paper. It was Constant Lounsbery. This was a great surprise to me as I had been looking for Constant Lounsbery since Rita's death in 1929. I had wanted to thank her for the very touching piece she had written about Rita then in the Paris *Herald Tribune.* I left a note for her there in Ceylon.

And there in Ceylon I received word from Gandhi that he would see me. I had written him before coming to India, but his answer had followed me around from one place to another and now, sadly enough, I did not have the money or the energy to retrace my steps and go north to him. Besides I felt that having seen the Maharshi, my cup was already filled and, in a sense, brimming over. I wired my regrets, thinking I would see him the next time I went to India. Alas. Had I known I surely would have made the effort.

Consuelo was there in Ceylon with me. Together we sailed on the S.S. *Victoria* from Colombo, the same ship we had arrived in India on. Two days later it stopped in Bombay. Consuelo couldn't make up her mind whether or not to get off and stay on in India a few weeks longer. At the last minute she got off and I sailed alone back to Europe.

Before leaving the ashram I wrote down several questions for Guy to ask Bhagavan that I had not had a chance to ask myself. I had been bothered by the fact that so many saints and enlightened people had been ill and suffering physically. I asked, should they not have perfect bodies and why do they not cure themselves? In Europe I got a letter from Guy saying he had discussed my question with Bhagavan. He wrote, "Bhagavan told me to tell you that the spiritually perfect person need not necessarily have a perfect body. The reason, as he explained it, is very simple. You see, the ego, the body and the mind are the same thing. The spiritually perfect person, like Bhagavan, is above these three things. Consequently he has no body to heal, neither a mind—or ego—to heal it with. He is beyond all this because it is illusion. He is living in Reality. Christian Scientists can take the mind and heal the body—for they are the same thing. American Indians heal, too, in this manner. It is faith healing. But if the spiritually perfect person is sick in body it is because the body is working out its Karma. Bhagavan gave an illustration of Karma, which he says is like an electric fan and must just run its course, only gradually ceasing even after it has been turned off. He says the mind is born into illusion and builds a body and a world to suit it—that is, a world that it has *earned* and *deserves* (by its Karma). Bhagavan, knowing the body and the mind to be *illusion,* cannot experience any bodily ailment or discomfort. *We* make him suffer pain, loss of weight, etc. It is in *our minds not his.* He is bodiless, actually is, though you and I cannot realize this as a fact."

In another letter Guy answered my questions, which led to others. He wrote down my questions and Bhagavan's answers.

Question: Is reincarnation a fact?

Bhagavan: You are incarnated now, aren't you? Then you will be so again. But as the body is illusion then the illusion will repeat itself and keep on repeating itself until you find the Real Self.

Question: What is death and what is birth?

Bhagavan: Only the body has death and birth, and it [the body] is illusion. There is, in Reality, neither birth nor death.

Question: How much time may elapse between death and rebirth?

Bhagavan: Perhaps one is reborn within a year, three years or thousands of years. Who can say? Anyway what is time? Time does not exist.

Question: Why have we no memory of past lives?

Bhagavan: Memory is a faculty of the mind and part of the illusion. Why do you want to remember other lives that are also illusions? If you abide within the Self, there is no past or future and not even a present since the Self is out of time—timeless.

Question: Are the world, the mind, ego and the body all the same thing?

Bhagavan: Yes. They are one and the same thing. The mind and the ego are one thing, but there is no word to explain this. You see, the world cannot exist without the mind, the mind cannot exist without what we call the ego [itself, really] and the ego cannot exist without a body.

Question: Then when we leave this body, that is when the ego leaves it, will it [the ego] immediately grasp another body?

Bhagavan: Oh, yes, it must. It cannot exist without a body.

Question: What sort of a body will it grasp then?

Bhagavan: Either a physical body or a subtle-mental-body.

Question: Do you call this present physical body the gross body?

Bhagavan: Only to distinguish it—to set it apart in conversation. It is really a subtle-mental-body also.

Question: What causes us to be reborn?

Bhagavan: Desires. Your unfulfilled desires bring you back. And in each case—in each body—as your desires are fulfilled, you create new ones. You must conquer desire to be absorbed into the One and thus end rebirth.

Question: Can sex change in rebirth?

Bhagavan: Oh, surely. We have all been both sexes many times.

Question: Is it possible to sin?

Bhagavan: Having a body, which creates illusion, is the only sin, and the body is our only hell. But it is right that we observe moral laws. The discussion of sin is too difficult for a few lines.

Question: Does one who has realized the Self lose the sense of "I"?

Bhagavan: Absolutely.

Question: Then to you there is no difference between yourself and myself, that man over there, my servant, are all the same?

Bhagavan: All are the same, including those monkeys.

Question: But the monkeys are not people. Are they not different?

Bhagavan: They are exactly the same as people. All creatures are the same in One Consciousness.

Question: Do we lose our individuality when we merge into the Self?

Bhagavan: There is no individuality in the Self. The Self is One— Supreme.

Question: Then individuality and identity are lost?

Bhagavan: You don't retain them in deep sleep, do you?

Question: But we retain them from one birth to another, don't we?

Bhagavan: Oh, yes. The "I" thought [the ego] will recur again, only each time you identify with it a different body and different surroundings around the body. The effects of past acts [Karma] will continue to control the new body just as they did the old one. It is Karma that has given you this particular body and placed it in a particular family, race, sex, surroundings and so forth.

Bhagavan added, "These questions are good, but tell de Acosta [he always called me de Acosta] she must not become too intellectual about these things. It is better just to meditate and have no thought. Let the mind rest quietly on the Self in the cave of the Spiritual Heart. Soon this will become natural and then there will be no need for questions. Do not imagine that this means being inactive. Silence is the only real activity." Then Guy added, "Bhagavan says to tell you that he sends you his blessings."

This message greatly comforted me.

On my way back to Europe my boat stopped at Port Said. I landed there and motored across the desert to Cairo where I stayed three days and then caught the ship again when it docked at Alexandria.

In Cairo I stayed at the old famous Shepheard's Hotel. I spent one day in the museum seeing the Tut-Ankh-Amon collection, and the second day I rode out by camel to see the Sphinx and the Great Pyramid. When I reached the Pyramid it was nearly sunset. There was no one around except my own dragoman and one or two Arabs sleeping against their kneeling camels. I decided to climb to the top of the Pyramid. Although it towered above me, tapering off into the sky, and looked terribly high, I did not realize how high it was until I started climbing. I started out briskly but after a certain distance I grew tired and my pace slackened. The steps of the Pyramid are very narrow and eroded, but I was determined to reach the top. Thoroughly exhausted, I finally did. The sun had already gone down. I turned and looked down the steep and awesome slope of the Pyramid. Suddenly I was overcome by the most frightful vertigo. My head swam and I felt that I was going to plunge to my death. I crouched on the narrow steps and clung to the top of the Pyramid so fiercely that my nails broke against the stone and my fingers bled. I could not bring myself to look down again. An agonizing fear took hold of me. I felt cold sweat pouring over my face, neck, and back. I became hysterical. What was I to do? I knew if I let go I would fall, but I also knew I could not hold on much longer. I closed my eyes. I remembered what the Maharshi said—to dive deep into the Spiritual Heart. I summoned every faculty and all power within me and concentrated on the Heart. Suddenly I saw it, like a great light, in my mind's eye. In the center I saw the Maharshi's face smiling at me. Instantly I felt calm. I turned and looked down. Far below I saw a man waving at me. I loosened one hand and held it over my head, then I waved back. The man began calling someone else. Another man ran to him. Swiftly they began to climb. They climbed expertly and fast but it seemed hours to me. Probably it took them about thirty-five minutes to reach me. One man had a rope. He tied it around my waist and gently stroked my face. He mumbled some words that I could not understand, but I knew they were kind words to encourage me. Between them, each one holding the rope as though we were mountain climbing, we began to descend. Eventually we reached the bottom safely.

Some time after this I was told by an enlightened person that climbing the Great Pyramid was considered in ancient Egypt one of the "fear tests" which students had to pass in order to be initiated into the great religious mysteries. Aspirants were required to climb to the very top of the Pyramid, and if on reaching the top of it he or she could conquer fear, this particular test was won.

Forty-Five

Back in Hollywood from India in the Spring of 1939, I felt very changed. All my values were different. I wondered why I had ever let Hollywood "get me down" or why I had ever cared whether I made a success in the studios or not. I rented a house near the sea with lemon trees around it. The blossoms were in full bloom when I moved in, and I can recall their fragrance distinctly. It was a new house and no one had ever lived in it. I was glad of this. The only trouble was that it was too large for just Anna, Chotzie and me. Bambina had died when I was in India. When Anna broke this news to me I was greatly saddened. She was eighteen years old, but I had hoped she would live until my return. I kept her basket, her blanket, and her toys in my room and I would not let Anna take them away. Then a strange thing happened. I was motoring home one evening in quite a heavy fog, and suddenly saw something gray running just a little in front of my car. I slowed up, thinking it was a rabbit. Then it disappeared. I stopped, fearing I would run over it. In the fog I could just dimly see the side of the road. I opened the door. Something darted in and jumped onto my lap, and that "something" began madly licking my face. I put on the lights and saw it was a puppy Bedlington terrier, a female, and exactly the same coloring as Bambina. Of course I took her home with me, and when I opened the door of the house she rushed upstairs and ran directly to Bambina's basket and got into it. I called Anna and when she saw her, she cried, "She's a small Bambina!" To me she was not only a small Bambina but she *was* Bambina. This puppy had all her habits. Bambina loved bananas. This dog ate one as soon as I gave it to her. Bambina also liked brandy, which is very unusual for a dog. This puppy lapped it up greedily. She was at home in Bambina's basket, played with her toys, and obeyed me just as Bambina had done. I called her Scampi and strangest of all, Chotzie behaved with her as she had with Bambina.

At this same time Greta rented a house on North Amalfi Drive just up the road from me, but across Sunset Boulevard. This boulevard divided Amalfi Drive into North and South. On the same road, down nearer the sea, Maria and Aldous Huxley had a house. Maria was Belgian. She was fragile and charming-looking, quick, intelligent and responsive. We were friends and I was fond of her. When she died a few years ago it made me extremely sad. I was fond of Aldous, too, and still am. I have the greatest admiration for his amazing erudition and prodigious knowledge and I don't think I have ever known anyone who knows as much, intellectually, as he. No need to have a dictionary or encyclopedia if you live near him! He can answer any question on any subject and tell you the meaning and origin of any word. Often in those days we used to go for walks together just before or after sunset. When I was alone with Aldous I used to ask him endless questions on all sorts of subjects. I always felt he knew so much that I shouldn't spend a second with him without digging some rare piece of information out of him. Added to this, I thought him very attractive.

Not far away, in Santa Monica Canyon, lived Eva Hermann. She was a German painter who had been well known in Berlin for her caricatures. A lovely and sensitive person, she was a great friend of the Huxleys, who introduced me to her. I saw her often those last years in Hollywood and we have remained warm friends.

On the beach in Santa Monica Anita Loos lived, and next to her the Albert Lewins—Millie and Allie—had a house. I have known Anita since the early twenties. No need to describe who she is. She has been famous the world over ever since she wrote *Gentlemen Prefer Blondes*. I have always had a great affection for her and an admiration for her brains, her quick wit, and her dynamic energy—all wrapped up in her small, unique personality.

The Lewins lived in a modern house designed for them by Neutra. Like Anita's, it was right by the sea with the beach in front of it. They always allowed me to use their house to dress in when I went swimming.

People said then that Millie looked like a Renoir, but I thought she was far more beautiful.

During the first few weeks I was in my new house Anna and I noticed a great many ants. They came into the library in a steady stream through the long French windows, across the floor, up one side of the mantel, down on the other, and out of the room through a window on the opposite wall. They marched in strict formation and I was fascinated by the incessant procession. I was quite convinced that, like extras in the theatre who are supposed to be marching soldiers and appear on the stage and then run behind the backdrop to reappear again and give the impression of numbers, the ants were doing the same thing, putting on a show for me.

The owner of the house came over one day and when she saw the ants, she said she would send an exterminator to do away with them. My blood ran cold at the thought of killing my little marching friends. I hastily told her not to bother, that I would get rid of them. She departed, saying she would come back in a week, and if my method hadn't worked she would try hers. After she left I turned over in my mind what my "method" could be. Knowing that ants are very intelligent, I hit on a plan. I closed the door of the room and sat down in front of the mantel. I first made myself inwardly quiet and did some slow breathing exercises. Then I dove deep into the Spiritual Heart and tried to contact the Self. Then I called on all the Enlightened Ones. I asked their help. Then I spoke out loud to the ants. I spoke slowly, distinctly, and softly. I told them that they were in great danger and would surely be killed if they did not go away. After saying all this, I began saying over and over again, "Please leave the house," as though I were chanting or repeating a mantram. After about fifteen minutes the line of ants turned and began marching toward the window through which it had entered. When I had seen the last one disappear, I called Anna and explained what had happened. We never had another ant in the house.

One day a remarkably handsome young man, Ronnie Elliot, brought Ona Munson out to my house. They wanted to hear about my experiences in India. I had not seen Ona since I had met her at Lubitsch's house with Greta. This meeting made us great friends. After this she came often to my house, and as she was living in Hollywood and loved to come down to the sea, she often came to spend the night when she was shooting at Republic Studios in San Fernando Valley.

That spring and summer of 1939 was a happy time. I, like most people, did not foresee the impending war and for me personally it was a happy time because Greta was happy. Never since I had known her had she been in such good spirits. She had begun shooting the first gay picture she had ever done, *Ninotchka;* and Lubitsch was directing it. "The first time I have had a great director since I am in Hollywood," she said.

Greta was a changed person. She used to come for me as usual after shooting, and we walked in the hills. At least I walked, but she more often ran and danced. She laughed constantly and she used to repeat the question "Why?" as she did in the picture. She would imitate Lubitsch's accent and ask over and over again "Vhy? Vhy?" She acted out scenes for me from the picture, and some days she would really be Ninotchka. It was fascinating to see how by playing a gay role rather than a sad one her whole personality changed.

The studio ran an advance ad before the picture was released. It read, GARBO LAUGHS. When I saw this it made me sad. It made me sad to think that all the years she had been in Hollywood she had never been permitted to laugh in a picture, and that the fact of her laughing should be so featured and considered remarkable. I felt the studio had kept her in a strait jacket, and I knew only too well the tragic effect it had had on her health.

Late in the summer after she had finished shooting, I took her up to Gaylord Hauser's house high up in the hills back of Beverly Hills. It was a very nice house with a beautiful view, a swimming pool, and a badminton court. Gaylord and Frey Brown, who lived with him, are both very good-looking men and I liked them, and I was sure Greta would. At first she did not want to meet them but I tempted her to their house by saying they would have a wonderful vegetable meal for us. Greta and I were confirmed vegetarians by this time and Gaylord had promised he would have a vegetable lunch for us. He kept his word. We had a delicious lunch served charmingly on the terrace, and afterwards swam in the pool and played badminton.

Shortly after this the four of us took a trip to Reno, Nevada. We motored across the desert, stopping at various places on the way. The scenery was magnificent and, of course, the weather was perfect and full of sunshine. In Reno we went to a big rodeo, which Greta and I did not like, as we hated to see the steers and calves thrown by the cowboys. At night we went to some kind of a gambling place which was very tame and not at all what Greta and I had hoped such a place in the "Wild West" would be. We drove back to Hollywood over some mountain passes in the Sierra Nevada—a breath-taking sight. Gaylord and Frey are delightful companions and the trip was a great success.

Iris Tree was in Hollywood then. She had been there for some years and was always a source of amusement to me. When I was in my former house, before going to India, she was living in a trailer. She came one day and asked me if she could have a bath in my house. To my surprise she got into the tub with her underclothes on and washed herself and them at the same time. Afterwards she went out into the garden and stretched out in the sun to dry herself and her clothes. She said, "It's so much simpler to wash and dry yourself and your clothes at the same time."

When I had the house on Amalfi Drive she was living in a little shack on the beach near Malibu. I went to see her and found an old car was at the door. Iris told me she was leaving in half an hour to go to Ojai, adding calmly, "I am giving up this house and taking everything with me except the furniture." I looked around. Nothing was packed and I saw no sign of boxes or valises. She caught my thought. "Don't worry. I'll be ready," she said, and proceeded to spread out a huge sheet on the floor. She went to the cupboard and gathered up her dresses and clothes and threw them onto the sheet. Then she took all the spoons, knives, forks, cups, dishes and pans from the kitchen and tossed them onto her clothes. Finally she picked up all the remaining things: sponge, toothbrush, books, magazines, ashtrays, and put them on top of everything else. This was all done in a very few minutes. Tying up the four corners of the sheet together she carried the bundle out to the car. "See what a quick packer I am!" she said, in her soft beautiful voice. I could not contradict the statement.

Ganna Walska, celebrated as a singer and for her beauty, had bought a lovely house in Santa Barbara during this period. She is Polish by origin, but is now four times more American than most Americans, having had four American husbands. One of them was the famous millionaire, Harold McCormick from Chicago, who was a backer for the Chicago Opera Company. She owns the Champs-Élysées Theatre in Paris which, among other things, he bought for her. Harold was a friend of Abram's. I thought him kind and liked him because he gave no evidence of his vast wealth.

I met Ganna some years ago in Paris when Eva and I were there with my *Jehanne d'Arc*. She gave a large lunch for us in her house, but after walking round the block several times, we ended by not going to it. We saw so many people arriving and they all looked so dressy and grand that we just turned and fled. I was afraid Ganna would never forgive me, but when I met her some years later she never mentioned it. We have a number of interests in common—among them, Eastern religions. At this particular time she had a friend of mine, Theos Bernard, staying with her.

Theos was a young American lawyer from Arizona. He was blond, blue-eyed, and handsome and he looked like an athlete. But this was far from what he actually was. He was spiritually connected with the East and had remarkable knowledge in Eastern teachings and Yoga. He was an exponent of Hatha Yoga and could take the postures, perform purification practices and breathing exercises, as well as any Yogi.

In Tibet he met the Dalai Lama at a time when this was a rare accomplishment for anyone. Tragically enough, after the war he went to India and returned again to Tibet. He was killed there in some mysterious way, the details of which are conflicting.

I had another friend by the name of Bob Abbot who had a beautiful ranch on the Mojave Desert just outside of Victorville. Bob was tall, handsome, and full of fun. I often went out to the desert to stay with him and I felt absolutely at home there. It is strange, but sometimes, maybe only once in a lifetime, you find a place which you feel is part of you—which belongs to you and where you belong. I felt like this on Bob's place in the desert. There was nothing grand about it except the desert itself and the range of mountains in the distance, and perhaps the swimming pool. That was unique. It was certainly as long as a city block and nearly as wide. The water that poured into it came from a mountain stream, and its temperature could be regulated. Swimming in it right there in the heart of the desert in moonlight or full sunlight was an experience.

The ranch house was simple but furnished with taste. I had a room which Bob always kept for me, with the bed placed so that I could see the rising sun over the desert. Bob owned a great deal of land on which he raised alfalfa.

There were cows on the ranch and also an aviary, where Bob raised canaries. Of course, there were horses and I used to ride off every day into the desert. One day as I was riding at a leisurely pace, I passed an old Indian on foot. We greeted each other and I was conscious that he gazed into my eyes in a most penetrating way. He stopped and I pulled up my horse. "Do you know that you are a water-finder?" he asked. "I never make a mistake. When I look into a person's eyes I can tell. Would you like me to prove that you can find water?" Of course I said yes. He led me to a grove of Tamarisk trees and cut off a branch that looked like a fork and gave it to me to hold, with the two points of the fork pointing downward. "Follow me," he said. "I know where water is on every inch of this area of the desert. We will see what happens when you come to a place where it is." We walked solemnly, I with the branch bent low over the ground, and the old boy leading my horse. Suddenly, after about half an hour, the branch twisted and turned in my hand, and bent under me with such force that I fell to my knees. The Indian cried out, "I knew it, here is water!" We tried it again further on and again I was pulled to my knees and again he cried, "Here is water." There was no doubt that I was a "water-finder."

Other curious things happened on the desert. One evening, in the dusk, I was taking a walk and came upon a coiled rattlesnake just in front of my feet. I stopped dead, the toes of my sandals not an inch away from him. As he reared his head I quickly bent over him. I was not at all frightened and said softly, "Hello, old boy. How are you?" He sank down and I passed around him. I will never forgive myself for telling a cowboy my experience. He rushed for a flashlight and a gun. I heard a shot and he returned with the dead snake over the muzzle of his gun. I felt like an accomplice in a crime.

One time I took Greta to the ranch with me. Bob was away and he said we could stay there as long as we wanted to. When we reached the desert a sandstorm came up. The blowing sand was so dense and sharp that we had to stop the car and get down on the floor with handkerchiefs over our mouths, and the rug over our heads. When the storm passed we found that the sand had taken every bit of paint off the car. Our hair, ears, and clothes were full of sand and our skin was horribly dry. I had wanted to give Greta a holiday, but it certainly started off badly. The desert can be friend or foe.

One day I got a call from Gabriel Pascal in New York. He was broke and said that the Sherry Netherlands Hotel where he was staying would not let him leave with his luggage until he paid his bill. He said he had a ticket for California and the possibility of a job there, and he asked if he could stay with me as obviously he could not afford a hotel. I, of course, said yes, and he arrived the next day with a brief case in his hand and his shaving brush and toothbrush in his pocket. He said that in a few days he would be able to raise the money to pay the Sherry Netherlands and have his things sent on, but that until he got his clothes he did not want anyone to know he was in Hollywood, except Greer Garson. He added that he was madly in love with Miss Garson and wanted to marry her. As Gaby always insulted people he was generally in hot water. Eventually his clothes did arrive and he went to Metro-Goldwyn-Mayer where he had hoped to get a job as a producer. Nevertheless, he promptly insulted Louis B. Mayer and lost any chance of a job. After that he decided to return to London and film another Shaw play.

Before he went he asked me if he could charge some things to me. He wanted to bring a picnic basket to Miss Garson's house and said he intended to ask her to marry him. He went to the village and returned with several dozen red roses and a huge basket in which he had fruit, vegetables, and a turkey. "I will pay you for all these things when I get some money," he said childishly. I put my arms around him and laughed. "Tell that to the birdies," I said. Then I added, "You can consider all these things, especially the turkey, as a wedding present." He went upstairs, came down with his hair brushed and shining with brilliantine, and gathered up the flowers and the basket. Miss Garson was then living with her mother and Gaby said, "I am not frightened of Greer but I am of her mother."

As he drove off, looking very nervous, I called after him, "If the mother throws you out of the window when you propose to Greer, be sure to bring back the flowers and the food. We'll have a picnic here."

Within a couple of hours the poor, sweet man returned, looking very glum and depressed without the flowers or the basket. "Greer won't marry me," he said.

I opened a bottle of champagne and wished him better luck next time, which indeed he had. Not long after this he was consoled. He married Valerie Hidveghy, a beautiful Hungarian actress.

Forty-Six

At the end of the summer of 1939 I moved to another small house belonging to Elissa Landi's brother. It was high up on a hill on Napoli Drive with the garage at the bottom and you had to walk up sixty-seven steps to the front door. I used to go down those steps day and night and up them two steps at a time. I had a large bedroom with a porch off it and I could see from my window the mountains on one side and the sea on the other. At night the nightingales sang so loudly in the trees outside my window that I kept little pebbles to throw at them when they got too boisterous.

Nazimova had come to Hollywood and was living in one of the bungalows of the Garden of Allah Hotel. This hotel had originally been her own home and she called it then the Garden of Alla. When she sold it bungalows were built in the garden around the swimming pool Alla had designed. It was a sad thing for her to have to live there in a small bungalow in the garden of her own house. When I moved to Napoli Drive she came out and helped me arrange my furniture. I remember how remarkably agile she was at lifting things.

Gladys Cooper lived in a house just across the road, and by some kind of strange acoustic effect I could hear her voice distinctly when I was in bed and she was in her garden. She had chickens and Welsh corgi dogs and sometimes as early as six or seven in the morning she would be out there feeding and talking to them. No matter how quietly

311

she talked it sounded as though she were right there beside me. I had met Gladys with Ivor Novello in London many years before and had thought her remarkably beautiful, as everyone did. To then be thousands of miles away from London, in bed in a little house on the Pacific Palisades in California, and suddenly hear her most individual and attractive voice right beside me, and sometimes even waking me up, was indeed weird. I was too shy to tell her about it, but I wrote Ivor in London and told him. All the years I was in that house, until I left it in 1944, I heard Gladys' voice beside me every morning.

In September 1939, when war was declared in Europe, I was in a desperate state of mind. I cursed myself for not having stayed in France or England when I came back from India. To be caught again in America in another war was more than I could bear. I was terrified for the safety of Baba and Freddie and their two children, and I was terrified, too, for the safety of all my friends in France and England. Today I cannot say that I had the "good fortune" to escape being bombed in the war because I do not feel like that and I never did.

Hollywood changed completely during those war years. It suddenly became flooded with Europeans, refugees who had fled from their various homelands. Among the first celebrated ones to arrive were Igor Stravinsky and his wife Vera. Igor said, "I fled from Russia to France where I became a French citizen. Now I have fled from France to the United States where I shall become an American citizen. This is my last move. Three countries in one lifetime are enough."

I was happy to have them in Hollywood. During those war years I felt they were my family. I used to go to their house continually, and often we would sit up late into the night drinking tea and discussing the news. Igor was like a child. He was excited to see how quickly everything grew in Southern California. He is a great lover of birds and he was always pointing out to me the different ones that flew into the garden or perched on the trees. His favorite was the hummingbird. Lots of them came for the honeysuckle that grew on his porch.

Many artists swamped Hollywood then who had nothing to do with films. They came out there either as refugees from Europe or (if they were Americans) because they could not go to Europe. Various colonies of all nationalities sprang up—French, German, Austrian, Italian and English, besides its own very special artists—actors, directors, designers, painters, sculptors and musicians. During the period of the war it was a fascinating place and a great international center.

One of my favorite refugees at that time was Galka Scheyer. Galka was German and because she was Jewish, she had, fortunately, left Germany at the beginning of Hitler's rule. She came to Hollywood in the mid-thirties and built an extremely modern house high up in the hills off Sunset Plaza Drive. The house literally hung from a cliff and dominated a magnificent view, overlooking all of Hollywood, Beverly Hills and Santa Monica. In the distance one could see the sea. Many people were afraid to go over this road, especially at night, and would not go to see Galka. I took Rose Adler, the famous French bookbinder, over it one evening and she nearly had a heart attack. Often when the rains came and part of it was washed away, I left my car and braved it on foot. But Galka lived there fearlessly, surrounded by her collection of modern paintings and taking her daily bath in a little pool partly hidden by bamboo trees, which she shared with the birds.

She was an amazing person. To the casual observer she was physically monstrous. Her head was too large and her body ill-shaped. She dressed with the most appalling bad taste. She also murdered the English language and spoke with an accent as terrible as Lubitsch's. Yet if you knew the real Galka you forgot all this. She was extremely sensitive to beauty and fought passionately for it in all things—except her own person. But I believe her lack of taste in dressing came from a state of hopelessness about her own looks. Loving beauty as she did, she suffered from her looks and in a kind of violent and pathetic protest made herself appear worse than was necessary. But her shining spirit made up for all this. Many evenings we sat on her terrace with that fantastic view miles below us and watched the lights come on as far as we could see, talking of art—modern art, for this was Galka's passion. When France fell and I nearly had a breakdown, it was to Galka I went and sobbed my heart out—and it was she who comforted me.

In Germany she had been a great friend of the Blue Four Riders: Kleè, Kandinsky, Feininger, and Jawlensky. When she came to the United States they made her their representative. She brought with her many of their best paintings and had them in her house. She also had several fine Picassos, Braques, and a number of other first-class modern painters.

The beautiful Negro dancer Katherine Dunham stayed with Galka once for several months, and my friend Consuelo Sides stayed with her the summers of 1940 and 1941. Consuelo, Galka, and I used to motor some Sundays over to Ojai to hear Krishnamurti talk. Other times I went with the Huxleys. Krishnamurti lectured out under the trees as they do in India. These talks were always exciting as he is dynamic—in fact, atomic. As scientists have split the atom on the physical plane, he has split the core of thought on the spiritual plane.

Then Sir Charles and Lady Mendl descended on Hollywood with their entourage, including Elsie's lovable companion and secretary, Hilda West, and her adopted son, Johnnie McMullin. Elsie tried to bring an atmosphere of Versailles to her house, a rather difficult thing to do so close to Sunset Boulevard. Catherine, Baroness d'Erlanger, opened a night club, which was much more to the point.

All kinds of art collections had sprung to life in Hollywood. Edward G. Robinson, Charles Laughton, and the Maitlands all began their acquisitions during this period. Of course there was the Arensberg collection which was started in 1913. This was then one of the greatest modern collections in the world, comprising eight hundred paintings, including the famous "Nude Descending the Stairway" by Marcel Duchamps which caused such a sensation in its day. Mr. and Mrs. Arensberg hung this collection in their own house and it covered every inch of their walls. You found a masterpiece in the kitchen or a bathroom as well as in the drawing room.

During the summer of 1941 Greta went before the camera for the last time. She acted in a film by the name of *Two Faced Woman*. I was terribly upset when I heard she was going to do this story. The same plot had already been used twice in the silent films with other actresses in the title role. Why this old chestnut was dug up again for her I will never know. It was a dull story in the silent days and remained the same when she played it. The studio made her feel that she should do a film that would appeal to the American market, which meant appealing to a very low standard as far as Greta was concerned. Except for the big cities she has always been too European for the American taste. She was too mysterious, too much of an enigma for the small towns in the United States. The average person likes to identify himself with the character he sees on the screen and the average American man did not feel that Greta was "cute" enough for him. If unconsciously he recognized her artistry, at the same time he felt as uncomfortable when he saw her acting as he would have felt in her presence. And although the American small town woman secretly admired Greta she was also baffled by her. What relation had Mrs. America to a Viking's daughter whose soul was swept by wind and snow?

And yet there is a paradox in all this because Greta's influence eventually spread all over America, as it did over the whole world. At no time in the history of the world has one woman so vitally influenced so many other women. Because for the first time in history, thanks to the medium of the screen, millions of people could be reached, Greta reached them. Her beauty and artistry stirred them. She stirred and influenced not only women but men, and she inspired artists. In the thirties and forties she completely influenced fashion. Women the world over copied her straight, long-hair style. Her type of beauty became the prototype for this period. Even the dummies for women's clothes in the shop windows of America, England and France were made to resemble her.

But the studio did not sense all this. They argued on a low level. In their view an artist must be pulled down to the public. At the time of *Two Faced Woman,* when because of the war they were unable to sell Greta's films to the European market, they did not have the vision to know that if she had been given the right story she could have raised this same public up to her own level, and made money into the bargain. But who is blinder about money than a so-called business man? Call in a poet and his vision will often make more money than a business man, that is if he cares to bother about it.

So Greta was prevailed upon to do this film. When it was released at the end of December 1941 not one critic had a good word for it. The Catholic church banned it because the hero of the story, played by Melvyn Douglas, falls in love and has an affair with his wife's supposed sister. The picture deserved reproach, not on grounds of morality, but because it was an insult to anyone of even the most retarded mentality. Oscar Wilde said, "A book is neither moral nor immoral, it is either good or bad." In this case, what applies to the book applies to films.

Greta was humiliated by the reviews and by the furor created by the women's clubs. To my way of thinking all this was a tempest in a teacup and as stupid as the picture itself. But I think Greta's regret was more in her own soul for having allowed herself to be influenced into lowering her own high standards. She said, "I will never act in another film."

Since then many writers have sent me manuscripts asking me to give them to Greta. Producers and directors have called me or cabled me thinking I might persuade her to do a picture with them. A few years ago Jean Cocteau begged me to intercede for him. He wanted to write and direct a picture for her. To all entreaties of this kind I have been entirely indifferent just because I have seen her suffer too much in pictures. I would only want to see her return to films if a great universal role could be written for her in a significant story. I would want her to have a producer with vision, a perfect director, an amazingly talented camera man, and a great artist to create sets and costumes. Where would anyone find such a set-up? I believe today, in her mature years, Greta could give the most moving and inspired performance of her life. But why should she unless things are perfect for her? She has already contributed enough of herself to art in our era. She and Duse are the two greatest actresses of our century, and the two who will be long remembered.

Many things have been written and said about Greta, most of them false because few people know her. In writing about the end of her film career, who can doubt that she will go on influencing and inspiring people for years even if she never does another film in her life? I believe that she will because her legend will live.

Like many great artists Greta is often superficially child-like. At the same time, on a deeper level, she has what I would term a "soul quality" so profound that it seems to take her out of life and it accounts, I think, for her remoteness. She is Nordic and it is surprising how true she runs to type. She is reticent, but the stories about her shyness are incorrect —she is never shy. She is emotional and fears showing it. When she is among people she can be gay and full of fun but alone she tends to become serious and melancholic. I understand this because Spaniards too are like this.

The important thing is that Greta was born an artist. She did not become one. Such true art as Greta's has no "becoming." As an innate artist it must have been frustrating for her to have lived with a conventional family and in the surroundings of her childhood and adolescent life. In Stockholm she worked at jobs that had no relation to her soul and aspirations. Until she met the great director, Maurice Stiller, she had no true contact with art, though she was acting in the Royal Academy in Stockholm at the time that he met her. After her first success in "Gosta Berling" in Sweden under Stiller's direction, and after her first success in Hollywood in "The Torrent" she sky-rocketed to fame overnight. How much it is to her credit that in spite of this fame and amazing beauty, in Hollywood, of all places, with adulation and every frivolous snare laid at her feet, she kept her dignity and led a solitary life.

She not only lived a solitary life but she lived an austere and simple one. Despite the claims of vulgar writers and fan magazines in their distorted books or articles as to what her butlers, valets, chauffeurs, secretaries and servants have written or reported about her, the fact is that in the many years I was in Hollywood she had exactly three servants. Two of them were maids—first Whistler, and then Gertrude. James was her only chauffeur. I am convinced that these three people were always loyal to her, and never discussed her or gave out any information about her. I feel this should be stated in view of the many stories given out by Greta's "phantom" servants.

She never went to nightclubs and she never allowed producers or directors to overstep their professional relation to her. I remember well once when Louis B. Mayer sent her an enormous basket of flowers. When the florist's boy came with it she told her maid not to accept it. Her thought was, "What right has Mr. Mayer to take the liberty of sending me flowers?" She did not have the slightest fear of offending the head of her studio and such a powerful man as Mr. Mayer. Her sense of personal privacy was so strong that she thought it an offense for anyone to send her flowers or presents whom she had not accepted as a friend. I think life has since mellowed this attitude somewhat, but it was very strong then.

It has been said that this sense of privacy and Greta's wanting to be "alone" was a pose that her agent, Harry Edington, prompted by the studio, cooked up for publicity. This is sheer nonsense. No one who has known Greta and her *unfailing* honesty could ever believe that she could at any time put on an act. She has suffered immeasurably from publicity and newspaper men. I can vouch for this. In the days when she received thousands of fan mail letters a week she suffered from them. She never opened them and they were burned on the back lot of the studio. I know these letters caused her sleepless nights. She worried about the senders even though she would have no part of them. Once when I said to her that perhaps these poor fans had a need to write to her, she answered, "But what right have they to intrude in my private life?"

Another time I persuaded her to go with me to see The Blue Boy. When we got to the Huntington Library a group of children were in the gallery. One of them spied Greta and rushed at her for a signature. The others followed and crowded around her. If they had been lions about to tear her to pieces she could not have been more frightened. I saw her poor beautiful little face twisted in fear as she backed against the wall. Then, before I could reach her, she rushed through the circle of children and out of the museum. James was sitting in the car a little way down the road. She fled to the car shouting to him to start. She opened the door as the car moved, jumped in, and in shutting the door

318 / Here Lies the Heart

caught her finger in it. Far down the road James stopped for me. Her finger had been badly smashed. She was sitting on the floor weeping hysterically—not because of the pain but because of the children. "I can't *even* go to a museum way off here in Pasadena without having people surround and torture me," she cried. I tried to explain that they were only children who meant no harm, but it was no good. I wished that some of the people who said she put on an act could have seen her then.

Her real tragedy is that she is a lone wolf. No matter how much she may love a person and try to hold onto that person's life and be part of it, in the end she has to let go and pursue her own lonely course. People have sometimes said that she has little talent for friendship. Her problem is that her standards of friendship are so high that few people can meet them. In her self-imposed isolation she cannot understand a friend who has a need to go about socially and perhaps partake of the innocent frivolities of life. To her, and rightly so, life is a serious matter. She is a Virgo, Virgos are often over critical, high strung and intolerant. They are also very analytical. Greta analyzes everything as if she were holding a magnifying glass up to life. Her analyses are sometimes wrong, but I once said of her, "No matter how wrong she is, in her error she is more right than people who are right."

She has, what I consider a very striking quality, a deep purity of intention in all that she does. I believe her own greatest problem and one that causes her untold unhappiness is an underlying suspicion toward people and life itself. This trait, I am told, is a Scandinavian characteristic and is perhaps more emphasized in Greta than in many Scandinavians. Latins are just the opposite. We flow more readily with life than the Nordic race and are more out-going. We are willing to take a chance and throw our caps over the mill. Greta takes few chances. She continually draws back, and when she moves she moves cautiously and then is tortured with regret, convinced she has made a mistake.

But in this matter of suspicion Greta is again a paradox, as she is in most things. She will often be suspicious to the last ditch of someone who is *really* her friend, and give her confidence to someone who has not got the slightest bit of her interest at heart. Her judgment can often be unstable and unsound.

Greta can more thoroughly evoke an emotion of pity and defense than anyone I have ever known—at least she can in me and, I think, this is the case in other people, too. Though there may be nothing particular to defend her against, I want to defend her, to protect her, to take her part. This may be because there is a strange sadness in her, underlying everything she does. This sadness is lurking beneath the surface, even at her gayest moments. It is a sadness that makes me continually conscious of the eternal sufferings of all creatures. There is something cosmic about it—something that keeps me constantly aware of fundamental and serious values. It awakens in me a great sense of compassion —a readiness to forgive her any shortcoming—a desire to take upon my own shoulders her slightest pain or sorrow. I have often analyzed this sadness in her and I. believe it is a quality of all great souls. I say "quality" because it *is* a quality. Any attribute which lifts the spirit to higher things and penetrates it to deeper things is a quality. Greta, in her art and in her life, does just this. This is the hold, I believe, she has had on the public. Seeing her on the screen people have felt this lifting of the spirit—this contact with mystic forces that they, themselves, could not even understand. And yet, she has never played in a film in which the role lent scope or dimension to this quality. Being so much a part of her it came through anyway, in spite of the role.

Greta's art and character deserve far more appreciation than I can give it in these few pages in this book. There is so much more that I could continue to develop and analyze about this inexhaustible subject on the artistic, human and mystical level. I feel I have only scratched the surface in giving this slight picture of her as an artist and as a person. I have said nothing of Greta's mystic quality, which is extremely strong, and which, in spite of her lack of understanding of it in herself, controls most of her motives and actions. She is unconsciously suspicious of this, too, and tries to suppress it and fight against it. If she would give herself completely over to it and be always guided by it, I believe she would spiritually and mentally integrate and come powerfully into her own. She will one day—without the slightest doubt.

To know Greta—one must know the North. She may live the rest of her life in a Southern climate, but she will always be Nordic with all its sober and introvert characteristics. To know her one must know —*really know*—wind, rain, and dark brooding skies. She is of the elements—*actually* and *symbolically*. Forever, in this present incarnation, she will be a Viking's child—troubled by a dream of snow.

Forty-Seven

In March 1940 I went to New York for a few weeks, as the Museum of Costume Art (since moved to the Metropolitan Museum from Rockefeller Center) had an exhibition of Rita's clothes which were part of her wardrobe from 1900 to her death in 1929. Fortunately I had kept all these things. Since then I have divided this collection between the Metropolitan Museum, the Museum of the City of New York, and the Brooklyn Museum, and donated it in Rita's name.

The exhibition was arranged by Irene Lewisohn, Aline Bernstein, and Polaire Weissman and it was very well done.

Frank Crowninshield, who had been the editor of that stimulating magazine "Vanity Fair" and who in himself was a famous character, a gracious person and a great patron of the arts, and who was known as "Crownie," opened the exhibition. Three thousand people came to it the first day and we had to call the police to keep the clothes and laces from being handled. It is interesting to see how people always respond to a romantic personality. Crownie wrote in the catalogue:

> On viewing the costumes worn by Rita de Acosta Lydig, one is impressed by the fact that they belong to no period. They are the expression of a great individualist bent not only on personal adornment, but on acquiring and displaying to greatest advantage ancient materials, rare laces, brocades and velvets, in themselves works of

art. Thus she developed a style of dress to which she remained faithful despite changes of fashion. It is interesting, moreover, to note that she never had one thing of a kind; in other words, that every model in her wardrobe was duplicated by the dozens with only slight variation in material, lace or design.

The whole collection has a quality of extravagance that reminds one, perhaps, of the Renaissance—certainly it has no parallel in the costumes worn today.

Beautiful and original though they are, one is conscious that these clothes depended for their real life on the romantic and striking personality of their wearer.

During the summer of 1941 Eileen Garrett came out to Hollywood. She is a unique person and is usually considered the greatest medium in America. She is also many other things and has a variety of talents as editor and publisher of "Tomorrow," a quarterly review of psychical research, president of the Parapsychology Foundation, noted author of a number of books. She has experimented in extra-sensory-perception at Duke University with such leading minds on the subject as J. B. Rhine and Gardner Murphy, and she has lectured at many universities, on related subjects such as Spontaneous Phenomena and Unorthodox Healing.

When she came to Hollywood she looked me up and I took her down the road to meet Aldous Huxley. They became friends and when Aldous experimented with the drug mescalin by taking it and writing a book about it, Eileen was instrumental in the project. She was planning that autumn to publish the first number of the magazine, "Tomorrow," and to start the Creative Age Press. She asked me if I would go to New York and become associate editor of the magazine. When the time came I decided to accept this offer. Leaving my little family with Anna in my house on Napoli Drive, I left for New York.

Happily, by this time America had come into the war. In spite of it the winter was not an unhappy one. Eileen has great charm and intelligence as well as plenty of humor and wit. Working for her was very pleasant although I don't think I was too good at the job. The magazine at this time published stories as well as articles. I at least got Aldous Huxley, Thomas Mann, and Igor Stravinsky to contribute to it. And for a South American number, I translated some articles from the Spanish and also a beautiful poem by the Chilean poet Pablo Neruda about the fall of Stalingrad. At this time the Russians were our allies and one could comfortably write about them. I received a charming letter of congratulation about this number from Mrs. Roosevelt. But, a few years ago, when that horror McCarthy began accusing writers of being Communists because they wore red ties or bought red roses, I was afraid the F.B.I. would dig up this poem and draw it to his attention—especially as Neruda had by then become an avowed Communist.

Harold Vursell and Jack Sullivan were editors on the magazine at the same time I was. Eileen and I used to go out with them often at night. Usually we went to a restaurant that Cole Porter backed, called 123, where a friend of mine, Roger Stearns, played the piano. It was good to see my friends in New York again, but I missed the California sunshine and I was homesick for what I called "my little brood and family"—Anna, and my dogs. When May came I was glad to return to Napoli Drive.

Unfortunately, with the entry of the United States into the war, things changed greatly out there, especially for those who lived directly on the coast and near the beach as I did, as there the Japanese threat was much closer. Truckloads of Japanese were being transported, and this made a big difference to California as almost all the field workers, florists, gardeners and fishermen were Japanese. My own gardener, a sweet little old man, was taken off, and I was fearful for Anna as she was German and had never taken out United States papers, although she had been in California since 1930. Like all enemy aliens outside a camp, she had to report to the F.B.I. every day and observe a curfew.

Greta had moved to Beverly Hills and I missed her very much, but I seldom went far from home, except to the village for food, as most shops would not deliver because of the petrol shortage. The Huxleys had gone to live on the desert in a place called Llano, near Victorville. I managed to go there once and Aldous took me for a walk on the desert. We came to an old Indian cemetery and sat down on one of the graves where we discussed the Christian Mystics and Aldous told me a lot about Catherine of Siena. He said he hoped to write a book about her. He was eating, then, only food cooked in a manner which he called "natural." This meant by the sun's reflection in a mirror.

The worst problem for me at this time was Anna. Well-meaning friends told me that the reason I could not get a job in the studios was because I was protecting and befriending a German. I understood the attitude of the studios. Most of the producers and directors were Jewish, the war news was terribly frightening to them and I did not expect them to understand how I felt about Anna. But she had been with me nearly all my years in California and I could not help putting human values and friendship before anything else. I was determined to stand by her at any cost. I consulted Aldous. Fortunately he was of my opinion, although even his disapproval would not have influenced me. But I was hurt when a few friends began keeping a strange and guarded silence on the subject. I withdrew more into myself and stayed more and more alone.

Janet Flanner came out to visit her mother in Altadena, and she stayed a week with me. I remember sitting by the fire drinking rum, and talking nostalgically of France. One starless, pitch black night I was coming home and in order to see the keyhole I struck a match. Ten minutes after I was in the house I heard motorcycles coming up the road. I looked out and saw two officers starting up my steps. Anna was in bed and I rushed into her room, sure they were coming for her. With my heart in my mouth, I said, "Have you any German literature of any kind? If you have give it to me *at once!*" Poor Anna, who had gone white, dove under her mattress and produced a very old and torn German Bible. I snatched it from her and hid it under a sofa in the drawing room just as the officers began banging on the door. I opened it. They entered the house, and said, "Who lives here?" "I do, with my maid." They looked sharply at me. "You don't look American. Are you an American?" I told them I was, but I thought, since I was sure they already knew it, I better make a clean breast of Anna. I told them she was German. "Which one of you has been signalling?" I was mystified. "No one has been signalling." "There was a flash of light at this doorway not more than fifteen minutes ago," he insisted. Then I remembered striking a match to see the lock. I finally satisfied them and they drove away on their motorcycles. I retrieved the Bible and took it back to Anna who was lying in bed crying.

But not long after this something happened which made me think I must come to a drastic decision. One morning after lunch I went down to the garage where Anna's and my, rarely used cars were standing. I drove mine out and went to the village in it. About an hour later I returned and as I came over the hill I saw smoke near the house. As I drew nearer I saw fire engines in front of it; smoke was pouring out of the garage. Later empty kerosene cans were found in the field nearby. Whoever had done it had waited for me to take my car out, but it was very sinister, and made me realize that feeling was mounting against Anna in our vicinity. As I stood by the window in the darkness and watched the smoldering embers, I asked myself with some fear, how much longer could I protect Anna?

Shortly after this I was told that the Office of War Information was starting the publication of a propaganda magazine called, "Victory," in New York, and needed editors. I applied for the job, and after making out dozens of governmental papers, I got it. When I broached the subject of my departure to Anna, she said that she had saved up a little money and would like to buy a little place of her own in the desert. Anna knew the country near Victorville and after some exploring we found a place for sale in Lucerne Valley with forty acres, a small house, electricity, and a well. It was very low-priced and had a magnificent view. I knew she would not be out of a job as there was a great need for workers on the ranches since so many men had gone to war.

The last night before I left Hollywood for New York, Anna and I slept on the floor on our coats. The poor dogs were bewildered and could not imagine what we were doing. As the curtains were all gone, so we lay in the dark and watched the great searchlights sweeping the sky for enemy planes. I felt desperately depressed, and I knew Anna did too. She had permission to motor me to the station in Pasadena and then to motor herself out to the desert. When the train pulled out from the station I saw the anxious little faces of my brood peering out of the car, wondering where I was going. Anna was standing on the platform with tears pouring down her face. I rushed into my compartment and wept bitterly myself.

From my bedroom window of my New York flat, 471 Park Avenue, I could see the rooms in the Ritz tower that faced north. Greta had also come to New York and from one of these rooms we used to signal to each other at night with lighted candles. Why we weren't arrested for showing lights I will never know.

I reported for work on "Victory" and met Frances Keene, one of its editors. She is a lovable and remarkably intelligent person and it was a joy to find that she, also, had a flat in my building. But it was a sad time. No one actually knew which way the war would turn, although no one expressed the opinion that the Allies could lose it.

I had very little sleep at this time as I got up at four in the morning and wrote letters to Europe and various articles for myself. Far into the night I made up packages to send to Europe. My living room looked like a grocery store. Sometimes I went to Eyre de Lanux's flat near me on Fifty-sixth Street and we made up packages there. Eyre is celebrated for her beauty. She is warm and unconventional and a talented painter.

She had lived a great many years in France and like me felt very close to it. We were both counting the days until we could return to what we called our "homeland."

My brother Ricardo died that winter. I had seen little of him over the years, but his death made me extremely sad. He had a brilliant mind, good looks, amazing charm, and was considered one of the best tax lawyers in New York. President Roosevelt was a friend of his and had offered him a distinguished government job. But for some unknown reason he began to drink. Spaniards just cannot drink, especially hard liquor. Unlike the British and the Americans who can pour down cocktails, whisky, gin, and brandy continually, and still survive—if rather badly—the Spaniard who drinks just does not survive *at all*.

Walking home the night I saw him dead I was plunged into despair. It was cold and drizzling. As I went along the dark streets I came upon a policeman. He was huddled up against a building with the drizzle dripping from his cap and raincoat. He looked cold and lonely. We were the only people on the street so I stopped and spoke to him. "Officer," I said, "what do you think about death? Where are we all going in this beastly war?" "Lady," he answered, "I'm no intellectual. It's hard for me to think about these things. But come to think of them now, I guess we're all damn well going to hell." I walked on. He was no comfort.

My sister Maria was living in New York that winter with her husband, Teddy Chanler. They had a flat on Fifty-fifth Street, not far from mine. Maria was under a great strain with Ignacio in the Air Force, and I tried to see her as often as I could and talk to her about things outside the war; and when I was lonely and depressed myself it was good to be able to drop in for lunch or dinner at their flat.

After work, or sometimes during the lunch hour, I went to America House to see Alfred Stieglitz. He was old then, and not too well, but his mind was unfailingly brilliant and it was always stimulating to listen to him. By métier, he was a photographer, but he was also what I would call an artist of life. He only saw life in terms of art. It was he who introduced Cezanne, Picasso, and the Cubist painters to America. He also discovered Marin and Georgia O'Keefe who later became his wife.

They often asked me to lunch on Sundays. After lunch Stieglitz and I would sit and talk. I have always loved capes, especially black ones, and have worn them all my life. Stieglitz loved them too. When I went there for lunch we always tried on each other's capes. The last time I saw him he was in bed wearing a most beautiful white linen night shirt.

As I do, he loved black and white, and, with his white hair, he looked best in them. I never get over missing both Stieglitz and O'Keefe. Sadly enough, he died. O'Keefe now lives in New Mexico.

Ten days before the end of the war in Europe Baba wrote me a pathetic letter. She said she thanked God that it was nearly over and that her husband Freddie was safe. He was coming home the second it was over and she was counting the days. Baba had done wonderful work during the war and had been through terrible bombings. I knew how tired she was and what a lift it would give her to have her Freddie home again as they were the closest couple I had ever known. Three days before the end of the war I got a cable from her. It said: "Freddie killed yesterday." I simply could not take it in or believe it. But it was only too true. Fortunately, Baba's marvelous Catholic faith and her indomitable courage pulled her through this tragedy.

Just at the end of the war Mádge Garland came to New York. It was wonderful to see someone from England and to see Madge for herself. Then, almost immediately and to my great joy, I got a job to go to Europe and write articles for a syndicated newspaper. I could not have gone otherwise, as without a definite job no one was then issued a passport. I sailed on the first boat I could get on.

Forty-Eight

The ship I sailed on had been a troopship and this was her first voyage since the war as a passenger boat. She was still stripped of furniture and comforts. There were no carpets, deck chairs or table cloths, and the china and glassware was a mixture of any old thing the company could pick up. No one complained. We were all too happy to be going back to Europe. I had eight Mittel-European women in my cabin and we slept on a sort of mattress-hammock arrangement hung from the ceiling. They all smoked, ate fruit, and hung their rather suspect underclothes on a line across the room at night. Luckily my berth was nearest the porthole and when the smoke got too thick and the odor too high I opened it. In one chorus they complained, but I gazed out the porthole and pretended not to hear them. When they rang for the stewardess to tell her what a monster I was she sided with me. She was a Canadian and used to good fresh air. I could see she wanted no truck with these ladies.

It was already night when we reached Paris although we had been in the train since early morning. As most of the tracks were being laid down new, and the bridges were still makeshift and unsafe, the train had to creep along. To my great surprise Alfredo Sides, Rose Adler, and René Gimple were at the station to meet me. Marie Laurencin had sent René Gimple in her place as she was not well enough to come. Cars were very scarce and there was practically no petrol, but these

three thoughtful people had managed to rent a car so that I could get
my luggage to Alfredo's house on the Quai where he had offered me a
flat. But I had an unfortunate accident. A steel-wheeled hand truck
piled high with luggage ran over my foot before I had time to get out
of the way. The pain was excruciating. Everything went black before
my eyes, but I managed to conceal it from my friends. Knowing all
the strain and suffering they had been through, I didn't think it sporting
to make a fuss over a crushed foot when we were seeing each other for
the first time after years of separation. As we walked toward the car I
looked behind me and saw a trail of blood! I pulled myself together
violently and got in without anyone noticing that my shoe was completely torn away at the toes and covered with blood.

Alfredo had written that the flat he offered me was empty and I
thought he meant no one was living in it. It was indeed empty, in the
barest sense of the word. There was nothing in it at all except an army
cot with a blanket thrown over it. Evidently an American G.I. had left
these two things. There was no hot water, which I had expected, but I
had at least counted on sheets and towels. Alfredo moaned that the
Germans had taken all of them, but when I went up to his flat I noticed
he had plenty of both!

I slept under my coat that night with my painful, bloody foot wrapped
in a silk scarf. By morning it was horribly swollen all the way up to the
knee. At great expense I got a car from the Ritz Hotel and went out to
the American Hospital in Neuilly. Three toes were crushed and the nails
gone. I was always proud of my feet and for one week I had to hire a
car every day to drive to the hospital and have my foot dressed and it
was another two weeks before I could really walk on it.

To get food you had to know someone in the country, deal with the
black market or go to very expensive restaurants.

But one day my generous friend, Iya Abdy, called me in great excitement. Her maid had a friend in the country who was willing to sell a
chicken. Iya had sent her off by train to get it. It was to arrive in time
for dinner and I was invited. I had not tasted meat since 1933 but I felt
this was no time to refuse it. I rushed across the Tuileries gardens to
Iya's flat. Her son George was there, very excited about the chicken.
He was a son by Iya's first husband, who was Dutch, and he had such
an impossible name and George had such trouble with it that he eventually changed it to Gaynes. George has his mother's good looks and is
extremely handsome, tall, and well built with really golden hair. He has
a marvelous singing voice and is a talented actor. Since those days he

has gone far in his career. We gathered around the dining room table and waited for the chicken to appear. Iya had paid a good sum for this birdie, and run-down and hungry as I was, I hoped I would be forgiven for planning to eat him with relish. Proudly the maid brought the poor thing in on a silver platter. George rose to carve him. He tried once and then twice. He said there was something wrong with the knife. He was given a sharper one and with great exertion hacked off a few pieces. We bit into them with no success. I put mine back on my plate. "I hate to be unkind about this poor old fellow, but I'm afraid he was killed before the war of 1914," said I. "This is what comes of dealing with the black market," said George. Iya called in the maid and said, "Give this bird to the birds." Solemnly and sorrowfully he was carried from the table. On the way home I said to myself, "Let this be a lesson to you for trying to eat your fellow creatures."

A few days after this I saw the first carloads of cauliflowers coming in from the country to the Paris markets. People lined the streets to watch them. I must say I never thought cauliflowers could look so beautiful. They were piled high in neat pyramids and their leaves were fresh and green. I had a lump in my throat as they passed, and one man took off his hat. It was interesting to see him do it because he made the gesture quite unconsciously. I look upon cauliflowers very differently since that day. At the time I was sending two or three stories a week back to my newspapers and the entrance of the cauliflowers into Paris was one of them.

One day Bébé (Christian) Bérard came for me and took me out to lunch. We sat for a long time over our coffee and talked of the war and its influence on art. Bébé thought that the trend in romantic art would change to a brutal realism. I did not think, at the time, that he was entirely right but now I am inclined to believe he was. I asked him to walk with me to the Rue du Bac. I spoke of the many people I had known on this street—Isadora, Teddy Gerrard, Dorothy Ireland, Mimi Franchetti, Nazimova, Greta Cooper, Dollie Wilde, Jacques Rigault, Gerald Kelly—all of them dead. He shivered and said, "Let's get away from here. This is a street of ghosts." How unknowing we are, for we did not know how soon he too, would be dead.

I went to see Marcel Herrand in his flat. He and Jean Marchat were still producing and acting in the Théatre des Mathurins. He described to me all the vicissitudes he had passed through during the war and how, in spite of everything, he and Jean had managed to keep the theatre going. He had sent me a wonderful cable during the war which had deeply touched me. I told him that afternoon how much it had meant to me. He did an imitation for me again of Etienne de Beaumont. It seemed like old times.

Of course I saw a lot of Marie Laurencin. Having lost her own flat during the war, she was living, oddly enough, in a small house belonging to Etienne de Beaumont. And, naturally, I could not return to Paris without going to see my favorite fortuneteller—Sheilah Hennessy. I met Aileen, her sister, for the first time. Droll, and very much "une type," Aileen has many qualities to make her endearing.

Soon afterward I went over to London to see Baba and the children. Our reunion was, of course, a sad one. It was difficult not to continually talk of Freddie. I saw Quintin Tod, who took me around the city and showed me the worst bombed spots; Gabrielle Enthoven, Ivor Novello, and many other old friends. It was exciting to see them again, but so emotional that I felt like weeping most of the time. Before the war, Tamara Karsavina and her husband, Bengie, had been living in a charming house in Regents Park. Now they were in a flat. Bengie did not seem well and I sensed Tamara's anxiety about him, although she did not express it. Bengie was so considerate it would have worried him to think he was making anyone anxious. But I was anxious about him too.

I went down to the Midi to visit an American friend of mine, Isabel Pell. When the war broke out Pell, as her friends called her, was down there in the South and refused to leave. She stayed on and worked in the Resistance, and was decorated by the French Government. She was a lovable person; the quality I liked best about her was that, like Mary Garden, she always made me believe in myself. At one time in New York when I was going through a bad period, she sent me a gardenia every morning with some absurd thing written on the card, and she often came for me in a chic white Sunbeam and drove me to the country. She predicted I would look back on that bad time and feel it had taught me a lot, and she was right.

When I got off the train at Cannes, there was Pell on the platform, but her car was no longer a shining white Sunbeam; it was a small. shabby French vehicle and as it panted up the hills toward Grasse and she talked to it lovingly, I soon found out that it was dearer to her than any other car she had ever had and not to be exchanged for a Rolls Royce.

Pell's house, then, was high up in the hills overlooking Grasse. It had a magnificent view and from the terrace we could see the Mediterranean. After the strain of Paris and London it was paradise. She led me to a lovely tiled floor room where the shutters were closed just enough to allow the sunlight to play on the floor, and to let that wonderful heat of the Midi during the summer months, seep into the room. I reacted to it like a cat to catnip. Heat gives me vitality. And there was the sea. From my window I could behold its blueness and even smell it. Pell is dead now, but I look back on those two weeks and bless her for them. I bless her not only for the joy I had then but because I met a wonderful friend in her house.

Besides myself she had two other guests, Anne Francine and Claire, the Marquise de Forbin. Anne is a statuesque American singer who worked with the U.S.O. during the war, and later sang with great success at Monseigneur in Paris.

Pell said Claire had gone to Cannes and would not be back until dinner time and she hoped I would not mind dining with her alone as Anne and she had a dinner engagement.

After they had left Claire arrived. Once or twice during the war I had seen her name mentioned in the American newspapers as one of the French women doing remarkable work in the Resistance movement. But as I did not know anything more about her than this I had not formed any impression of her. When, however, she came into the house this evening and introduced herself to me I was at first struck by her extreme fragility. She was so thin and looked so ill that I wondered how it was possible for her to actually be alive under these conditions. I saw at once, however, that she had great nervous vitality—even a kind of nervous strength.

It was moonlight. After dinner we went out and sat down on the terrace. Far away we could see the Mediterranean shimmering like quicksilver. I noticed then how really beautiful Claire was. Her beauty was not that of a glamour girl—far from it. It was a beauty born of race—of heritage—of a long and ancient line. I noticed the formation of her small skull, the delicate modeling of her brow, the exquisite chiseling of her nose. I thought of a woman I had seen on a fresco in Pompeii. She could have been this woman. She told me of her life. Her own name was Claire Charles-Roux. She was born in Avignon, but brought up in Morocco as her father had been aide to Marshal Leyhauty. She spoke with emotion of her father. He had been killed in the first world war. He had taught her to love horses and made her ride Arabian ponies bareback on the desert. I found out later that she excelled in a number of sports. She swam like a fish, skied beautifully and could ride any horse. Some days later when I saw her in a bathing suit I noticed her

legs were developed above the knees. This puzzled me. I knew that the
legs of ballet dancers were often developed below the knees but I asked
myself what could develop legs above the knees? Then I remembered
about the bareback riding. This was the answer.

I found out later from other people how courageous and extraordinary
she had been during the war in the Resistance and what a help she had
been to the American Army when it arrived in the Midi. She was later
given a citation by the Strategic Services Unit of the United States Forces
in the European Theatre.

That first evening we had been speaking French but when Pell and
Anne returned Claire suddenly began to speak English. She spoke it
quite fluently but I wanted to laugh because she used phrases and words
that she had evidently picked up from the G.I.'s. These phrases and
words did not at all go with her distinguished looks. To hear her talk
about "guys," "dolls," and someone being a "louse" was startling
enough, but when she began using really tough words and phrases it
was funny. Pell drew me aside and said, "Don't correct her. It's such
fun when she comes out with these astonishing words in front of prudish
people. She's learned English from the G.I.'s and half the time she
doesn't know what she's saying."

Alas, everything changes! She speaks perfect English now, but sometimes I miss her tough remarks.

Gaylord Hauser and Frey Brown turned up at Pell's house when they
heard I was there. Gaylord had come to lecture in Paris. He liked
Claire and was disturbed at her lack of weight. He wanted to take her
in hand and fatten her up. ".With what?" we said. But I made a resolve
then to get her to New York.

Back in New York, I kept my resolve and persuaded Claire to fly
over before Christmas to spend at least six weeks with me. She arrived
Christmas Eve, the day the great blizzard of 1947 started, and on this
first trip to the States and New York she never saw the city except without taxis, without buses, and buried in snow. But we had great fun. I
took her to a Christmas Eve party that night and everyone adored her.
Before I knew it she was being dated up by all the men. When we left,
long after midnight, we were still able to get a taxi as it had been snowing only a few hours then, and I took her to see the Christmas tree in
Radio City. For someone who had been through five years of war, who
had slept in the woods, in cellars and even sewers, who had been cold
and hungry and faced every kind of danger, to suddenly see this great

lighted tree through the falling snow was like a miracle. She burst into tears, and I wept too.

I became obsessed with the idea of making Claire gain weight and feel well. I woke her up at least once, and sometimes twice during the night, and gave her cereals, fruit-juices or milk. I made her stay in bed late in the morning and fed her every known food that I felt was healthy for her. Whatever maternal instinct I possess came out during those weeks.

She said she had never been so happy. Sleighs with horses appeared that winter, and we went for a sleigh ride around the park. When we went to the theatre to see Lillian Gish, we took the Third Avenue elevated. It was the only thing running. The cars swayed and bumped along (it was falling to pieces and has since been torn down), and in the stations there were still the old iron stoves with people crowded around them trying to keep warm. Many an old fur cap which had been in mothballs for years came out of the attic that winter complete with ear flaps, and women put shawls over their heads. Claire looked around and said, "But this can't be New York. We must be in Odessa!"

I took her backstage to meet Lillian who left the theatre with us. Dressed in heavy boots and a great fur cape, with snowflakes falling on her face, Lillian looked very beautiful and every inch an orphan of the storm. Of course we had to walk home, but that only gave me a fine excuse to feed Claire again when we got there cold and shivering. When the six weeks was over and Claire had to go back to Paris for a job, she had gained sixteen pounds and had to have her clothes altered. I was very happy, especially as the same syndicated paper sent me back to Europe soon again.

That summer, I went to Venice and there met my two good friends, Loren McIver and Lloyd Frankenberg. Loren is what I would call a lyric and poetic painter. Since then she has had many exhibitions and the Metropolitan Museum bought a painting she did of Venice at this time. This was their first trip to Europe, and as Venice is one of my most beloved places it was great fun showing them around.

Back in Paris Bluet Gaubert, a charming French friend of mine, introduced me to Eleanor Lutton who has a glorious natural voice and had come to Paris for singing lessons. We met often at a dreary tea room in the Rue Monthabor because it was the only one in Paris that occasionally served one brioche apiece with tea. Eleanor is great fun

334 /   *Here Lies the Heart*

and strikingly handsome. I took her to sing for Muratore who was enchanted with her voice.

I had met Muratore in Paris the year before the war when Mary Garden had taken me to his studio. I had given her my play, "The Mother of Christ" to read, and she suddenly said she would like to have it produced in Paris and play the part herself. She thought Muratore could play the part of Pilate. It seemed a little wild to me to have two great opera singers in a play without music, but Mary is such an artist that I felt she wouldn't cast herself in such a role without knowing what she was doing. I was not, however, so sure of Muratore. We went to see him and discuss it. He was enthusiastic but the war came and the idea was abandoned. He talked about it the day I took Eleanor to sing for him, and said he regretted it had never come to pass.

Loren and Lloyd were returning to New York and they said, before going, they wanted to meet Brancusi. As he had no telephone we just went to his studio on a chance of finding him in. I had known him in the twenties but I had not seen him since he had grown old. When he opened the door it was clear that he had suffered a great deal during the war and this had prematurely aged him. His hair had grown white and he appeared quite feeble. He had on a soiled white smock and his hair, face, and beard were covered with little flakes of white plaster. His entire appearance made him seem like a ghost. Even the studio was ghost-like, as all his works, many of them huge, were covered with white sheets. The studio was icy cold and felt like a tomb.

We hesitated in the doorway, embarrassed at disturbing him, but he made a weary gesture with his hand and beckoned us to come in. I explained that Loren was a painter and greatly admired his work. Lloyd added that we all admired it and asked if we might see some of it. Silently, like someone risen from a death bed, he shuffled across the room and slowly began removing the sheets from his various works. Lloyd moved forward to help him. One by one his magnificent works appeared as the sheets fell away. Some were in stone, some in brass, some in wood, and some in marble. They were all highly finished with an extraordinary patina. As each sheet slid to the floor, he ran his hand lovingly over the surface. We were tremendously impressed and he felt it. For a fleeting second his face lighted up. No one spoke. How could we? Anything we could have said in this studio would have been trivial. We were well aware that we were seeing the lifetime work of a genius. Finally Lloyd asked, "Were you able to work during the war?" He answered, "I lived here in this studio with practically no food, but each day I managed to polish with my hands some piece of work. See, how smooth this is." He tenderly indicated the surface of a stone piece. Lloyd drew a package of cigarettes from his pocket and offered him one. The old man sadly shook his head. "I am too tired to smoke," he said.

Forty-Nine

I was staying at the Crillon that autumn. I had one of the small rooms with a balcony on the fifth floor that looked over the American Embassy. It faced West and got the light of the setting sun and from it I could see the Tour Eiffel. It also had a wood-burning fireplace, and I lighted it often at night as the hotel was still poorly heated. Greta came over for a short time and had a room not far from mine on the same floor. I stayed on because I had promised Claire to go with her to Avignon where she was born.

Before we left, Bébé Bérard came for me one day and we lunched at a small restaurant—La Grenouille—which Bébé loved. At this restaurant I dropped a little mirror I carried in my bag. It fell at Bébé's feet and broke into pieces. He was terribly disturbed, and said some misfortune would come to him. I remembered Igor Stravinsky telling me how superstitious Diaghilev was about breaking mirrors, and that, when he did break one, he never rested until he had thrown the pieces into flowing water. Flowing water, he believed, counteracted any misfortune the broken mirror could cause. To make Bébé feel at ease I suggested we go to the Seine and throw the pieces into it. He jumped to his feet and we rushed to the Quai. I gave him the pieces, and when he had thrown them into the river he looked relieved. I laughed and said, "You know, it was I who broke the mirror. You haven't worried at all about the misfortune that might come to me."

He looked childishly repentant. I took his arm and said, "Oh, well, never mind. I don't need a river because I just can't have any bad luck with you. We always have too good a time together." This was the last time I saw him alive. We finished lunch and parted in the street. I told him I was going to Avignon and he said we would go antique hunting again when I returned. Alas, if we only could have.

Claire and I went first to Nimes, then to Arles and Les Saintes-Maries-de-la-Mer in the Camargue, and finally to Avignon. She took me to the house where she was born and to the Eglise Saint Pierre where she was christened and married. She bought a photograph of the baptismal font and wrote on the back of it, "Here is where I let out my first loud yell when salt was put on my tongue. I must have spit out wisdom then, which accounts for the later visit in a long white dress."

After my visit to Avignon with Claire, I took a train back to Paris. It came from Marseille and I chose an unfortunate compartment. After Lyons, when everyone was asleep and the compartment was in total darkness except for the little blue night-light overhead, a man quietly opened the door. He was wearing black glasses and a cap pulled well down over his eyes, and he held a revolver in each hand. Three young men in the compartment jumped to their feet as they woke up and saw him in the doorway. He fired at all three. Two were killed instantly and the third died later in the hospital in Lyons. An old man, the other occupant of the compartment, turned on the lights and rang the emergency alarm. The man who had done the shooting (afterwards called the "bandit of Marseille" by the newspapers) jumped off the train, broke his leg, and was captured in a field. I read some months later that the poor devil was hung. He was no bandit, but an unbalanced casualty of the war.

The three men were detectives sent by the government to Marseille to break up a black market ring. They had large sums of money on them which the so-called "bandit" had been tipped off about. When they jumped to their feet to attack him, he lost his head. There was only one relieving incident to this tragedy—he dropped his guns behind him in his flight. When I saw them lying on the floor, I covered one with my handkerchief and the other with my scarf. I knew that fingerprints on a gun should not be touched. When the police arrived they were amazed. They said it was a very intelligent thing to have done, but they looked at me suspiciously for having done it. "How did you know about covering the guns?" one of them asked.

"I have been a writer in Hollywood and I have seen enough gangster pictures being produced out there to make me a full-fledged detective and a policeman rolled into one," I told him.

But I had a bad reaction from this melodramatic little adventure. When the train arrived late in Paris (the police had held it up for several hours) I had a high temperature and went to bed in the Crillon. A doctor came and said I had "shock." For the first time in my life I developed a bad earache and had to be given large doses of penicillin. I became a bit delirious, and half in this state, and half asleep, I had a dream.

I dreamed I was in Tibet. It was interesting that I knew it was Tibet as I have never been there, but I was fully aware that it was this country. I was walking along a white road in brilliant sunshine. The road stretched out before me, winding up into the mountains, the highest peak of which was covered with snow. The air was so clear and rare that as I walked I felt as if I was flying. At first as I walked, there was no one in sight. Then, suddenly, at a distance on the road, I saw a woman coming toward me. She walked freely and beautifully, and she was dressed in a sort of purplish blue Chinese gown embroidered in gold. As she drew close and passed me on my left side, I noticed her slanting eyes seemed almost closed. She smiled faintly when she was directly beside me, but she did not turn her head. I wanted to turn and look after her, but I dared not because I knew she would be aware of it. I walked on a little further with a great feeling of well-being. Then I woke up.

As I lay in bed I felt extremely happy. Although I still had pain in my ear it did not seem to matter. When the doctor came he remarked my good spirits. I said, "I have been to Tibet." He did not answer and probably thought I was still delirious. I knew it was no use trying to explain.

Some days later Dilkusha de Rohan rang me on the telephone. I told her I was fed up with staying in bed. She suggested that I go with her to a friend's for dinner. The friend's name was Poppy Kirk and she was an excellent cook. (I learned later that Poppy's real name was Maria Annunziata Sartori—what a shame to have changed it!) Her father of Italian descent was born in Philadelphia from a family who had been Americans for several generations. Poppy was the only child of his second marriage and her mother was British. She was born in Italy—in Leghorn—but she was brought up in the international sets of France and England.

We went to Auteuil, stopping on the way to pick up Mary Busch and an Indo-Chinese poet—Pierre Dodinh. When we arrived Poppy was in the kitchen and called out to us to take off our coats. As I am always very sensitive to voices, I like to hear a voice before I meet the person it belongs to. Poppy has a charming one, and her English is English, although she was born and brought up in Italy. The room we were in was lighted only by candles and when she appeared I thought for a second that I wasn't seeing clearly, or that I was dreaming again. She was wearing the same Chinese gown the woman in my Tibetan dream had worn and in fact she was the same woman. There were the same slit, half-closed eyes, and the same faint smile. I was actually so stunned by this encounter that it was difficult for me even to shake hands with her. She was so busy preparing dinner that she was unaware of my emotion, but when we sat down at the table and I remarked on her gown, she said, "I always wear Chinese gowns. I love everything oriental. In fact, I sometimes think I really am oriental." She did not have to say this to make me believe it.

When we left she told us she was going to the United States within a week, first to Washington and New York, then on to join her husband in Mexico City. She had been working with Edward Molyneux, but had given up the job, for a while anyway. I gave her my address and she said she would look me up after the New Year.

That week Bébé Berard died. Boris Kochnow, whom he lived with, telephoned me the shocking news. I went over at once and saw poor Bébé lying dead on his bed. I simply could not take in his death or believe it. He always seemed so part of life—so part of the artistic life of Paris—so part of my own life in Paris. His funeral services were at Saint Sulpice. And never, even for a great statesman, have I seen so many flowers. I was told that every flower shop in Paris had been emptied. I sat through the High Mass feeling very despondent because, somehow, I identified Bébé's death with the breaking of my mirror.

On Christmas Day Jean Cocteau and I flew to New York together. We had a miserable trip because the heating apparatus in the plane broke down. Luckily, we were the only passengers, so we took all the blankets and piled them on. I was afraid Jean would smother under his mountain of coverings during the night. But worse was to come for him. When we arrived in New York he found he had forgotten his vaccination certificate. No amount of pleading with the officials would let him off. They dragged him into a room, took off his coat and vaccinated him then and there. He was horribly frightened and it was no small ordeal after a freezing flight.

My wonderful friend, Marion Stevenson, was waiting for me in my flat. Although it was the day after Christmas, she had thoughtfully decorated a small tree for me and arranged flowers in my rooms. Greta was next door in the Ritz Tower and she came in to have tea with us. She had never met Marion and I could see she was intrigued by her. She looked at her closely, frankly staring at her the way a child sometimes stares. Then she said to Marion, "May I ask you a personal question?" Marion was puzzled, but answered, "Of course. I have no secrets from Mercedes." I couldn't imagine what Greta was going to bring forth. Rather shyly, she asked, "Are you a virgin?" Marion laughed. "Do you know, I am seventy-six years old and I have never really thought about that question. But come to think of it now, I *am* a virgin." Greta gazed at her in wonderment, and said, "How extraordinary."

After this conversation I always had great fun with Marion. When I rang her on the telephone I used to ask, "Is this the Virgin speaking?"

Just before New Year's I had a letter from Poppy Kirk who was in Washington saying she was coming to New York soon. I invited her for dinner and got tickets for *The Mad Woman of Chaillot*. Although we had had a magnificent dinner the night I had been to her flat, I did not realize she was a celebrated cook and known as such far and wide. During the war, with several other women, she had cooked for hundreds of British officers a day at the National Gallery in London, and with practically no ingredients, managed to vary their food and give them such good dishes that this particular canteen became famous.

What got into me the night Poppy came for dinner, I'll never know. I decided to cook her a dinner. When she arrived I was in a nervous state. I had been cooking since three o'clock! She looked indulgent but politely said nothing. She even more politely ate my dinner and pretended she thought it exceptionally good. I am ashamed to say what a simple dinner it was. As it turned out, she could have cooked it in thirty minutes with only one hand and her eyes closed.

We went sightseeing the next day, and just before sunset, around the Reservoir for a walk. It was bitter cold, but the sky was flame pink as the sun went down. Over the water the lights in the windows of the tall buildings began to come on and she was enchanted. Dressed in a grey tweed suit she walked with the ease and long strides I had seen in my dream. I said, "Now you are walking as you did in Tibet." I told her

about my dream. She was tremendously interested, and said that her
father, whom she adored, had encouraged her at an early age to feel
oriental and to like Eastern things. When she was a small child he used
to wrap her naked in an ice cold, wet sheet and make her create enough
heat in her own body to dry it. This is an exercise practised by Yogis
in the Himalayas. Poppy didn't know this and was amazed to hear it.
She said her father had made her sit quietly alone in her room, making
her mind blank. This is another Yoga practise—emptying the mind.
She did not know where her father had learned these practises, but they
gave me an even stronger impression that she had been Tibetan or
Chinese in another incarnation.

I introduced Poppy to my friends. Marion adored her and from old
trunks where she had been hoarding treasures for years she produced
Chinese shawls, bits of exquisite silk, a paisley bedspread, a crystal
necklace, lace baby dresses (which she said could be made into blouses)
and heaven knows what else, and gave them to Poppy. They were
constantly in a huddle over bits of lace or some Victorian piece of
jewelry. At a party given by Kay and George Sakier, she wore a white
Molyneux evening dress. Kay and George were living in a studio over
a stable, lit by candlelight, and when she came into the room everyone
stopped talking. Kay said she was fascinating. She should know, as she
is the able fashion editor of "Mademoiselle" under her own name—
Kay Silver. Kay herself is a combination of a successful career woman
and a bashful child. Blonde and pretty, she often, at her own parties,
wears Nineteenth Century dresses which suit her very well. George is
a painter, dark as Kay is blonde. He has been art director of both *Vogue*
in Paris and *Harper's Bazaar* in New York. He is sensitive, intelligent
and has the qualities that make him companionable to women.

I introduced Poppy to another friend of mine, Eleanor Cooley. I met
Nell through Natasha Rambova when I wanted her to look up an aspect
of my astrological chart. She had no time to do it then, and said she
knew only one astrologer she would trust to do it for me. Nell is warm
and intelligent and a profound student of esoteric teachings. I often
discuss complex problems with her.

Poppy was having such a good time that she stretched out her visit
for a month, but finally the day came when she had to leave for Mexico.
I rented my flat to Carol Channing and her husband and flew back to
Paris.

I heard from Poppy often. She seemed restless and did not like
Mexico. In the meantime I went out often to Senlis to see my friends,

the Ericksons who had a lovely house out there and what was even more "lovely" was its atmosphere of perennial hospitality. There is no one more hospitable in the world than Lee Erickson. The household consisted then (before Eric's sad death) of Lee, Eric, their daughter Charlotte, and three French poodles, one of which had a gentle habit of biting people. At one party he tore off a lady's skirt and left her standing rather exposed and extremely embarrassed, but these were only minor inconveniences compared to the warmth, affection, and good food of this house. Apart from Eric's fine portraits, he had over a number of years contributed fashion drawings to *Vogue* which in my opinion greatly enhanced the prestige of that magazine. But I always jokingly told Eric that his true fame came from the chic manner in which he could wear a bowler hat! No one could wear one as he did.

I went two or three times a week to Marie Laurencin's studio and sat with her while she painted. Suzanne made tea for us and one day she took some rather monstrous photographs of Marie and myself. Marie was terribly upset at this time that she had lost her apartment at 1 rue Savorgnan de Brazza, near the Champs de Mars. Everything in it was hers—her furniture, even her personal things, and her books. I think she cared more about losing her books than anything else. During the war some people moved into the apartment, which Marie had unfortunately left vacant. When the war was over they would not move out. Marie started a lawsuit but it trailed on and on and made her terribly unhappy and nervous. She was also hurt that the government did not force these people out. She talked to me about this and said, "After all, I am an artist who has brought France some réclame. In my old age the least they can do is to return me my home." Had she had the money to bribe the officials she probably would have won the suit. I believe all the nervous strain of this suit caused her death. Not long before she died she did recover the apartment but, it was too late. She was too ill to care.

One day in the bus I ran into my beloved friend, Alice Toklas. I had not seen her for a long time and this chance meeting was very fortunate. She was wearing what I called "a Knight's hat"—a hat dripping with plumes. I felt she should have whisked it off her head and bowed low with it to the floor when she said good-bye to me. But she did better than that. She invited me to lunch. Whoever reads this has, I hope, also read the wonderful cook book written by Alice B. Toklas. If they have done so they will know why I looked forward to this lunch. Alice completes the trio of the three best cooks in my life—Marlene, Poppy, and Alice.

But let no one think that I only went to see Alice for food. I would gladly starve for a month for one hour's conversation with her. She has the quickest and most intelligent mind I know. And what is more, she has untold kindness, and the good manners of the heart. I do not know anyone with more exquisite manners, which spring from her extreme preoccupation with the welfare of others, and also from her rare sensitivity. When I am away from her I look forward to her letters which I am fortunate enough to receive quite often. They look as if they were written with the eyelash of a fly. The letters are so small and so delicately shaped that she could easily write my full name and address on a postage stamp. I am always fascinated by them and when I get a letter from her I often sit and gaze at the writing for a long time before opening the envelope. I have studied handwritings and Alice's denotes what she is: beautifully modest, religiously humble, sensitive to an extreme, artistic, full of awareness, alert, tactful, forceful, unswerving to principle, generous and kind. These are just a few of the traits her writing reveals. She is a continual "event" in my life, in her letters or in person.

At this time Basket was still alive. Basket was a dog—I would prefer to say a person. He was a large white poodle. He had belonged to Gertrude Stein and I suspect that Alice not only loved him for himself but also for his association with Miss Stein. At this time he was exceedingly old, blind, and frail. It was strange, but whenever I saw him I felt I was "dreaming" him. I never felt he belonged on this plane.

I suddenly had a letter from Poppy saying she wanted to return to Paris and suggesting we share a flat together. I put in a long-distance call to Mexico City and we decided she would fly to Paris as soon as I found an apartment.

Then began the hunt for one! I could have found a needle in a haystack with my eyes closed more easily than an apartment in Paris at this time. I wore the soles off my shoes running from one apartment house to another. I ascended and descended in shaky old lifts. I walked up and walked down dozens of stairways a day. I stopped unsuspecting concierges who were beating their rugs in the street and asked them if they knew of any apartment in their quartier. I made the sound of a thousand-franc note under their noses. All to no avail. Finally, in despair, I gave up. That same day Claire rushed in to see me. She had heard of

344 / *Here Lies the Heart*

a small flat on the Quai Voltaire that we should go and see at once. "Not a stone must be left unturned," she said, using a stock phrase she had picked up from a book of English expressions.

"Well, you go and turn the stone," I said, "and if there isn't an old moth-eaten carpet under it, I'll consider looking at the flat. At present I'm tired of dingy stairways and nasty smells."

Claire was exasperated. "I've worked hard to find out about this flat. You simply *must* look at it," she moaned. Just for deviltry and not to seem to be giving in too easily, I said, "If there is a butterfly in the flat of any kind, I will take it without even looking at it. But if not I will come away at once." Claire looked puzzled and produced a bit of G.I. slang. "Are you nuts?" "No, I just mean what I say. Who can tell? There may be a butterfly painted on a lampshade, or there may be an ashtray with a butterfly on it, or there may be just some old dead butterflies with pins through them on the wall in a frame. You know the kind. You've seen them in every stuffy house."

Claire shook her head and mumbled, "Come on." We proceeded out of the hotel, into her car, across the Place de la Concorde and on to the Quai Voltaire. We stopped at number five. Entering the house I perceived a beautiful stairway but no lift. "Just as I thought—no lift," I grumbled. At the top of the fifth floor, I said, "Remember about the butterflies. No butterflies, no apartment."

Claire gave me a withering look as we went down a small corridor. She knocked at a door. It was opened wide by a woman, and we stood on the threshold gasping. All four walls of the room were covered with butterflies and in the center of the room, on an easel, there was a huge oil painting of butterflies. The woman saw our look of amazement and said, "I am a painter of butterflies. Won't you come in?" I moved not a muscle. I just said, "Madame, I will take the apartment. Please draw up the paper."

How I got it ready in the short time I did, I will never know. Let it never be said that the French cannot work quickly. True, the flat was small. There was only a bedroom, a living room, and a kitchen. I had a modern toilet put in the hallway and a bathtub in the kitchen. The rooms were attractively shaped as they had dormer windows. And the living room had a charming Louis XVI mantle and fireplace. Luckily, the rooms were at the back of the house and faced south and got full sunshine when there was any. I had all the walls painted white and book cases built in. Two friends of mine, Andrew Shunny and Charles Maguire, helped me furnish it. I had long yellow linen curtains made for all the windows and we picked up old pieces of furniture in antique shops. When Poppy arrived it was filled with flowers, and fortunately it was a sunny day. Of course it was just a modest little place but it was gay, clean, and amusing. Poppy brought a lot of things from Mexico which suited it. Silver plates, tin candelabras, printed Madonnas, colored paper flowers and all sorts of nonsense that gave it a special playful character of its own.

Spring was sweet in the little flat. As well as being a good cook, Poppy has a genius for flowers and always arranges them beautifully. The place was a mass of flowers inside and we had flower boxes at the windows. She made different colored dinners. She would have an all pink dinner. The flowers on the table were pink, the soup was pink— borscht or tomato. There would be radishes on the table and we might have shrimps with rice, beet salad, and strawberries or raspberries for dessert. Nothing was allowed on the table that was not pink except bread, rice, and butter. And, of course, we had vin rose. A green dinner was the easiest: pea soup, artichokes, spinach and string beans, a green salad and mint ice cream. Yellow was easy too. Melons, all kinds of soups are more or less yellow; then there are squash, corn, sweet potatoes, and chicken. We called chicken yellow. And for dessert there were cheese, apricots, bananas, or even peaches. Eggplant, purple plums, purple grapes, prunes and cabbage came under the purple dinners.

All this Poppy did with the greatest of ease. She often came home from having worked all day at Schiaparellis and while taking a bath and making up she not only cooked a marvelous dinner for six or seven people but she also arranged the table so beautifully that the mere sight of it so stimulated the guests' appetites that they could hardly wait for dinner to be served. But while they were hungrily eyeing the table and drinking their cocktails, Poppy would appear looking utterly charming in one of her Chinese gowns and giving the impression that she had never been near a kitchen, much less having coped with fifty or more tiresome and exacting women clients all day at Schiaps, having probably run up and down the stairs one hundred times and answered the telephone dozens of other times, having had to make choice of materials and possibly having had to assist Schiap personally in various ways.

Poppy is deliciously unique. I have never met anyone in the world remotely like her.

George Sakier came to Paris that spring. He was not well and he came often to our flat to lie down. Poppy cooked for him and he told her how attractive she was. Then Poppy got ill. She had caught some kind of a germ in Mexico so I had them both ill on my hands. One day when I tried to take Poppy's temperature she snatched the thermometer out of my hand and smashed it against the wall. George called out from the other room. "Never let a woman with even a drop in her of Italian blood get anything breakable in her hands." The rest of the time I lived with Poppy I remembered this advice.

We had a happy summer. We did not go away and it was lovely when everyone else did. We seemed to have Paris to ourselves. We walked down by the water's edge on the quais, we went to the flower markets, and we sat in the sun. We went to concerts, sometimes dined late at our favorite restaurants, and a great deal of the time we did just nothing. But Poppy began to get restless and said she must work again. We viewed our finances and decided she had to. She had not been brought up to work and had only begun to when her first husband left her without any money and a small son. I hated to see her start working again. She considered returning to Edward Molyneux, but one day by accident she ran into Schiaparelli, who immediately offered her a job as a sort of general manager of her shop. Poppy and Schiaparelli have very much the same taste and artistically see things with the same eye. Also, Poppy had known Schiap a long time and was fond of her. Then too, she liked the location of the shop on the Place Vendome. Altogether she was not unhappy about the job, but I was suddenly left alone all day. I had been most of my life alone, but these few months with Poppy had spoiled me. I thought of getting a job myself, but I had free-lanced so long that I dreaded again being stuck in set hours. Greta came to Paris in the beginning of September and we took long walks in the Bois and the Tuileries Gardens.

Then it began to rain and the days were dark and cold. In the midst of this dreary weather the concierge's wife died. She had been ailing for some time and I often went in to see her. A few days after the funeral I met her on the stairs. Of course I knew it was only her astral body, but it had a very disturbing effect on me. I became very nervous and I hated being left alone in the flat and going up and down the stairs. Poppy saw my state of mind and suggested we move. A small hotel on the Quai farther up—the Bisson—had just been opened and a friend of mine, Eric Charrel, was living there. Eric was the original producer of the *White Horse Inn* when it was first done in Germany. He had also produced that beautiful film, *Congress Dances*. He suggested that Poppy and I go to this hotel. So we took a little suite there and furnished it with a good many of our own things. We had a beautiful Christmas.

We carried home our own tree and Poppy decorated it entirely with paper butterflies. She can cook on a candle and in some extraordinary way she cooked delicious meals for us on some kind of a makeshift burner and a small electric stove. This stove regularly blew out the fuses in the hotel. Undaunted, Poppy would fix the fuses with hairpins and suddenly the lights would go on again. She has green thumbs for flowers and plants and red thumbs for fuses!

But after Christmas I became ill. I am a creature of the sun and continual dark days and rain get me down. Next I heard that Eleanor von Mendelssohn had killed herself and this had a terrible effect on me. Ona Munson and Eugene Berman came to Paris and lived in Alice de Lamar's flat a few doors away from us in Alfredo Side's house. Ona hated Paris. She did not feel well either and talked constantly about how she wished she was in New York. When I went to see her I was unable to cheer her up and unconsciously she communicated her unhappiness to me. I always left her feeling worse myself. I began having terrible headaches and a recurrence of my old time depressions. The hotel was badly heated and I was often cold. Poppy had so much work to do at the shop that many evenings she did not come home until seven. I began writing articles, and in order to be warm, I wrote them in the American Cultural Centre on the Faubourg Saint Honore. But this was no solution to my depressions so I decided to go to New York and see my beloved doctor, Max Wolf. Max was not only my doctor but he and his wife Edith were also my friends. Schiap was sending Poppy to New York in six weeks, so it was just a matter of going a little sooner. When I reached New York I came down with a bad case of shingles.

Of course, Marion came and took care of me. I was so ill, she stayed with me night and day at first. But as I got better she came only in the afternoon and stayed until about eleven. She was a night owl. When she left me she would say she was going over to walk on Broadway. This was actually true. She loved walking at night on Broadway. Often, in the old days, before I went to Hollywood and when I was a night owl too, we used to walk together on Broadway sometimes as late—or as early—as dawn. She would hold my arm and say, "I must hang on to you so that no one will pick you up." I answered, "If there is any picking to be done it will be you who will be picked."

I had a letter then from Gabrielle Enthoven in London saying Quintin Tod had died. He had died in his sleep. He had written me only ten days before, saying he wished he could leave England for a long time.

Then one day I had a far greater blow, but I know I should not have regarded it as such. Bhagavan Ramana Maharshi died on April fourteenth. He had said, "I am going away. Where could I go? I am here." By the word "here" he did not imply any limitation. He meant rather, that the Self *is*. There is no going, or coming, or changing, in that which is changeless and Universal. I should not have regarded his death as a blow. How could I lose him? How can one lose anyone? How can one lose that which is Eternal? It is only in the first shock, and gripped in the illusion of death, that one grieves for the physical presence.

Yet, millions in India mourned the Maharshi. A long article about his death in the *New York Times* ended with "Here in India, where thousands of so-called holy men claim close tune with the Infinite, it is said that the most remarkable thing about Sri Ramana Maharshi was that he never claimed anything remarkable for himself yet became one of the most loved and respected of all."

His death was remarkable. My friend, the celebrated French photographer, Henri Cartier-Bresson, and his wife Ratna, were there at the time. They told me that at six P.M. of the evening of his death, he gave Darshan to a great number of people, who, hearing he was dying, had come long distances just for the last Darshan. A short while before the actual minute of his death, he had the doctor put his body in the Lotus posture. The resident devotees came in one by one, touched his feet, and had their last Darshan. Then Bhagavan asked the doctor to feel his pulse. He said, "When it stops, you will know my physical organism has come to a standstill." At forty-seven minutes past eight, and without any movement, Bhagavan's heart stopped. At this same second, a bright ball of light rose from his head and was observed moving slowly across the sky. For ten to fifteen seconds it trailed across the sky. It passed to the Northeast and dipped into the peak of Arunachala. Many people saw it, and many more people saw its reflection, even as far as Madras, and felt what it portended. Both Henri and Ratna Cartier-Bresson saw it and said there was no doubt about this phenomenon.

I did grieve at first because of a feeling that I would not again be able to be in the physical presence of Bhagavan. I regretted not having flown over to see him before the end, but I had no idea it was so close. Then one day in meditation, I felt his Spiritual Presence so strongly that I never grieved again.

Poppy had, in the meantime, come to New York. After some weeks when she had finished the job for Schiap, we flew back to Paris. She had two surprises for me. While I was in New York she found a lovely duplex apartment on the Quai Saint Michel, and she had found a little farmhouse in Normandy. The apartment had a large studio on the top floor with a balcony all the way around it, and on the roof there was a terrace. The floor below had a living room, a study, a large bathroom, kitchen and bedroom. As this block of houses is on a hill we could see all over Paris from the studio floor. The Seine lay at our feet and directly opposite was the Notre Dame. It was a lovely location because it was so easy to get to the flower market right near Notre Dame.

The farmhouse in Normandy was a find as it was charmingly furnished with Provincial furniture. It was in a small village called Aincourt, not far from Magny-en-Vexin. Besides two farms owned by peasants, we and the Dreyfus family (of the famous Dreyfus case) were the only people in the village. A mile and a quarter away there was another village called Parne, which boasted a twelfth-century church and a cafe. This village had no running water in the houses. Everyone drew water from a pump in front of the church. The Dreyfus house and ours were the only ones for miles around with running water, and of course that did not mean hot running water. I thought I could organize a petition to the Government to have running water installed in the houses in Parne but the peasants did not want it. They shrugged their shoulders and asked, "Who wants running water?" And yet the two poor women (one very old) who kept the cafe had to go in every kind of weather with a bucket to draw it at the church just to wash their glasses.

But we were very happy in this farmhouse. It was surrounded by fields in which there were cows. This delighted me, but Poppy was frightened of them, at first, when they came close enough to chew our flowers and shrubs. At night they coughed and sneezed loudly which always made me laugh. They sounded like very old men clearing their throats. We spoke of them as "the girls."

At this time Poppy came in one day when we were at the apartment with something bulging from her pocket. She said, "You don't know what I have in my pocket." I said, "I'll bet I do—a Siamese cat." I was right. She produced a tiny Siamese kitten. I decided to call her "La Linda," after my grandmother. She was very delicate as her mother had not been fed properly. Poppy had bought her from a concierge on the Quai. She was inclined to be humpbacked. But we fed her the best food and fussed over her. We became doting parents. We went every week end to the country and sometimes, in summer, we motored down every evening and came back to Paris in the morning. Luckily Linda loved motoring. If she was up a tree and we wanted to get her down, all I had to do was turn on the motor and she would rush down and make a dive for her seat in the car.

That August in 1950, Gabrielle Enthoven died. After Ivor's death, followed by Quintin and finally Gabrielle, London never seemed the same to me again.

Often friends turned up in Paris. I used to say it was like a corridor because people were continually coming and going. For this reason I always feel that Paris is the most restless city in the world. While Poppy and I were on the Quai Saint Michel friends were always arriving from America or England. Greta came to Paris a number of times during those years. I used to drive her around in a Hillman car that Poppy and I shared. I love driving in Paris because one has to be so much on one's toes. I remember dashing Greta around the Place de la Concorde and recalling our slow-paced driving in Hollywood. "No getting out to pick flowers here," I said.

Malvina Hoffman has a house in Paris and I often drove her various places. We went a number of times to the foundry on rue Leplanquais where she had all her sculpture cast in bronze. This was the foundry of Eugene Rudier—considered the Master Founder. Rudier cast for Rodin, Bourdelle, Despiau, Maillol, Renoir, Daumier, and Degas. In recent years he cast for such modern sculptors as Matisse, Henry Moore and Zadkine.

It is an interesting fact that Rudier signed his name under Rodin's name on everything he ever cast for him. This, it is said, gives Rodin's bronzes more value since they bear the Master Founder's signature as well as his own. Rudier was unquestionably the greatest bronze founder of this century and the last. Rodin said of him, "I create in plaster. Rudier then takes my creations and gives them flesh in bronze." He died in 1952.

Two English friends of Poppy's came from London to stay a week with us—Mrs. Winifret Game and her daughter Barbara Neill. I discovered that Mrs. Game is Eastern in her way of thinking. Perhaps this is why she is so wise. Without actually being a Buddhist, like myself, she tries to follow the Eight Fold Path.

While we were still in this apartment Eva Le Gallienne came to dinner with us bringing her friend the English stage director Margaret Webster with her. The evening passed pleasantly and we laughed about the old days of *Jehanne d'Arc*.

Natasha Rambova also came to Paris. I did not know she was there and I was sitting in the sun in the Tuileries Gardens. I was not at all thinking of Natasha, then suddenly I saw her standing before me exactly as though she was flesh and blood. This appearance lasted only a split second, but long enough for me to notice her clothes. I got up, walked to the Quai and along it. Just in front of the Institut de France Natasha actually came toward me in the flesh and dressed as I had seen her ten minutes previously.

In 1951, Baba and my niece Mercedes were living in Paris in Passy, as Mercedes had a job at the British Embassy. On the ninth of April Poppy and I had tickets to fly back to New York, as she was scheduled to do a job there for Schiap. Frederick came over to Paris on a few days leave from the Navy. The night before he was to return we all went out to an Austrian restaurant for dinner. We had vodka, a good wine, chicken paprika, strudel and all the things that go with it, and a very happy time—at least until the moment Frederick announced he had volunteered for an assignment on a submarine called the *Affray*. He had already told Baba and she was very upset about it. Frederick argued that there was more danger in crossing a Boulevard in Paris on foot than going down in a submarine. He said this submarine had every modern safety device. He drew a plan of the *Affray* on the table cloth and showed us where all these safety devices were. His eyes shone as he talked and I could see he was terribly happy about the whole thing. "But if there's no danger why did they call for volunteers?" I asked. To this question he had no answer. He tossed it off lightly and just said, "Oh, they always ask for volunteers if a job's outside the usual routine." Looking back on it now I don't think either Baba or I could possibly have persuaded him not to make this trip. Poor boy, he probably also thought that by volunteering for this assignment, which was obviously a dangerous one no matter what he said, he would advance his promotion and make more money with which to help Baba. After dinner he put Poppy and me into a taxi. It was raining and I called out to him not to wait. I never saw him again.

On the morning of April seventeenth, after I had returned to New York, I received a cable from Baba just saying, "Frederick lost on *Affray*—Mercedes and I flying London—there is still hope."

Poor Baba sitting in her room in Paris had turned on the radio and heard the Affray was lost. She and Mercedes flew to London waiting forty-eight hours in the Admiralty Office only to be told at the end the ghastly news that the submarine could not be recovered. What courage that waiting must have taken! But Baba, like all of my family, has always had courage.

Fifty

When Poppy and I returned to Paris, Baba and Mercedes were back again in their flat in Passy. To me the tragedy of Frederick and the Affray seemed a bad dream. But to them I know it did not even seem a nightmare—it was just a ghastly reality.

That summer Poppy took a few weeks holiday. We spent it in the little house in Aincourt. Although we were delighted to have these uninterrupted weeks in the country, I think the happiest one of us was Linda. With the good food and care we gave her she had developed into a beautiful little creature with amazingly beautiful big blue eyes. She is a great talker—as many Siamese are and often she has had a number of impolite things to say whenever she dislikes someone. She loves cars and when driving she likes to lean out the window and feel the wind whistle through her long whiskers. She also enjoys flying. She sits quietly, attentive to all that is going on. There are no flies on her! She purrs a lot and I think it is her way of making music.

At this time Schiap had some problems of her own and came to stay a week with us to get away from people and to rest. Otherwise, we had no other visitors except Poppy's cousins, Mick and his wife, Kitty, who came once or twice for the day. Mick is like a brother to Poppy. He is Sir William Meiklereid and at this time was British Minister in Paris and later was the British Ambassador to Luxembourg.

I look back to those days in the little house in Aincourt, and to the

352

farm country spread out around it with great nostalgia. I have a deep fondness for Normandy. Somehow, its soil speaks to me more than any part of France.

The following winter I went often to Gretz, to the Ramakrishna Centre, to see a beloved friend—Swami Siddheswarananda, a very remarkable man. With the help of Monsieur and Madame Sauton the Swami founded the Centre there. Not long after this Monsieur Sauton died, but Madame Sauton remained with the Swami, and became the "Mother" of the Centre. She is called Mammaji by all the friends and disciples. She is a beautiful person, physically and in her character. She ran the Centre for the Swami, who until the moment of his death in April 1957, established a cultural centre there. People of note from every country went to see him. He attracted scientists, philosophers, poets, musicians, writers—in fact, every kind of artist or thinking mind.

In May of 1952 I knew that Marion Stevenson was very ill. She had been writing me and trying to conceal it, but she did not fool me. Besides I knew her condition from her doctor. I decided to fly back to New York to see her. It was not too soon. In the hospital she said, "Tell me the truth. Am I dying?" For a second I thought of lying to her, but I had never lied to her before. I did not lie to her then, and I am thankful I didn't. I answered, "Yes, darling, you are dying, but don't be afraid. There is nothing to fear. Death, I am· sure, is no different from life. I will becoming along soon, too, and we will be walking on Broadway again." She smiled faintly. Then I said, "But whatever happens I know God has his arms around you." This time she really smiled. Her face became radiant. She said, "Yes, yes. That's it. God has his arms around me." She closed her eyes and went into a coma. She died an hour later.

When the doctor came I told him what I had said to Marion and what her last words had been. He said, "How wonderful that you told her the truth. I wish everyone would do this to people who are dying. It would help them to die. Dying people are very sensitive. They know when they are being lied to, and, I believe, half the time they pretend to swallow what they are told about getting well and all that nonsense just to make it easier for their family and friends. To die, being told the truth, is what everyone would want." I am glad he told me this. I believe it is an important thing to know.

While I was still in New York after Marion's death I heard that Abram's wife had died. I went to Old Lyme, Connecticut, where he was living in the country. I found him not very well and I was disturbed by the fact that all his paintings were in a barn where there were mice, bats, and a leaking roof. Many of them were in very bad condition from exposure and dampness. There were about thirty or forty paintings. I got a van and brought them all down to New York where I left them with my friend, Dick Pleasant, who allowed me to hang them in his flat so I could judge their condition.

Then I flew back to Paris. Poppy and I had lost the house in Aincourt because the owner wanted it herself, but in the meantime she had found another one beyond Saint Denis and Orgival. It was attractive, and, it could be said, more so than Aincourt. But I missed our fields and the "girls." We went out to it every weekend during the summer and autumn, but then Poppy gave it up as she knew Schiap wanted her to work for her in New York that winter.

In September I heard that Muriel Draper had died. Muriel and I were friends for many years. She was an outstanding figure in New York and Europe because of her vibrant and arresting personality, and for her interest, in what I would call humanity at large. Unfortunately for her at this time she did not take into account that McCarthy was spreading his slime all over the United States, and that the House Un-American Activities Committee was just as apt as not to label a woman "pink" because she used pink powder. As a result when Muriel *was* labeled "pink," she was not prepared for all that went with it—social ostracism, criticism, and the cancelling of her passport. She might have borne these things had they not affected her son Paul, the remarkable dancer and artist. At this time he was at the peak of his career and as unconcerned with national affairs as his mother was concerned with them. His career was blocked and he was unable to continue dancing in the United States. All this had a terrible effect on Muriel. She died of a stroke brought on by anxiety, but, I believe, she died of a sad heart. Right or wrong, she was a casualty of the Cold War. There have been many such casualties here in the United States—victims of misplaced patriotism, and unintelligent nationalism. I have known several.

At the end of November, when it was time to go to New York, we gave up the apartment on the Quai and with Linda flew to New York. We lived at first in my flat.

This winter I had the great privilege of meeting and studying with Doctor Suzuki. I went to many of his classes in Columbia University. Doctor Daisetz Suzuki is the greatest living authority on Zen Buddhism and it is mostly through his writings and teachings that the western world has recently become conscious of Zen.

Zen often seems in contradiction, but it is just this contradiction which gives the spiritual "shock" so necessary to shatter ignorance. "Where Buddha is do not stay, where Buddha is not, pass on quickly," is an example of Zen contradiction.

At the lectures, Mihoko Okamura sat next to Doctor Suzuki taking notes for him. She was then not more than nineteen years old. She is slender and small, like many Japanese women, but the shape of her face —oval and finely carved—and the texture of her skin—white as a magnolia flower—are unusual. At the lectures I was impressed by a kind of radiation Doctor Suzuki projected. In fact, I was so caught up by this radiation of goodness which came from him that often I lost track of his words. I thought about these two people so apparently close in spirit and so far apart in age. (Doctor Suzuki was then eighty-eight years old.) Then one day I was walking up Third Avenue before the elevated tracks had been torn down and coming toward me were Doctor Suzuki and Mihoko—"Miho," as I call her. They glided toward me and in just this way seemed to come into my life. We met there on that shabby avenue and smiled at one another. They invited me to tea.

When Miho took me into Doctor Suzuki's study he was seated behind a large desk dressed in Japanese costume. He is small and has bright intelligent eyes overhung with amazing eyebrows which stand out from his brow like great wings. On his desk and round the room many books were piled high. Miho brought in tea. We sipped it and spoke of cats. Doctor Suzuki had heard of Linda. Miho called in their cat, Peter. She explained that he was only an "alley cat," not meaning that she loved him any the less because of this fact. We all agreed about his nobility of spirit. Then we talked of tea and flowers. Finally, we fell into silence. There was no need to talk. Doctor Suzuki's goodness and soul-rareness so filled the room there was no need for words. Before leaving he gave me one of his books and wrote an inscription in it for me. When I got home I saw the inscription was in Chinese. I called Mihoko and jokingly said, "Tell Dr. Suzuki that, as clever as I am, I do not understand Chinese. Ask him what he has written in my book." Mihoko returned from discussing the matter with Dr. Suzuki. She said he has written an early Zen saying "Mountain is mountain, water is water."

In the spring Poppy's son, Victor Montrezza, came back from Roumania where he had been working for the State Department. He was young and had been unhappy, and virtually in exile, as one is when serving one's country behind the Iron Curtain. Poppy thought she should live with him. She found a flat in my building during the summer, but in the winter they took another flat on East Thirty-fifth Street. Then came the problem—who would keep Linda? We both loved her. Poppy generously left her with me. She bought an enchanting little Pekinese fellow whom we christened Cherry Blossom and a little later I gave her another Pekinese—Lotus Blossom. This boy is breathtakingly beautiful and so good and gentle that we are constantly touched by him, although, at odd moments, we secretly admit to each other that he is, perhaps, the village idiot. Brains are not his strong point. But Poppy adores him just the same, and I am a runner-up for his heart and paw!

As a roundup of, what I call, "my first hundred year plan," I would like to say that Abram has married a third time and is very happy. He married Marion Skirten, a wonderful and charming person.

Anna still lives on the desert in California but, one by one, the little brood have died. She used to sign all their names to my Christmas and birthday cards, but, over the years, each name has dropped off until now she only signs her own. I shall never forget my "little family." They were a vital part of me in younger days.

Happily, old friends still remain in my life—Vouletti, Audrey, Hope, Claire, Poppy, Natacha, Greta, and many others.

Linda is now nine years old. She grows steadily each day in wisdom and mischief. She is my "dream-girl,"—and completely rules my life.

The circle closes in. I am once more living alone. I am reminded of a Spanish saying: "Whichever way the monkey jumps he always sees his own tail." But I cannot really say I am alone. How can I? I have my Linda, and, despite the many years behind me, I feel now, as if I am only beginning life. I feel this because I believe I have arrived at a true consciousness of the meaning of life. That meaning to me lies in the practice of the art of the complete gift of myself in all that I do. This, I have found, is the only way to bring life *alive*. I have never had any desire for money, but now I have no desire for possessions of any kind, or for fame, or even for any further friendships. I only desire to *achieve* life—not in taking from it—but, in whatever small way it may be granted to me, *to give to it*. But even this desire I know I must also overcome. I must learn just simply and quietly *to be*. To cease trying. Then it may be given to me to mount even further than the very last step —beyond giving or taking—to mount into the realm which encompasses the Whole.

As I finish this narrative, I feel I have in some measure fulfilled Granny Pop's wish that I should write my life, though I have failed to carry out her other wish—that I should keep notes. I have never kept notes on any subject in all my life, and I have not done so for this book. Nor have I at any time kept a diary or even an engagement pad. At odd moments I have written down my appointments on little slips of paper—and promptly lost them. Everything I have written here (except quotations from letters, cards, catalogues, newspapers, and so forth) I have drawn from memory. I may have made mistakes in some dates or minor incidents, but if so, I do not too much regret it since I feel that I have held to the spirit of my statement if not to the letter.

Perhaps, we all have to write such a book as this in some one of our incarnations. I hope I shall never have to do so again. It has taken too much out of me. One should brood over such a book for years, adding to it and then eliminating; polishing it as one polishes an old piece of wood. To dash it off is not good. I can see why Jung makes many of his patients write their lives. Somehow, after doing so, it puts one's life behind one. It is like closing a door in an old house, throwing away the key and starting out on the road. But plunging back in the subconscious and remembering incidents long since passed is, many times, very painful.

Today, I realize that my view of life is very different from what it was when I was young, or what it was a few years ago, or even only yesterday. Life is nothing but a continual process of change. Thanks to my many mistakes along the way, I have learned some lessons.

I have written in these pages about people as I believed I knew them, but I must, in a way, apologize for this because, in the final analysis, who knows another person? Like myself, are they not continually changing and are they not different people today? Can anyone know another person without continually evaluating and constantly taking new measure of him or her?

I recall one of the wisest things George Bernard Shaw ever said. He was asked, who knew him best in all the world. He answered, "My tailor. Because every time he sees me he takes new measures of me."

If I have written about anyone in this book without taking his or her new measures, as of the day, or, even, as of the very second, I write, I hope I will be forgiven.

Many people I have written about in this book are now dead. Death—that supreme sculptor—has chiselled much of my heart away with the dying of each one. And yet the core of my heart remains. It remains to battle, to struggle, and ever to seek peace. Perhaps just this lesson I in the end must learn: that struggle itself is the peace of life, and that real peace—that envied peace—belongs to another shore. Another shore so close that it is within ourselves. But we must become mariners to reach it. We must cross the sea of our own natures to reach that peaceful shore where dwells our Divine Soul.

Is there anything outside ourselves? Do we not hold within our own hearts the Belovéd, and Life and Death? And do we not hold within our own souls the Divine Self? But the illusions created by both Life and Death must initiate us into their dark mysteries before we can comprehend all this. And it may bé, too, that in this initiation we cannot reach our full maturity until we have bled deeply from a wound, pierced far into the garden of our hearts by the hand of the Belovéd. Until we have gone in despair and loneliness through foreign lands, and heard the echoes of our once cherished dreams proclaimed in the mouths of gossipers and vulgar people—distorted—deformed—until we ourselves no longer recognize them.

So at last we are forced to return to some simple thing we once loved —perhaps only the delight in a streak of sunlight across the floor.

But in this a small contentment: to know that some things are together and hold forever tightly, and some things are never to be more than dreamed.

Index

HOMOSEXUALITY

Lesbians and Gay Men
in Society, History and Literature

Acosta, Mercedes de. **Here Lies The Heart.** 1960

Bannon, Ann. **I Am a Woman.** 1959

Bannon, Ann. **Journey To a Woman.** 1960

Bannon, Ann. **Odd Girl Out.** 1957

Bannon, Ann. **Women in The Shadows.** 1959

Barney, Natalie Clifford. **Aventures de L'Esprit.** 1929

Barney, Natalie Clifford. **Traits et Portraits.** 1963

Brooks, Romaine. **Portraits, Tableaux, Dessins.** 1952

Carpenter, Edward. **Intermediate Types Among Primitive Folk.** 1919

Casal, Mary. **The Stone Wall.** 1930

Cory, Donald Webster. **The Homosexual in America.** 1951

Craigin, Elisabeth. **Either Is Love.** 1937

Daughters of Bilitis. **The Ladder.** Volumes I - XVI. Including an **Index To The Ladder** by Gene Damon. 1956 - 1972. Nine vols.

Documents of the Homosexual Rights Movement in Germany, 1836 - 1927. 1975

Ellis, Havelock and John Addington Symonds. **Sexual Inversion.** 1897

Fitzroy, A. T. **Despised and Rejected.** 1917

Ford, Charles and Parker Tyler. **The Young and Evil.** 1933

Frederics, Diana. **Diana: A Strange Autobiography.** 1939

Friedlaender, Benedict. **Renaissance des Eros Uranios.** 1904

A Gay Bibliography. 1975

A Gay News Chronology, 1969 - May, 1975. 1975

Gordon, Mary. **Chase of the Wild Goose.** 1936

Government Versus Homosexuals. 1975

Grosskurth, Phyllis. **John Addington Symonds.** 1964

Gunn, Peter. **Vernon Lee: Violet Paget, 1856 - 1935.** 1964

A Homosexual Emancipation Miscellany, c. 1835 - 1952. 1975

Karsch-Haack, F[erdinand]. **Das Gleichgeschlechtliche Leben der Naturvölker.** 1911

Katz, Jonathan. **Coming Out!** 1975

Lesbianism and Feminism in Germany, 1895 - 1910. 1975

Lind, Earl. **Autobiography of an Androgyne.** 1918

Lind, Earl. **The Female-Impersonators.** 1922

Loeffler, Donald L. **An Analysis of the Treatment of the Homosexual Character in Dramas Produced in the New York Theatre From 1950 to 1968.** 1975

Mallet, Françoise. **The Illusionist.** 1952

Miss Marianne Woods and Miss Jane Pirie Against Dame Helen Cumming Gordon. 1811 - 1819

Mattachine Society. **Mattachine Review.** Volumes I - XIII. 1955 - 1966. Six vols.

Mayne, Xavier. **Imre: A Memorandum.** 1908

Mayne, Xavier. **The Intersexes.** 1908

Morgan, Claire. **The Price of Salt.** 1952

Niles, Blair. **Strange Brother.** 1931

Olivia. **Olivia.** 1949

Rule, Jane. **The Desert of the Heart.** 1964

Sagarin, Edward. **Structure and Ideology in an Association of Deviants.** 1975

Steakley, James D. **The Homosexual Emancipation Movement in Germany.** 1975

Sturgeon, Mary C. **Michael Field.** 1921

Sutherland, Alistair and Patrick Anderson. **Eros: An Anthology of Friendship.** 1961

Sweet, Roxanna Thayer. **Political and Social Action in Homophile Organizations.** 1975

Tobin, Kay and Randy Wicker. **The Gay Crusaders.** 1972

Ulrichs, Carl Heinrich. **Forschungen Über Das Rätsel Der Mannmännlichen Liebe.** 1898

Underwood, Reginald. **Bachelor's Hall.** 1937

[Vincenzo], Una, Lady Troubridge. **The Life of Radclyffe Hall.** 1963

Vivien, Renée **Poèmes de Renée Vivien.** Two vols. in one. 1923/24

Weirauch, Anna Elisabet. **The Outcast.** 1933

Weirauch, Anna Elisabet. **The Scorpion.** 1932

Wilhelm, Gale. **Torchlight to Valhalla.** 1938

Wilhelm, Gale. **We Too Are Drifting.** 1935

Winsloe, Christa. **The Child Manuela.** 1933